D0212420

VILLA JULIE COLLEGE LIBRARY
STEVENSON, MD 21153

T. S. ELIOT'S DRAMA

A Research and Production Sourcebook

RANDY MALAMUD

Modern Dramatist Research and Production Sourcebooks, Number 2

William W. Demastes, Series Adviser

GREENWOOD PRESS
New York • Westport, Connecticut • London

Library of Congress Cataloging-in-Publication Data

Malamud, Randy.
   T. S. Eliot's drama : a research and production sourcebook / Randy
Malamud.
      p.   cm.—(Modern dramatist research and production
sourcebooks, ISSN 1055-999X ; no. 2)
   Includes bibliographical references and index.
   ISBN 0-313-27813-X (alk. paper)
   1. Eliot, T. S. (Thomas Stearns), 1888-1965—Dramatic production.
   2. Eliot, T. S. (Thomas Stearns), 1888-1965—Dramatic works.
   I. Title. II. Series.
   PS3509.L43Z715   1992
   822'.912—dc20   91-46960

British Library Cataloguing in Publication Data is available.

Copyright © 1992 by Randy Malamud

All rights reserved. No portion of this book may be
reproduced, by any process or technique, without the
express written consent of the publisher.

Library of Congress Catalog Card Number: 91-46960
ISBN: 0-313-27813-X
ISSN: 1055-999X

First published in 1992

Greenwood Press, 88 Post Road West, Westport, CT 06881
An imprint of Greenwood Publishing Group, Inc.

Printed in the United States of America

The paper used in this book complies with the
Permanent Paper Standard issued by the National
Information Standards Organization (Z39.48-1984).

10 9 8 7 6 5 4 3 2 1

72155

For Daniel, Judie, and Lisa Malamud

Contents

Preface

T. S. Eliot's poetry has been extensively covered by scholarship and bibliographies; his plays have a less coherent critical discourse. This book, I hope, will help to establish an orderly foundation for the study of Eliot's drama.

A chronology lists the most important events of Eliot's life and career, and the introduction surveys Eliot's literature and details his movement from poetry to drama.

Each of Eliot's seven plays is the subject of a separate chapter, which begins with a list of characters and a synopsis of the plot, followed by a production history that lists dates, places, casts, and production staffs of major peformances, as well as other relevant details (where available) that will help readers visualize, as much as possible, the nature of the play in performance. In the section headed "Critical overview" I present a summary of reviewers' reponses; a survey of scholarship regarding that play; and textual notes and allusions. The final section gives a publishing history.

I intend these chapters to serve as fairly comprehensive introductions to each play and the relevant critical reaction and performance details. I quote from numerous representative critics, reviewers, actors, and directors in each of these chapters. Though my intention is to provide an objective overview of the most important material, there is obviously an inherent bias: the sources quoted are, simply, the ones I judged most interesting, helpful, and original. Since the bibliography consists of over 600 entries, there are some—which certainly may be of considerable value—that are not specifically cited elsewhere in my text; the reader is advised not to overlook these sources simply because I have not referred to them in the chapters on the plays.

Appendix I lists additional dramatic, musical, film, and television adaptations of Eliot's work, including, most prominently, *Cats*; and gives locations of photographs of various productions of the plays. Another important vantage point on secondary sources for Eliot's drama is the chronological development—trends and changes—of the criticism. Appendix II provides a key (organized by the number assigned to each secondary source in the bibliography) to the year in which each item was published, so that one may trace the evolution of scholarship over the years. Appendix III lists productions and credits for major productions.

A Note on Bibliographic Codes and Organization

Primary source material—Eliot's plays, essays on drama, and interviews—is identified by numbers prefaced with a "P." Manuscript and archival collections are also listed in the bibliography of primary sources. In Appendix III the codes enumerate major productions of each play (P1—P7).

Reviews are marked by the preface "R" in the bibliography of secondary sources, and scholarly criticism is marked by numbers prefaced with a "C." Reviews are grouped by play (in section I); for each review I have identified the production (or text) discussed therein. Scholarly essays, books, and sections of books are organized by the individual play they examine, where relevant (in "Secondary sources," section II); scholarship about two or more plays, and of Eliot's drama or dramatic theory more generally, is in the final grouping (section III) of the bibliography of secondary sources.

Throughout this book, each reference to a source listed in the bibliography includes a parenthetical citation of the source's code number. The Author Index, additionally, lists each source by page number and code number.

Acknowledgments

I am immensely indebted to Deborah Browning, whose tireless and meticulous research assistance was invaluable in compiling, organizing, and annotating the bibliography. Her commitment to sound methodical scholarship was a constant support.

I thank Deans Robert Arrington and Clyde Faulkner, of Georgia State University's College of Arts and Sciences, for various assistance including summer research funding and released time; and the office of Vice President for Research Cleon Arrington for two GSU Research Grants.

Virginia Spencer Carr, chair of the English Department, has provided me with countless forms of support and encouragement; I am grateful to her for creating and maintaining a department conducive to energetic and enthusiastic scholarship. Dorothy Sussman and Patricia Bryan moved mountains that needed to be moved, against seemingly unconquerable forces of inertia.

Matthew Roudané generously read a draft of this book; I hope some of his expertise has rubbed off on it. I thank Dabney Hart for sharing with me her wide knowledge of British theatre; for reading my work with a fiercely incisive editorial eye; and for lovely dramatic conversations across the corridor. I am indebted to Marilyn Brownstein, Greenwood Press's senior editor for humanities, and series editor Bill Demastes for their help and tolerance throughout the course of this project.

This project tested the resources of several libraries and librarians: I am grateful for the access to materials and research assistance provided by the New York Public Library's Main Research Library and its Berg Collection; the Billy Rose Theatre Collection, the Rodgers & Hammerstein Archives of Recorded Sound, and the Theatre on Film and Tape collection at the NYPL Performing Arts Research Library at Lincoln Center; Emory University's Woodruff Library and reference staff; Georgia State University's Pullen Library and its stellar reference staff; and finally, Jane Hobson's tremendously helpful interlibrary loan office at Pullen Library, including Marjorie Patterson, Matt Stinson and Lois O'Shea, *sine qua non*.

I thank Scott Gissendanner for serving as my interface with hardware, software, laserprinters, and various other technical entities beyond my scope; James Poulakos, in relief, was similarly instrumental.

T. S. Eliot dedicated *The Elder Statesman* to Valerie Eliot, "to return as best I can / With words a little part of what you have given me"; in the same spirit I acknowledge my debt and appreciation to Wendy Simonds.

Chronology

1888   Thomas Stearns Eliot born 26 September in St. Louis, seventh and final child of Henry Ware Eliot, a merchant, and Charlotte Champe Stearns Eliot, a schoolteacher and a Christian poet.

1905   Publishes poetry in school magazine, *Smith Academy Record.*

1906   Matriculates to Harvard College, where courses of study include Greek and English Literature, French Prose and Poetry, German Prose and Poetry, History of Ancient and Modern Philosophy, Latin Literature, History of England.

1907   Begins publishing poetry in the *Harvard Advocate.*

1908   Encounters Symbolist poetry via Arthur Symons's critical study.

1909   Receives B.A. (though he graduates with the class of 1910), and begins M.A. course at Harvard, with classes in Chaucer, Drama in England from the Miracle Plays to the Closing of the Theatres, Romantic Poetry, French Literary Criticism, Allegory, Philosophy of History, and Florentine Painting. Teachers include Irving Babbitt and George Santayana. First reads Ezra Pound's poetry. Begins writing poetry that will appear in his first collection.

1910   Studies at the Sorbonne in Paris, where he attends Henri Bergson's lectures.

1911   Receives M.A. First visits London, then travels to Munich and Northern Italy. Returns to Harvard to begin doctoral course in Philosophy. Studies Indic Philology, Sanskrit, Indian Philosophy.

1913   Reads F. H. Bradley's *Appearance and Reality*.

1914   Meets Bertrand Russell at Harvard. Appointed Sheldon Travelling Fellow in Philosophy, and plans to spend next academic year at Merton College, Oxford. Tries to attend summer school in Marburg, Germany but school is canceled, forcing departure for England, upon outbreak of World War I. Meets Pound in London.

1915   Meets Vivienne Haigh-Wood, a governess, whom he marries two months later at Hampstead Registry Office. *Poetry* publishes "The Love Song of J. Alfred Prufrock" and three other short poems; *Blast* publishes "Preludes" and "Rhapsody on a Windy Night"; and *Others* publishes "Portrait of a Lady."

1916   Begins teaching at Highgate Junior School. Through Clive Bell, begins to meet members of the "Bloomsbury Group," including Lytton Strachey, Roger Fry, and (in 1918) Virginia and Leonard Woolf. Sends thesis (*Knowledge and Experience in the Philosophy of F. H. Bradley*, published in 1964) to Harvard advisors, intending to sail to America for his final defense, but ship's delay leads to cancellation of plans.

1917   Begins working as a clerk in the Colonial and Foreign Department of Lloyds Bank. *Prufrock and Other Observations*, first collection of poetry, published (with Pound's secret financial support). Appointed assistant editor of *The Egoist*.

1919   Henry Ware Eliot dies, thinking his son's life is ruined. The Woolfs' Hogarth Press publishes *Poems*. Announces intention to write what will become *The Waste Land*, fragments of which he had been compiling for at least four years.

1920   The Ovid Press publishes *Ara Vos Prec*, and Knopf publishes the first American edition of his work, *Poems by T. S. Eliot*. Methuen Press publishes *The Sacred Wood*, his first collection of critical essays. Through Pound, meets James Joyce.

1921   Suffers nervous breakdown; takes leave of absence from Lloyds and goes to rest at Margate. From there, travels to Lausanne for two months of treatment under Dr. Roger Vittoz.

1922   Returns to London with a draft of *The Waste Land*. Founds and edits *Criterion*, which he uses as a prominent organ for his literary and critical writings. *The Waste Land* appears (after extensive editing by Pound) in October in *Criterion* and *The Dial*.

1923   Vivienne's frail health degenerates, compounded by colitis and depression, taking a heavy toll on Eliot and possibly reawakening his religious sensibilities.

1925   Hired by Geoffery Faber to be a director at his new publishing house, Faber & Gwyer (in 1929, Faber & Faber). "The Hollow Men" published.

1926   First part of *Sweeney Agonistes* published (followed by the second part in 1927) in *Criterion*.

1927   Rejects his Unitarian upbringing (which had long troubled him because he felt its Puritanical origins refuted the reality of sin, and because he found it bland) by becoming confirmed in the Church of England as an Anglo-Catholic after a secret baptismal ceremony at Finstock Church, Oxfordshire. Vivienne leaves England for nine months of medical treatment abroad following a breakdown upon the death of her father. Renews youthful acquaintance with Emily Hale, a drama teacher. Becomes a naturalized British citizen.

1928   Publicly announces conversion in the Preface to *For Lancelot Andrewes* by declaring himself "classicist in literature, royalist in politics, and anglo-catholic in religion."

1929   Charlotte Champe Stearns Eliot dies.

1930   *Ash-Wednesday* published. Through George Bell, Bishop of Chichester, meets E. Martin Browne, director of religious drama for the diocese, who will direct all his plays except *Sweeney Agonistes*.

1932   *Sweeney Agonistes: Fragments of an Aristophanic Melodrama* published as a book. Accepts Charles Eliot Norton professorship at Harvard for 1932-33 academic year, where his lecture topics include the work of Sir Philip Sidney, Shelley, Keats, and the formation of a poet. Visits Emily Hale at Scripps College, Claremont, Calif.

1933   American tour includes appearances at Princeton, Yale, Smith, Bryn Mawr, Vassar (where *Sweeney Agonistes* is first produced by Hallie Flanagan's Vassar Experimental Theatre), Buffalo, Minneapolis, St. Louis. Separates from Vivienne.

1934   *The Rock: A Pageant Play* is presented and published. Active involvement in Group Theatre, which presents a production of *Sweeney Agonistes* that is acclaimed by avant-garde audiences.

1935   *Murder in the Cathedral* debuts at Canterbury Festival and is published; moves to London's Mercury Theatre. *Sweeney Agonistes* moves to the West End for a limited run.

1936   Returns to see family in New England. Federal Theatre Project sponsors New York debut of *Murder in the Cathedral*, which is also presented in London's West End, broadcast on B. B. C. radio, and televised. "Burnt Norton" published.

1938   Vivienne placed in Northumberland House, a London institution for certified patients, probably a result of collaboration between Eliot and her brother; she had seen her husband only once since his departure for Harvard in 1932 and would not speak to him again before her death.

1939   *The Family Reunion* premieres and is published. *Old Possum's Book of Practical Cats* published. Moves out of London to avoid German bombing. *Criterion* ceases publication.

1940   "East Coker" published. With the emigration of several noted poets (Auden and Isherwood to America, MacNeice to Ireland) and the recent death of Yeats, as well as the popular reception of his latest poems and his powerful stature at Faber & Faber, Eliot rises to a position of preeminence in England's literary establishment. Wartime service includes a post as air-raid warden, and as a fire watcher from the top of Faber & Faber's office building. First (amateur) American productions of *The Family Reunion* given by college troupes.

1941   "The Dry Salvages" published.

1942   "Little Gidding" published.

1943   *Four Quartets* published as a whole.

1945   Travels to America, where he campaigns for the release of Pound, accused of treason during World War II, who is declared insane.

1946   Moves in with John Hayward, friend and literary advisor.

1947   Vivienne dies. Relationship with Emily Hale begins to dissipate, lingering on until it finally terminates with Eliot's 1957 marriage. *The Family Reunion* is revived for the Edinburgh Festival, which will present the debuts of all Eliot's subsequent plays; play also has its New York debut.

1948   Awarded the Nobel Prize for Literature (in honor of which a Stock-holm production of *The Family Reunion* is staged), and the Order of Merit from King George VI. Received in private audience by Pope Pius XII. Accepts appointment at Princeton's Institute for Advanced Studies.

1949   *The Cocktail Party* premieres in Edinburgh (published 1950). Mary Trevelyan first proposes marriage. Tours Germany, lecturing on European unity.

1950   Visits the University of Chicago as poet in residence. Hires Esmé Valerie Fletcher as his secretary at Faber & Faber. *The Cocktail Party* opens on Broadway (where it wins three Tony awards), then in the West End.

1951   George Hoellering's film version of *Murder in the Cathedral* debuts at Venice International Film Festival (general release in 1952).

1953   Lectures at Washington University in St. Louis, recalling his boy-hood there, and visits Boston and New York. *The Confidential Clerk* premieres in Edinburgh and London (published 1954).

1954   Broadway premiere of *The Confidential Clerk*.

1957   Marries Valerie Fletcher, 38 years his junior, at St. Barnabas Church, Kensington, ten years to the month after Vivienne's death.

1958   *The Elder Statesman* premieres in Edinburgh and London (published 1959).

1961   Last public lecture given at University of Leeds.

1962   *Collected Plays* published (excluding *Sweeney Agonistes* and *The Rock*).

1963   American premiere of *The Elder Statesman* in Milwaukee. Carol H. Smith publishes *T. S. Eliot's Dramatic Theory and Practice*, a major critical study.

1964   Meets Groucho Marx. Awarded the American Medal of Freedom at a cermony in the American Embassy in London.

1965   Dies at his home in London on 4 January. Body is cremated and an urn with his ashes is taken to St. Michael's Church, East Coker, the village from which Eliot's ancester Andrew Eliot sailed to New England in 1699. A memorial service is held in Westminster Abbey, where a commemorative stone is later placed in the floor. London memorial program, "Homage to T. S. Eliot," includes a revival of *Sweeney Agonistes* with a new jazz score by John Dankworth.

1970   *Murder in the Cathedral* presented in Canterbury Cathedral to mark the 800-year anniversary of Becket's martyrdom.

1971   Valerie Eliot edits and publishes facsimiles of the original manuscripts of *The Waste Land*, revealing much about the poem's genesis and Pound's influence, and stimulating interest in autobiographical aspects of Eliot's life.

1981   Eliot's poetry returns to the London stage in *Cats* (Broadway opening in 1982; in 1983 he posthumously wins the Tony award for musical book, and shares with Andrew Lloyd Webber the award for score).

1988   Among the issues raised during centenary commemorations of Eliot's birth are his anti-Semitism, his biases relating to issues of canon formation and literary criticism, and his treatment of and attitude toward women (including his first wife). Many of the newest critical trends seem hostile to Eliot's literature and his critical orientation. Valerie Eliot's edition of her husband's letters through 1922 confirms the writer's carefully-cultivated poise in his private life.

Introduction

Intellectual and Poetic Foundations

Thomas Stearns Eliot rejected his midwestern Unitarian upbringing, leaving his native St. Louis for the more refined intellectualism of Cambridge, Massachusetts; after five years at Harvard he rejected that milieu, too, for Europe. His poetry, at the forefront of the modernist movement, is the work of an expatriate in the process of relocation: it reflects an attempt to locate both the poet and his tradition in a place and time of uncertain definition, amid the turmoil of the modern age. His drama, though, may be classified as staunchly English. It comes out of the final phase of his creative career in which he found himself, for better or worse, firmly situated in contemporary London (heir to the legacies of England's period of unparalleled dramatic glory, the Elizabethan age), and firmly ensconced in the upper ranks of the English literary establishment.

During his boyhood at the close of the nineteenth century Eliot tried to embrace a severe and saintly Christian sensibility, reacting against the middle-American Unitarianism that he felt—guided by Henry Adams's critique—was tainted with a falsely smug calm. An early poem, "The Death of Saint Narcissus" (withheld from *Collected Poems*, though a section of it and much of its sensibility were integrated into *The Waste Land*), shows Eliot's attraction to the lives of the martyred saints: rejecting the Dantean horrors of contemporary urban life, with its physical and spiritual torpor, the poem's hero becomes a dancer to God. Masochistically embracing the trials of the martyr—hot sand, piercing arrows—he is fulfilled by the pain that transcends secular banality. The image recurs in "The Love Song of St. Sebastian" (unpublished), in which physical beauty is subsumed by extravagant self-maceration. Another influence toward religious discipline was the didactic spiritual poetry of his mother, Charlotte Champe Stearns Eliot.

The familiar title character from "The Love Song of J. Alfred Prufrock" defines and pervades the sensibility of the poetry that marks the beginning of Eliot's canon. Prufrock is afflicted by a terror, or perhaps a range of interrelated terrors, ranging from mild distaste for social rituals to paralyzing fear of being unable to function in the modern world. The poems were written from 1909-15 (published in 1917 as *Prufrock and Other Observations*), as Eliot pursued his undergraduate and master's level studies at Harvard and completed his doctoral dissertation while traveling in Europe and in residence at Oxford. Eliot never formally defended his thesis, *Knowledge and Experience in the Philosophy of F. H. Bradley*, probably because he had come to doubt the importance of an academic career by the time he completed his work. It was published just before his death, with a preface stating that he could no longer understand what he had written; but the philosopher Josiah Royce, who was familiar with the thesis when it was written in the 1910s, had identified it as the work of an expert.

Elements of Eliot's philosophical background appear prominently in his poetry: Bradley's dictum on the "finite centre"—the idea that we live in a solipsistic universe, in which no one can communicate with anyone else—is cited as an endnote to *The Waste Land*. Bradley's *Appearance and Reality* led Eliot at least to consider whether there might be some absolute truth in a realm that escaped the realities of quotidian experience, though in his poetry he generally rejects that possibility. Bergsonian flux of time and memory contributes to the ominously uncertain and surreal atmosphere of these poems. The exotic transcendence embodied in Indian philosophy offers Eliot at least the possibility of finding some coherence amid Western exhaustion. Irving Babbitt's emphasis on classical reason and balance adds a comforting philosophical foundation. The vestiges of such an academically philosophical underpinning are perhaps all that prevent the poetry (and the poet) from sinking into an incomprehensible void in which the orderly entity of verse would be incommunicable.

Recurrent themes that delineate Eliot's poetic voice include the barren hostility of the city; the vacuity of high social mores; a sense of inane, skewed, incomprehensible, or anarchic moral foundations and secular habits; a fear or hatred of women and their power to intimidate the kind of man who inhabited Eliot's verse; and starkly banal horror, often muted or repressed but flaring to the surface in moments of heightened terror that loosely evoke the piercing arrows endured by the martyred saints of Eliot's early poetry. The settings evoke the genteel cosmopolitan heritage of Harvard and the European capitals, but this heritage is overshadowed by the more oppressively mundane realities of the streets and drawing rooms that obsess the poet. Poems such as "Rhapsody on a Windy Night," "Portrait of a Lady," and "Hysteria" starkly assert the unsettling condition of the status quo—a modern condition Eliot depicted as universal, though current critics have come to see his cry as more of a desperate lament that his own privileged position within the Western tradition was becoming endangered.

Moments of resolution or of the possibility for a deeper intellectual response to the modern dilemma surface tentatively and enigmatically, as in the final troubled cogitations of "La Figlia che Piange," which holds out the feeble possibility of recapturing artistic beauty; in the tinkling laughter—submarine and profound—of the philosopher (who is an incarnation of Bertrand Russell) in "Mr. Apollinax," which is, however, profaned by his audience's incomprehension at afternoon tea; or in the awareness of redemption lurking in the mermaids' song at the end of "Prufrock," powerless though it seems amid the drowning reality of human voices.

Eliot's study of Symbolism colors his first collection of poetry: its dreamy overdetermined imagery is eloquently unfettered. Newspaper readers sway like ears of corn in "The *Boston Evening Transcript*"; the damp souls of servants sprout at gates in "Morning at the Window"; a gentleman caller dances like a bear, chatters like an ape in "Portrait of a Lady." In his next collection, *Poems 1920*, the smoothly irreverent Symbolism develops into a more harshly fragmented sharpness. The spiritual and aesthetic dryness of the title character in "Gerontion," for example, makes the language and imagery of that poem subtly more desperate, more ruthlessly expository of his barren condition (and manifestly hopeless of escape) than in "Prufrock" or "Portrait of a Lady." Gerontion's despair is inscribed within, and determined by, the impersonal forces of history and tradition; he is more pointedly forced to confront the magnitude of his (and humanity's) failure.

Four poems in this collection are in French, in a voice of tamed lassitude. With a nod, perhaps, to Gustave Flaubert (along with the forebears of French Symbolism—Stéphane Mallarmé, Jules Laforgue, and so forth), Eliot rather passionlessly uses them to sneer at the bourgeoisie. Seven of the poems are written in an unnerving quatrain—some in a neurotic voice, some infused with an intentionally and densely obscure pedanticism (and, one might argue, all on a continuum Eliot thus establishes between neuroticism and pedanticism: deriving from a conception of the subject's alternating inability to function normally in society on the one hand, and society's hapless inability to approach the vatic on the other hand). Three of these poems explicitly—and perhaps the others implicitly—contain the figure of Sweeney, representing a loose association of distasteful characteristics that culminate in the persona highlighted in Eliot's first dramatic work, *Sweeney Agonistes*. An amalgam of hostility, misogyny, and calibanish brutality, the sensibility of Sweeney infuses these poems with a repugnant realism seemingly irreconcilable with the classicism of Irving Babbitt that Eliot had clung to in his younger years.

The Waste Land

In the early 1920s, Eliot felt oppressed by a wife he considered threateningly unstable (and who was, certainly, frequently ill); he had married Vivienne Haigh-Wood impulsively in 1915, perhaps to shock his family, or to avoid returning to America by rooting himself in the country he would later adopt as his own. He was disappointed by what he deemed an insufficient stature in contemporary literary circles. Virginia Woolf had tried to raise funds to provide Eliot with a fellowship so he could quit his draining job at Lloyds Bank—settling the international debts of post-war Europe—and devote all his energy to poetry, but Eliot rejected the plans because Woolf was not able to guarantee what he considered a sufficient salary. Domestic and personal pressures led him to take a leave of absence from his job in 1921, and retire to the beach at Margate for recuperation. From there, he went to Lausanne, Switzerland, to visit the nerve specialist, Dr. Roger Vittoz. Under his care Eliot apparently endured and recovered from some sort of nervous or emotional breakdown; more significantly for literary history, he returned to England in 1922 with a draft of what would become *The Waste Land*.

Ezra Pound incisively edited the text, paring down Eliot's ornate narratives, parodies, and descriptions, and leaving the manuscript at a taut 433 lines that embodied the concise, stark vision of a post-war European culture pathetically fragmented though tentatively redeemed by a mystical sensibility imported from the Hindu *Upanishads*. The poem is the nadir of Eliot's pessimistic scorn for the world that surrounds him. He details the crumbling of former imperial greatness from Alexandria to London, and the consequent emptiness of contemporary life. Drawing heavily upon myths and archetypes and making copious cultural allusions, Eliot constructs a waste land so profoundly far-reaching that escape seems hopeless, and pointless.

The villians in his scenario range from provocatively sensual queens to neurotic housewives; from rapists to sleazy travelling salesmen; from polluted rivers to the dizzying panorama of noisy traffic-filled London streets; from the cosmopolitan European aristocracy to lecherous bored clerks. One may detect in this grotesque cast of characters and settings the germ of a dramatic panorama—or perhaps more accurately, a parody of dramatic interaction: no character truly communicates with any other, and the sense of advancing dramatic plot or action (such as the quest archetype) is generally a cruel illusion. Still, the poem's title in an early draft was "He do the Police in Different Voices"—an allusion to the character of Sloppy in Charles Dickens's *Our Mutual Friend*, who read the police news with different voices for each person involved, thus turning a flat account into a kind of dramatic interaction. *The Waste Land*, though no more technically dramatic than Sloppy's police news, may nevertheless embody a chorus of voices that Eliot tries somehow to wrest into drama; perhaps because drama offers the potential for social redemption in a way that a bland listing of crimes (in Sloppy's newspaper, or in Eliot's cataloguing of modern cultural and intellectual "crimes") does not. In a 1953 monograph, *The Three Voices of Poetry*, Eliot writes that he has come to see a dramatic element in his early work and that possibly he always aspired to be a dramatist.

The final section of *The Waste Land*, "What the Thunder Said," embodies visions of calming watery redemption; an empty chapel that may offer a degree of refuge or respite; and the loose skeletal outlines of a coherent philosophy of life that provides some control. It ends, though, in a babbling devolution, a Lear-like resignation to defeat, a descent into Gothic madness. Certainly Eliot's aesthetic of despair hits bottom in the poem; perhaps, though less assuredly, the poet may have attained a glimpse of redemption by having undergone his Dantean trial.

Immediate and international acclaim followed the publication of *The Waste Land*.   "Mr. Eliot's poem—kaleidoscopic, profuse, a rattle and rain of colors that fall somehow into place—gives us the malaise of our time, its agony, its conviction of futility," writes the founder and editor of *Poetry*, Harriet Monroe (21 [March 1923]: 325). The *New York Times Book Review* (26 November 1922) states that the poem "is marked by an intense cerebral quality and a compact music that has practically established a movement among the younger men" (12). In *Dial* (December 1922), Edmund Wilson writes that "Mr. Eliot, with all his limitations, is one of our only authentic poets. . . . The poem is—in spite of its lack of structural unity—simply one triumph after another." In *The Hidden God*, Cleanth Brooks remembers his first impressions of the poem: "I wrote that it was 'perhaps' the finest poem of the generation but conceded that it was 'the most significant in that it gives voice to the universal despair or resignation arising from the spiritual and economic consequences of the war, the cross-purposes of modern civilization . . . ' et cetera" (C273, 68-69).

In 1925 "The Hollow Men" presented one last appraisal of modernity, in the mode of *The Waste Land* but stripped down: tamer, shorter, more detached, less of an assault on cultural or aesthetic sensibilities. That year Eliot left Lloyds to take a job at Faber & Gwyer (later Faber & Faber) as poetry editor, a position he would occupy for the rest of his life and which he would use to advance the careers of numerous younger poets such as Stephen Spender, W. H. Auden, Louis MacNeice, Thom Gunn, and Ted Hughes, among others.

A secret conversion to Anglo-Catholicism took place in June 1927 and was announced publicly in *For Lancelot Andrewes* (1928), in which Eliot labelled himself "classicist in literature, royalist in politics, and anglo-catholic in religion." His next poem, *Ash-Wednesday* (1930), is replete with the spiritual serenity that Eliot seems to have found in religion. The poem begins with a stance of resignation, contentment, and informed philosophical inquiry into and definition of the external world. The language is hypnotic: oblique (in the way that scriptural texts may be, reflecting human inability to comprehend divine mysteries) and incantatory.

Early Drama

Sweeney Agonistes was written in the mid-1920s, certainly reflecting Eliot's pre-conversion sensibility. As early as 1924, Eliot told the novelist Arnold Bennett, as recorded in Bennett's journals, "he had definitely given up that form of writing [i. e., poetry] and was now centered on dramatic writing" (3.52).

It seems incongruous that Eliot nurtured *Sweeney Agonistes* through the early and mid-1930s—a period when he was ardently working on devout religious drama (*The Rock* and *Murder in the Cathedral*), poetry (*Ash-Wednes-*

day and "The Ariel Poems"), and non-fiction prose (*Thoughts After Lambeth, After Strange Gods*)—by reprinting what he called "Fragments of an Aristophanic Melodrama" in book form in 1932, six years after the two parts had been published in *Criterion*; allowing and assisting with productions of the play in 1933 at Vassar College, and in 1934 and 1935 under the aegis of Rupert Doone's avant-garde Group Theatre; and making available to the Vassar production's director, Hallie Flanagan, an additional 25 lines of unpublished manuscript for the play. An epigraph added in 1932, from St. John of the Cross, suggests something of a process of Christian cleansing and regeneration which figures to a certain extent in the play; but *Sweeney Agonistes* is much more prominently a desperate, bawdy, crude celebration of animalistic torpor than it is an incipient attempt at control through spiritual determination.

One wonders how Eliot could have tolerated Sweeney after his conversion—he may have seen *Sweeney Agonistes* as a kind of penance for his earlier period of futile desperation; and perhaps he realized that even amid the serene spirituality of Canterbury Cathedral and Thomas à Becket's devotion, there exists an incarnation of Sweeney (in the Tempters, and even, to some extent, in Becket himself).

Neither *Sweeney Agonistes* nor Eliot's next dramatic work, *The Rock: A Pageant Play* (1934), was a dramatic *tour de force*, though *Sweeney* caught the attention of the European avant-garde and *The Rock* heightened Eliot's prominence among the Anglican community. Both works are far from conventional—they are both extreme: extremely stylized social combat in the first, and extremely formulaic Christian propaganda in the second. Neither play sought or attained a mainstream theatrical audience. In neither play does Eliot exhibit a strong sense of control over the drama: he dispersed few solid directions to his producers about how to stage *Sweeney Agonistes*, and was plagued by having to work with an enormously large cast (mostly amateur) of actors and production personnel on *The Rock*, which made it difficult to exert any feelings he might have had about exactly what shape the pageant was to take.

Yet both these works brought him to the stage, which represents a vast transition from the solipsistically interiorized and private world of his earlier poetry. For the first time Eliot concretely confronted a form of art (about which he had been theorizing in numerous critical essays for more than a decade) predicated upon a social situation—an audience, and a team of artists. And, as his later efforts from the 1930s through the late 1950s demonstrate, the move to the theatre was one to which Eliot had fervently committed himself. The early plays proved to be finger exercises for the more sustained efforts that would culminate in his five major plays: *Murder in the Cathedral* (1935), *The Family Reunion* (1939), *The Cocktail Party* (1949), *The Confidential Clerk* (1953), and *The Elder Statesman* (1958). The *Sweeney* fragments show Eliot's preparation for later drama through experimentation with basic spoken rhythms and with the ritualized nature of rhythm (what he called, archetypally, "the beating of a drum") as a foundation for verse drama. The dialogue—the patter of two prostitutes who share a flat, and of a room full of party guests—is raw, yet striking and surprisingly potent. Eliot begins his dramatic enterprise of creating different atmospheres of social interaction onstage, and tempering his traditionally finely-crafted poetry (elegant, Parnassian, unapproachable) with an element of more commonly accessible humanity.

In *The Rock*, Eliot begins to use choral drama—a chorus being the consummate expression of the social component of drama—which explicitly figures in *Murder in the Cathedral* and *The Family Reunion*, and less prominently, though still significantly, in *The Cocktail Party* (where the chorus appears in stylized prayer rituals). Eliot developed the chorus in his drama, writes Clifford J. Webster, to present "truths, eternal verities that cannot be represented directly to the spectator. Their blunt manifestation only detracts from their impression on his mind. . . . The artist has created a finer, subtler mode of expression [in the chorus], capable of arousing the desired response in the observer. . . . No longer do we follow the drama as detached, external observers, but find ourselves personally injected into the thrills and anxieties of the action. This production of the spectator's mind into another sphere is made possible by the intercommunication set up by the chorus between the figures of the play and the audience" (C395, 42).

Because *The Rock* was a fund-raising effort for a church-building drive Eliot merges the dramatic and Christian traditions, as he continues to do more intricately and more successfully in all his later plays. While much of the pageant's script is, to its detriment, a collaborative effort, and contains large passages of fairly predictable and sluggish language, there are nevertheless isolated passages (especially in the choruses) in which Eliot does seem to have discovered an effective mode of verse drama, one that conforms to the intricate theories of poetic drama he had been formulating since the early 1920s. In *The Rock*, Eliot began a close collaborative relationship with the actor and director E. Martin Browne, who was to direct all Eliot's plays except *Sweeney Agonistes*.

Additionally, Eliot may have learned from *The Rock* what *not* to do in a play. For example, in *Poetry and Drama*, written 17 years later, he advised against interspersing prose and poetry on stage. (The prose passages spoken by the Cockneys in *The Rock* had been, by general acclaim, among the least successful elements of the pageant.)

Murder in the Cathedral is "the first crest of Eliot's dramatic achievement," writes Nevill Coghill in the introduction to his edition of the play, "and it is interesting to stand on the crest and look back over the paths by which he seems to have reached it and see the pattern of a growing design furthered by accident, a design that begins in a sad, liberal agnosticism and steadily strengthens into the positive grief-in-joy and joy-in-grief of Christianity" (C56, 10). Threads of this pattern "are perceptible in Eliot's earliest published poetry" such as "Prufrock" and *The Waste Land*, "both of which pose a problem in the purpose of life and begin faintly to formulate a solution. . . . At last they took fully Christian shape in *The Rock* . . . which has the air of a trial run for *Murder in the Cathedral*" (11). In the mid-1930s and early 1940s, Eliot was hovering between poetry and drama. *Murder in the Cathedral* was performed frequently during that time, and Eliot spent five years drafting and reworking *The Family Reunion*. At the same time, he was bringing his poetic oeuvre to a close with *Four Quartets*—"Burnt Norton" was published in 1936, "East Coker" in 1940, "The Dry Salvages" in 1941, and "Little Gidding" in 1942. Besides a very conscious sense of closure to Eliot's poetry writing, these poems offer an antithesis to the tormenting solipsistic visions of his earlier poetry. They embody a sense of serenity, drawing upon a Christian (and Buddhist) submission of personal will, with its trials and limitations, to a larger guiding force. The aura of the Annunciation chimes through the poems; an apocalyptic sensibility, too, is present: England was, after all, under horrific bombardment by the Nazis as Eliot wrote the wartime *Quartets*, and prospects seemed bleak for the Allies across Europe.

But in a periplus through time, and aided by a river-force evocative of Hermann Hesse's spiritually-endowed rivers and the sacred Ganges from Part V of *The Waste Land*, Eliot commits himself to fare forward in a spirit of humble endurance. The rose of Dante's *Paradiso*, promising the ineffable splendor of heavenly ascension, infuses recurrent garden imagery. Eliot productively nurtures "moments" of simple and tranquil calm; these moments join together like the rose's enfolding petals to create a valuable sense of experience, upon which Eliot imposes a pattern, a form, that will reveal some higher meaning—of the poem, his career, and his life. A state of grace is imagined, variously described as a cyclical unity, a still point, or simply concord.

The war redirected Eliot's attention from playwriting to poetry which was beneficial to his dramatic career, he said in a *Paris Review* interview, because he was kept from writing a successor to *The Family Reunion* too soon. Though he realized immediately that the play had problems, he felt it was better to wait several years before returning to it so he could come to the theatre fully prepared to start afresh (P67, 60). Another important event that took place in the hiatus between his third and fourth plays was the death in 1947 of Vivienne (from whom he had been estranged for 15 years), which seems to have freed him from a sense of guilt and failure about their marriage.

The *Quartets* are better poems because of his having worked on *Murder in the Cathedral* and *The Family Reunion*, Eliot stated in the *Paris Review*, since his playwriting experience led to a simplified language and a speech which is more conversational and more accessible to his reader (63). The *Quartets* contain stylistic echoes of the language and sensibility Eliot would use in his final plays: there is a cessation of horrific hostility; a resigned acceptance of the nightmares of the past; and a determination to live out the last phase of life in a simple state of beneficence. The poems' comforting Christian consolation and their insistence on the possibility of a meaningful social enterprise point to themes that are further explored in *The Cocktail Party*, *The Confidential Clerk*, and *The Elder Statesman*. More explicitly, a few of the images

Eliot uses to stake out a future course in *Four Quartets* portend his dramatic mission. In Part III of "East Coker," for example, Eliot tells his soul to wait in stillness, giving itself over to the darkness of God (which promises eventual enlightenment), as in a theatre one sits in the dark waiting for the scene to be changed. The religious vision is the next scene Eliot awaits—both allegorically and literally, as he begins to craft his own dramatic "scenes" that promise an enlightened vision.

In Part II of "Little Gidding," Yeats's shade accompanies Eliot on a pre-dawn tour of London's present ruin, detailing for him the gifts reserved for the aged poet: the final of these is the pain of reenacting everything he has done; the shame resulting from the motives thus exposed; and, ultimately, the awareness of things done badly—which harm people—though these things had once been thought virtuous. Eliot's drama certainly reenacts the pains of human (especially marital) communion and compassion that he had so assuredly denigrated in his earlier poetry. Certain motifs, as important as a reemergence of ghosts from the past or as simple as an automobile accident, are reenacted in several of the plays. (The plays themselves reenact Greek dramatic models.) The plays are full of shame at what is reenacted—Harry's ancestral guilt in *The Family Reunion*; Edward and Lavinia's selfishness in *The Cocktail Party*; Claverton's profligate and insensitive youth in *The Elder Statesman*. The shame is compounded, as Eliot explains in "Little Gidding," by motives late revealed—the conventional dramatic techniques of discovery and self-recognition are at the heart of each play (prominently in *The Confidential Clerk*, for example, as Colby comes to a shocked revaluation of his world and the values of his patrons and family after revelations about his long-obscured childhood). Reverberating throughout *Four Quartets* is the motto Mary, Queen of Scots embroidered on a tapestry as she awaited execution: "In my end is my beginning." The *Quartets* present the end of Eliot's poetry and the beginning of a new voice ensconced in the social endeavor of drama.

Dramatic Theories in Practice

"The most useful poetry, socially, would be one which could cut across all the present stratifications of public taste. . . . The ideal medium for poetry, to my mind, and the most direct means of social 'usefulness' for poetry, is the theatre" (*The Use of Poetry and the Use of Criticism* [London: Faber & Faber, 1933, 152-53]). The strength of drama, Eliot continues, is that it operates successfully on several levels, such as plot, character, conflict, rhythm, and a more deeply and sensitively intricate meaning. The viewer who misses some of these levels is still able to enjoy others without detraction.

Eliot embraced drama as a means to stimulate his creativity, Marjorie J. Lightfoot argues. She cites numerous critical essays from as early as the 1920s—such as "'Rhetoric' and Poetic Drama," "Prose and Verse," "The Poetic Drama," and "The Possibility of a Poetic Drama"—in which Eliot frequently refers to the expressive artistic powers of drama as paradigms for literary success: for example, discussing drama as the ideal form for expressing natural human emotions; and as a genre giving special needed attention to the role of the audience (C341, 120).

In *The Music of Poetry* Eliot identifies the task of modern poetry as a search for a proper contemporary colloquial idiom—nineteenth-century verse plays such as Shelley's *The Cenci* were failures, he writes, because they presented merely poetic declamations, not real people in natural situations—and Ronald Bush argues that "An impulse to *himself* express a 'commonplace message' in a language any educated person's mother could understand was one of the dominant aims" of Eliot's work in the plays beginning with *The Rock*, and also in *Four Quartets*, which are influenced by this demand that his language communicate to an audience on the simplest of levels (C283, 161). In *Poetry and Drama* Eliot stresses his belief that drama must be modern, relevant, and accessible to an average and widespread mass audience—"people living in houses and apartments like ours, and using telephones and motor cars" (P55, 87). Certainly, though, some aspects of his plays seem to undercut this sensibility: his stylized early work, the historical and spiritually elevated setting of his saint's play, the mythic foundations of his later plays.

William Skaff argues that Eliot in his playwriting attempts to approach the origins of all art: "If art is essentially ritual, as Eliot has learned from his examination of primitive experience, then the principal way to make modern art express its unconscious origins is to make it more ritualistic: by investing it with a structure recalling the death-rebirth pattern of primitive rites and ancient drama, with a rhythmic stylization similar to the modern ballet, and with a savage, serious humor and social awareness like the music hall. Since drama evolved out of primitive religious ritual, Eliot was continually preoccupied throughout his life with reinvigorating the modern dramatic form, especially by reinstituting poetry as a dramatic medium" (C379, 99). The pervasive use of Greek dramatic sources in the plays, and the use of choruses in the earlier plays, accord with Skaff's assessment of Eliot's dramatic intentions: the reincarnation of classical myth certainly provides a strong link with primitive ritual. Eliot cautioned against making too much out of this connection, though, in his *Paris Review* interview: he said he did not consider the Greek originals as models, but only points of departure (P67, 61). Probably his discussion of Joyce's borrowing, adaptation and invigoration of Greek sources in *Ulysses*, as described in his 1923 essay "Ulysses, Order, and Myth," applies to his own use of Greek sources: there is a kind of continuous parallel between the present and past, though the modern artist—while drawing on the past work for a sense of continuity, tradition, and structure—need not be too closely or literally tethered to the antecedent.

Rudd Fleming characterizes the Hellenic influence in Eliot's plays, in his "passage from Aeschylus to Euripides to Sophocles. The baroque style of *Murder in the Cathedral* and, to a diminishing degree, of *The Family Reunion*, corresponds to the metaphorical, imagistic richness of the style of Aeschylus; the extremely flat style of *The Confidential Clerk* and, to a less degree, of *The Cocktail Party* corresponds to the colloquial flatness of Euripides' dialogue. . . . Eliot's Greek model for *The Elder Statesman* was. . . Sophocles, and, of the three Greek tragedians, it is Sophocles who best renders the pure, imageless, non-metaphorical music of human intimacy. It is, therefore, harmonious with Eliot's whole development as a prosodist that he should have finally turned to Sophocles of the *Oedipus at Colonus*, where dramatic prosody reaches a peak of naturalness and flexibility" (C245, 60). (For more detailed examination of the Greek influences in Eliot's final four plays, see the section in the discussion of each play entitled "Textual notes and influences.")

Skaff cites aspects of ancient dramatic ritual in Eliot's plays: the pervasive jazzy influence of the music hall (which Eliot explains in "Marie Lloyd," was "one of the few surviving rituals in modern life") and the drum beat in *Sweeney Agonistes*; the masks in *The Rock*, and the prominence of the chorus revived from ancient classical models; the Greek notion of dramatic ritual sacrifice in *Murder in the Cathedral*; the patterned revival of Aeschylean rituals in *The Family Reunion*; social customs that suggest religious ritual in *The Cocktail Party*.

But Skaff writes that Eliot's drama "actually appears to be an offshoot of a more compelling and pervasive effort to revive an art form closer to the true nature of his creativity, poetry" (C379, 101). Noting the dramatic character of his early poems, Skaff asserts, "Eliot would certainly have felt that poetry expresses the most intense emotion only within a dramatic situation consisting of a persona whose identity is separate from the author's, and who addresses other characters and an audience according to particular circumstances dictated by plot action. This notion that poetry is inherently dramatic stayed with Eliot throughout his life" (103).

In *The Invisible Poet*, Hugh Kenner sees the dramatic career as a natural outgrowth of Eliot's sensibility. "If, at about the age of thirty, a poet has devoted intellectual passion to Francis Herbert Bradley's exorcism of the common-sense world (reduced phase by phase to Appearance merely, but capable of approximating Reality by a feat of self-transcension), then we need not be surprised to find that poet, at about the age of sixty, contriving plays. In the theatre we are all Phenomenalists; it is the perfect Bradleyan form. A make-believe world cut out of darkness by judicious prearrangements of spotlights . . . in which salaried persons whose habitual selves are concealed manipulate other selves equally makeshift through factitious, imponderable psychic business; in which all is Appearance mimicking for two hours a continuous Present (it will be exactly repeated tomorrow night), yet enacting an ideal Transcience (we have neither time nor will to deceive ourselves with analysis), and presenting in terms of Immediate Experience whatever self-transcendence of the merely apparent it is capable of according us" (C330, 327-28). Almost too neatly Kenner thus argues not only that Eliot's drama is the logical culmination of his career, but more provocatively, that all Eliot's earlier poetry—with its strikingly prominent poses, self-consciously created conceits of form, and insistent demand for a "stage" on which the material could be most suitably "performed"—aspires to the solid conventions of theatricality.

Michael Goldman explains Eliot's drama by what he calls "a theory of ghosts": "The structure of each of Eliot's plays is built on a double manifestation of ghosts. At first, the play appears to be haunted by spirits that, though still in some respects disconcertingly archaic, still bear a clear relation to our own familiar ghosts—the ghosts we have been accustomed since Ibsen to recognize both in drama and in our lives. Gradually—and this is the fundamental process of Eliot's drama—the ghosts are revealed to be very different from what we took them to be. The original ghosts seem to vanish with an ease that is again disconcerting, but their vanishing proves to be a deeper haunting, more personally directed at the audience. . . . The most intense and usually the most effective part of Eliot's drama is not the demonstration that the new ghosts are different, but the manifestation of their true power to haunt—their power to haunt in their true capacity" (C307, 157-58). In *Murder in the Cathedral*, for example, the Tempters—ghosts of former desires—at first appear to be the antagonistic forces, but Becket later learns that his real struggle is the temptation to do the right thing for the wrong reason. In *The Cocktail Party*, the Guardians first seem determined to harass and humiliate Edward with their cryptic power over his embarrassing situation; though they finally turn out to be angels rather than pests, their power to haunt Edward endures. Grover Smith, in the same vein, writes that it is not "surprising that his ghosts have nothing to do with spiritualism and the séance-room. They are manifested to clarify the known, not to expose the unknown" (C249, 233).

In "Eliot and the Living Theatre" Katharine J. Worth writes, "Eliot's plays must be seen in the context of the living theatre, not as an extension of the poetry and the dramatic theory, nor as a special kind of activity called 'religious drama'" (C403, 148). This is in contrast to, for example, the sensibility of one of the most prominent scholars of Eliot's plays, Carol H. Smith, who writes that she is "not primarily concerned with an evaluation of Eliot's works by current theatrical standards" (C382, ix). Noting that Eliot rejected the audiences who might attend his plays "to be patiently bored and to satisfy themselves with the feeling that they have done something meritorious," as he writes in *Poetry and Drama* (123), Worth asks, "Must they always be performed in what Ivor Brown jocularly called 'the crypt of St. Eliot's' and have they no relevance to the development of the modern theatre? Are they quite out of the main stream, as far out as the plays of Masefield, Drinkwater and Stephen Phillips are now seen to have been?" She answers: "I do not believe that we have to answer 'yes' to these questions, though much of the existing criticism . . . forces us to do so by emphasizing so heavily moral patterns, Christian solutions and thematic progressions. What in my view emerges as theatrically interesting, and what gives Eliot a place, however tentative, in the main stream, is his feeling for alienation and violence, his gift for suggesting metaphysical possibilities in the trivial or absurd and his exploration of new dramatic means for working upon the nerves and pulses of an audience" (124).

"The sense of many people that the plays are a weaker branch of the Eliot tree," writes Ronald Peacock, "tends constantly to obscure the fact that the impulse in Eliot to drama was exceptionally deep and strong" (C362, 97). Attention to the breadth of Eliot's copious critical essays on drama, and to the energy he invested in them, shows that "In his writing and thinking as a whole, as a single activity flowing into diverse channels, there was a greatness of outlook, a powerful radiation of ideas about the fundamental problems of interpreting life, society, the human conflicts, that quite transcends the limits of his lyric poems and cries out for a broader mimesis of life" (97-98); this broadness, Peacock writes, could be provided only by drama.

Eliot's "urge to drama was a profound instinct," Peacock continues. "He was searching for the canvas, the landscape of manifold human conflict, which would be an adequate representation of human involvement, and which he could impregnate with his interpretations of existence. Eliot . . . saw very soon that the drama was the only extended form available to him if he wished, as he did, to move beyond his 'first' voice (meditative) and give a picture of society, of men and women with their actions and conflicts, in situations of suffering and guilt, and in a relation to society as a whole and its values" (98). Arnold Hinchliffe writes that "the work of T. S. Eliot represents the most complete attempt to construct a theory of drama since Dryden" (C317, 38).

Eliot's drama is often seen as being constructed on different levels, as he himself described in *The Use of Poetry and the Use of Criticism*. Speaking of *Sweeney Agonistes*, he writes that the central character's consciousness was meant to be on the level of the most intelligent members of the audience, and his speeches would be addressed more to the others, who were visionless, though meant to be overheard by the more insightful. The more intelligent should have an understanding with Sweeney, while the others would relate more clearly to the characters that surround him (153). In this sense, writes Seán Lucy, Sweeney "is the ancestor of Harry in *The Family Reunion*, of Celia in *The Cocktail Party*, and of Colby in *The Confidential Clerk*" (C342, 183): all are characters who will have a special resonance for the most insightful audience members.

Carol H. Smith uses a theory of levels as the basis for her study of Eliot's plays. All his plays , she writes, confront   the plight of a person who perceives a divine order, but, forced to live in the natural world, must somehow integrate both realms. To express this theme, Eliot crafted what Smith identifies as "a multi-level drama" to lead his audience from a mundane perception of reality to an awareness of a new transcendent one, which is nevertheless extant within the natural world (C382, viii-ix). In a similar vein, Patrick Roberts writes: "The theme of the relationship of the two worlds, material and spiritual, the natural and the transcendent, is ubiquitous in Eliot's drama; his efforts are always directed toward bringing them into creative interaction with each other, and his development as a dramatist is essentially a record of his attempts to bridge the gulf that, in his experience, opens between them" (C148, 183).

In *English Dramatic Form*, M. C. Bradbrook presents another schema of different dramatic levels: "Eliot learnt from the French theatre of the 'thirties that irony could be strengthened by setting together ancient heroism and modern triviality; it gives what Yeats termed 'an emotion of multitude'—like that of plot and contrasted subplot. The spectator is forced to respond in two different ways simultaneously to the same situation, and so his own personal interpretation is stirred up" (C270, 162).

Richard Wasson argues that Eliot's drama has an intentional and important dramaturgical self-awareness, embracing dramatic rhetoric as he himself described in "'Rhetoric' and Poetic Drama." "Eliot's drama constantly reminds the actor that he is playing a role" (C393, 233). Because his characters "learn that the real plot is controlled by powers not really on but off-stage," they come to "recognize the existence of a script" (235). Wasson calls Harry, from *The Family Reunion*, "quite a dramatic theorist," whose role is to remind the audience "first that the theatre is artificial, the real forces are off-stage, and second, that in life as in a theatre ultimate reality is off-stage" (235).

The Cocktail Party "begins with a story about tigers and with conversation about the ability of particular characters to tell stories and mimic others," Wasson continues, because "they all want to write their own play. That issue is quickly resolved—Sir Harcourt-Reilly emerges not only as playwright but as director" (236). Reilly's psychoanalytic sessions have "appropriated the drama of therapy to the rhetoric of theatre, and the sessions, theatrically speaking, form a play-within-a-play. Reilly carefully directs an elaborate sequence of entrances and exits and discusses with each character the role he has played and will play in the drama. Such manipulation of action on the part of a 'real' therapist would probably have bad results and destroy the whole sense of trust; but it is precisely the kind of manipulation Eliot thinks necessary to good drama" (236-37). In *The Confidential Clerk*, Sir Claude "tries to write a comedy in which his bastard son can inherit his business and estate. He carefully prepares for his wife's entrance and instructs Eggerson and Colby on the roles they are to play. But he is a bad playwright; even worse, he is a bad director, and ends up by creating bad actors" (238), pointing to the need for a playwright of greater integrity; Colby comes to fulfill this role.

Reception

Large audiences followed the development of Eliot's playwriting career eagerly and enjoyed his plays roundly. What might be defined as a quasi-intellectual audience—knowing they were supposed to admire the Nobel laureate, but finding his early poetry inaccessible—found plays like *The Cocktail Party* calming and thankfully serene after *The Waste Land*; and found the social medium of the theatre a palatable respite from the younger Eliot's prophetic insistence on solipsistic disintegration. Some scholars, too, saw Eliot's star continually ascending; Denis Donoghue, for example, argues that each of his plays is an improvement on the previous one (C290). Peter Kline's critical praise typifies the substantial chorus of voices that lavished boundless adulation on Eliot's drama: "though Eliot's drama deals with a very narrow range of human experience, it brings to the stage a depth profounder than anything previously realized in successful drama. What Eliot has achieved, in effect, is a solution to the human dilemma, and although this solution may be limited to the author himself and is at any rate extremely cryptic at best, it is a powerful directing force which leaves its mark on drama as a whole" (C332, 458). Eliot's unique strengths, Kline writes, include his "spiritual and philosophical impact" (458), and his profound and concentrated focus on "a single instant of apprehension" (459). Eliot "has given us a modern sense of the kind of integrity that is necessary" for superlative drama: each of his plays is great as a "result of the greatness of the experience behind it" (472).

Bernard Bergonzi, on the other hand, calls the final plays "irredeemably trivial," and writes in 1972 that "it is, by now, a common opinion that Eliot's theatrical development in the fifties was a move in the wrong direction, after the promising dramatic experiments of the twenties and thirties" (C266, 189). Such an attack is typical of those by critics who expect or demand the same approach and sensibility in Eliot's later work as in his earlier career.

Indeed, a considerable segment of Eliot's original loyal audience had followed his guidance through waste lands and felt disappointed or betrayed by the writer's widespread public acclaim. Discussing Eliot in a parody of the poet's own verse (apparently a popular contemporary diversion—there are several examples of such parody), a *New Statesman* writer satirized the fame Eliot reaped on the Broadway stage with *The Cocktail Party*:

> This is the vulgarist success, blasting
> A hitherto immaculate reputation,
> The voice
> *Par excellence* of the waste land and the wilderness.
> Can the exalted oracle rejoice
> Who, casting
> Pearls before swine, wins swinish approbation?
> *Tereu*, twit, twit, this metaphysical mime
> That should have been
> The most distinguished failure of all time
> Proves quite the opposite.
> Between the conception and the reception, between
> The curtain calls the Shadow falls—
> The deep damnation of a Broadway hit. (In C277, 247)

More harshly, William Barrett laments "the embarrassing and delicate situation of the master at the height of his fame and influence at the very moment when his creative powers and energy appear to be at their lowest ebb. Many years ago, it seems, we were undergraduates, and Eliot's name was a secret and holy conspiracy among us against our teachers of English literature and the tastes they taught. Since then we have seen his influence spread abroad, and his figure become entrenched in the academy itself; this influence has been immensely valuable, and it is hard to imagine what we might be without it; but every influence is exclusive in some directions, and so we have seen this one too become in time stiff and rigid" (C162, 359).

On the occasion of the American premiere of *The Confidential Clerk*, a *New Yorker* review titled "The Importance of Being Eliot" gives a sense of his presence at the height of his dramatic fame. Though Wolcott Gibbs finds the play an unsuccessfully jumbled bag of goods, he admits that the author—not completely deservedly—is "something of a legend in his lifetime, as nearly infallible as a mortal man can be. He is assured not only a large, ready-made audience for any work of his but also one of a peculiar quality, since it comes intellectually captive to the theatre, already more than half convinced. It is touchingly grateful for trifles, fearful of even the idea of being bored, nervously alert to detect secondary meaning whether they exist or not. An author could hardly ask for more than this cultivated obeisance" (R175).

Reviewing Eliot's final play, *The Elder Statesman*, Alan Brien in *The Spectator* objects even more aggressively to what he characterizes as unmerited adulation: "Somehow Mr. T. S. Eliot melts the marrow in the bones of critics. When Don Quixote de la Faber comes blindly clanking across the waste land, the fog streaming from his outsize armour, the gallant yeamen of England break their pencils across their knees and throw themselves beneath his proud hooves. They are so afraid that they will miss the point that they desperately make all the points he muffed. They rewrite his plays for him. They magnify his puppets into people. They create an imaginary genius called 'T. S. Eliot—playwright' and clamber over each other to worship at the shrine of the Invisible Dramatist" (R190, 305). Critical hostility against Eliot is developed at greatest length in *The Myth of T. S. Eliot* (C370), by Rossell Hope Robbins, but most critics and readers cannot so unilaterally dismiss him as an emperor wearing no clothes.

Between the extremes of adulation and disappointment at Eliot's dramatic career, there is a middle way. John Bayley typifies the engagement and tempered interest evoked by the oeuvre—provocative, but not wholly satisfying—published in 1962 as *Collected Plays*: they "have the look of an experiment that has been brought to some kind of conclusion. A way of trying it, not very satisfactory, as their author might say. . . . as a playwright Mr. Eliot—it is one of his most engaging traits—seems politely to co-opt the interested spectator to stand beside him in the wings and to contemplate in a deprecatory, quizzical head on one side sort of way, the shortcomings of the piece and the laborious technical problems it posed. . . . all he seems to expect is a mild mutual collaboration at the end of which he and his ideal audience will turn their heads towards one another as they stand together and regretfully, amusedly, thankfully, comprehendingly, shake them" (C263, 3).

And Ronald Peacock diplomatically offers this assessment of Eliot's drama: "It may be that the unifying of many strands of feeling and experience in the picture of life presented in Eliot's plays admits of approval in theory without being unchallengeably successful in dramatic practice. But the attempt to express this in drama by a combination of realistic modern setting and emergent myth is unique and, because of the range of experience and thought involved, infinitely interesting" (C364, 71).

Noting that the plays today "are commonly either ignored or treated as an appendix to Eliot's main poetic achievements," Carol H. Smith writes that "This perception of his plays as secondary plagued Eliot himself during his lifetime, despite their popularity and his many assertions regarding the importance of drama both for his time—a formless age—and for his own poetic development" (C381, 162). Contrary to some sentiments, Smith argues, Eliot's playwriting was not a hobby or a distraction to occupy the time of an exhausted poet: "The fact is that Eliot, except for the hiatus between 1924, when he wrote the *Sweeney Agonistes* fragments, and 1934, when he agreed to write the choruses for *The Rock*, steadily pursued his own program of dramatic education and experimentation throughout his long career. Moreover, there is clear evidence that he regarded as one of his most important accomplishments the development of a conversational dramatic poetry that would attract lay audiences to poetic drama" (162).

Playwriting provided Eliot with the order and form that he increasingly demanded of his mature work, Smith asserts. "Drama represented to Eliot a literary form with a special mission. The playwright could, he believed, create an artistically ordered world within the play and at the same time unite all levels of the audience in a communal experience. Most important of all, drama could re-create for the modern audience what Eliot . . . believed to be at the heart of both drama and religion—the secular death and spiritual rebirth of the hero" (163).

Style and Genre

Eliot's verse drama can be categorized into three different styles that evolved from the 1920s to the 1950s. The first of these, most pronounced in *Sweeney Agonistes* (and, to the disappointment of some critics, relatively repressed in all the other plays) is Eliot's vintage modernism. This embodies the voice, diction, and tenor of his poetry as seen in the tawdry bleak banality of the final third of "A Game of Chess"; the empty horror from "Gerontion" and "The Hollow Men"; the ominous Dantean terrors of *The Waste Land*; the insecurity and social fragmentation from "Prufrock" and "Portrait of a Lady." *Sweeney Agonistes* bears the imprint of a language Eliot carefully cultivated to convey the difficult condition of the modern world (examined at greater length in my chapter on Eliot in *The Language of Modernism* [Ann Arbor: UMI

Research Press, 1989])—a language that aesthetically co-opts the harsh disjointed confusion which so many modern artists found so pervasive.

The second style, which most affects *The Rock* and *Murder in the Cathedral*, is one of mystical spiritual incantation—an attempt to transcend, purify, redeem, perhaps repress, the language and tone of Sweeney's modernism. Obviously *Murder in the Cathedral* is more successful than *The Rock* in this regard, but there are important moments in the pageant as well: the expressionist confrontation between the Redshirts and Blackshirts and its aftermath dramatically asserts a newly-created aesthetic sensitive to the importance and delicacy of a productive social commonweal. Eliot's courageously trite resort to appeals for British/Anglican stamina and respectability (in the characters of the Cockney workmen) is also indicative of his imperative in this period: to displace Sweeney with whomever might offer a productive vision of spiritual regeneration, whether Thomas à Becket the heroic martyr or Ethelbert the prosaic flat caricature.

Eliot's third stylistic phase is seen in *The Confidential Clerk* and *The Elder Statesman*. Eliot's tone in those plays is quotidian and unassuming, signifying that his characters have learned to live their ordinary lives in meter. The loose poetry reflects a kind of orderly control—certainly not a very obtrusive order or form, since the plays' poetry is not profoundly striking; but a form that is nevertheless insistently present as the characters go about their daily business. This style is appropriate to the later comedies of identity, which are resolved with relatively less torment or trauma as compared with Eliot's difficult earlier resolutions. In their mechanical, pragmatic determination, these comedies are refreshingly formulaic. The late style is evocative of certain passages of *Four Quartets*—not the passages of incisively existential ontological querying, but rather, the poetry of concord and consort that is the consequence of the philosophical quest: a well-earned equilibrium.

The Family Reunion and *The Cocktail Party* are perhaps the most interesting plays because they do not fit neatly into this schema of stylistic development. Basically, they straddle the second and third categories, but there is always the possibility of the first rearing its ugly head—though in the event this never really happens, still, it could—turning the plays into "Sweeney Erect." What would the Eumenides have said if they could speak? (Perhaps something out of the most horrible passages of *The Waste Land*?) Would Edward have "done his wife in" (as Sweeney fantasizes doing) if Julia and Alex hadn't come to calm him down? Such inescapably persistent modernist tensions underlie all Eliot's plays to some extent, and these two most prominently.

M. C. Bradbrook in *T. S. Eliot* suggests a slightly different anatomy of the dramatic canon—linking *The Family Reunion* and *The Cocktail Party* with *Murder in the Cathedral*—writing that the three middle plays "form a closely related group; all . . . are built on a contrast between the man who sees and the rest who are blind" (C272, 38). The action in all these plays is slight, she writes: "A single moment of choice, the Kierkegaardian choice, is set before the main character; the rest of the play leads up to and leads away from this moment" (38-39). And Robert A. Colby, writing of *The Confidential Clerk*, presents another paradigm: "His typical plot situation now, as [in *The Family Reunion*] is the "reunion"—a group of individuals, related in some way to each other, separate and then come together again, sobered, sophisticated by an emotional experience they have all shared, presumably better oriented to each other and the world" (C235, 802).

From *The Family Reunion* through the end of his dramatic career, Eliot's plays presented at least the veneer of comedy, which bore a sometimes strange relation to the other more sober dynamics of spirituality, pathos, uncertainty. (See, for example, the "Critical reaction" section in the chapter on *The Cocktail Party* for discussion of whether that play is in fact, as Eliot claimed, a comedy.) Noel Coward, for decades the West End's preeminent comic dramatist, certainly exerted a stylistic influence: Eliot's dry, subdued, cosmopolitan tone, with its clipped yet resonant wit (occasionally giving way to a mild slapstick) evokes the tenor of Coward's comedy. P. G. Mudford reconciles Eliot's use of the "high comedy" mode with his more serious dramatic intentions: "the humorous revelation of individual folly, through behaviour and situation, raises social and moral issues which are themselves often seen in the perspective of some further metaphysical belief. And it is the presence of such a belief, however subtly indicated, that allows these issues to be treated with comic levity" (C352, 127). The plays "provide that combination of pleasure and interest which belong to a literary and dramatic kind rarely achieved: laughter at human folly, delight in comic situation, seriousness of viewpoint—and a restraint of feeling that enables us to enjoy the comedy without losing sight of its more sombre implications" (140).

As a poet writing plays, Eliot was most consciously placing himself within a centuries-old tradition of verse drama, dominated by the Elizabethans. (See the introduction to the annotations of Eliot's essays on drama, in the bibliography of primary sources, for more detailed consideration of Eliot's links to Shakespeare and the Elizabethans.) At the same time, though, Eliot was involved in a genre that had a limited but notable contemporary resurgence. Pound took Eliot to see a performance of W. B. Yeats's *At the Hawk's Well* in 1916, which may have been the impetus for Eliot to envisage his own revival of poetic drama. E. Martin Browne, Eliot's director, discusses the difficulties and drawbacks of verse drama: "It has long been in disuse, and has been regarded with suspicion both by actors and audiences. The actor thinks it is difficult to 'play.'. . . how can he make [lines of poetry] sound like the speech of a real person? Not only are the technical demands of verse, in breathing, diction, gesture, exacting as well as unfamiliar: when they are fulfilled, the result, as he fears, may be a barrier against the audience. It is more difficult, so many playgoers feel, to 'suspend disbelief' in a character speaking verse" (C275, 197). To overcome these problems, "dramatic verse must have two things: a speech-rhythm which seems natural to actors and audience, and the power to express individual character. These in addition to what is required of all stage-dialogue, that it should speak with immediately apprehensible point and clarity."

Today, Salmon writes, verse drama plays are regarded as "period pieces in a theatrical museum" (C373, 87). The genre arose to challenge the prevailing naturalism; verse playwrights claimed that a condition of dramatic stagnation could be overcome only by means of the very consciously aesthetic device of poetry. Poets from Masefield to Eliot believed "the only remedy for this artistic paralysis was a massive injection of verse plays into the main arteries of the theatre's system." Salmon quotes from a program at the 1932 Cambridge Festival Theatre, explaining how the theatre could accomplish the invigoration of dramatic expression: "Drama is words and movement. If movement must be given more expressive form, so must words. Words in expressive form are poetry. The English stage demands poetry" (88).

The tradition of poets in the theatre, of course, has a rich lineage in the nineteenth-century work of Byron, Shelley, Keats, Southey, Blake, Wordsworth, Scott, and Coleridge, and is obviously indebted to the golden age of verse drama in the Elizabethan and Jacobean periods. Early twentieth-century audiences had seen an attempted revival of verse plays by such Georgian poets as John Masefield, John Drinkwater, Lascelles Abercrombie, and Gordon Bottomley.

With their interest in the Japanese Noh play, Pound and Yeats brought to the theatre a poetic sensibility of stylization, imagism, aestheticized visual effect, and resonant dramaturgical economy. They intended their discovery and transplantation of the genre to restore a sense of almost sacred power and ritual to contemporary drama. Yeats's "plays for dancers," highly formalized productions involving masks and musical choruses, included *At the Hawk's Well* and *The Only Jealousy of Emer*. For his company at Dublin's Abbey Theatre, he wrote and produced a range of verse plays ground in Irish myth and mythography.

Toward the end of the period *l'entre deux guerres* verse drama gained a following, abetted by such institutions as Rupert Doone's Group Theatre (which offered avant-garde poetic drama by Auden and Isherwood, MacNeice, and Spender) and Ashley Dukes's Mercury Theatre. The Mercury, Salmon writes, "between 1933 and 1939, was particularly hospitable to verse plays" (89). Successful American verse plays included Maxwell Anderson's historical chronicles from the 1930s, such as *Elizabeth the Queen* and *Mary of Scotland*, and Archibald MacLeish's 1935 *Panic*. In England, in addition to numerous religious verse plays emanating from the Canterbury Festival, the 1930s and 1940s featured Christopher Fry's *The Boy with a Cart*, *A Phoenix Too Frequent*, *The Lady's Not for Burning*, and *Venus Observed*. Other prominent verse plays at the Mercury after Browne took over its helm in 1946 included Ronald Duncan's *This Way to the Tomb!*, Gilbert Horobin's *Tangent*, Norman Nicholson's *The Old Man of the Mountains*, Donagh MacDonagh's *Happy as Larry*, and Anne Ridler's *The Shadow Factory*, which "carries a strong element of social conservatism that flavors the work of all the Mercury poets, whose ideas and whose verse seem to owe much to T. S. Eliot," writes Gerald Weales (C394, 229).

Less successful dramatic verse ventures also surfaced during this period: In *Modern Verse Drama* Arnold Hinchliffe cites, for example, Stephen Spender's verse play *Trial of a Judge*, in which "The verse does nothing beyond produce a kind of elevated atmosphere," and a coterie of "verbally indulgent" poets—e. e. cummings, William Carlos Williams, Robert Lowell, Wallace Stevens—who came to the theatre to make a second reputation, but whose efforts were more dramatic poems than true drama, and who never discovered significant audiences (C317, 27).

Mid-century verse drama, though prolific, has come under considerable contemporary attack—its swift disappearance is taken as a sign of its want of enduring substance. In this vein, M. C. Bradbrook defends Eliot in *English Dramatic Form*: he "should not be held responsible for Christopher Fry—who probably would have written in any case—but seen rather as an indirect influence behind the very different work of Pinter or Albee" in terms of the incisive element of caricature (C270, 171).

By the late 1950s—exactly when Eliot ceased writing plays—verse drama disappeared from the contemporary theatre. Salmon calls the 1956 production of John Osborne's *Look Back in Anger* the catalyst for terminating verse drama: "by the shock of that crucial event and what followed from it, the modern play in verse in Britain was put to flight." (C373, 97) Poetic drama "sank back into the shadows, to be replaced . . . by the burst of energy" embodied in such drama as Osborne's, Edward Albee's, and Arthur Kopit's.

The Plays

Sweeney Agonistes

Characters
Dusty. Doris. Wauchope. Horsfall. Klipstein. Krumpacker. Sweeney. Swarts. Snow.

Synopsis
Subtitled "Fragments of an Aristophanic Melodrama," the play is divided into two parts, headed "Fragment of a Prologue" (which Eliot wrote to the play's first director he did not think very good) and "Fragment of an Agon." The first of two epigraphs is taken from the *Choephoroi* of Aeschylus: "You don't see them, you don't—but I see them: they are hunting me down, I must move on"; Orestes utters this as he flees the psychological terrors of the Furies. The second epigraph is from St. John of the Cross: "Hence the soul cannot be possessed of the divine union, until it has divested itself of the love of created beings."

The play begins in a frenzied confusion of short, clipped sing-song lines, *in medias res*. Dusty and Doris are young working women, probably prostitutes, sharing a flat. They worry about who can be trusted to take care of them: Pereira is judged untrustworthy, while Loot (i.e., Lieut.) Sam Wauchope, a Canadian, is seen as a kind-hearted and safe fellow. Periera calls on the telephone, and Dusty makes an excuse for Doris; it seems that the vaguely-defined connection between the women and Pereira involves some power he holds over them: perhaps because he pays their rent, perhaps due to something more illicit.

Dusty and Doris draw cards, evocative of the tarot scene in *The Waste Land*. The King of Clubs, the first card drawn (symbolic of God, or of an anti-God, various critics argue), represents either Pereira or Sweeney: the two seem interchangeable. Other cards evoke aspects of Dusty and Doris's social lives, from trivial parties, presents, or quarrels, to more ominous forebodings: estrangement, death. The women act as if they are simply whiling away time playing a harmless game; the drama, though, evokes a more sinister foreshadowing of the condition of modern society—made all the more dangerous because Dusty and Doris are more consumed with their dates for the evening and an impending party than with the condition of spiritual dryness that the oracular Eliot depicted in his earlier poetry.

The chatter ends when Sam comes by with Captain Horsfall and two American businessmen, Klipstein, and Krumpacker, for the informal party. The knocks on the door (in the published text represented in all capital letters, portentously dragged down for five lines) announce the end of the card reading and the beginning of the party, though the mystery of the two of spades—the coffin—and of other queer prophecies remains unresolved.

The "party" is about 50 lines of small talk, in which we learn that all four men served together in World War I. They reminisce briefly about previous escapades, and anticipate future amusements in London under Sam's stewardship. As earlier there was an unsavory hint about Dusty and Doris, here there is a risqué suggestion about what the men will be doing to entertain themselves in London—a place they see as too slick and gay to settle down in, but perfectly fine for an jazzy adventure on the town. The first fragment ends thus, with the possibility that some disreputable adventures might begin at the party.

"Fragment of an Agon" opens with all the same characters as before, bolstered by Sweeney, Swarts, and Snow, presumably at a later stage in the party (though Sears Jayne claims this fragment takes place at Sweeney's pub [C25]). Sweeney and Doris banter, mixing flirtation and aggression, about his plan to take her away to a far-off island. Sweeney casts himself as cannibal and Doris as missionary; the island is both idyllic—bountiful and removed from the decadence of society—and dangerously isolated, at least for Doris. Sweeney is entranced by the idea of life on the island consisting of nothing but birth, copulation, and death; Doris rejects this life (perhaps out of a survival instinct that Sweeney threatens, or perhaps only because she would be bored there with no prospects of parties) in spite of a sensuous seranade sung and acted out by all the other men, evoking the lush atmosphere of bamboo, palm trees, and soothing sea sounds.

For Sweeney this island represents the essence of life; for Doris, though, it evokes death. Sweeney tries to reconcile this disparity, or perhaps just to play on her words, by asserting that life is the same as death. (Sweeney's discussion of birth and death and his sense of knowing more about this topic than any other person at the party have led some critics to interpret his demeanor in this scene as Christlike.)

Doris tries to fend off this conversation, remembering the card of the coffin she had drawn earlier, but Sweeney proceeds with the story of a man—perhaps himself—who killed a girl and kept her body for months in a bathtub, immersed in lysol, while he continued with his daily routine. Offhandedly he remarks that every man, at some time, needs to kill a woman.

The macabre story sparks a bit of gossipy banter from the other guests, but Sweeney uses the story as a springboard from which to expound his philosophy of life and hints that his point is so lofty as to defy mere language; his philosophical abstractions briefly seem to transcend the inanities of a boozy party, though they are at the same time mired in the discourse of the scene's inescapably common brashness. The murder, Sweeney explains, called into question for the murderer who was alive and who was dead; the murderer felt estranged from quotidian society (recalling Doris's drawing of the card of estrangement earlier), and in a surreal limbo between life and death.

Sweeney himself, as his story concludes, is cognizant of the party that is the immediate reality, and the necessity of such day-to-day struggles as paying the rent, which was Dusty and Doris's main concern at the beginning of the play. At the same time, though, he has brought death to the party, and simultaneously brought—albeit clumsily and cruelly—the uncomfortably unanswerable question of what life means, and what the value is of their inane amusements. The earlier allure and exuberance of the party in the foreground has been tainted by the introduction of cannibalism, grisly tabloid murders, and an existential miasma. In a final chorus that combines a *danse macabre* with echoes of Gilbert and Sullivan's *Iolanthe*, the four ex-soldiers describe the nightmarish horror of not knowing whether anyone is alive or dead, and the play ends with the same configuration of "knocks" as in the first fragment—this time, the knocks of the hangman coming to lead away the condemned prisoner. The final effect is one of dimly perceived terror amid a dissipated dithyramb.

Production History

The play was first produced on 6 May 1933 at the Vassar Experimental Theatre, Vassar College, Poughkeepsie, NY, directed by Hallie Flanagan. The performance was part of a program called *Now I Know Love*, composed largely of a sequence of mimes set to music by Quincy Porter. Eliot wrote to Flanagan with some details about how he envisioned the production: characters should wear masks, with characters in old masks acting young and vice versa; the diction should not have much expression; light drum taps should accompany the play, especially the Chorus, which should sound like a street drill; the characters should be seated at a refectory table in a shabby apartment, and Sweeney should be scrambling eggs (a mythical icon of regeneration, an image Eliot would use again in *The Cocktail Party*). The play should be stylized like a Japanese Noh drama, he felt (C382, 62). Emphasizing the ritualistic aspect of this play, and indeed of all drama, Eliot wrote Flanagan that she should read Francis Cornford's *The Origins of Attic Comedy* before producing the play. Eliot also pressed Flanagan to study W. H. Auden's drama; in her book *Arena*, she quotes him as telling her, "Anyone who liked Sweeney could have a lot of fun with Auden's *Dance of Death*" (6). For the Vassar production Eliot wrote another 25 lines of script to complete the second fragment, in which an old gentleman enters after the knocks at the end of the final chorus.

Flanagan rejected many of Eliot's suggestions regarding atmosphere; Eliot, who attended the premiere, found Flanagan's rendition of the play quite different from his own intention but approved of it, and thought her vision of the play was perhaps even better than his own. The next day, in an address to Vassar students (given on the set where the play had been presented the previous night), Eliot discussed the play. To a student who asked if the production had been what he expected, he responded with a line he would later use in *Murder in the Cathedral*: "The moment expected may be unforeseen when it arrives." Another questioner, referring to Sweeney's compulsion to murder a girl, asked the author, "Mr. Eliot, did you ever do a girl in?" Flanagan recorded that "Mr. Eliot looked apologetic and said, 'I am not the type'" (C15, 138-39).

Sweeney Agonistes was performed starting on 11 November 1934 by London's Group Theatre, which Eliot had joined that year. Eliot influenced the plays written for the company and was instrumental in publishing them. The Group Theatre was perceived to have leftist leanings, certainly incompatible with Eliot's professed sentiments, though he appeared committed (if cautiously) to its work. Michael Sidnell describes Eliot's influence in the Group Theatre: "In opposition to the sensuousness, didacticism and immanence of Brechtian theatre, Eliot emphasized the word and the symbolic relation of the stage to reality. Under his influence, Group Theatre plays and productions tried to accomodate poetry and symbol on the one hand with song, dance and parable on the other" (C29, 259).

Rupert Doone, who had begun his career dancing for Sergei Diaghilev in the Ballets Russes and was the Group Theatre's most prominent leader, directed the production at the Group Theatre Rooms. (Doone's other productions for the company included Auden's *The Dance of Death*; Auden and Christopher Isherwood's *On the Frontier: A Melodrama in Three Acts*, *The Ascent of F6*, and *The Dog Beneath the Skin*; Louis MacNeice's *Out of the Picture*; Jean Cocteau's *The Human Voice: A Play in One Act*; and Stephen Spender's *Trial of a Judge*.) Desmond MacCarthy describes the Group Theatre performance of *Sweeney Agonistes*: "I found myself in an L-shaped room on the third floor, round which seats had been arranged leaving an empty space in the middle, where stood a table with some drinks on it and some unoccupied chairs. It was in this space that the performance took place. We, the spectators, were in the position of Elizabethan swells; we were sitting on the stage itself. . . . Into the darkened room, or rather into a little pool of light created by one lamp overhead, came two young women wearing masks; their masks bore a grotesque resemblance to a commonplace kind of prettiness." The actors retired "offstage" by stepping out of this pool of light. MacCarthy notes "Doone's device of turning the audience itself into a kind of chorus (the actors were sitting among us)," and dragging the spectators into Sweeney's sordid world (R7).

In 1934, Eliot had discussed with Doone the possibility of writing a new play for the Group Theatre, but Eliot's career proved to turn away from

Doone's brand of experimental drama. A scenario called "The Superior Land-lord" (described in Sidnell pp. 100-102 and 262-65), outlines a more complete version of a Sweeney play; an earlier title for the same work was "The Marriage of Life and Death: A Dream." This sketch may have been the new play for the Group Theatre that Eliot contemplated. Eliot referred to "Fragment of an Agon" when it was published in the *Criterion* in 1927 as being from *Wanna Go Home, Baby?*, possibly a working title for the same project.

William Alwyn wrote the music, "a dreamy South Seas background to Sweeney's confrontation with Doris" (C29, 105), and Robert Medley was responsible for masks and decor. The play featured Ruth Wynn Owen as Dusty, Isobel Scaife as Doris, Mervyn Blake as Sam Wauchope, Desmond Walter-Ellis as Klipstein, John Ormerod Greenwood (a Group Theatre founder) as Krumpacker, Patrick Ross as Horsfall, Doone as Snow, and John Moody as Sweeney. Two performances were announced, and a performance intended to be the final one was added in December, due to the play's enthusiastic reception; W. B. Yeats and Bertolt Brecht were present at the December presentation (C29, 103). MacCarthy broadcast a story about the play after that performance, and the Group Theatre added additional performances in January and February of 1935 as a result of the favorable publicity. Doone added a violent conclusion to his production, based on Eliot's poem "Sweeney Erect," and did not use the passage Eliot had written for Flanagan. Doone's ending presents Sweeney chasing Doris around the table, razor in hand; the audience hears a police whistle, a scream from Doris, a knock at the door, and then blackout (C29, 106). Yet Lyndall Gordon sees this ending as a mistake: Presenting the implication of a literal murder, she writes, "only obscures further the hidden life of penitential torture" (C309, 64).

On 1 October 1935, *Sweeney Agonistes* opened at the Westminster Theatre, London, for 15 performances, sharing a double bill with W. H. Auden's *The Dance of Death*. The cast was the same as at the Group Theatre Rooms, except for the substitutions of Richard Schjelderup as Wauchope, Peter Copley as Klipstein, and Stefan Schnabel as Krumpacker. The program carried a producer's note: "My production is concerned with morals as well as aesthetics. I have sought to criticise the conventionalities of modern behaviour with its empty code and heartiness—immoral, but never immoral enough—decaying, but so long in dying. I see Sweeney himself as a modern Orestes (the only three-dimensional character in the play). The rest are conventionalised conventional characters—The Eumenides or Bogies of Sweeney's persecution."

Doone used a series of blackouts to emphasize the play's fragmentary nature, giving the effect of an Expressionist montage. Sidnell hypothesizes that the success of this effect may have influenced Eliot not to further integrate the fragments that remain of the play into any larger work. The production reflected the aesthetic Doone had learned from Diaghilev and Cocteau (with whom he had collaborated), involving an avant-garde combination of all the arts, and the necessity of considering theatre as a dramatic community, a cooperative social force. Gordon describes Doone's vision of the play: the characters were all "projections of Sweeney's mind: they were his bogies on a darkened stage. Even when they unmasked at the end, they were scarcely human. Sweeney alone did not wear a mask, but appeared as a sinister clerk in pin-striped trousers and steel spectacles" (63).

In January 1942, Cleveland College's College Square Players presented the play, directed by George R. Kernodle, as an opener for Marlowe's *Dr. Faustus*. Eric Bentley produced the play in the library of Schloss Leopolds-kron, Salzburg, in the Spring of 1949. Of that revival, he writes, "the castle library made an admirable auditorium for the play, perhaps a better one than a real theatre would have. Our not having a stage seemed also no disadvantage. There was a dais for Doris' couch, and enough space in front of it for Swee-ney to walk forward—it seems good to have Sweeney walk, as it were, out of the frame of the picture and into (i.e., towards) the audience" (C14, 390). Any sympathetic production, he adds, will highlight "the explosive effect of the various entrances. The most explosive of all entrances is, of course, that of Snow and Swarts as minstrels in black face. . . . An essential part of the musical episode is the silent figure of Sweeney. In fact the episode seems to bring to birth, as a sort of protest against its frivolity, Sweeney's long, cli-mactic speech" (390-91).

Judith Malina directed the Living Theater Company in a production at New York's Cherry Lane Theater that ran from 2 March to 18 May 1952. The show was part of a program that also featured Gertrude Stein's *Ladies' Voices* and Pablo Picasso's *Desire*. Walter Mullen starred as Sweeney, Christina French as Dusty, Shirley Gleaner as Doris, Mihran Chobania as Wauchope, J. E. Duane as Klipstein, Angelo Laiacona as Krumpacker, Henri Sulaiman as Swarts, and Cecil Cunningham as Snow. Settings and constumes were by Julian Beck.

The play was produced at Wesleyan University's '92 Theater in May and June 1952 and revived there the following year. Ralph Pendleton directed the show, and Richard K. Winslow conducted the musical score as performed on piano, tympanist, celesta, and saxophone. William Dobson played Sweeney, Marjorie Rice played Dusty, and Lena Sinagulia played Doris. Winslow converted the play into a chamber opera that was produced by the Opera Workshop at Columbia University's Brander Matthews Theatre in May 1953. Felix Brentano staged the opera, the cast of which was composed of students.

Rupert Doone directed *Sweeney Agonistes* at Morley College in the mid-1950s; musical direction was by Winifred Radford.

In London, Peter Wood produced a revival with a jazz accompaniment by John Dankworth (who conducted his own score) and settings by Bridget Riley; it was presented on 13 June 1965 at the Globe Theatre under the direction of Vera Lindsay (who as Vera Poliakoff had acted for the Group Theatre in the 1930s, and had led an attempt to revive the ensemble as Group Theatre Productions in the 1950s). The singer Cleo Laine played Dusty, Anna Quayle played Doris, and Nicol Williamson played Sweeney. That performance included the passage Eliot wrote for Flanagan's 1933 production.

The *New Yorker* review describes the spectacle of the set at the Globe: it was "acted against a projection screen on which a luminous disc of brilliant spots and other optical razzle-dazzle . . . constantly changed color." Dankworth's score "provided the perfect nervous, titillating obbligato to the chatter of the two whores." Sweeney is described as dressed "in shirtsleeves and a dirty red waistcoat, with a bowler hat pushed back from his round, intelligent face" (R9). The play was part of a "Homage to T. S. Eliot" (who had died six months earlier) by the Stage Sixty Theatre Club to benefit the London Library, of which Eliot had been president. The evening began with Igor Stravinsky's requiem for Eliot, and also featured Peter O'Toole reading "The Love Song of J. Alfred Prufrock," Lawrence Olivier reading "Little Gidding," and Groucho Marx reading from *Old Possum's Book of Practical Cats*.

In August 1972, New York's Jean Cocteau Repertory performed *Sweeney Agonistes* along with a dramatic presentation of Sylvia Plath's poems. In May 1974, the same company again performed the play, directed by Eve Adamson. Along with Samuel Beckett's *Act Without Words II*, it was part of a program called *Astonishments*. Design was by James S. Payne, and sound and music were by Coral S. Potter.

Richard Williams directed the Birkenhead Exchange company's *Sweeney Agonistes*, in a program also featuring Adrian Mitchell's *In the Unlikely Event of an Emergency*, at London's Old Red Lion Theatre beginning 4 August 1988, starring Maggie Saunders as Dusty, Liz Brailsford as Doris, Iain Armstrong as Wauchope, Michael Rigg as Klipstein, Christopher Snell as Krumpacker, Mark Lindridge as Horsfall, and Jack Ellis as Sweeney. Music in the style of Kurt Weill was by Stephen McNeff, decor by Simon Ash, and costumes by Hilary Peyton.

On 24 April 1989, in celebration of Eliot's centennial, The Chameleon Theatre Company presented a concert reading directed by Cash Tilton and with music composed and directed by John M. Cook, at New York's Penta Hotel.

Critical Overview

Performance Reviews

Nevill Coghill remembers the Group Theatre production as being "performed with an exquisite blend of violence and restraint. The cool, rich, level voice of Mr. Doone as Snow saying 'Let Mr. Sweeney continue his story' sent a shudder down my back. He offered an almost entirely different interpretation of the play to that I had worked out. As he presented it, it was a study in the psychology of a Crippen; he made it seem that we were all Crippens at heart" (C16, 117). (Dr. Hawley Harvey Crippen was an American, who had once lived in Eliot's birthplace of St. Louis, convicted of murdering his wife and burying her dismembered body in the basement of his London house; the 1910 case drew extensive publicity.)

Desmond MacCarthy, reviewing the same production in *The Listener*, writes that "*Sweeney Agonistes* belongs to that part of Mr. Eliot's work inspired by his negative impulse, the impulse to contemplate the sordid" as opposed to more comfortingly sedate works such as *Ash-Wednesday* and *The Rock*. Of the performance MacCarthy notes, "One of the defects I noticed . . . was that this ominous close, this knocking at the last, was not emphatic enough." The play, as he perceives it, eschews realism: "In performance, the realism became largely symbolic, and this effect was strengthened by all the characters save one [Sweeney] wearing masks" (R7).

"It was good broad character-acting we saw," the reviewer for *Punch* writes, "and the gulf was not between Sweeney and all the rest but between the three persons [Sweeney, Dusty, and Doris] and the background of horrible disembodied caricatures. But *Sweeney Agonistes* produced like this is an arresting spectacle. I thought the producers were a little unsparing in their copious use of effects, piling black caps on death masks lest the point should be missed that behind the masks of conventional heartiness and pleasure there is nullity" (R13).

George W. Bishop, in the London *Daily Telegraph*, calls the 1935 Westminster production "one of the most extraordinary [plays] ever seen in London. . . . [it] defies description, and calls for little attention. It is dull and pretentious, and as far as I was concerned . . . quite pointless" (R3).

Surveying the past theatrical season, Michael Sayers observes in *Criterion* that while the Westminster production "was on the whole adversely received by the critics," nevertheless "It seemed to me that our only hope for a poetic theatre lay in the work of the Group. According to the critics the first presentation was pretentious, degenerate, asinine, gauche, insincere, propagandistic, crude, sordid, stupid, hysterical and altogether in bad taste. All of which was rather encouraging" (R10, 657); unfortunately, Sayers continues, the Group Theatre's subsequent programs that season were dull and conventional.

Richard Winslow's 1953 student production at Columbia "turned out to be a rather interesting operatic experiment, though nothing more," writes Douglass Watt in *The New Yorker*. "I was impressed by Winslow's ingenuity in giving 'Sweeney Agonistes' a semblance of form." The performance "proved so persuasive that I am ready to accept it as an approximation of what Eliot had in mind when he wrote the poem. It also suggests why he didn't feel like elaborating on it, for once the garrulous Sweeney has succeeded in putting a chill on the evening . . . the party is done for and there just isn't any place to go but home. Making the best of the egocentric and unappetizing leading character, the composer has written a lively and effective score, which has the virtue of always seeking to clarify the drama instead of adding new subtleties. Following the dialogue with exactitude and intelligence, it adopts whatever style seems to be called for—a melodious duet for some soul-searching observations exchanged by Dusty and Doris, a music-hall song for Wauchope, and so on—and at times it simply gets out of the way altogether and lets the singers speak their lines. Winslow's score, arranged for an orchestra consisting only of piano, celesta, pedal timpani, and snare drum, is not especially distinctive in itself, but it is admirably theatrical and appropriate" (R11).

Katherine J. Worth describes the 1965 production: "it came over as an exhiliratingly open piece of theatre, with its evocative changes of rhythm, its easy, swinging movements out of dialogue into soft shoe turns and musical comedy numbers" (C404, 58).

In *Show Business*, Victor Lipton describes actors in black leotards in Eve Adamson's 1974 production "reciting the familiar, haunting lines with clarity, and confronting one another with verve and fine energy. Its highlight is the section, 'Under the bamboo tree,' which is incanted well and amusingly" (R6).

Christopher Edwards in *The Spectator* calls Richard Williams's 1988 production "a genuine collector's item . . . urbanely brittle—despair and disintegration, cocktail-party loucheness and a dash of the criminal under- world. . . . The production does not try to make too much sense of Eliot's unfinished and uncommunicative fragment, but it does manage authentically to recreate its stylish mightmare quality" (R5). In the *Independent* Paul Arnott calls the musical accompaniment "discordant . . . violent efforts from piano and cello," and writes that the play "reeks of murderous men and tropical parks. It is the 1930s and the language often seems to fall between Berkoff and Pinter underscored by music which is half beat, half shriek. For those who do not know their Eliot it may well prove incomprehensible" (R1).

Scholarly Response

The special quality of *Sweeney Agonistes*, writes Katherine J. Worth, "springs from the skillful turning of elements derived from a warm, popular art"—the underlying music hall vaudevillean sensibility—"to effects of isola- tion and disorientation. It is an exercise in black comedy whose success depends upon the sustaining of the popular note just long enough for the distortion to register. Heavily syncopated rhythms suggest sexual excitement passing into a state of hysteria and spiritual panic. The jovial nightmare song from Gilbert and Sullivan takes a sickening lurch into real nightmare, convey- ing in musical terms the experience Sweeney cannot find words for, the swallowing up of the known by an unknown world" (C403, 128).

William V. Spanos characterizes the play as a crucial example of literature of the absurd, and explains how it relates to other absurdist texts: "As in Kafka's novel *The Trial* and so much of the drama it has influenced—Ion- esco's *Victims of Duty* and *Amédée*, Pinter's *The Room* and *The Birthday Party*, Frisch's *The Firebugs* and, in a wider context, Dürrenmatt's *The Visit*, to name but a few—the first part of Eliot's *Sweeney* . . . begins in a seedy apartment in the modern urban wasteland, the lonely inhabitants of which are expecting, though trying desperately to suppress their consciousness of, the imminent knock on the door. Like K's reaction to the mysterious intruders who arrest him one fine day and *Amédée*'s to the growing corpse in the next room, Dusty and Doris, the dislocated tenants of the postwar London flat, regard the mysterious Pereira, who is unpredictable and untrustworthy, as a demonic pursuer threatening their physical and spiritual security. . . . Thus in *Sweeney*, as in the existential literature of the absurd, the flat, the 'home' of modern man, assumes the character of a place of refuge from the dark and ominous outside world. It becomes, that is, an ironic symbol of the flimsy barrier erected by the modern scientific world view and its technology against the irrational; and the mysterious intruder, the agent who reminds the tenants of the contingency just beyond the locked door of their objectified world and just below the surface of their positivized consciousness, becomes an embodiment of the absurd or Nothingness, which has its radical source in the finality of death" (C32, 9-10).

Dusty and Doris are like a duo of Samuel Beckett characters, Spanos continues, who "rely on each other to act out meaningful or, at least, amusing and thus distancing dramatic illusions in their obsessive efforts to evade the meaninglessness of life in the precincts of eternal recurrence—'the zero zone'—or, rather, to evade the dread of Nothingness that threatens to break through the surface of their boredom . . . so Eliot's ladies see Sam and his friends as means of escaping consciousness of their predicament in the erosive circularity of life in the wasteland, which Sweeney focalizes later" when he talks of the inescapably banal cycle of birth, copulation, and death (10).

Numerous critics address the pervasive effect of the play's ritually stylized rhythm: Ronald Bush writes that Eliot's essays during the early 1920s "advocating the ritual-like stylization in drama, the cinema, ballet and poetry" were "drawing him inexorably toward the sketches" that became *Sweeney Agonistes* (C283, 81); the choruses of "The Hollow Men," too, anticipate the play's tone (97). Gareth Lloyd Evans probes beyond a focus on rhythm generally to the nature of the language itself: the play "has an insidious beat, but it only becomes completely hypnotic in its effect because of the interplay between the beat and (firstly), verbal repetitions and (secondly), the sound of words. 'Pereira' is like a rattle of kettledrums: 'How about Pereira?', 'What about Pereira?', 'You can have Pereira,' 'He's no gentleman, Pereira.' Throughout *Sweeney*, this interplay . . . goes deeper than the creation of a generalized emotional reaction in the listener; it helps to create character. Notice how in Dusty's speeches the repetitions and the emphases on 'I think' and 'I hope' and 'she says' and 'she hopes,' and 'mustard and water,' not only give a remarkable impersonation of real speech, but help to identify the flapdoodle mind of the speaker" (C295, 146). Evans calls Eliot's "ear for contemporary idiom and mode" the play's most important technical feature.

Andrew K. Kennedy, similarly, calls the play "most successful as an experiment in speech, or more precisely, in turning speech into rhythmic sound effects. . . . We are meant to experience the play upon our pulses. . . . we should recall how many of the elements in the short play are language-as-sound: the constant repetition of names, questions and greetings, for phonic play ('Good bye. Goooood Bye'); the telephone bell's 'Ting a ling' and the 'knock, knock' woven into the texture of this dialogue (spelt out as fourteen lines); Sweeney's speech, about *his* unutterable experience, merging into crooning ('We're gona sit here and have a tune'); the six visitors, with the unnecessary names, forming a broken chorus even before the burst into jazz song and the final nightmare-chorus. The spirit of the Hoo-ha's pervades this work" (C328, 101).

"The most signal failure among Eliot's attempts to have a character function on more than one plane," Grover Smith writes, "occurred in his skit *Sweeney Agonistes*. . . . [Sweeney] has to exist on a level of understanding or experience beyond the comprehension of some of the thickish members of the audience. But actually Eliot devised a character who utters gnomic statements about life and death without convincing one that he knows more than such people about what he is saying" (C383, 112).

But Lyndall Gordon disagrees, finding the play indeed set "on two distinct levels. Sweeney's state of spiritual terror was to address itself to what Eliot envisaged as a small receptive elite in the audience, while, theoretically, the 'literal-minded and visionless' sector [Eliot's description] would share the responses of their counterparts on stage: for them, the fortune-telling games of the tarts, the party songs of the Jazz Age, and murder as mere thriller. This superficial action is a cover for the fact that the core of the play is non-dramatic or, rather, pre- and post-dramatic: foreboding and remorse" (C309, 63).

Kinley Roby finds Sweeney a pilgrim figure trying to find truth. The murdered girl in the bathtub evokes a "macabre baptism, with Lysol rather than God's grace serving as the preserving agent" (C27, 13). She is a sacrificial reminder of the humanity that "the man in his pilgrimage, in his entrance into the dark night of the soul, has cast off" (23-24). Yet in the murderer's evocation of Eliot's epigraphs, Roby posits, the play may have a germ of optimism: "Orestes found deliverance and St. John found God. Perhaps the man in Sweeney's story will be equally successful in his quest. Sweeney, the man in the play who knows more than the others, will become Agatha in *The Family Reunion* and Julia and Harcourt-Reilly in *The Cocktail Party*" (25).

Morris Freedman finds, in the portrayal of the presumably Jewish bordello clients Klipstein and Krumpacker, a continuation of the anti-Semitic characterizations present in some of Eliot's other prose and poetry of this period. "Love in Eliot is always sexual . . . his attitude is either of resigned acceptance of its 'inhuman' machine-like practice or repugnance toward what he takes to be dissoluteness. All of his creatures, one way or another, are contemptible or pathetic in their sex habits, but a special condemnation seems to be reserved for the emotionally vulgar Jews" (C20, 201).

While "no one on stage has the faintest idea what Sweeney is talking about," writes Hugh Kenner in *The Invisible Poet* (C330, 222), his character represents "the objective correlative of a terrible thirst for metaphysical purity. . . . Sweeney, in fact, has undergone the process Eliot characterized as 'the frightful discovery of morality'" (227-28). *The Family Reunion*, Kenner asserts, completes the task Eliot left unfinished in *Sweeney Agonistes*.

Carol H. Smith finds the jazz age setting, like Eliot's affinity for the music hall, evidence of his early compulsion to find a large popular audience for his theatrical writing. The play's pervasive rhythmic strain represents Eliot's belief that rhythm is at the core of the ritual of drama, she writes, citing as evidence Eliot's 1923 essay "The Beating of a Drum"—Eliot later wrote in *The Use of Poetry and the Use of Criticism* that "poetry begins . . . with a savage beating a drum in a jungle" (155)—and his 1926 introduction to his mother's poetic drama, *Savonarola*, where he writes that such facets of modern life as the combustion engine have contributed a new and pervasive rhythmic sensibiltiy to our lives. The play's strong debt to jazz rhythms, writes Freedman, reflects the culmination of Eliot's experimentation using jazz to evoke the authentic idiom of vulgar dialogue. "The jazz rhythms marvelously enhance the spiraling quality of increasing stupor and confusion as the crowd gets more and more drunk. . . . Sweeney repeats the phrases in typical drunken fashion. He has got hold of an idea and keeps saying it aloud with awe" (C19, 429-30).

Sweeney, Smith argues, represents "natural man experiencing the agony of human deprivation and guilt. . . . suffering from an awareness of his lustful nature" (C30, 92), and embodying the Christian path toward spiritual suffering and salvation. The play's grotesque exaggeration reflects, "more clearly than anything Eliot has written, his state of mind and the state of his painful marriage during the years before his separation and conversion. . . . Eliot never again expressed the mood of anxiety and isolation so directly, nor so clearly identified the spiritual and sexual, although several of the later plays hint at this identification" (97-98). The play's importance, she argues, is Eliot's willingness to give voice to the character who had broodingly but silently haunted several earlier poems: "the challenge of letting Sweeney speak" (C381, 164).

T. H. Thompson argues that the play is Sweeney's confession of the murder of Mrs. Porter from *The Waste Land*, and that all Sweeney's appearances in Eliot's previous poetry provide clues to this crime (C33). Gordon confirms that in the typescript scenario of the play Sweeney appears to shoot Mrs. Porter (C309, 60).

D. G. Bridson finds the play dull and banal, though perhaps intentionally so; he admires only its rhythm: "This is pure barrel-organ, and with its constant repetition in Music-hall crosstalk, makes no bad medium for the whole" (R4). George Barker writes that *Sweeney Agonistes* demonstrates "poetry dissolving into a condition of exquisite, and perfectly lucid, decay. About it I perceive a pallor not only of subject, but as well of treatment. Eliot has contrived as deathly an elegy of his poetic decease, as he composed triumphal ode of his birth, *The Waste Land*" (R2).

Marjorie J. Lightfoot contrasts Eliot's early dramatic sensibility as manifested in this play with his later development: "Early, he held that verse drama should emphasize its differences from the naturalistic prose drama then popular; later he tried to adapt naturalistic conventions to his own ends and to keep the audience from being conscious—or at least self-conscious—that it was listening to verse drama. Accordingly, the early experimental plays . . . exhibit such attention-getting devices as a chorus, caricature, soliloquy, lyric duets, elevated rhetoric, and formal ritual," while the later plays avoid such devices (C341, 119-20).

What Eliot meant by calling the play an "Aristophanic Melodrama" is open to critical debate. "We are probably not meant to place a strict interpretation upon the word 'Aristophanic,'" writes David E. Jones. "Certainly, the resemblance to Greek Old Comedy does not go deep. The 'Fragment of a Prologue' performs the same general functions as the Aristophanic prologue; it sets the scene, creates a mood, and initiates the exposition. The 'Fragment of an Agon,' however, does not follow the carefully articulated form of its prototype. There is essentially no conflict because there is no mutual understanding, no common ground, so to speak, upon which contenders could meet in debate" (C325, 27).

But Nancy D. Hargrove finds the play Aristophanic "in its satire of the present age, in its mixture of comedy and tragedy, and in its use of the structure of Old Comedy. It is a melodrama," she adds, "in its presentation of exaggerated emotions and situations and in its use of songs" (C22, 166). Carol H. Smith, too, finds the play Aristophanic "in that it combines a comic surface of social satire with the ritualistic celebration of death and rebirth which Cornford found to underlie comedy" (C382, 58). Herbert Howarth suggests an echo of Laurent Tailhade's *Poèmes aristophanesques*, caricatures of the generation of 1900 (C322).

Perhaps because Eliot included *Sweeney Agonistes* in his collected poems (the only dramatic work aside from choruses from *The Rock* included there), some critics treat it as a poem rather than a play. "*Sweeney Agonistes* nominally marks the begining of Eliot's career as a dramatist," writes Elisabeth Schneider, "but among his plays it has no sequel"; and as an "unfinished poem," it also "proved rather a dead end, related more nearly to parts of the later fragment *Coriolan* than to anything else that followed it" (C28, 95).

Sears Jayne, reading the work as a poem, considers it "at least as 'finished' as most of Eliot's poems," especially if one pays attention to "the integrity of the verse-blocks of which the poem is built"—Jayne considers this unity of the verse-block a "basic principle of Eliot's poetry" (C25, 100). Eliot may have abandoned the idea of more fully developing the work, Jayne argues, because it "so accurately represents the average American's reaction to British life. The play may originally have been projected as a satire not merely on modern life in general, but on modern British life in particular. If so, Eliot's acceptance of British citizenship [in 1927] would explain his loss of interest in the work" (106).

Peter Ackroyd surmises that the work remained unfinished, or disintegrated, because "the novelty of the enterprise proved too much for him—he could not find an existing literary model from which he could draw strength and inspiration" (C255, 191). But David Galef argues that the play's unpublished final fragment lends a sense of structural completion and unity to the project. "The addition, written mostly in prose, is explicitly Christian and shifts the thematic structure toward spiritual rebirth, away from an arrested halfway state" (C21, 497); this fragment, along with a projected structure sketching "a Prologue, a Parados, an Agon, two Parabases, two Scenes, a Chorikon, and an Exodus. . . cohere in what amounts to a progression: the presentation of the world, the mind's confused terror in attempted withdrawal, and the eventual redemption of the soul. The sequence amounts to a journey that, as with most of Eliot's religious rites, must be performed in isolation" (497).

Jonathan Barker explains how the titles mislead many readers: "To define a work in its sub-title as 'Fragments' unfortunately militates against us considering it as a whole and worthy of our full attention: 'Fragments' carries with it the hint of 'failure.' Even more tentative is the repetition of the word in the titles of 'Fragment of a Prologue'—which seems to indicate that, as a Prologue is only the introduction to a work, the fragment of one leads *less* than nowhere—and 'Fragment of an Agon,' to which the Prologue leads. In fact *Sweeney Agonistes* is no more a fragment than *The Waste Land* which Eliot also named thus in its final lines: 'These fragments I have shored against my ruins'" (C13, 103).

Yet Gordon minimizes Eliot's concern with whether or not *Sweeney Agonistes* was, or would be, completed. She cites a letter he wrote to Flanagan in 1934, telling her he did not know if or when there would be more to the work, but seeming more immediately concerned with something else he was writing, that he called something new yet of the same kind; Gordon identifies this new enterprise as *The Family Reunion*—like Kenner, seeing important themes from that play germinating in *Sweeney Agonistes*.

The essential poetic point, Jayne asserts, is "the modern disease . . . [of] the difficulty of communication among human beings, and especially of poetic communication. It is Mr. Eliot himself who complains in the poem that he's 'gotta use words' when he talks to us; the struggle which is the subject of the poem is the poet's own struggle; it is Sweeney's voice and Sweeney's vocabulary we hear, but it is Mr. Eliot's Agon" (C25, 114).

While Jayne writes that the full title of the work in *Criterion*—*Wanna Go Home, Baby?*—implies that the play's language is that of a London pub, Barbara Everett calls this erroneous because the *OED* Supplement lists "baby" in the slang sense of "girl" only as an American usage before 1930. The title, then, suggests "an Americanism all the more highlighted by its linguistic formality: cadenced, derisive and self-conscious. The 'Americanness' of *Sweeney Agonistes* is indissociable from its meaning" (C18, 246). Other American elements in the play include the jazzy tone; the "stacatto machine-gun fire exchanges" of Dusty and Doris's stychomythia and Sweeney's gangster argot, all evocative of Chicago mobsters of the 1920s; the fact that the party never seems to leave Doris's flat to drink, further evoking "the time and place of the speakeasy, the private club and party of the Prohibition period"

(253); and stylistic echoes of such vintage American writers of the period as Anita Loos and Ring Lardner.

The importance of the play's American sensibility, Everett writes, is that Eliot begins his playwriting career "making a dramatic voice for himself by 'calling in the new world to redress the balance of the old,' writing, one might say, a European tragi-comedy in American. . . . It brings together a great if largely 'dead' European culture with a vital if debased modern American speech" (251).

Marianne Moore writes in her review of the play: "When the spirit expands and the animal part of one sinks, one is not sardonic, and the bleak lesson here set forth is not uncheerful to those who are serious in the desire to satisfy justice. The cheer resides in admitting that it is normal to be abnormal. When one is not the only one who thinks that, one is freed of a certain tension. Mr. Eliot is not showy nor hard, and is capable at times of too much patience; but here the truculent commonplace of the vernacular obscures care of arrangement, and the deliberate concise rhythm that is characteristic of him seems less intentional than it is. Upon scrutiny, however, the effect of an unhoodwinked self-control is apparent" (R8, 109).

Textual Notes and Influences

Virginia Woolf's diary entry for 20 September 1920 mentions Eliot's intention to write a verse play inhabited by four characters of Sweeney. Peter Ackroyd writes that a letter from Eliot to Wyndham Lewis in September 1923 shows he had begun the work by that time. To Arnold Bennett, Eliot said in 1924 that he "wanted to write a drama of modern life (furnished flat sort of people)," as Bennett recorded in his diary (3.52); this probably reflects the genesis of *Sweeney Agonistes*. Eliot may have sent Bennett a scenario or drafts of the play. Hans Hauge argues that Eliot sent Bennett a draft not of *Sweeney Agonistes*, but rather of a prose sketch called "On the Eve: A Dialogue" (possibly written, at least partly, by Vivienne Eliot), published in the *Criterion* of January 1925, which may itself be the genesis of *Sweeney Agonistes* as it portrays "furnished flat sort of people"; "On the Eve," too, may anticipate a few details of *The Family Reunion* and *The Cocktail Party* (C23).

In the final brief fragment Eliot wrote for Flanagan's production an old gentleman enters, resembling Father Christmas, carrying an alarm clock and an empty champagne bottle. He speaks of time and of waiting nihilistically at the depot—by a heroic statue of the Paraguayan General Cierra, the presence of which is a mystery—for lost trains carrying the last souls. Sweeney banters briefly with him, posing questions that are partly evocative of zen philosophy, and partly rambling nonsense; the old gentleman answers them in similar vein, evoking the omnipotence of the forces of time and possible biblical archetypes of quest, fruition, and the cycles of life. He departs as the alarm clock goes off.

This figure's entrance "brings a slowing of the pace," writes David Galef. "The jazz rhythm is gone and the religious tenor is finally out in the open; the fragment's end has a judgmental note" (C21, 505). Explicating this fragment, Galef writes, "the champagne bottle and the alarm clock will appeal to the clownish element in the audience, along the lines of Eliot's dramatic levels. On the other hand, there is the empty bottle, devoid of spirits, the alarm clock ready to signal the annunciation. . . . the word *cierra* does mean 'he [she, it] closes or shuts down' in Spanish. General Cierra represents something greater than Pereira. In the context, *cierra* is the spiritual end of things, the end of the body's reign as the soul departs" (505-506).

Galef notes correspondances between the final fragment and a play of Auden's: The old gentleman's "resemblance to Father Christmas may be in part a borrowing . . . of Auden's character Father Christmas in *Paid on Both Sides*," which Flanagan had produced two years earlier. "Auden's Father Christmas makes an address to the audience in much the same manner as Eliot's character introduces himself and announces the time. Both plays telescope birth, life, and death; both Father Christmas and the old gentleman are somewhat farcical—both characters borrow from the English mummers' plays" (505).

Herbert Howarth discusses the play's influence on contemporary writers: "Rupert Doone's Group Theatre, that quickest force in the London of the thirties, was the result of the impact of Sweeney on Auden and his friends. It filled them with Eliot's own passion for a new poetic drama and told them how to re-energize the theatre. They saw how to use speech, speech rhythms, speech echoes in their poetry. They saw how to use song and dance. . . . The reiterated, monotony-laden, doom-laden *Birth, and copulation, and death* led to the style of ferocious indictment of the world-as-it-is which became the staple of half the poetry of the thirties." The style of comic animosity—"the comedy augmenting and directing the animosity"—infiltrated the literary establishment, Howarth writes: "Auden and Day Lewis pounced on the style and developed it. Grigson adopted it as editor and critic. Dylan Thomas integrated it into his poetry and scripts. It was the hard-hitting in Kenneth Allott, Orwell borrowed from it. Lawrence Durrell took it into his violent caricature. It persisted in the so-called Angry Young Men" (C322, 336-37). Joanne Bentley makes further claims for the play's influence, quoting a *New York Times* article as stating that "without *Sweeney Agonistes*, the works of Samuel Beckett, Harold Pinter and Sam Shepard are unimaginable" (C15, 135). In the same vein, William V. Spanos writes that Eliot's concerns in *Sweeney Agonistes* "are surprisingly similar to those of post-Imagist 'existential' writers such as Samuel Beckett, Eugène Ionesco. Harold Pinter, Günter Grass, and Charles Olson, who speak to and in the idiom and rhythms of man in the 1960s" (C32, 8).

By the time *Sweeney Agonistes* was published in 1926 and 1927, Sweeney was already a prominent (and provocatively elusive) character in Eliot's poetry. Although F. O. Matthiessen writes that Sweeney of the play "is so different a character from the 'apeneck Sweeney' of the poems that Eliot might better have given him a different name" (C347, 159), most critics consider the dramatic Sweeney character a continuation of the poetic one. He is lowbrow and harsh; comic, though nobody else laughs at him as much as he seems to enjoy his own private and depraved humor; sensual, but prone to dangerous, distasteful, inappropriate passions; unpleasant, but someone who must be reckoned with if one is to understand the depraved condition of contemporary London because he is, besides everything else, simply the quintessential modern man.

Sweeney's activities in his various incarnations throughout Eliot's work "tend to require a minimum of energy and to be trivial and mundane in nature," writes Nancy D. Hargrove; and his physical descriptions and positions "suggest his vulgarity and fleshiness. Typically, his positions are relaxed or reclining (implying slovenliness or laziness), often with legs or knees spread apart (a posture considered impolite, crude, or sexually suggestive at the time these works were written)" (C22, 150-51). Though not all these characteristics are explicit in *Sweeney Agonistes*, some directors have used such details from the poems to help depict Sweeney on stage; the poems, thus, may serve as a kind of stage direction, which is absent from the play itself.

Some critics have found Sweeney not completely objectionable—engaging, sympathetic, even heroic, sharing something of the divine. Such readings though, must be predicated upon the vision Eliot himself presented, in *The Waste Land* and elsewhere, of a harsh, perverse, cruelly combative and barren world; that is to say, Sweeney is heroic to the extent that Eliot has warped his audience's sense of what heroism means in the modern world.

In "Sweeney Erect," Sweeney appears cast in an artistic montage of a wild classical landscape. While he is potentially mildly heroic, he is more prominently animalistic and possessed of an aggressive, offensive, instinctually base sexuality; and he emotionally abandons the victims of his sexuality. As the title implies, he is essentially no more than a phallus, and thus comprised of all the wanton and distasteful aspects Eliot associated with sex. Sweeney is shown performing a post-coital ablution while surrounding characters in a dimly banal boarding-house setting try to maintain their fragile equilibrium. He is partly tragic, partly evil, and seems as if he should be a negligible component of any serious poetic vision—but Eliot cautions, in a parenthetical quatrain, that Ralph Waldo Emerson (representing the thinkers acclaimed as brilliant by previous generations) could not know the human condition because he did not know Sweeney.

Doris from *Sweeney Agonistes* (that is, she is the same character just as Sweeney from the poems seems generally to be the the the Sweeney of the play) appears in this poem. She seems to be a prostitute, clean and calm—thus in contrast to the clean but deadly Sweeney—but also somehow in complicity with the title character. (Doris lends her name also to the title of a grouping of three short poems—published in 1924 as "Doris's Dream Songs"—reprinted in *Collected Poems* as "Eyes that last I saw in tears," "The wind sprang up at four o'clock," and Part III of "The Hollow Men.") While Doris restores a balanced peace to the ugly scene, Eliot seems to reject the idea that such a scene is deserving of any calming element; it would perhaps be better if the erect Sweeney simply finished his destructive emotional terrorism at once, rather than being assuaged and allowed to continue his rampage.

In "Mr. Eliot's Sunday Morning Service," Sweeney appears only briefly as a boor—again, though, a clean one, as he sits in his bath—indifferent to (or uncognizant of) an intellectually wrenched ontological and spiritual consideration that surrounds him in the poem. Sweeney's existence may imply that the church has failed and is spiritually corrupt because it cannot effect the salvation of the most slovenly of souls.

In "Sweeney Among the Nightingales" (London's prostitutes were called "nightingales"), the title character is a sort of vulgar master of ceremonies for a panorama of sprawling, shadowy, tortured characters; he simply laughs, cruelly or pathetically, at the surrounding surreal horror. Like *Sweeney Agonistes*, "Sweeney Among the Nightingales" begins with an epigraph from Aeschylus (though here in the original Greek, rather than translated as for the play): "Ay me! I am deep smitten with a mortal blow" is the Loeb translation of the phrase Eliot takes from the *Agamemnon*; it is Agamemnon's cry of death. "The action and atmosphere of Eliot's poem portend a similarly treacherous attack upon Sweeney," writes Jane Worthington (in Roby 240); she finds other Aeschylean parallels in this poem, strengthening the connection between Eliot's development of Sweeney and his interest in Greek tragic drama. Like *Sweeney Agonistes*, "Sweeney Among the Nightingales" is haunted by the obscure suggestion of murder.

In *The Waste Land*, Sweeney appears in Part III in a similar guise: as the poet confronts the depths of modern degradation in a filthy wasted landscape, Sweeney intrudes amid the mindlessly busy noise of the city, celebrating spring (the lifegiving potency of which Eliot feels has been nearly destroyed by modern depravity) by visiting a brothel.

The Sweeney character is certainly a kind of silent presence even in poems in which he does not appear—though Emerson was oblivious to him, Eliot knows that Sweeney casts a long shadow across all the most horrific modern montages: the settings from "Preludes" and "Rhapsody on a Windy Night" through "Gerontion," *The Waste Land*, and "The Hollow Men."

Eliot described Sweeney to Nevill Coghill as "a man who in younger days was perhaps a professional pugilist, mildly successful; who then grew older and retired to keep a pub" (C16, 119). The "Apeneck Sweeney" as described in "Sweeney Among the Nightingales," writes Jonathan Morse, is clearly "an Irishman, one of the monsters who shambled through the nightmares of literary America during the second and third quarters of the nineteenth century. Sweeney is physically and morally repulsive, but his repulsiveness is generic, not individual" (C26, 137). Morse credits Thomas Nast's editorial cartoons with defining this lower-class character: "a squat, barrel-chested Celt. . . . He is usually carrying either a shillelagh, a rosary, a policeman's club, or a bottle; he is always pug-nosed, beetle-browed, and unshaven, with tiny, deep-set eyes and a wide, lipless mouth full of pointed teeth" (138).

Such a clearly-engrained stereotype was "immediately accessible as a vehicle" for Eliot, who lived in a milieu "in which it was socially acceptable to speak one's prejudices aloud. . . . [and] in which snobbery and exclusiveness were almost de rigeur" (136). Eliot's character, then, comes to *Sweeney Agonistes* laden with the burdens of fierce class fear and loathing, social scorn, and Anglocentric bigotry. Before he even sets foot on stage, Sweeney embodies an explosive and foul persona.

The play shows the influence of Yeats's *Plays for Dancers*, Michael Sidnell writes (C29, 92); Eliot's grotesque modernism is a counterpart to Yeats's mythical actions. Katherine J. Worth, too, calls the play "a Yeatsian concept of total theatre, full of primitive power" (C403, 124). Eliot may have had in mind, Worth conjectures, Yeats's use of drum, gong, and zither in *At the Hawk's Well* when he planned his own strongly percussive play. She also cites the influence of Cocteau (who wrote frequently for *Criterion*, the journal that Eliot helped found and edit and that first published *Sweeney Agonistes*) "prophesying the future role of 'le cirque, le music hall, le cinmatographic.' The ideas were in the air, but no one saw further into them than Eliot" in *Sweeney Agonistes* (127). Worth notes echoes of "the world of Jack the Ripper or of the Grand Guignol Theatre—which was active in London in the Twenties," and of the Berlin work of Brecht and Weill (C318, 63, 77). Carol H. Smith mentions Eugene O'Neill's 1920 play *The Emperor Jones* as "an earlier and more successful experiment in the use of drum-beats and primitive dramatic rhythms" (C382, 49).

Grover Smith notes parallels between the play and *The Great Gatsby* (which Eliot had been sent by F. Scott Fitzgerald and had read three times): a humorous telephone conversation; characters who exposed the tragic side of the jazz age, illustrated with songs from the period; the exotic serio-comic similarities of the names of Eliot's Klipstein and Fitzgerald's Klipspringer (C383, 114). He also conjectures that Eliot's Sweeney might be based on the nineteenth-century fictional character of Sweeney Todd—the demon barber who killed his clients to make meat pies; or, he might allude to a witness, M'Sweeney, that Dr. Crippen was unable to produce at his murder trial, implying that Eliot's Sweeney is merely a witness to the whole nightmare of this drama.

Elizabeth Sewell draws parallels between the play and Lewis Carroll's *Alice* novels, including "the executioner who haunts *Sweeney Agonistes* among the playing-cards as he does the Queen's croquet game; the echo, also in *Sweeney*, of the riddle of the Red King's dream, 'If he was alive then the milkman wasn't'" (C376, 52). Ronald Bush sees an echo of Dostoevsky's *Crime and Punishment* in the story of the murdered young woman, linking her also with the array of emotionally and literally assaulted women in *The Waste Land*, and Harry's murdered wife in *The Family Reunion*. Lightfoot explains the traditional significance of the play's drunkenness: "a routine of the music-hall, [it] was used for satire and criticism, as it had been used for centuries in comedy" (C341, 121).

Elisabeth Schneider sees the germ of the play's dialogue in *The Waste Land*, though she finds the poem's dialogue unsuccessful. Noting that Eliot had initially titled *The Waste Land* "He do the Police in Different Voices" (meaning to indicate a kind of dramatic chorus, a social panorama of voices), she writes, "in the end the only passages conspicuously answering to that intention were the scenes involving Madame Sosostris and Lil" (C28, 94); those passages, though, provide the opening for his attempt, better realized in *Sweeney Agonistes*, to depict the authentic rhythm and voice of dialogue.

Sears Jayne explains more allusions: the lyrics to Wauchope and Horsfall's song are based on a song published in London in 1905 by Bob Cole and J. Rosamund Johnson called "Under the Bamboo Tree," containing the lines that appear in the play about how one live as two and two as one. The character of Periera may have been an ironically inverted allusion to Bishop Henry Horace Pereira, Honorary Chaplain to Queen Victoria and a leader of the temperance movement, who died in 1926. The coffin card Doris draws represents London, Jayne writes. Wauchope, then, being (as Krumpacker mistakenly calls him) "a real live Britisher . . . is apparently dead, and Horsfall, who says not a word, must be dead, too. . . . The ironic equivalence between life and death is brought out here in the fact that the two soldiers who have been engaged in killing are now engaged in loving and are so represented in the cards by the Knave of Hearts" (C25, 110). The character Snow is presumably black, writes Morris Freedman, "for Eliot has a stage instruction: 'Snow as Bones,' Mr. Bones being one of the traditional pair in a Negro minstrel show" (C19, 429).

The play's debts to the biblical story of Samson (Judges 13-16) and to Milton's dramatic rendition of that story, *Samson Agonistes*, are intricate. In *Milton's Debt to Greek Tragedy in "Samson Agonistes,"* William R. Parker identifies some Greek underpinnings of Milton's version: a fusion of Greek and Christian ideals; the drama of regeneration "largely confined to the hero's soul" and dependent upon the hero's faith in himself and in God; the fluidity and free rhythms of Milton's verse which show the influence of the Greek chorus; and the firmly Aristotelean structure. All these influences in turn infuse Eliot's play to some extent. "Agonistes" denotes an athlete struggling for a prize in an Olympic game, or "agon" (which could mean any gathering, or assembly, but, by extension from the Olympian sense, with the more likely overtone of contest or struggle—hence "agony"), but also, Merritt Y. Hughes notes in the introduction to *Samson Agonistes* in his edition of Milton's *Complete Poems and Major Prose*, with metaphorical connotations of a Socratic champion of truth, and, later, the Christian athlete of whom Augustine wrote in *De agone Christiano*. (Several critics have noted that many of Eliot's later plays, particularly *Murder in the Cathedral*, function more clearly as agons—or at least more literally—than *Sweeney Agonistes*.)

Like Milton's Samson, writes Nancy D. Hargrove, "Sweeney is a sinful being who experiences conflict and is spiritually isolated from the other characters by his insights" (C22, 165). Charles Lloyd Holt sees both Milton and

Eliot creating an agonist "unable to sublimate, save in death, his appetite for women"; Milton's hero, though, ends his tragedy with a heroic finish, while Eliot's ends with a psychotic nightmare. Holt also points out the Aeschylean parallels indicated by the epigraph from the *Choephoroi*: "we remember the Eumenides and the retribution they represent. We remember at the same time the KNOCK KNOCK KNOCK and the door that must be opened" (C24, 130-31).

In a 1936 interview with Irish Broadcasting (discussed by A. Walton Litz in his introduction to a lecture of Eliot's in *The Southern Review* 21.4 [October 1985]: 875), Eliot stated that this play was written in two nights between 10 p.m. and 5 a.m., "with the aid of youthful enthusiasm and a bottle of gin."

Vivienne Eliot saw the 1935 Westminster revival of the play and, according to Lyndall Gordon, "she wondered how she had managed not to faint at the 'absolute horror of the thing'" (C309, 58). Perhaps she saw an autobiographical element of her husband in the misogynistic Sweeney; Gordon writes that the tempestuous early years of Eliot's marriage form a background to the play (52).

Publishing History

The text was first published in *Criterion*—"Fragment of a Prologue" in 4.4 (October 1926): 713-18, and "Fragment of an Agon" in 5.1 (January 1927): 74-80. Faber & Faber published the play in December 1932 (where the title *Sweeney Agonistes* is given for the first time), containing the two epigraphic quotations that did not appear in *Criterion*. It was reprinted in *Collected Poems 1909-35* (London: Faber & Faber, 1936; New York: Harcourt, 1936), in the section headed "Unfinished Poems"; in *The Complete Poems and Plays* (New York: Harcourt, 1952); and in *Collected Poems 1909-1962* (London: Faber & Faber, 1963; New York: Harcourt, 1963). The play was not included in Faber & Faber's 1962 *Collected Plays*.

When *Sweeney Agonistes* was reprinted in John Hampden's *Twenty-four One-act Plays* (London: J. M. Dent, 1954), a note was added: "The author wishes to point out that *Sweeney Agonistes* is not a one-act play and was never designed as such. It consists of two fragments. But as the author has abandoned any intention of completing them, these two fragmentary scenes have frequently been produced as a one-act play."

The 25 lines Eliot wrote for the 1933 Vassar production of the play have never been published in any collections of his writing, but they are given in Hallie Flanagan's *Dynamo* (New York: Duell, Sloan, and Pearce, 1943), 82-84; in Joanne Bentley's biography of Flanagan (C15), 136-37; and in Carol H. Smith's *T. S. Eliot's Dramatic Theory and Practice* (C382), 62-63.

The Rock

Characters

Chorus. The Rock (later St. Peter). Workmen, including Alfred, Ethelbert, and Edwin. Unemployed. Saxons. Mellitus (first Bishop of London). Monks. Sabert (King of London) and retinue. Contractor. Rahere and Men. Agitator. Israelites. Nehemiah. Shemaiah. Messengers. Danes. Redshirts. Blackshirts. Plutocrat, Flash Ladies, Gunmen. Bishop Blomfield, Attendants, Knights Templar, Candidates. Young Man and Woman of the time of Richard Coeur de Lion. Elderly Merchant and Family. Mrs. Ethelbert. Major, Millicent, Mrs. Poultridge. Preacher of Reformation times. King's Officer. Mourners. Craftsmen. Fisherman. Archbishop, Abbot of Westminster, Queen Anne. Dick Whittington and his Cat. Wren, Pepys, Evelyn. Servant.

Synopsis

Part I opens with a Chorus lamenting the prominence of the secular—ideas, action, experiments—over the spiritual, and the movement away from God. Churches have become superfluous remnants, they complain: useful in a small traditional way, but otherwise unimportant. The Rock appears, affirming the pragmatic realities of humankind but proclaiming the need to recognize the eternal Christian condition: the struggle between good and evil. Workmen chant of the constructive glory of building new churches, but the unemployed respond with despair at their own misfortune.

These choruses give way to a tableau of Cockney workmen—Alfred, Edwin, and Ethelbert—building foundations, who will reappear throughout the pageant in prose interpolations. They discuss the difference between building a bank and building a church, concluding that a church is not just another edifice of bricks and mortar but a unique social and spiritual undertaking. Their discussion gives way to the entry of a group of Saxons—the first of the pageant's continual temporal fluctuations—discussing the introduction of Christianity to England. Though some of them are wary of the new religion a humble preacher wins them over and instructs them to build their first church.

The Chorus returns to remind the present-day congregation of its noble roots and its need to preserve that heritage by forever building churches, continuously affirming the temperament of the early Christian founders.

As the Cockney workmen continue to build the foundation they find that the ground is swampy and will require unforeseen labor, at a greater cost to the already-meager subscription funds, to complete. The site is pragmatically impractical, but essential to the church's mission because it is the only available plot of land in a neighborhood that is currently without a church. Rahere, a monk from the time of King Henry, enters to inspire the builders with his story of having founded and built a church (also on a marsh, both literally and figuratively) in his own time. Rahere implores the builders to have faith in their enterprise and the Chorus rebukes those who abuse the gift of religion, reminding them that the commonweal cannot function as a merely commercial enterprise whose ultimate ideal is to create the perfect refrigerator.

The next challenge to the church construction comes from a Marxist Agitator who stirs up a crowd by arguing that funds for the church would be better used for housing, and that the church hierarchy wants to keep the masses ignorant and superstitious while they themselves get rich. The builders do not address his arguments, but merely explain that there are enough building materials to put up houses as well as churches, and treat him as an eccentric fanatic. The Chorus introduces a community of ancient Israelites rebuilding the temple in Jerusalem against the threats of enemies who prefer, like the modern-day Agitator, that the temple not be built. The pageant draws on the Old Testament sense of fierce determination and its trust in the favor of God. The Agitator continues ranting about impending revolution, when churches will be transformed into clubs and museums; he spouts the kind of Marxist platitudes and terrorist threats most calculated to incite a capitalist ecumenical society. The next tableau depicts the Danish invasion of England and persecution of early Christians, to remind the audience of the threat posed by forces opposed to Christianity.

As the Chorus laments the lack of social commitment to the church but determines to persevere, a military brigade of Redshirts (communists) enters proclaiming that they can laugh at God because production has risen 26 percent. Next the Blackshirts (fascists) enter, espousing support of some generalized cause but tossing out anti-Semitic invective against this one. The Chorus despairs of help from any militaristic group, looking for relief to a Plutocrat who poses as a conciliator. He pays lip service to the church's glory and panders to the Redshirts, the Blackshirts, and the mob that finds religious precepts inconvenient. Extolling the power of gold, he introduces his flunkies bearing a golden calf, which incites the mob to a chaotic frenzy. The Rock appears, speaking of his vast experience of suffering, and closing Part I by rising above the hellish spectacle. Though the condition is now one of darkness, The Rock knows there shall be an eventual resurgence of light.

The Chorus at the beginning of Part II combines a conflated retelling of the Judeo-Christian stories of genesis and the path toward spiritual righteousness with abstracted images that describe Eliot's sense of contemporary spiritual confusion. Amid the presence of atheism, usury, and lust, the Chorus sinks to its pessimistic nadir. The Rock combats this lethargy, pointing to the omnipowerful prospect of the eternal world against which the immediate world wanes; London's nineteenth-century church builder Bishop Blomfield is brought in to provide a more concrete and personal inspiration. His message echoes that of all the pageant's other transhistoric testimonials: conditions have always been tough for those who fought for the church's survival, but the fighters have always been victorious. Despite lax clergy, anti-ecumenical reformers, and spiritually destitute congregations, the missionary church has persevered, Blomfield counsels (and the Chorus affirms).

Next comes a young man from the time of Richard Coeur de Lion, about to embark on a Holy War in Jerusalem—dreaming of the triumph of Christendom, as well as of glory and plunder—and soothing his family's fears. A church tableau interrupts as the congregation recites in Latin the confident words of prayers including the *Vexilla Regis Prodeunt* and *Pater Noster*. The contemporary Cockney church builders return, praising the miraculous success they have had in finishing their construction and crediting the assistance of all the historical Christians who have spiritually aided their labor. The foreman's wife Mrs. Ethelbert steps forward, having watched her husband's labors proudly, and the group raises a toast to the church's strength.

The Ethelberts sing a music-hall style ballad celebrating their humble and dedicated services to society and the church. Yet when some high-society onlookers show up, they denigrate the new church for not looking gothic, not having ivy-covered walls or stained-glass windows. In response Millicent emphatically defends the new church's simple English plainness against high-church sensibilities, calling church decorations vulgar and loathsome idolatry, and arguing that church money would be better spent on such things as libraries and health centers. As the fashionable Mrs. Poultridge is satirized for her obsession with ornament to the exclusion of weightier spiritual matters, so too is Millicent, despite the sensible elements of her low church social gospel, satirized for her fervent antipathy to the aesthetic delicacies and treasures of the English religious tradition.

Against the background of a Lutheran hymn, a Reformation-era preacher inveighs against graven images and luxuriant religious artifacts; a crowd removes such objects taken from churches and officers impound them for the King's treasuries, while the preacher warns of God's wrath in harsh Protestant invective. The Chorus, though, refutes such religious intimidation and speaks instead of the spiritual honor of creating, stone by stone, a Temple which complements the spiritual grandeur of God as, in people, the worlds of spirit and body are united. In response to the preacher's dismal prophecies of wailing, gnashing, and grinding, the Chorus extols the joyful communion of saints.

In the final appearance of the modern-day church builders, the pageant shows an array of stone-carvers, book illuminators, and other religious craftspeople putting the finishing touches on the church; the Cockneys march off to a pub to celebrate the completion of their work. The Chorus speaks of sanctifying the edifice and invokes the sanctity of earlier churches. The Rock appears as St. Peter, who tells a Thames fisherman he has personally consecrated the Abbey Church of St. Peter at Westminster. A ballet interlude depicts the legend of Dick Whittington—the poor Midlands boy, who had nothing but his cat, was lured to London by the sound of church bells and ultimately rose to the position of Lord Mayor—in dedication of the rebuilding of the Church of St. Michael, Paternoster Royal.

The final tableau concerns Christopher Wren's construction of St. Paul's (London's most renowned cathedral, which rose like a phoenix after the great fire of London), and his humane and informal discussion of the architect's role in the life of the city. After a procession of thanksgiving to St. Paul's the Chorus invokes, as its conclusion, an image of the completed church as a light on the hill amid a world of confusion and darkness. The Rock reminds the audience that the church is only a reflection of God's greater glory and light; a bishop invokes a closing benediction for London, church, and God.

Production History

The Rock: A Pageant Play opened on 28 May 1934 at Sadler's Wells Theatre, London, where it ran for thirteen performances to audiences of up to 1,500 each night. The large-scale production had 22 scene changes, a cast of over 300 actors (mostly amateurs from local parishes, including such notable church officials as Dr. A. F. Winnington-Ingram, Bishop of London), a choir, and an orchestra of 40.

Director E. Martin Browne observed that the need to treat volunteer actors respectfully often precluded the kinds of cuts and script adjustments a professional production would have demanded. Many reviewers noted that the actors seemed under-rehearsed, though not the Chorus: the *Church Times* review calls it "magnificently trained. . . . the chorus, with its clear enunciation, its variety of tone, its emphasis and its pointed hits, gives direction to the play. In spite of its physical immobility, it is the chorus that gives the pace to the action of the players" (R22, 83).

Eliot was involved in at least some aspects of the play's production and rehearsal, as he was to be with all his later plays, though Browne characterizes him as restrained and unobtrusive in terms of his "theatre-decorum." Martin Shaw, who had spent his life studying and revitalizing English Church music, collaborated as musical director—"the whole piece was conceived in terms of music as well as of words," Browne writes (C277, 12).

Stella Mary Pearce designed the costumes; her husband Eric Newton, a painter and mosaic artist, designed the set. The Chorus wore "half-masks, Greek in inspiration," writes Pearce; their robes were "stone-coloured, to suggest both the Rock of St. Peter and the stonework of the Church. Their costumes were . . . made of stiff unwashed natural hessian-sacking" (C358, 99). Since the pageant "represented each stage in the building of Christianity in England," she continues, "I had decided that each procession should have its own colour-scheme. The Saxons, for instance, were all in fairly dark blue, with pale blue hair and faces. The appearance of each procession was too brief for differentiations of character to be possible. The nineteenth and twentieth century women had to be grouped together at the end, so that a loosely controlled colour-scheme had to be used for them. As for the craftsmen and women who were building and decorating the modern church, these were in off-white, again to fit in with the new white church which was being created—white wigs and faces" (101).

The Plutocrat was played by the Rev. Clarence May, a popular West End preacher who often used current plays as the texts for his sermons (C277, 10). Ethelbert the foreman was played by Vincent Howson, an East End vicar who had previously played with Sir Frank Benson's Shakespearean Company; Howson extensively rewrote and adapted his part to improve on what he considered Eliot's inauthentic Cockney jargon. (For a comparison between Howson's Cockney dialect in the final script and Eliot's own attempts at this style, Browne reprints part of the workers' first scene as Eliot had written it in *The Making of T. S. Eliot's Plays* [C277], 15-16.) Phyllis Woodcliffe played Mrs. Ethelbert.

One part of the play that Eliot especially liked, Browne writes, was the music-hall ballad sung by Ethelbert and Mrs. Ethelbert—a variation on "At Trinity Church I met my doom." Eliot "always had a great partiality for the music-hall" (12); his essay on the death of popular entertainer Marie Lloyd details his appreciation of the vital community values he felt were fostered by the music-hall.

The Chorus—led by Janet Lewis and Stewart Cooper—"was conceived as a group of impersonal, abstract figures," Browne writes. "Wearing half-masks and stiff robes which allied them to the rock-foundation on which the church was being built and to The Rock himself, they spoke with the voice of the poet" (C277, 18). This may explain why Eliot felt this portion of the pageant was most worth preserving and reprinting; though it also represented a kind of dramatic failure, he writes in *The Three Voices of Poetry* (P57), since the Chorus members did not have any voice or character of their own.

The device of the chorus had returned to fashion, Browne writes, with Gilbert Murray's translations of Greek plays in the first decade of the century, and had become "almost an essential part of the poets' equipment in writing plays" (18) in the period after World War I. Yet Eliot's version of choral drama "owes little to the Greek chorus, still less to the abstract No," Browne explains. "It is inspired rather by the Hebrew prophets, whose direct address it adopts, whether in scathing denunciation or earnest exhortation of the people of God, or in prayer or praise to God himself. The versification also recalls the Hebraic parallelism" (C281, 83).

The Chorus represents a turn away from the Shakespearean tradition in poetic drama and a return to ritual and communal forms of drama; its popularity was bolstered by the growing study of speech and elocution in education courses. Browne calls the choruses "the most dramatically vital part of the play. They combine prophetic thunder with colloquial speech; and they use the orchestra of varied voices, male and female, to create continual dramatic contrast" (20). Critical opinion about the choruses generally accords with Grover Smith's: "Musically, whatever their dramatic deficiencies, these rank among Eliot's best poems. . . . By their imagery the choruses frequently recall Eliot's other poetry, with numerous echoes of *The Waste Land* in particular" (C383, 174). Browne notes that the review in *The Times* credits the Chorus with unifying a play beset by uneven acting and certain overlong scenes: "The chorus would come between, and by their beauty of speech and variations of pace impart a new impetus" (R24, 32). Francis Birrell praises "the crashing Hebraic choruses . . . the most prolonged effort the poet has given us since *The Waste Land* . . . admirably suited for dramatic delivery, and, unlike most modern poetic drama, really written to be spoken as well as read."

The Chorus was trained and coordinated by Elsie Fogerty, principal of the Central School of Speech and Drama, and her colleague Gwynneth Thurburn; the two were at the forefront of English oratorical studies at the time. The smooth execution of choral passages, Browne writes, owed much to the intimate familiarity the Chorus members had with each other as a group—they were students of Fogerty and Thurburn, and had worked together in other productions. The *Blackfriars* reviewer describes the Chorus as "seven men and ten women, masked, in dull gold draperies" (R24).

The July 1934 *Blackfriars* review captures the pageant's vast sense of spectacle, describing the interlude preceding the Cockney workmen's final appearance: "a mime of singular beauty, showing the dedicated craftsmen at work upon the new church. Their hair and faces are whitened, so that they seem statues; they stand as statues, and as the music progresses, turn by turn they come to life and then are again still, so that movement passes visibly in a circling wave: the sculptors hammer at the chiselled crucifix, the fresco painter awakes to paint, the weavers of vestments sway rhythmically about their loom, the metal workers complete a chalice, and lastly the illuminator, sitting at a desk, lifts her brush."

Critical Overview

Performance Reviews

The *Listener* review finds Eliot successful in his attempt to create a comfortable modern verse drama: while the play's verse models range "from the measures of the Psalms to those of the music hall . . . the point is that they are familiar rhythms, to which the audience's ear is attuned. And so, either sung, or spoken with beautiful clearness by the Chorus which links up the scenes, they present no difficulty in acceptance." The tone is compared to "the smart rhythms of *Sweeney Agonistes*, or the clear lines of the 'Journey of the Magi'" (R28).

In the London *Daily Telegraph*, too, J. E. Sewell lauds Eliot's new work: "His pageant-play, unlike his earlier poetry, is pellucidly clear, but it is no less startling than *The Waste Land* in its poetry, its imaginative brilliance, and its satirical force. . . . It is all tremendously alive, tremendously exhilirating." The Chorus, Sewell writes, is composed of "sharp, stabbing, challenging phrases" (R18).

J. Isaacs, surveying Eliot's drama in 1951, offers a reminiscence: "I remember very vividly the audience of *The Rock* at Sadler's Wells in 1934. It was the first time poetic drama had really come to the people. It was a simple and devout audience, a rapt and uncomprehending audience, moved by the liturgical patterns, laughing uneasily at the human lines as if they were afraid of being caught laughing in church. . . . It was an audience of church workers, of mothers' outings, of shepherds and their flocks, and a few 'highbrows' like myself, who were moved by the echoes of the Book of Nehemiah . . . highbrows who responded to topical Audenisms . . . or were flattered by recognizing a clerihew in the Christopher Wren scene" (C324, 152-53).

The choruses, according to the *Times Literary Supplement* review, "prove the most vital part of the performance. . . . They combine the sweep of psalmody with the exact employment of colloquial words. They are lightly written, as though whispered to the paper, yet are forcible to enunciate . . . . In *The Rock*, Mr. Eliot's success is certainly lyrical; the action scenes have immaturities and faults, for which, on account of collaborators, he may not be entirely blameworthy. The Cockney humour is often curiously feeble; sometimes alien points of view, such as the Agitator's, are thinly projected. But with his use of the chorus he has regained a lost territory for the drama" (R21). In the despondent voices of the Redshirts, Blackshirts, the Plutocrat, and some of the choruses, the *TLS* finds an evocation of the pessimism of *The Waste Land*. The *Times*, too, notes that Eliot's rhythm in the choruses was "haunted by the whimper already familiar, as if even now he was unable to get away from the futility against which he has reacted so bitterly" (R20).

In *New English Weekly*, though, Michael Sayers criticizes the lack of "that precipitation of the spirit without which stage dialogue is tedious and flat. His verse 'stays on the ground'; it walks, with irregular steps, in a circle. It does not stir us by a bold advance. . . . Its emotional gamut is restricted, dropping from satiric levity down to hopeless despondency, but reaching neither really comic impetuosity on the one hand, nor tragic contemplativeness on the other hand." The dialogue, Sayers finds, is filled with "melodramatic utterances" and "mediaeval platitudes decked out in canonicals" (R17). *Adelphi* reviewer Harry Thornton Moore writes, "The author of *Prufrock* should have had a sufficient sense of humour, the author of *For Lancelot Andrewes* should have had too much intelligence, and the author of *The Waste Land* should have had enough poetic feeling, not to have committed a thing like *The Rock*" (R16).

The review in *Everyman*, like many other mixed appraisals of the performance, lauds Eliot's creative experimentation, however mitigated its success:

"The admiration of the honesty and courage needed to emerge from the study to engage in such a broil must condition all criticism of *The Rock*. . . . [Eliot] understands his own genius best, and the ways of a serious experimenter are always worth watching, even when they give the impression of being wrong ones" (R27). The *Catholic World* reviewer writes that the "weakness from the dramatic standpoint lies in the number of Mr. Eliot's words though they are always interesting in themselves and full of sound spirituality" (R26).

In *The Spectator*, Derek Verschoyle finds the content unconvincing. Considered as an *apologia* for the campaign of church-building in the context of the conflict between the church and the world, "the case for neither of these opposed causes is conclusively stated. Mr. Eliot's defence of the Church is based rather on invocations than on definition, and he seems reluctant to commit himself to logical justification. For the most part the Church's cause is assumed and not stated, and at times Mr. Eliot's unwillingness to substantiate his beliefs makes him appear to be doing little more than strike an attitude. His picture of the society in which the Church must work is simplified and thereby distorted. He satirizes Fascists and Communists, plutocrats and social parasites, but admirable as much of his satire is it is not conclusive. The elements in society which he satirizes do not represent the only, nor even the main, reasons for indifference to the Church today. Acceptance of Fascism or Communism is for many of their followers the result, not the cause, of dissatisfaction with the Church. The causes in many instances lie elsewhere; in, for example, despair of the Church's attitude towards such questions as Housing and Population. Mr. Eliot does not touch upon the latter problem, and only deals fragmentarily with the former. And he neglects altogether opposition to the Church which has other than a materialistic basis" (R19).

(Eliot responded in a letter [P41] to the next issue of *The Spectator*, stating that Verschoyle's assumption that the play was an *apologia* was an unfair and imprecise characterization—the campaign needed no apologia, and had he written one it would have been a prose pamphlet; he considered what he had written an advertisement.)

The *Blackfriars* review of July 1934 epitomizes the tone of reviews emanating from a predominantly religious sensibility: "That one who is perhaps the greatest of our living poets should lend a docile pen to write, and, he admits, rewrite under the direction of the organizers of the scheme, is an example of literary humility so rare as to deserve all reverence" (R24).

Scholarly Response

Eliot's effort in this play is "so unfortunate," Grover Smith writes, "that scarcely anyone could have predicted for him a successful future in theatrical writing" (C383, 171). Smith allows that "what Eliot wrote was subject to criticism by various kinds of expert people, with the natural result that a good deal of it is mediocre at best. Eliot cannot be censured for having missed an adequate conception of characters he did not invent." Still, he may be only "barely acquitted, on grounds of piety, of having abused his talents with such hackwork. It could appeal only to people in want of no convincing."

Carol H. Smith finds in *The Rock* an example of Eliot's theory of dramatic levels: the prose passages represent the surface of the drama, with the added dimension of parallel incidents from the past, "one of Eliot's favorite methods of conveying simultaneous analogy and irony." Flat characters create a "stylized surface which would not interfere with the symbolic level below the action." The Chorus is both a vehicle of social commentary and, along with The Rock, a "dramatic instrument for piercing through the level of the surface action to the level of the philosophical and theological implications of the action" (C382, 86). Smith sees anticipations of themes that will be more fully developed in *Murder in the Cathedral* (and to some extent in all Eliot's later plays): the idea of the suffering of the person who acts; the need to perfect the will; the conflict between temporal and church forces. In the choruses she finds a continuation of the attention to unifying dramatic rhythm as begun in *Sweeney Agonistes*.

R. P. Blackmur, like Smith, sees an attempt to create a drama on different levels but judges it unsuccessful: "the fact is that the level of interest appealed to by the whole play is too low to make passage to the higher levels natural. The general level lacks emotional probability and therefore lacks actuality. It is dead level writing. The reader satisfied with the dead level can hardly be expected to perceive, even unconsciously, the higher levels; and the reader interested in the higher levels cannot but find his interest vitiated by finding it constantly let down." Blackmur concedes that "At Sadler's Wells it may have been magnificent, but not because of Mr. Eliot's poetry; and as it is now, a reader's text, what was important and the very life of the performance—the incident, the fun, the church-supper social comment, and the good-humoured satire—reduce the effect of the poetry because it points away from the poetry instead of towards it. Bad verse cannot point to good poetry, and there is here the first bad verse Mr. Eliot has allowed himself to print, as well as his first bad jokes" (C267, 257).

David Ward calls the work "a failure, an uneasy association of modes in which a crude expressionism alternates with rather flaccid experiments in the choric mode. Eliot's ear for the rhythms and intonations of British working class speech which had served him well in *The Waste Land* II fails him: the language of the workmen in *The Rock* is self-conscious parody, and though Eliot's intention is far more sympathetic to his subjects than it is in 'A Game of Chess,' the final result is a far more contemptuous debasement of the dialect than in *The Waste Land*, where the cockney speech at least has a kind of vigorous flatness and sloppiness" (C391, 180).

But Toby Olshin defends the play's integrity: it "can be considered a unified whole if the underlying theme of its various episodes is seen to be the vision of a timeless, invisible, and hierarchical order existing above and simultaneously with the 'timekept' visible order we know. The Church is the most important visible manifestation of this greater order for Eliot; the cyclic nature of its history makes it a perfect symbol of the invisible rhythm" (C37, 313). For example, though many of the pageant's scenes seem digressive or unconnected, even the Dick Whittington ballet, "considered something of a thematic excrescence, fits into the theme of the invisible structure which supports and envelops the whole if we keep the legend in mind. . . . Whittington is inspired by the Bow bells with the vision of himself as Lord Mayor. In a culture where the civic hierarchy is the earthly representation of the Heavenly, Whittington becomes the vision incarnate. As Lord Mayor, he rebuilds St. Michael, Paternoster Royal, and presents it to the city, just as Christ, at the top of the hierarchy, presented the Church to the world" (317).

The Rock "belongs to what Eliot himself called (in another connection) 'vision literature'" (314-15), Olshin writes. "The total drama is in the form of the Chorus's vision, and this contains several visions within it: the workmen's vision including the 'dream' of Rahere and the 'discernment' of Nehemiah as well as the false visions of the Redshirts and Blackshirts; the workmen's vision is followed by three more scenes depicting this same kind of prescience: the fisherman-dedication procession, the Dick Whittington ballet, and the Wren tableau. In every case, the seer of the 'true' vision achieves a momentary but deeply impressive insight into the invisible scheme by which the world is structured" (318).

Contemporary critics who compared *The Rock* to Eliot's earlier poetry found intellectual flaws and a lessening of concentrated intensity. In 1934, Conrad Aiken writes that he is "more than ever uncomfortable about [Eliot's] present predicament, his present position and direction." The pageant, along with religious poems such as *Ash-Wednesday* and "Marina" written after *The Waste Land*, indicate a "contraction of both interest and power," Aiken writes, and "a diminution of vigor and variousness: the circle has narrowed, and it has gone on narrowing." Of the choruses from *The Rock*, he finds, "one feels the cunning of the rhetoric and the rhythm to be almost too glib and easy, and as if usurping the place of what would formerly have been a richer and more natural inventiveness." D. W. Harding faults the pageant's "suggestion that the Church is the only alternative" to modern despair, "for his pleading relies upon false antitheses. It puts the plight of the uncultured vividly but it does not show what the Church would do for them" (C34, 180), resorting instead to sentimentality, banality, and blurry caricatures.

The Rock is unlike Eliot's later plays, Gerald Weales notes, in that "there is more social, even political content than one is ordinarily likely to find in an Eliot play. There is the direct satiric treatment of a variety of modern panaceas of the left and right. . . . *The Rock* is the only one of the plays that actively embodies social ideas—except by implication. . . . The plays that followed were to focus their attention more and more on the individual" (C394, 189).

The pageant's structure reenacts Eliot's theological argument, writes William V. Spanos. "Archetypal scenes from the past . . . are not presented chronologically, nor do they depict consistently the vicissitudes of the English

Church. Rather, ranging back and forth in time and place, they suggest a pattern of recurrence," thus reinforcing the pageant's moral that the church must be continually building because it is continually decaying. Its structure is "not merely progressive, but cyclically progressive, the end being a new beginning which incorporates all the past. Thus we see the contemporary action of the building of a church not only as a process moving toward completion that implies rest for the builders . . . but also, and more important in terms of the emphasis of the pageant, as a recurrent historical process related to the perpetual struggle of Good and Evil that requires, as The Rock says, perpetual commitment and labor on the part of the earthly builders" (C385, 66).

The pageant's spiritual argument, writes H. Pietersma, is that "in spite of all our feverish busyness, clever findings and learned calculations, we have no reason to be optimistic, for spiritually we are 'advancing progressively backwards.' . . . A man whose life has no spiritual center is a man whose life is utterly meaningless. . . . The whole of *The Rock* is essentially a call for consciously-lived Christianity" (C365, 21-22).

The choruses have attracted the most serious and substantive critical attention. Ronald Bush attributes special importance to the second verse paragraph in Chorus IX (about the transformation from imprecise language to a perfectly beautiful order of speech): Eliot there "hails incantation as the very 'soul' of poetry, foreshadowing 'Burnt Norton'"; he is thus "being drawn out of the orbit of Pound and Joyce and back into the orbit of the symbolists. . . . his growing passion for incantation attracted him to . . . Mallarmé" (C283, 122). This movement culminates in *Four Quartets* and, Bush notes, manifests itself also in Eliot's incantatory recordings of his poetry.

Arthur W. Fox, writing of the 1936 edition of Eliot's collected poems which includes "Choruses from 'The Rock,'" states that in the choruses "the reader can grasp much of his meaning and appreciate the fine flavour of his satire. But these are almost the only pieces in the volume which can be read from beginning to end with a sense of clear understanding" (C35, 24). Eliot embeds "in the midst of much biting satire . . . a distinct and noble message to his time" (32); it "is in the main perfectly clear in spite of its profundity. It attacks present-day problems fearlessly and with a certain sonorous music of its own" (38).

Textual Notes and Influences

F. O. Matthiessen writes that the work "is a pageant, not a drama. That is to say, its situation does not give rise to any intense struggle or conflict; its structure consists of a series of scenes of a related tone" (C347, 161). Eliot himself minimized the dramatic significance of the work: in a letter to *The Spectator* (P41), he writes that it made no pretense of being, as a *Spectator* reviewer had called it, "a contribution to English dramatic literature"; it was meant simply as a revue, with the only important dramatic goal being to show the possible importance of the chorus in drama. But Ashley Dukes, owner of the Mercury Theatre and an early advocate of Eliot's drama, sees in the pageant professional origins for Eliot's later work. "He learned from it something of the collaborative process of the stage; he became interested in the possibilities of the dramatic form; and in fact he was prepared for the writing of plays as perhaps no dramatist of our present century had been prepared before him. An Elizabethan spirit of respect for the poet combined with theatrical inventiveness began to be abroad" (C292, 112).

The Rev. R. Webb-Odell had been asked by the Anglican diocese of London to build and endow new churches, and decided on a theatrical pageant to help raise money for the Forty-Five Churches Fund. Such pageants (usually outdoors, with large processions celebrating the history of the locale) were traditional fund-raising institutions; to suit the lofty goals for this fund-drive, Webb-Odell had decided to stage the pageant in a London theatre. He approached E. Martin Browne, a director of religious drama, who suggested Eliot for the project. The fund-raising committee was hesitant: they saw him as "too modern: too difficult" (C277, 3-7). The *Blackfriars* reviewer (R24) writes that "each scene was sponsored by a London Anglican parish."

Eliot was given a scenario for the pageant by Browne and Webb-Odell, and, as he later wrote in *The Three Voices of Poetry* (P57), he merely filled in the words. The commission for *The Rock*, he explains in that essay, came at a time when he felt his poetry writing was blocked, or exhausted. He had also written in the Prefatory Note to the printed text that he could not consider himself the author of "the play," but only of the words.

Despite the hesitations of Eliot and others about the place of this work in his canon, Toby Olshin writes, "both its choruses and its prose dialogue . . . cannot be ignored as a part of Eliot's writing. . . . in a collaboration of this nature, the final work does not deserve dismissal because it is based on an idea originating with someone other than the author. Rather, it should be closely examined because an author's acceptance of a given form may be as revealing as his own writing. . . . In considering Shakespeare's use of Holinshed or the classical dramatists' use of religious myth, we normally study the elements in the given plot which appealed to them or focus our attention on their treatment of that plot. Let us use the same system for Eliot and realize that the nature of the given scenario touched something within him with sufficient strength to lift him from what might be called 'poetic depression'" (C37, 312).

In the one scene that Eliot did actually plot and write himself (at the end of Part I where the pageant returns to the twentieth century), he satirizes the increasingly-powerful contemporary ideologies of communism and fascism. Browne writes that this scene "makes use of the methods of the German Expressionists of the 'twenties, reminding one of some of the earlier plays of W. H. Auden and Christopher Isherwood who were influenced by them. It calls for precise and disciplined movement to match the suggestion of the mechanisation of thought inherent in the mass movement of the Red and Black Shirts" (C277, 10).

Eliot attended a performance of Auden's *The Dance of Death* while he was writing *The Rock*; Michael Sidnell asserts that Auden's play was certainly an influence, and perhaps even the inspiration, for Eliot's pageant (C29, 93). The Expressionist influence that Browne noted, Sidnell argues, is taken completely from Auden: "Eliot's ophidian Plutocrat . . . is a close equivalent of Auden's Theatre Manager . . . The Redshirts and the Blackshirts portrayed by Eliot . . . strongly resemble Auden's Chorus in its Communist and Fascist phases. As in *The Dance of Death*, Eliot uses choric formations, facile rhymes and broad caricature for his satiric effects" (96).

"The choruses of *The Rock*, which owe much to the rhythms of the Authorised Version, and to the Prayer-Book Psalms, have the simplicity of syntax, the emphatic repetitions, the rhythmical variety which choric verse must possess," writes Helen Gardner (C300, 133). Peter Ackroyd identifies the simple, direct language of Isaiah and Ezekiel as influences (C255, 213).

The legend of Dick Whittington and his cat, set to a ballet toward the end of the pageant, makes a brief reappearance in the poem "Gus, the Theatre Cat," in *Old Possum's Book of Practical Cats*: among Gus's grandiose anecdotal recollections from his dramatic career is one of having understudied the role of Dick Whittington's cat.

Some passages in the pageant, especially the workmen's mystification about economic dynamics, reflect Eliot's interest in the doctrine of Social Credit, as devised by Major C. H. Douglas and promulgated by Ezra Pound, among others, according to Ackroyd (221).

In *Unlocking the English Language* (London: Faber & Faber, 1989), Robert Burchfield writes, "A computer search of the electronically coded version of the *OED* revealed that there are just over five hundred illustrative examples in the *OED* drawn from the works of Eliot. . . . As it happens, the work most frequently quoted from—fifty-one examples—is *The Rock: a Pageant Play*" (75).

Publishing History

Faber & Faber published *The Rock* in May 1934, and Harcourt published the American edition later that year. Most, though not all, of the choral passages were reprinted in *Collected Poems 1909-1935* (London: Faber & Faber, 1936; New York: Harcourt, 1936), under the heading "Choruses from 'The Rock,'" and divided into ten separate passages; this is the only part of the pageant that remains in print. Six of these passages were reprinted in *Selected Poems* (London: Penguin, 1948; New York: Harcourt, 1967); the choral excerpts as in the 1936 edition—but not the remainder of the pageant's text—were reprinted in *The Complete Poems and Plays* (New York: Harcourt, 1952), and *Collected Poems 1909-1962* (London: Faber & Faber, 1963; New York: Harcourt, 1963). Nothing from *The Rock* was included in Faber & Faber's 1962 *Collected Plays*.

The Builders: Song from 'The Rock' an arrangement for chorus with music by Martin Shaw, was published in 1934 (London: J. B. Cramer & Co.); a setting for the second half of Chorus X was published in 1966 as *The Greater Light Anthem for Tenor Solo, Double Choir and Organ* (London: J. Curwen; New York: G. Schirmer).

Murder in the Cathedral

Characters

Chorus of Women of Canterbury. Three Priests of the Cathedral. Messenger. Archbishop Thomas Becket. Four Tempters. Attendants. Four Knights.

Synopsis

The play opens in early December 1170 with a Chorus of poor Canterbury women drawn to the Cathedral anticipating something momentous. They have been left to their own devices, in the cycles of quotidian peasant life, in the seven years since Archbishop Thomas Becket was driven into exile because of disagreements with his former ally King Henry II. Previously, serving as chancellor, Becket had been in Henry's camp; but when the King installed him as Archbishop, hoping to maintain secular control over religious affairs, Becket began to assert the church's independent authority. As Priests bemoan the confusion of temporal rule in the absence of religious authority, a messenger brings hasty notice of Becket's return from France. The Priests wonder about the terms of his return and the status of his disputes with the crown. The messenger informs them that Becket comes in assurance of his claims, and of his people's dedication to him, but with only a patched-up agreement with King Henry. Though the Priests are unsure whether the Archbishop's return will bring good or ill, they are confident that it will be an improvement over his seven-year hiatus. The Chorus, though, fears the return. They are afraid he brings death: that his destiny involves their doom, and threatens their quiet mundane stasis.

Thomas enters, with Christ-like serenity and tolerance for the fearful masses, speaking in the language of Christian paradox of their suffering and stasis as a pattern of action. He speaks with a foreboding sense of danger inherent in his return to Canterbury. As if in confirmation of external threats to Becket's leadership, a procession of Tempters arrives to challenge him. The First Tempter (like all of them, a figure from Becket's flawed past), evoking a previous period of easy intercourse between Becket and Henry, cajoles the Archbishop to revert to his earlier posture of secular accommodation and to abandon his newfound spiritual intensity. As Becket dismisses this temptation, the Tempter warns of the danger that will accompany what he calls the higher vices Becket intends—defiance of the King. The Second Tempter tries to lure Becket back to the world of secular and political power, in which he had once flourished. Acceptance of such power and prestige, he promises, embodies real glory; holiness, in contrast, involves only shadowy future prospects and grim earthly ones. Becket, replete in the supremacy of his archbishopric, proudly spurns him.

The Third Tempter, a blunt country lord, offers Becket a pragmatic alliance against the King to serve the anti-monarchial interests of both church and barons. The Archbishop haughtily rejects the coalition. The Fourth Tempter arrives—unexpectedly, Becket admits—with a temptation that is much closer to his own desires than the previous ones: he counsels Becket, with the same kinds of Christian paradoxes the Archbishop himself had used earlier, to anticipate and capitalize upon his impending martyrdom as the most effective way to vanquish his enemies and ensure his own eternal power. Thomas fears the temptation to pride and vanity; he deliberates with anguish to stave off the temptation, though he cannot reject it as explicitly as he had done with the first three.

The Chorus has a heavy, sickly presentiment; the Tempters, forming their own sort of chorus, exacerbate the uneasiness by speaking of humankind's unreality, disappointment, self-destruction, and delusion. Even the Priests fear Becket's excessively determined posture. The Archbishop himself, though, rises serenely above this as Part I ends—he places himself in God's hands, now sure of what he must do and what his struggle means.

The Archbishop's Christmas sermon forms a prose Interlude. He speaks of the connection between death and birth: the idea of an ending as beginning, as in the resurrection of Christ; the paradox of peace emerging out of war, and of joy springing from the sorrowful suffering of martyrs. With scant subtlety, Becket sets the stage for his own martyrdom.

At the opening of Part II, set on 29 December 1170, the Chorus continues waiting for the culmination of Becket's pattern of action but now with a more hopeful vision of a winter cleansing and renewal. The Priests, too, affirm the patterns of earlier religious heroes and hope for the appearance of an eternal design. Four Knights appear, urgently arrived from France, for business with the Archbishop on the King's behalf. Becket receives them cordially, and alone; they charge him with revolt against the King and his laws and personal disloyalty to the man who made him powerful. The Archbishop protests that he maintains his allegiance to the crown, uncompromised except for his obligations to his own order. The Knights taunt him; they say he has sown strife by suspending bishops appointed by the King and undermining the King's faithful servants. They relay the King's command that Becket leave England but he refuses to be separated from his flock any longer and invokes the higher authority of Rome.

As Becket exits the Chorus confirms its presentiment of this pattern of action: of the conflict between church and state, and the humiliation and death that will ensue. Thomas returns to calm the anxiety of the masses, promising that the completion of God's purpose will bring ultimate joy. The Priests fear the return of the Knights and urge Becket to retreat into the Cathedral for his safety. When he refuses, determined to wait in his hall for death, they forcibly drag him into the Cathedral where the Chorus prays for help from God. The Priests try to bar the entrance but Becket commands that the doors remain open; he tells them the spiritual power of the Church, not the stones and oak of the building, will protect him. As the doors are opened, the drunken Knights enter. Charging the Archbishop with treason, disobedience, arrogation of power, and appropriation of the King's funds, they demand Becket's contrition. The Knights attack and kill him as the Chorus laments the fouling of the land: the horror and sorrow that transcends anything they had experienced in their daily lives before Becket's return.

In a shocking contrast to the play's passionate crescendo, the Knights step forward to address the audience in prose rhetoric evocative of a sloppy after-dinner speech about what they have just done. They ask the audience to consider their side of the case. They were drunk only because they had to brace themselves for the unusual and unpleasant task of killing the Archbishop; they are four plain and loyal Englishmen, disinterested, only doing their duty. Though it was imperative that Becket be stopped they know they will be scapegoats and will probably be exiled without any reward for their services. The King, they argue, recognized the need to restore stability to England, and had envisioned a harmonious union of spiritual and temporal administration, but Becket had undermined that with his ostentatious and offensive spirituality. While they regret the violence, it was necessary for social justice. Finally, they argue (recalling the words of the Fourth Tempter) that Becket, in his monstrous egotism, provoked his own death, which should thus be considered the suicidal act of an unsound mind.

When the Knights exit the Priests lament the desecration, but realize that the church is strengthened by surviving persecution. They dismiss the Knights and other disbelievers as weak men and lost souls for whom the promise of future glory is irrelevant; and they offer thanks to God for having given them a saint. Above the strains of a choir singing the *Te Deum*, the Chorus closes the play praising God for the pattern of action that they have finally come to understand and accept. They know their Church has been enriched by the blood of a martyr, and seek forgiveness for having feared to surrender themselves to God's will; they ask for the mercy of God and Christ, and the prayers of St. Thomas.

Production History

An initial production of *Murder in the Cathedral* was planned, but canceled, by an offshoot of the Group Theatre (which presented *Sweeney Agonistes*). The company, called Poets' Theatre, would have presented a series of plays by poets including Eliot, W. B. Yeats, and W. H. Auden; that enterprise never materialized.

The play premiered 15 June 1935, giving seven performances at Canterbury's fourteenth-century Chapter House, 50 yards from where Thomas Becket was killed in 1170; the play might have been staged in the Cathedral itself, according to Browne, except that earlier attempts at dramatic productions there had proven acoustically impossible. In a 1937 address, though—reprinted in 1954 as *Religious Drama: Mediaeval and Modern*—Eliot offers another reason for not performing the play in the Cathedral: since not enough details are known about the historical event to reenact it accurately, it would have been in bad taste, and grotesque in effect, to present the play on the site of the original event.

Robert Speaight, who starred as Becket, describes the Chapter House: "The building has a certain Gothic bleakness, which was suitable enough to the play but which somehow forbade enjoyment" (C386, 72); he wore an Augustinian Friar's habit with a pectoral cross (which was unhistorical); he preached the sermon in a plain surplice and wore the pontifical cope and mitre for the murder (C108, 174).

The play was directed by E. Martin Browne, who also played the Fourth Tempter and Knight, and featured mainly local amateur dramatists (many of whom had religious vocations—Harold William Bradfield, for example, who played a Priest, later became Bishop of Bath and Wells). Browne revised Eliot's text slightly to enable the four Tempters to double parts with the four Knights, for production reasons. "It is easier to get a good actor to play a part which appears in both acts than a part which is confined to one," he explains (C276, 57); also, the doubling "helps the audience to grasp one of the main theses of the play by showing a parallel between the force that Becket is fighting within himself and the antagonists from without" (58). In 1958, though, Browne writes that "Mr. Eliot now prefers that [the Knights] should not" be doubled with the Tempters (61). Frank Napier played the roles of the Second Tempter and Knight; he also designed the set for a later run at the Duchess Theatre, including Norman architectural design to restore the medieval atmosphere lost when the play moved out of the Canterbury setting.

George Bell, who had seen and admired *The Rock*, commissioned the play for the Canterbury Festival of Music and Drama. The Canterbury Festival also produced plays by Dorothy Sayers, Christopher Fry, and Charles Williams in the 1930s and 1940s, and other versions of Becket's martyrdom: Laurence Binyon's *The Young King*, which depicts the reign of Henry II after Becket's death, and Tennyson's *Becket*. (Kenneth W. Pickering, in *Drama in the Cathedral* [C90], exhaustively examines the 20-year tradition of Canterbury Festival plays.) "To the theatre as it then was," Browne recalled decades later, "the play was a non-event. No manager came, or even sent a scout. The notices meant nothing because the Festival and its play were 'religious.' The only English theatre-man interested was Ashley Dukes, owner of the tiny Mercury in Notting Hill Gate." (C281, 94-95).

Stella Mary Pearce, who had also worked on *The Rock*, designed the costumes. Since the walls of the Canterbury Chapter House were distractingly painted in cold colors, costumes had to compensate for this distraction. "The only solution was to try to deaden the gentle brownish decoration on the natural stonework by using strong designs for the costumes, and by not being too narrowly historically accurate in their design," writes Pearce. "Had the production been planned for another setting, I should have produced very different designs" (C358, 102).

The Chorus, in sight for the whole play, was "given garments which provided for as much variety of appearance as possible. They had unshaped robes divided vertically into two shades of green and decorated with strong patterns in deep red and blue, giving the effect of figures of early stained glass, and allowing of constant change of colours as the figures moved from grouping to grouping" (C277, 62). Pearce writes that she found it impossible "to dress speakers of such complicated verse in naturalistic costumes. . . . At the same time, it seemed very important to save the audience from visual boredom and therefore, while keeping the Chorus in a single design, to be worn by all of them, I reversed the colours for half of them so that in grouping they could look either pale or dark" (C358, 102).

The Knights wore traditional medieval dress based on a reconstruction of the heraldry on the Black Prince's tomb of the actual murderers. Priests wore Benedictine habits and Becket wore a habit and a travelling cloak. The Tempters' costumes were dominated by bright yellow colors and included a suggestion of a modern-day type of each temptation, combined with the necessary medieval flavor: the First Tempter had striped trousers and "the top hat of the gay 'man about town'"; the Second had "a suggestion of medals on his breast," evoking a politician; the Third carried a stick to evoke a rough-hewn golf club, appropriate for a country lord; and the Fourth, "habited like Becket whose mind he inhabited, bore on his costume the palms and crowns of the martyrdom to which he tempted Becket 'for the wrong reason'" (C277, 62-63). Settings were by Laurence Irving.

Gwynneth Thurburn and Elsie Fogerty, from the Central School of Speech and Drama, trained the Chorus for the Canterbury production; they had also worked on the choruses in *The Rock*. As in that pageant the Chorus was composed of students from the school, though these were replaced (still under Thurburn's direction) as the play went on for longer runs. Thurburn was credited with acutely understanding the role of the chorus in performance. "The common impulse must be felt throughout by all," Browne writes. "Even when a single person, or only a small number, is speaking"—the eight voices in the original production only rarely spoke in unison—"the whole group must be involved in the feelings expressed. Thought and feeling must flow from one to another so that there is no break, nor differentiation in the experience. . . . Its essential function is to convey an experience felt in unity by all" (C277, 86). The Chorus is "the most important single factor in the success of the play from the author's point of view, and the most difficult," Browne writes (C276, 61). Speaight, though, found Thurburn's Chorus off-key: "Eliot's Women of Canterbury are types of the medieval poor and these dulcet-tongued damsels from South Kensington suggested neither poverty nor the Middle Ages. The difficulty is nearly insuperable, and Eliot used to say that the best Chorus he had seen was at the National University in Dublin where the Irish brogue conveyed an unforced impression of the 'folk'" (C108, 173).

As Browne toured the play in the 1940s through 1960s he added more variation to the choral acting: movement, for example, became freer. "At the Old Vic in 1953, Robert Helpmann showed the way with movement designed by his own balletic genius; but he showed also the dangers of allowing the movement to take precedence over the speech. Eliot must be served first" (C277, 88).

Following Becket's sermon in the Canterbury performance, Kenneth W. Pickering writes, "Eliot weaves the liturgy into the fabric of the play. . . . singers from St. Augustine's theological college were positioned in a gallery erected at the rear of the Chapter House and their plainsong mingled with the action on stage" (C90, 190).

The Canterbury production was an abridged version of the published text, since that performance was limited to 90 minutes. The only stage property was a simple throne. The Tempters entered from screens on both sides of the stage, and all other entrances were through the audience from the large oak doors at the back of the Chapter House (C108, 174). After the murder, Becket's body was carried out in a procession through the audience. Because stage exits were difficult, the original production sometimes featured as many as nineteen actors on stage at the same time. Though Browne writes that it was a strain for the bulk of the actors to remain "frozen" while a few engaged in lengthy dialogues, he felt that such a tableau was not dramatically unnatural because of the play's ritual aspect.

Writing of his interpretation of the role, Speaight identifies the sermon as the dramatic fulcrum of the play: "The dramatic force of the sermon struck me as soon as I had started to memorize it. The hieratic figure of the first act, with its rather laboured retrospections and its calm looking forward to martyrdom, imprisoned by the stiff rhythms of the verse . . . now became human and approachable. In stepping up to the pulpit Becket stepped down from the pedastal, and the actor was given a single opportunity for pathos" (C386, 72). Another moment of focused emotion in his role, Speaight writes, is when he tells his people he would probably never preach to them again. "Some people always held that the Becket of *Murder in the Cathedral* would never have faltered; others . . . regarded this as the best thing in my performance." The difficulty of acting in this play, Speaight asserts, is similar to the difficulty of acting in a play by Shakespeare: "In each case, the actor must create the illusion of life within a poetic convention. He must animate, but must not transgress, the rhythms of the verse which the author has put into his mouth."

Speaight performed extracts from the play at Dublin's Abbey Theatre later that year, and on 1 November 1935—All Saints' Day—the play opened with a fully professional cast at London's Mercury Theatre (which Ashley Dukes had opened as a forum for poetic drama) for 180 performances. Shakespeare's *Coriolanus* joined *Murder in the Cathedral* to inaugurate the Mercury's Poets' Theatre program. Speaight continued in the role of Becket; Alfred Clark was First Priest; Charles Petry was Second Priest; Frank Napier was Third Priest; Guy Spaull, G. R. Schjelderup, Norman Chidgey, and Browne were, respectively, First through Fourth Tempters and Knights (doubling roles); eight women from the Central School of Speech and Drama, under the training of Thurburn and Fogerty, played in the Chorus.

The Mercury Theatre's production copy of the script shows that the Chorus spoke in divisions, writes R. J. Clougherty, Jr.; other early performances also featured such choral divisions. Clougherty describes the effect of one such division: "The chorus part which stands out most for its musical effects is that which was read at the Mercury by Cecilia Colley. Five times . . . the line 'Living and not living' occurs; each time this line is delivered by Colley. When it is preceded by the line 'Yet we have gone on living,' as occurs twice in the play, this latter line is delivered by the Chorus as a whole. The result is that Colley's line comes across quieter and thus with a more ghost-like manner—like the conscience of the Chorus" (C55, 15).

Dukes took *Murder in the Cathedral* on tour to Oxford's Playhouse Theatre, Cambridge's Arts Theatre, and Dublin's Gate Theatre in the summer of 1936. Speaight recalls that the Dublin show had only modest audiences, since the Catholic populace was unreceptive to the traditionally Anglican story; the clergy were forbidden to see it (C108, 177). The play returned to the Mercury (which seated only 142); Dukes gave the proceeds of every tenth performance to Canterbury's Friends of the Cathedral. It then moved to the West End's larger and more established Duchess Theatre on 30 October 1936 for 113 performances; after a hiatus in February 1937, the play reopened the next month for fifteen more performances. Here, the Chorus was increased to nine and the sermon was embellished liturgically. Denis Carey took over the role of Second Priest.

During the four-month run at the Duchess the performance of 21 December was televised by the B. B. C. in a very early live television production for a series called *Starlight*. Browne writes that the televised production "marked the first experiment in super-imposition; each Tempter was superimposed on the image of Becket as he emerged into the archbishop's unconscious mind" (C277, 68). Also that year, B. B. C. radio's Dramatic Department broadcast the play. Val Gielgud, discussing that broadcast, praises Speaight as "a radio actor of vast experience," and writes that it "achieved over the air a success equal to if not surpassing its run in two London theatres" (C64, 111). In December 1965 the radio play was rebroadcast as part of B. B. C. Third Programme's series *The Thirties in Britain.*

In 1937, Queen Mary attended a performance at the Duchess Theatre. After the season was over at the Duchess the play toured in Leeds, Manchester, Glasgow, and Edinburgh. On 8 June 1937 it began a run of 35 performances at the Old Vic Theatre, London, with the same cast as the previous Duchess run. In July it was produced before the west front of Tewkesbury Abbey in Gloucestershire.

The American premiere was by an amateur company: Alan Merritt Fishburn directed the Yale University Theatre in a production that opened on 20 December 1935, starring Day Tuttle as Becket.

On 20 March 1936 the play began a limited engagement (due to extensive and intricate performance copyright negotiations) by the Popular Price Theatre—part of the Federal Theatre Project of the Works Progress Administration—at the Manhattan Theater in New York. People on relief were admitted free to the performance on certain nights (though on at least one night crowds could not be accommodated and 2,500 had to be turned away). The FTP later toured the play across the country, employing out-of-work actors. Hallie Flanagan, national director of the Federal Theatre, produced the play, which was directed by Halsted Welles; Eliot had promised Flanagan his first full-length drama after *Sweeney Agonistes*, which she had premiered at Vassar in 1933. Edith Isaacs credits Ashley Dukes's generosity in allowing the FTP's production "at a time when no New York dramatists of consequence would give the Federal Theatre a play" (R46, 255).

The production starred Harry Irvine as Becket; Tom Greenway, Joseph Draper, George LeSoir, and Robert Bruce as the First through Fourth Tempters, respectively; and Roger DeKoven, Stephen Courtleigh, Jon Loriner and Frederick Tozere as the First through Fourth Knights, respectively. Music was by A. Lehman Engel, and scenery and costumes by The Theatre Workshop under the direction of Tom Adrian Cracraft. A stark set evoked the cathedral's interior, with steps rising in the rear and two impressionistic evocations of Gothic windows; a sky appeared behind this. In the FTP's performance script (in the New York Public Library's Billy Rose Theatre Collection), the set is described as "neither the interior or exterior of the cathedral, but rather an impression of both." In the sparse property plot for the FTP production—typical of most productions of the play—the only items are a rosary and ecclesiastical ring for Becket in Part I, several sheets of parchment for the Interlude, and three ecclesiastical banners, nine long spears, and four daggers for Part II.

Flanagan (by then, Hallie Flanagan Davis) directed a revival of *Murder in the Cathedral* for the Vassar Experimental Theatre that opened in December 1941—eerily, as many would later remember, on the eve of the Japanese attack on Pearl Harbor. C. Gordon Post starred as Becket. Settings were by

Martin W. Fallon, and a musical score was composed and played by Chris Leonard.

Browne's full-scale Broadway production of the play starring Speaight opened on 16 February 1938. An English cast was brought to the Ritz Theatre by Gilbert Miller and Dukes after previews in Boston, but the show ran for only 21 performances—because of unresolvable production and business conflicts, Browne writes. Speaight calls the opening night "purgatorial" (C108, 188) and Broadway audiences unexcited; he blames Flanagan's earlier New York production for having stolen the thunder from this one.

During World War II the play was quite popular in England, presented in—among other makeshift venues—cathedrals and churches, schools, and an air-raid shelter. (In 1959, Eliot stated that he wrote the play as anti-Nazi propaganda: expressive of "the desire to save the Christian world from the attacks of rival secular ideologies," as Carol H. Smith interprets his statement [C382, 24-25].) Due to wartime austerity measures, the production was billed as an "emergency version" of the play, with a cast of only nine actors and Browne himself taking the role of Becket. As thus performed by Browne's Pilgrim Players in 1939, it was the first production given under the auspices of the Council for the Encouragement of Music and the Arts (CEMA), which was formed to prevent the eclipse of the arts during wartime. Other Pilgrim Players productions—most of which were religious—included André Obey's *Noah* and Yeats's *The Resurrection*.

In America the play saw frequent revivals by college troupes: at Poet's Theatre of Harvard in 1937; Amherst College in 1937; the University of California at Berkeley in 1938; the University of North Carolina at Chapel Hill in 1945; Hobart College in Geneva, NY, in 1945; Indiana University in 1952; Berkeley again in 1959; UCLA in 1960; Grinnell College in 1961; the University of Illinois in 1969; and the Juilliard School in 1976. As M. C. Bradbrook observes in *English Dramatic Form*, this play "may well turn out to be Eliot's most enduring stage success, for though not often professionally performed it can be successfully played by amateurs" (C270, 163).

After the war the Mercury Theatre revived the play for three months, and Eliot attended a performance of the play sitting in a stall with King George VI, Queen Elizabeth, and Princess Margaret. The Gateway Theatre revived the play in 1947 as part of the Edinburgh International Festival, with Speaight in the lead. That production moved in September 1947 to the Arts Theatre of Cambridge, where it played in repertory with *The Family Reunion*. Also in 1947, Rudolf Alexander Schröder's translation, *Mord im Dom*, played in Cologne, Göttingen, and Munich; German productions, Dukes notes, "are inclined to give an operatic importance to the production by their use of incidental music, and to indulge in choreographics both in the scenes of the Tempters and the Chorus" (C293, 116).

A French production of the play, *Meurtre dans la Cathédrale*, translated by Henri Fluchère, was given at the Vieux-Colombier in Paris in 1945-46, produced by Jean Vilar. In the winter of 1950, Speaight directed and starred in a French production—again using Fluchère's translation—at Theatre des Compagnons in Montreal.

In 1953 Robert Helpmann produced the play at London's Old Vic Theatre with Robert Donat, in his last role, as Becket; Lyndall Gordon writes that Eliot considered Donat, with his simple and devout sense of exaltation, the best actor he had seen in the role of Becket (C309, 36). Music was directed by Christopher Whelen; sets and costumes were by Alan Barlow. Paul Rogers (who would create the role of Lord Claverton in *The Elder Statesman*) played the First Knight; Newton Blick (Eggerson in the New York run of *The Confidential Clerk*) played the Third Tempter.

In 1960 the play was presented at the first International Festival of the Arts in Adelaide, Australia, directed by Hugh Hunt, and afterwards toured to Sydney. On 21 October 1965, Marigold Charlesworth's revival opened, starring Powys Thomas, at Toronto's Canadian Players Foundation.

On 18 June 1966 the play was revived at the American Shakespeare Festival Theatre in Stratford, Conn. John Houseman directed that production in conjunction with Pearl Lang, a choreographer who designed the Chorus's movements. Joseph Wiseman starred as Becket.

In 1967 Browne led a production at the Yvonne Arnaud Theatre in Guildford, and in 1970 he produced the play within the actual cathedral at Canterbury to mark the 800-year anniversary of Becket's martyrdom, starring John Westbrook and featuring Henzie Raeburn as the leader of the Chorus. (Modern sound equipment allowed the play's performance in the nave, which had been acoustically impossible in 1935.)

On 31 August 1972 the play was revived at London's Aldwych Theatre in a Royal Shakespeare Company production starring Richard Pasco. Terry Hands directed that production; Ian Kellam's music was directed by Gordon Kember. For his sets, designer Abdul Farrah "preferred suggestion to solidity, creating space with rough hessian and silver foil, raking his stage and 'paving' it with flagstones, one of which obligingly rose on a stalk to form Becket's pulpit," writes William Tydeman (C390, 73).

Gregory Abels directed a revival that opened 26 February 1981, for fifteen performances, at New York's St. Malachy's Theatrespace, starring Lee Richardson as Becket. The Stratford Festival's Avon Theatre in Stratford, Ontario, revived the play for its 1988 summer season, directed by David William and starring Nicholas Pennell as Becket.

Eliot wrote the screenplay for George Hoellering's 1952 film version of *Murder in the Cathedral* and spoke the role of the Fourth Tempter (as an off-screen presence). An opera based on the play, *Assassinio nella Catedrale*, set to music by Ildebrando Pizzetti, was performed at La Scala, Milan, in 1958, and at the Vatican before Pope John XXIII in September 1959. On 3 July 1962 that opera opened at Sadler's Wells in London, with Don Garrard as Becket and Colin Davis conducting the Sadler's Wells Opera Company.

Critical Overview

Performance Reviews

Conrad Aiken (under the pseudonym of Samuel Jeake, Jr.), writing of the Canterbury premiere in *The New Yorker*, calls it possibly "a turning point in English drama. . . . one felt that one was witnessing a play which had the quality of greatness. . . . One's feeling was that here at last was the English language literally being *used*, itself becoming the stuff of drama, turning alive with its own natural poetry. And Eliot's formalisation wasn't at all the sort of thing one has grown accustomed to expect of poetic drama—no trace of sham antique or artiness about it; nothing in the 'dead' sense, 'poetic.' No, the thing was direct and terribly real, the poetry of the choruses was as simple and immediate in its meaning as our own daily lives." The amateur cast, Aiken writes, "gave a performance that professionals might envy" (R49).

An article in the London *Times* about the play at the Mercury in 1936, after the first run had been in production for more than a year, testifies to its durability and shows how the performance matured as it developed. "After many repetitions the production has not become rigid or the cast in the least tired; on the contrary the whole performance has the smooth precision which the play seems to require, and that exact balance of dramatic emphasis and calm which is needed for its often bare and classical form. The chorus, above all, appear to have benefited by constant drilling; the speaking of verse in unison is an intensely difficult art, and though here everything is done to vary the monotony by a frequent distribution of the lines to single speakers or to pairs, the excellent timing is of great advantage to the performance. And when the chorus do speak as a whole they are most unusually careful to be neither sibilant nor artificially impressive in their accents" (R69).

Michael Sayers writes in *Criterion* of the play's possible impact on contemporary theatre: "It is a challenge, and it must be so recognized. In thought, anecdote and language it repudiates almost all the popular values, in life and theatre, of our time. It may occasion a revolution in popular thought and theatre through subsequent imitations, and by its direct influence similar to that brought about by the comedies of Shaw. Or it may go down to the popular limbo as one of the curiosities of a moribund theatre" (R60, 655).

When the production moved to the Duchess Theatre, Ivor Brown complains in *The Observer*, "The promotion of this play about Becket to the West End carries it one step farther from its original home, the scene of the crime. . . . Eliot's tribute to the martyr seems to require its surrounding of the actual fane and the Canterbury bells." The church atmosphere "was absolutely right for the original production but is not as effective in a lay theatre" (R38).

Ezra Pound's typically idiosyncratic reaction to the play is recorded in a letter he wrote from Rapallo, Italy: "Waal, I heerd the *Murder in the Cafedrawl* on the radio lass' night. Oh them cawkney woices. . . . Mzzr Shakzpeer *still* retains his posishun. I stuck it fer a while, wot wiff the weepin and wailin" (C266, 144-45).

"For all its occasional obscurity and frequent dullness," Richard Watts, Jr., writes in the New York *Herald Tribune* of the 1936 FTP run, the play "possesses dignity, thoughtfulness, and beauty" (R64). Welles's production is "striking and effective, even though it is sometimes managed too slowly and too much in a minor key to be completely satisfying." Brooks Atkinson, too, in the *New York Times*, finds Welles the guiding force behind this production. "It would be difficult to find a play that offered greater problems in theatrical expression. There is nothing but spirit and perception to lay hold of. But Mr. Welles has conjured out of the choral chants and the violent imagery a moving and triumphant performance. Where the verse is too compact Mr. Welles has found ways of loosening it, and he has caught in the apprehensive gestures of acting the brooding, forewarned doom of the play" (R32). In a later review of the same run Atkinson cites the impact of Engel's music: "To the formal church music which Mr. Eliot's text provides for, and which is glorious, A. Lehman Engel has added a sternly prescient score that cries a swiftly phrased warning and gives *Murder in the Cathedral* an audible architecture" (R34).

Like many critics, Watts uses the occasion to comment on the government's involvement in the theatre industry: "Despite all the criticism that has been leveled against the WPA drama, it is only fair to say that in its laborious sort of manner, the government theatre is getting off to an interesting start" (R64). In the New York *American*, Gilbert W. Gabriel agrees: "Of all that the Federal Project has done to date, this seems in many ways to be the bravest . . . certainly the justest and kindliest and—must I suffer martyrdom for saying this in these utilitarian-minded days?—the most artistic" (R42).

From another quarter, though, comes criticism of the WPA's support of the play; in the *Daily Worker*, Jay Gerlando writes that since his conversion Eliot has become "something of an encyclical writer," and his works "have convinced no one, except those who were already convinced. . . . One of his most ambitious rationalizations is *Murder in the Cathedral*, which by the Grace of God and the Roosevelt regime has become a part of the Federal Theatre Project. . . . Some of the speeches are beautiful as poems, but are based entirely on medieval philosophy and superstitions" (R43).

Reviewers of the 1938 New York production generally found it inferior to Flanagan's 1936 run. "In most respects the WPA did a better job," writes Arthur Pollock in the Brooklyn *Eagle*. "The production last night was fussy by comparison, a kind of intimate performance suggesting murder in a lobby rather than anywhere more spacious, and it had none of the sweep the humble actors of the WPA gave it and none too much of the clarity, either" (R55). Richard Watts, Jr., in the New York *Herald Tribune*, prefers the 1936 American cast to the imported one. "The local performance somehow gave it more dramatic vigor and showmanship. The current version is more in the nature of a dignified religious chant" (R65). Atkinson agrees with Watts's assessment, though he appreciates what Browne chose to emphasize in his production: "If the Federal Theatre production was more vividly theatrical, the present one is more fervently religious, showing a deeper comprehension of Mr. Eliot's worship and thought" (R33).

Reviewing the 1953 revival, Atkinson writes in the *New York Times* that Helpmann "has clarified and dramatized a familiar script that has always seemed a little uncomfortable in the theatre despite the terse beauty of the poetry." The play "may have been a religious rite when Mr. Eliot wrote it for performance in the Canterbury Cathedral more than twenty years ago. But it is a piece of magnificent theatre now" (R35). W. Macqueen Pope lauds Donat in the *Morning Telegraph*: his "beautiful voice gets full scope. It is like listening to lovely music" (R56).

Mollie Panter-Downes, in *The New Yorker*, describes the Knights' speeches in that production: they "deliver their Shaw-like apologia to the audience for their murder of the Archbishop in such a wildly comic parody of the supercilious B. B. C. Third Programme manner that it brings down the house (and almost puts the great stride of the rest of the play out of step)" (R53).

Martin Esslin criticizes Terry Hands's direction of the Chorus in the 1972 Aldwych revival. "Of course, any chorus in any play, whether ancient Greek or modern, is an exceedingly difficult, an almost insoluble problem. There are two choices open to the producer: he can *either* distribute the lines in such a way that the choral passages become a kind of realistic dialogue, a conversation between a group of individuals, or indeed, monologues of individuals who express their deepest thoughts and longings only to themselves. . . . *Or* the director can stylise his chorus to a point where all pretence at realism disappears, and the choruses become rituals, intoned or sung" (R41, 44-45).

"Hands has not plumped for either of these alternatives," Esslin complains; "he has stuck to the traditional compromise of figures who try to pretend they are real characters while at times unaccountably breaking out into unison, speaking like children at school who bawl out their lessons in rhythmic recitation. In this case the seven ladies of Canterbury sound as though they were reciting poems of T S Eliot which they had just learnt by heart. Their voices are far too middle class, their intonations far too Third Programme to make them believable medieval paupers of Canterbury. Why, then, try to make them dress up and behave as though they were just that? Moreover, if seven people speak in unison at normal volume the sound which comes out is far too loud to allow for any modulation and expressiveness; it just becomes a noise" (45).

Scholarly Response

The aspect of religious experience portrayed in *Murder in the Cathedral* is one "with which [Eliot] is obsessed" in all his work, writes Richard Findlater: "the crisis of doubt, the sense of guilt, the necessity of suffering, the experience of purgation, the subjection to the divine will and the immanent destiny. He presents the experiences on the road to God, as it were, never the arrival, the consummation, the ecstasy. It is the incarnation of these states of mind that appears to be his first consideration: the characters of the play are vehicles, and he deliberately restricts their dramatic life to a single dimension of intense awareness" (C296, 135).

Comparing this play with Eliot's earlier religious drama, The Rock, critics unanimously write that Murder in the Cathedral has a much clearer sense of unity and less blatant propagandistic overtones. While The Rock showed moments of insightfully pointed writing, Murder in the Cathedral sustains this throughout. Bernard Bergonzi compares the play with Eliot's other previous play: "Becket, like Sweeney . . . was possessed of a graver burden of consciousness than those around him" (C266, 146).

Though Eliot did not consciously develop this play out of a Greek dramatic model (as he did each of his subsequent plays), Leo Aylen calls the play "most near in spirit to Greek tragedy, of all the plays written in English or French this century. It is formally similar; it uses a myth in the same way as the Greek tragedies did, and the myth bears the same relation to the religion of Eliot's audience as the myths of the Greek poets did to their audience's religion. It is based on ritual, and the action is carried out principally by the chorus, not by an actor. It was performed at a festival, not before a theatre-going public" (C259, 325).

Stevie Smith finds the play "a remarkable evocation of Christian fears" (as Eliot himself must have envisioned when he considered calling the play Fear in the Way). It is "remarkable for the strength of these fears and the horrible beauty. in which they are dressed" (C105, 170). Smith conjectures that Eliot saw his time as one of godlessness, frivolity, uncertainty, and guilt, and intended the play as an antidote: "Look on this, it says, and reform yourself" (170). While writers may "take events and personages of the past and fit them to their uses," Smith writes that she objects to his use of historical semi- fictions to depict the weakening of the human spirit—the apotheosis of fear: "is it permissible to distort the truths of humanity and offend against them, to cover the needs of men with a meretricious coat, and to envisage with delight a dwindling of hope and courage?" (171).

Smith lambasts Eliot for exploiting a fear cloaked in historical inevitability rather than confronting a pragmatic and contemporary transcendence of fear. "It seems curious, condemnable really, that so many writers of these times, which need courage and the power of criticism, and coolness, should find their chief delight in terrifying themselves and their readers with past echoes of cruelty and nonsense, 'pacing for ever . . . in the hell of make-believe'" (174). She finds Eliot's tone severe rather than loving, citing as indicative of this his interpretation in the screenplay of Murder in the Cathedral of a key biblical passage: "It is a disputed biblical text . . . but a wise heart would have adhered to our English Bible's rendering." Instead of "on earth peace, good will toward men," as in the play, Eliot in the film changes this to "'peace on earth to men of good will,' which is a limitation and shrinkage of charity, for all men need good will, and most of all those who do not have it" (174).

John Crowe Ransom calls the play "a drama that starts religious but reverts, declines, very distinctly towards snappiness" (C92, 619), reflecting an inauthenticity or insincerity in Eliot's religious poetic tone; the play "might be very good by modern standards, but Eliot knows how weak are modern standards" (623).

Stephen Spender, though, is more appreciative of Eliot's goals and success in a Christian sense. "The true theme of Eliot's plays written after his conversion is the discovery by heroes . . . of their religious vocation. It is required of the hero that he perfect his will so as to make it conform completely with the will of God," he writes in "Martyrdom and Motive"; and this play is the one "in which these aims are revealed in a very pure state" (C111, 96-97).

Marianne Moore lauds Eliot's tone, technique, and style: "One may merely mention the appropriateness of verse to subject matter and the consequent varying rhythms; the unforced suitability and modesty of presentation; the evidence that originality is not a thing sealed and incapable of enlargement, but that an author may write newly while continuing the decorums and abilities of the past" (C83, 280). Of the play's overall effect, she writes, "Mr. Eliot steps so reverently on the solemn ground he has essayed, that austerity assumes the dignity of philosophy and the didacticism of the verities incorporated in the play becomes impersonal and persuasive" (281).

The play is "Eliot's most successful integration of his dramatic theories," writes Carol H. Smith. "The levels of the play are intrinsically unified by the skillful interweaving of Thomas' story with the imagery of Christ's Temptation and Passion and with the prototype formula of all religion and drama. The hierarchy of characters within the play who perceive the meaning of Thomas' death on their various levels helps to tighten the unity of the drama and to give it the stylized quality Eliot admires. . . . By demonstrating the changing attitude of the chorus . . . from a fear of spiritual realities and a disavowal of responsibilities to acceptance of and participation in both the sin and glory of martyrdom, Eliot has provided a highly effective vehicle for commentary on the action and participation in it" (C382, 110).

Eliot's stylistic and formalistic endeavours won a generally favorable reception: "Many people could have made a play out of Becket's murder—an instructive play, a witty play, a good thriller or a moral tale," writes I. M. Parsons. "Eliot has done more: he has reanimated a literary form"—dramatic poetry—"which in England has been dead or dormant for nearly three hundred years, and in doing so he has found himself anew as a poet, only with an added ease, lucidity and objectiveness" (R54, 1112). James Laughlin offers a critical appreciation of Eliot's form: "There is no fixed metre, but there is, in the best sense, a fine free metric. Mr. Eliot has been to school and knows his language-tones and sound-lengths as few others do. He can cut a line of sound in time so that it comes off the page to you as a tangible design. His cadences are soft and cool and flowing, but there is never an unnecessary word. The language is highly charged with meaning, but there is no looseness of rhetoric" (R50, 251).

F. O. Matthiessen writes that *Murder in the Cathedral* shows "a relative lack of density" compared with *The Waste Land*. "This is partly owing to the fact that in *The Waste Land* the poet employed symbols which maintained the action continually in the present at the same time that he was exploring analogies with the past. In the play, though centering throughout on problems that reveal the 'permanent in human nature,' he has not made that complete fusion. . . . the life represented is lacking something in immediacy and urgency" (C347, 11).

Denis Donoghue, too, finds the play unsatisfactory: "its text evades, rather than solves, the problems of dramatic verse; and . . . its structural flaws are similar to those of certain late nineteenth-century plays." He objects to the fact that a Canterbury audience, especially, would know the plot before the play began, thus eliminating dramatic force. The organization is "pedestrian. The play, in fact, consists of a number of expressive segments which are related only on the conceptual level: there is no unity of drama and metaphor." The choruses link the play together mechanically, he finds, but not organically. The play has meaning only when one brings in religious and socio-historical institutions that are alluded to within the text, Donoghue writes, which diminishes its integrity; it is "theology as drama, but the determining bias is that of the theologian" (C290, 83). And the play's language, which Eliot meant to revolutionize verse drama, is in fact only derivative of his earlier poetry, such as *Ash-Wednesday*, Donoghue argues.

If the play is dramatically deficient, as Matthiessen and Donoghue argue, Robert W. Ayers finds that it embodies a liturgical unity. Eliot had written in "A Dialogue on Dramatic Poetry" that the ceremony of the Mass typifies perfect and ideal drama, and Ayers sees *Murder in the Cathedral* as mimetic of the Mass. "The work was written not for performance in the theatre, but for presentation in the 'semi-liturgical setting' [E. Martin Browne's phrase] of the Chapter House. . . . And the possibility that Eliot was employing a liturgical form for those religious precincts on that occasion of religious celebration may first occur when we observe that the Interlude in the drama is a sermon on the Mass, and the congregation Thomas addresses in the Mass is the audience witnessing the drama" (C41, 580). The Mass consists of two parts separated by a sermon—the first part "is instructional and preparational," and the second part "is concerned with the offer of the sacrifice (Offertory), the sacrifice itself (Consecration), and the participation of the community in the sacrifice (Communion)" (580-81); this same pattern, Ayers writes, may be discerned in the play's structure.

Carol Billman explains another way in which the play depends upon a metaphysical structure for its unity. As medieval playwrights presented copious anachronisms to point out the insignificance of linear chronology from a spiritual perspective, Eliot similarly "illustrates his lack of interest in temporal history for its own sake." For instance, "His medieval characters time and again refer to subsequent periods in history. . . . Beyond such references that make modern audiences consider medieval figures and events from a distinctly *ex post facto* perspective, the four knights in the play actually violate linear chronology with 'platform prose,' as Eliot called it, addressed directly to the twentieth-century audience" (C45, 48). Eliot embraces what seems like ambiguity in a literal historical sense (though not in a spiritual one) to create a "poetic mystery play that does not declaim but suggests," Billman writes. The play "anticipates later twentieth-century historical drama like Friedrich Dürrenmatt's *Romulus the Great*, Bertolt Brecht's *Galileo*, and Albert Camus's *Caligula* in its incorporation of puzzling ambiguities and exploration of man's doubt-full struggle to find his place in history and the cosmos" (54).

The Chorus visually "suggests the collectivity, the generality of mankind, as distinct from its outstanding individual members—Thomas à Becket or Henry II," writes Pieter D. Williams (C117, 499). "The stasis of the Chorus, compared with the movement, sometimes violent, of other characters and groups of characters, helps to isolate them visually in the kaleidoscope of power politics and reinforces another salient theme: the permanence of common humanity, the impermanence of political and ecclesiastical systems. . . . The Chorus has learned a stoical submission to life, to that manifestation of the will of God—something which Thomas, when the play begins, has yet to learn. He has to achieve the passive attitude of the Chorus without its negative apprehension and fear of involvement" (500-501). Additionally, Williams cites the importance of the vocal role played by the Chorus: it provides a symphony of female voices, a balanced antithesis to the male voices of the Priests, Messenger, Archbishop, Tempters, and Knights.

Other functions of the Chorus, Williams continues, include serving "as an expository device, to give details of time, place, action and the dramatic possibilities of situations" that complement some of the other more abstract development. "Theirs is a sentient interpretation of events, in contrast to the cerebral interpretations of the Priests, and the blunt, matter-of-fact one of the Knights" (501). The Chorus helps delineate character, register emotion, and "is used to telescope into ninety minutes the last twenty-seven days of Becket's life by suggesting the passage of time" (502). It provides an important stable point of reference: "The relative stasis of the Chorus, and their advanced age, make them convincing observers and commentators. Theirs is the voice of experience, not of innocence" (503). And finally, the Chorus acts "as congregational representative for the audience, for England, for humanity. . . . This direct link the Chorus forms with the audience is important in controlling the emotional balance and patterns of the play. In the first half the audience identifies empathically with the Chorus, but at some distance from them; in the Interlude it merges its identity and emotions with those of the Chorus. During the second half . . . the Chorus shows the audience how they should react, and openly invites them to join in the paean of praise, a new *Te Deum*" (507).

The choral passages, writes Richard Badenhausen, are closely linked to Eliot's own voice—what Eliot in "The Three Voices of Poetry" called "the first voice," that of the poet talking to himself. The Chorus echoes Eliot's earlier poetic characters such as Prufrock, Gerontion, and Tiresias, who expose "the psychic strife in the poet's mind" (C42, 243).

Textual Notes and Influences

Browne writes that the title came from his wife, Henzie Raeburn. Eliot "had always wanted the ritual aspect of the play to be balanced by the homicidal; he was a devotee of Sherlock Holmes; and this title, with its sardonic implications, had a contemporary quality which would induce in an audience an attitude favorable to the acceptance of the ironies, particularly in the Knights' apology, as a natural part of the play" (C277, 55). The play's earlier provisional title had been *Fear in the Way*, and Eliot had also considered *The Archbishop Murder Case*.

In *Poetry and Drama* (P55) Eliot writes that the play's subject matter was unusually suitable for verse drama—thus, it served him well as an early exercise in writing in this form. His task was to find a diction that was neither archaic nor banal; poetry was, for him, a neutral style, committed neither to the present nor to the past. He felt compelled to avoid the influence of Shakespeare, which he saw as a hazard for nineteenth-century verse dramatists. Though he writes that a verse play should, generally, be entirely in verse, he excuses the two prose passages by arguing that Becket's sermon would not have been credible in verse, and the Knights' addresses are designed to shock the audience with their dissonance.

Also in *Poetry and Drama*, Eliot cites the influence of the verse of *Everyman* in this play's poetry. In an appendix to his edition of *Murder in the Cathedral*, Nevill Coghill discusses Eliot's debt to the medieval play: *Everyman* "yields a kind of verse-movement quite different in its effect from that of iambic blank verse; it is specially different in having the pleasing, natural jerkiness of conversation with its sudden surprises, while retaining a certain arbitrary rhythm or balance, helped by the emphases of rhyme" (146). The effect that Eliot sought to borrow from *Everyman* for *Murder in the Cathedral* is "one of living movement and emphatic speech, that tumbles as if by accident on to the happy rhythmical phrase and compulsive rhyme, unforeseeably, and yet with gratification of a certain indefinable expectancy" (C56, 149-50).

Eliot found in the Becket story, Browne writes, something timeless and absolute: "at the moment when he was called upon to write his play, he found that the basic conflict of the twentieth century came very near to repeating that of the twelfth" (C277, 36); the rise of fascism in the 1930s may be perceived as an echo of the social threats to Becket's devotion in the play, Browne asserts.

Browne writes that it was his idea to develop the Tempters' characters as a way of explaining Becket's conflict between spiritual obedience and social factors; and that Rupert Doone, who was working with Eliot on staging *Swee-*

ney Agonistes as he was writing *Murder in the Cathedral*, suggested that the Tempters appear as manifestations of Becket's internal psychological conflicts (C277, 43). Lyndall Gordon, though, argues that the germ of the idea for the Tempters predates Browne's suggestion; she cites preliminary notes for the play that mention contemporary authors who seem to be models for the Tempters. H. G. Wells, a "noted philanderer . . . represents the facile charms of the senses and good-fellowship" embodied in the First Tempter. Bertrand Russell "was the germ for the Tempter to power who speaks with pervasive reason." D. H. Lawrence was "the germ of the blustering boor," the Third Tempter, who is full of "rebellious heat." Irving Babbitt and Huxley (Gordon is uncertain whether Eliot means Julian or Aldous) are possible models for the Fourth and most complex tempter, the one who evokes a "substitute religion" (such as Babbitt's humanism). The significance of the Tempters' having their origins in writers, Gordon claims, is that "Eliot was pitting himself against rival opinion-makers" (C309, 30-31).

While Eliot was composing the play Browne had asked him to liven up parts of Part I; the director suggested that the Chorus and Priests make comments after the Tempters' speeches. To this end, Eliot drafted thirteen lines of response to the Tempters, which were later deemed unnecessary. The lines, though, later became (with small changes) the opening passage in "Burnt Norton." In *The Composition of Four Quartets*, Helen Gardner details how Eliot recycled what he called "bits that had to be cut out of *Murder in the Cathedral*" to form the germ of his 1936 poem, and thus of the whole of *Four Quartets* (C302). Also, Becket's last words to the Chorus before his martyrdom, "Human kind cannot bear very much reality" (69), are repeated as lines 42-43 of "Burnt Norton," Part I.

Eliot's manuscript sketches of scenes for *Murder in the Cathedral* are intermixed with drafts of lines for an unpublished sketch called "Bellgarde," which Gordon describes: "a man experiences 'leaping pleasures' that release him from a mood of futility, and reach a 'matchless' moment, then fade all too fast, 'impaired by impotence.' There is a dramatic arousal, and an even more dramatic collapse that seems psychological, not physical, for pleasure is almost at once eroded by a self-lacerating mind that worries over the experience until it is virtually destroyed" (C309, 47). She argues that "Bellgarde" is a likely source for "Burnt Norton"; its connection with the manuscript composition of *Murder in the Cathedral* suggests an influence on this play as well, and also a link—in terms of the quest for emotional fulfillment and resolution—between *Murder in the Cathedral* and "Burnt Norton."

Becket's stichomythic exchange with the Second Tempter echoes the riddle of the hidden treasure in Arthur Conan Doyle's "The Musgrave Ritual," as Grover Smith describes; he suggests Eliot's use of the mystery "was motivated by his appreciation of all ritual that involves treading a maze or threading a labyrinth" (C104, 432).

The Knights' song as they enter the cathedral, Browne notes, is influenced by Vachel Lindsay's "Daniel Jazz." Eliot's jazzy tempo here is evocative of

Sweeney Agonistes, though perhaps in its tenor of foreboding and mindless decadence more closely connected to the Shakespeherian Rag from *The Waste Land*. And as Eliot himself hinted in *Poetry and Drama*, the Knights' speeches after the murder are indebted to the tone of George Bernard Shaw's somewhat blasé and banal Epilogue in his 1923 play *Saint Joan*.

Several critics compare the play to *Saint Joan*—Mark Van Doren writes that Eliot's play "is both higher and thinner [than Shaw's]; higher because it rises above the merely political problem of obedience to authority, and thinner because theology must always be thin on any stage" (R63, 417). Clifford Davidson asserts that Eliot "had apparently consciously attempted to set aside the kind of treatment that George Bernard Shaw had given to St. Joan and tried instead to establish some continuity with medieval tradition, which he wished to treat with integrity. . . . Eliot's play represents a study of a historical martyrdom in a play which is far more serious than any other English drama on such a topic since the end of the Middle Ages" (C58, 160).

Of the Apology of the Knights, Herbert Howarth writes, "With its buffoonery, its parody of the British speech-making styles, its cracks at British institutions in the favorite British mode of self-criticism, it looks back to the deliberate buffoonery of *The Orators*" (C322, 338), W. H. Auden's 1932 rhetorical satire. As with Eliot's two previous plays, comparisons were made between *Murder in the Cathedral* and Auden's drama. In an article reviewing Eliot's play along with *The Dog Beneath the Skin*, Gregory Stone writes that "Mr. Auden is not only less of a poet than Mr. Eliot, he is also less alive. Awareness of the facts of the moment can be accompanied by ignorance of the more lasting facts which explain them, and the realist with a quick eye for surface details may know nothing of reality. . . . Mr. Auden's timeliness is the timeliness of fashions that change with the seasons, of newspaper headlines that are dead when they are but a few hours old; whereas the insight that probes the constant urges of man's spirit throws a light on the present moment that no record of surfaces can equal. The eternal is forever timely" (R62, 127-28).

J. T. Boulton discusses Eliot's debt—both for content and direct appropriation of language—to the narrative of Edward Grim, a contemporary of Becket's who was present at the murder and is considered the best authority (C47).

"Eliot may well have known that plays on the subject of St. Thomas Becket existed in the middle ages," writes Clifford Davidson; well-known studies such as E. K. Chambers' 1903 *Medieval Stage* disclose that such saint's plays "were apparently staged at King's Lynn in Norfolk in 1385, where persons were paid for 'playing the interlude of St. Thomas the Martyr,' and at Canterbury itself, where a 'pageant of St. Thomas' was recorded in the sixteenth century on one of his feast days, thought . . . to be 29 December, until the suppression of his cult" (C58, 153).

Eliot also knew Tennyson's *Becket*. That play enjoyed a popular run in the 1890s starring Henry Irving and Ellen Terry, and, more recently, had been presented in the Canterbury Festivals of 1932 and 1933. "It is reasonable to assume that Eliot had this work in mind when deciding on the composition of his own play," David Seed argues (C100, 42). Eliot's divergence from Tennyson, besides his rejection of blank verse, can be seen in Tennyson's desire "to produce a work of documentary accuracy," with attention to the external historical situation, as opposed to the way in which Eliot "pruned away most of the issues dealt with by Tennyson, focusing instead on Becket's martyrdom" (44-45). (Still, in *Poetry and Drama*, Eliot faults even Tennyson's history, criticizing him for tampering unscrupulously with the documents available.)

Ashley Dukes remembers how the contemporary political climate affected the play: "Other things conspired to remind us of the play's actuality; indeed it was never allowed to become historical drama for a moment. Hitler had been long enough in power to ensure that the four knightly murderers of Becket would be recognized as figures of the day, four perfect Nazis defending their act on the most orthodox totalitarian grounds. Echoes of one war and forebodings of another resounded through the sultry afternoon" (C293, 114-15). Dukes also notes an unintentional resonance in the play: King Edward VIII abdicated his throne during the play's West End run, adding an ironic potency to several lines about the transience of the temporal sovereign's rule.

The play's hero, sharing Eliot's first name, is "not unconnected with the author himself, who has some special awareness of which others are deprived and yet whose great strengths are allied with serious weaknesses," writes Peter Ackroyd (C255, 227). Gordon, too, notes autobiographical overtones: Eliot found in Becket "a model who was not so different from himself. Here was a man to all appearances not born for sainthood, a man of the world . . . who moved from worldly success into spiritual danger. . . . Eliot said that a bit of the author may be the germ of a character, but that, too, a certain character may call out latent potentialities in the author. *Murder in the Cathedral* was a biographical play that had its impact on Eliot in shifting the balance of his new life from the shared course of love to the lone course of religious trial" (C309, 28).

R. J. Clougherty, Jr., analyzes the division of speeches by groups and individuals within the Chorus in the production copy for the Mercury Theatre run; he argues that they are authoritatively Eliot's divisions, though no published texts except that of the screenplay indicate such divisions (C55).

Publishing History

Faber & Faber published the play in June 1935, and published three more editions with minor authorial changes over the next three years; Harcourt published the American edition in 1935. The play was reprinted in *The Complete Poems and Plays* (New York: Harcourt, 1952), and *Collected Plays* (London: Faber & Faber, 1962). Faber & Faber published the screenplay in

1952 (for which director George Hoellering was listed as co-author), as did Harcourt. That edition contains a preface by Eliot.

Grover Smith (C383, 180-81), Browne (C277, 72-79; reprinted as "The Variations in the Text" in David R. Clark's *Twentieth Century Interpretations of Murder in the Cathedral*), and Robert L. Beare (C264, 39-47) detail the differences among various published texts. Kenneth W. Pickering (C90, 181-85) focuses on variants between published versions of the play and an acting edition Faber & Faber published for the Canterbury Festival performance. A. J. Turner argues that Eliot's revisions for the fourth edition (1938) were meant to efface the sense from earlier editions that "Becket was no passive sufferer, but an active provoker of his death" (C113, 51); deletions include some of Becket's most bombastic rhetoric.

In 1965, Faber & Faber published "an educational edition" of the play with an introduction, elaborate notes, and supplementary essays on the play's historical background, the versification of *Everyman*, and Tennyson's *Becket*, by Nevill Coghill. Eliot gave the introduction his approval but died before the completion of the other editorial matter; Coghill writes that Eliot directed him "to show how the action and dialogue were faithful to historical truth. He also asked me to illustrate the derivation of the verse from *Everyman*" (C56, 20).

The Family Reunion

Characters

Amy, Dowager Lady Monchensey. Ivy, Violet, and Agatha, her younger sisters. Col. the Hon. Gerald Piper and the Hon. Charles Piper, brothers of her deceased husband. Mary, daughter of a deceased cousin of Lady Monchensey. Denman, a parlourmaid. Harry, Lord Monchensey, Amy's Eldest son. Downing, his servant and chauffeur. Dr. Warburton. Sergeant Winchell. The Eumenides.

Synopsis

Amy sits in the drawing room of her country house, Wishwood; she watches the evening fade thinking of the excitement and confidence of the past, eager for the coming of Spring. Agatha, Ivy, Violet, Charles, and Gerald drily discuss the nature of the country life they have led and the uncertain prospects for the younger generation. They all seem complacent—well-suited to their lives, ensconced in their routines—though mildly irrelevant. Amy's three sons, Harry, Arthur, and John, are due to arrive for her birthday dinner: she has arranged the reunion hoping to keep the family centered at Wishwood. They have not come together for eight years; Agatha warns of the pain inherent in facing the changes from the past and building a future upon that changed past (though Amy denies any change).

Family discussion reveals that Harry (now Lord Monchensey), about whom Agatha is most anxious, lost his wife a year ago. Apparently she was swept off a ship's deck during a storm; the family considers her disappearance a relief, and plans to avoid referring to it when Harry arrives. Amy describes the dead wife as vain, cosmopolitan, and thoroughly unsuitable for Harry, whom she intends to take command at Wishwood. Yet while the matriarch seems in control of the drawing room setting, other members of her family, forming a chorus, reveal the more pervasive sense that they are ill at ease: like amateur actors, who do not know very accurately what will happen in the scenes to come. They feel Amy's reunion is a farce.

Harry enters nervously, complaining that the undrawn windows expose the family to the harsh eyes of the world. He sees something haunting outside the window: something he knew was approaching him as he traveled the world, which has finally appeared at Wishwood. As Amy tries to reconcile Harry to settling at Wishwood, where she says nothing has changed, Harry points out the inevitable changes that have actually occurred (to which they are all oblivious), and the inexplicable but tremendous changes in his own life during the past eight years. The family is muddled in a nostalgic, unreal past; only Agatha seems to understand Harry's vision of the present as a Dantean horror, evocative of the most horrible venues from *The Waste Land*—incomprehension, purposelessness, numbness, and awful anagnorisis.

Brutally and cold-bloodedly, Harry describes pushing his wife overboard to reverse the direction of the senseless present; Charles dismisses the story as a fancy. Agatha asserts that Harry possesses a fragment of the truth about his past and urges him to continue the difficult task of determining and understanding the entire truth. As Harry exits, the rest of his family, trying to smooth over an unpleasant past, assumes that Harry is psychologically delusional and that his desire to escape from his wife convinced him that he actually killed her. They suggest that Dr. Warburton, an old family friend, be invited to dinner to examine and cure Harry. They interrogate Harry's servant Downing, who was on the cruise, about what happened but he only compounds the confusion. Trying to restore Harry to what it sees as the comfortable normalcy of their own world, the family instead becomes combative and suspicious of each other; Harry's instability has infected them.

Mary, Harry's second cousin—who resembles him in her confusion about the present—complains to Agatha that Amy has brought her to the reunion only to marry Harry and chain him to Wishwood. Though Mary wants to leave Agatha implores her to stay and, like Harry, confront reality and discover truth at the old estate. Harry and Mary discuss their memories of an unhappy childhood at Wishwood, where everything was arranged simply and perfectly but without human reality or enjoyment. They come close to explaining their discontent and sharing a bond of communication but neither is able to make a completely genuine commitment to this; Harry then has a vision of the Eumenides through the window (though Mary does not see them), haunting him with the recollection of his past failures and his inability to come to terms with what he has been.

Warburton arrives for dinner, though Arthur and John remain absent. As Part I ends, the family-Chorus fears the impending change much as the Chorus of Canterbury women feared Becket's return at the opening of *Murder in the Cathedral*; Agatha invokes a sort of prayer that they can transcend their falseness and repression.

After dinner Warburton tries to reconcile Harry with his mother's vision of life. Harry lashes out against her and the pain she has caused him throughout his life. He wants to know about his father, who disappeared quietly from Wishwood when Harry was a child. Warburton declines to go beyond a mannerly reference to Harry's parents' mutual separation. He warns Harry that Amy's fragile health demands a calm continuation of the status quo and acquiescence to her wishes.

A police sergeant brings news that John has had an automobile accident and suffered a minor concussion. Warburton rushes off to examine him while Harry muses that there probably is not much difference between John's consciousness and unconsciousness. As Amy goes off to sleep, Harry chides the rest of the family for being obsessed with irrelevant details and petty gossip—such as his own behavior and Arthur's drunkenness and irresponsibility—and oblivious to the larger important patterns of life. Agatha counsels Harry to go beyond merely noting the family's stupid malice; he must try to penetrate the private worlds of fantasy and fear and learn to suffer more rather than taking refuge in self-pity.

Arthur calls to inform the family that he, too, has been in an auto accident, and asserts that newspaper accounts of his reckless driving and attempts to evade police are mistaken. Gerald and Charles anticipate the embarrassment connected with the incident, deploring the modern disregard for the privacy of the aristocracy; the Chorus speaks, forebodingly, of the inevitable accumulation of reality in an old house: the knowledge of agony, loathing, sorrow, deception, that must ultimately issue forth into the light, however long it is genteelly denied.

Finally Harry confronts Agatha: he speaks of his isolation, numbness, and degradation. The family at Wishwood is stultifying his attempts to discover the reality of his past, present, and future; he implores Agatha to divulge the mystery about his father. She tells of his father's weakness and his loneliness with his young wife. When Amy was pregnant with Harry his father had plotted, pathetically, to kill Amy and the child she was carrying. Agatha, who in some sense had loved Harry's father and the unborn child, had forestalled the murder attempt, which she says certainly would have been bungled anyhow.

Harry fatalistically understands now a vision of reconciliation—sin and expiation—and acknowledges that perhaps his own "murder" was only a fantasy like his father's. This understanding (of his family, and of what Wishwood stands for) is, for Harry, an end and a beginning. He feels himself free from his pursuing demons and prepared to live a public life. When the Eumenides reappear Harry is not surprised or frightened, but ready to confront them: ready, even, to follow them—that is, to pursue and explore his painful memories—instead of being chased by them. Seeing that Harry has confronted reality, Agatha sends him off from Wishwood to find his reconciliation. Harry settles Wishwood upon John, who is much better suited to the country home.

Amy castigates Agatha for having taken her son from her as, 35 years ago, she had taken her husband. Amy admits she had known of Wishwood's unquiet ghosts, but had tolerated them so Harry could come back to live there, and had herself planned to reconcile Harry with his past. Amy is bitter at what she considers Agatha's selfish meddling but Agatha maintains that Harry's departure is ultimately destined, and that the resolution of his quest rests in another world. Mary believes Harry is in danger from this other world, but Agatha—convinced, perhaps, by the Eumenides—knows that Amy's and Mary's terms of safety and danger have a different meaning in the world to which Harry journeys.

As Amy imagines her future crumbling like the walls of Wishwood without a master, Harry enters to reassure his mother that John will take care of the home and that he will be safe on his journey. Amy tells the others Harry is going off to become a missionary; Harry responds evasively, though it is clearly true in some sense. Some of the relatives seem vaguely cognizant of Harry's vision but they realize they are destined in their old age to continue inhabiting the world of Wishwood. Mary asks Downing to take care of Harry on their journey; he responds, enigmatically, that he is quite sure Harry is on the verge of transcending the life that had haunted him for so long. After Harry's departure Wishwood life continues normally. John is healing, Arthur is prevaricating about his troubles. Amy discovers that the clock has stopped—perhaps gracefully and soothingly announcing a cessation of traumatic change.

The Chorus explains its reaction to the modernist angst that the evening has brought: it is unsettling to look through the same window and see a different landscape, or to climb a stair and find oneself descending. But acts of God defy human understanding; the family at Wishwood has learned that its attempts to arrange things perfectly cannot last. The play concludes with the family discussing arrangements for Amy's funeral—but the event of her death is tremendously understated, indicating the lesson that has been learned: acceptance of a higher force that rules their lives, determination to undertake a pilgrimage of expiation, and the promise of ultimate redemption.

Production History

The Family Reunion opened on 21 March 1939 (on the "vernal equinox" which had been the play's subtitle in draft) at the Westminster Theatre, London, under the direction of E. Martin Browne; 38 performances were held. (John Gielgud had expressed interest in co-directing the play and starring as Harry, but plans for this never materialized; Gielgud did, though, later perform in several broadcast versions of the play.) Michael MacOwen, one of the Westminster's managers, had led an acclaimed production of Eugene O'Neill's *Mourning Becomes Electra*—like Eliot's play, a modern adaptation of Aeschylean themes—in 1937.

The cast included Browne himself as Dr. Warburton, Michael Redgrave as Harry, Helen Haye (who traditionally played aristocratic roles) as Amy, Browne's wife Henzie Raeburn as Ivy, Catherine Lacey as Agatha, Marjorie Gabain as Violet, Colin Keith-Johnston as Gerald, Stephen Murray as Charles, Ruth Lodge as Mary, Pamela Kelly as Denman, Robert Harris as Downing, Charles Victor as Winchell, and Audrey Alan, Helen Latham, and Diana

Nicholl as the Eumenides. (Murray, though, suffered a breakdown before opening night so Browne played Charles for the first four weeks of the play's run, with George Woodbridge taking over the role of Warburton.) Decor was by Peter Goffin and costumes were by Stella Mary Pearce, who had also designed the costumes for *The Rock* and *Murder in the Cathedral.*

The introduction of choral passages—spoken by the same actors who play Harry's family—was marked by "changes in convention so definite as to compel the audience to notice them and to say to itself: 'Now we have a chorus'" (C277, 127), Browne writes. On reflection, he admits, this seems to be a mistake; choruses should not so obviously recall traditional Greek antecedents, but instead the characters should "slide almost imperceptibly into concerted speech," connoting naturalistically their common emotions of fear or dread. Changes of lighting to highlight the choral passages are probably unnecessary, Browne writes, and must be delicately imperceptible if used; musical accompaniment, too, would be misleading and distracting. Lyndall Gordon, though, cautions against considering Browne's directorial analyses and decisions too weightily: "Browne misconceived the play from the start," she writes, "when he praised the reality of the family and criticized non-realistic scenes" (C309, 82).

The play's first American performances were by amateur college troupes: Robert Klein directed the American premiere at Wells College's Macmillan Hall on 8 June 1940 with an all-female cast: Nancy Genet starred as Amy, and Elizabeth Capstaff as Harry. Klein wrote in a director's note to the program that the play was "of our time. . . . Eliot has attempted to represent that trend in our modern life which forces the imagination and the intelligence of the individual into the mould of mass belief, which crushes personal initiative and substitutes totalitarian action." On 8 November 1940 the Harvard Dramatic Club presented what was billed as "an experimental production . . . by T. S. Eliot '10" [i.e., alumnus, class of 1910]. S. Roger Sheppard and A. George Rock directed that production, with original music by Alan Sapp. A note in the program explained that Sapp's music "highlights and intensifies the choral passages and gives an undertone of beauty to the lyrical poetry." Subsequent productions by college companies included Owen Dodson's at Howard University in July 1952, and Leslie J. Mahoney's at the University of California at Berkeley in July 1957.

Browne revived *The Family Reunion* in London, opening on 31 October 1946 at the Mercury Theatre with a cast including Alan Wheatley as Harry, Eileen Thorndike (Sybil's sister) as Amy, Frank Napier (who had played the Second Knight and Second Tempter in the original production of *Murder in the Cathedral*) as Charles, John Burch as Gerald, Catherine Lacey repeating her creation of Agatha's role, and Henzie Raeburn again playing Ivy. In the bleak post-war years fuel shortages and electricity supply cuts were common, and the play occasionally had to be performed by candlelight.

Pearce designed sets and costumes for the Mercury revival, which was difficult because so much was in short supply due to post-war shortages; she could buy hardly any clothes, and many other things necessary for her designs were either still being rationed, or had only recently been (C358).   She describes the set design: "The Mercury Theatre stage was very small—12 feet high, only about 18 feet wide and not very deep.   To suggest a country mansion, therefore, meant that it was essential either to put the action in the corner of a large room, or in a small ante-room, but at the same time to suggest the size of the house by large, handsome doors and windows.   In view of the eerie plot of the play, I felt the décor of the room should be dark, though not of course black. . . . I was able to get enough dark blue scenic paint to cover the walls" (106).   She used a large marble bust as the only prominent decoration, to suggest that the family was old and established.

About the costumes at the Mercury, Pearce writes, "At the time it was written, before the War, it would have been natural for a well-placed upper-class family to dress for dinner every day.   I therefore dressed Harry and his uncles in very dark blue (which appeared black) for both day and evening, merely giving them dinner jackets and off-white shirts for the evening.   The women were a different problem: although they lapsed into chorus from time to time, they could not be dressed uniformly, for their individual characters were clearly defined and differentiated in the text.   I therefore decided that each should wear a single colour, suited to her character. . . . Violet . . . hard and severe, I put into dark grey; Agatha, warm-hearted and understanding, I dressed in a sort of orange tan; Ivy, the sentimental aunt, was in pale pink.   The important character, the girl Mary, seemed to be right in palish blue.   Since the background was almost black, and since all the men wore dark suits, these colours were of great importance in forming a colour-scheme, and were particularly telling and significant" (107-108).

Pearce writes that she received no advice about how to present the Eumenides.   Independently, she decided Harry was haunted by, perhaps, Amy, Agatha, or Mary; thus, she costumed the Eumenides as life-sized, somewhat bird-like dummies, dressed in the colors of the characters she felt were haunting Harry.   The audience, she explains, had no idea what the implications were supposed to be, so after the London run she decided to scrap them and substituted three dangling drops of crystal.

The Birmingham Repertory Company presented the play in 1946. Browne's 1947 revival at Scotland's Gateway Theatre as part of the Edinburgh International Festival's opening season featured Patrick Troughton as Harry, Yvonne Coulette as Mary, Raeburn as Agatha, and Thorndike again as Amy. The success of that production led to an enduring connection between Eliot and the organizers of the Edinburgh Festival: each of his subsequent plays had its premiere there.   In September 1947 Browne's production moved to the Arts Theatre of Cambridge, where it played in repertory with *Murder in the Cathedral*, starring Robert Speaight.

Also in 1947 the play had its New York premiere at the Cherry Lane Theatre.   Frank Corsaro directed the production which starred the actress

Olivia as Amy, Laviah Lucking as Ivy, Roberta Unger as Violet, Roberta Dixon as Agatha, Jeffrie Weaver as Gerald, James Linn as Charles, Julia Meade as Mary, John Christie as Harry, and David F. Perkins as Warburton. Settings were by Michael Mear. The play's program carried "a word from the director" that seemed like a kind of apology for Eliot's drama: "Considering the high esteem [*The Family Reunion*] has achieved in discerning theatre circles . . . the paucity of performances it has achieved in this country is scarcely comprehensible—or must I reiterate a tired phrase and blame our so called devotion to 'slavish commercialism.'"

In December 1948, Eliot attended a performance of the play in Stockholm presented to celebrate his award of the Nobel Prize for Literature. (Eliot humorously described the presentation of the Furies at that production to his friend, Mary Trevelyan, as reported by Gordon [C309, 87-88]: they "had appeared as a sort of rugby team of fifteen huge leprous giraffes, swarming out when the bookshelves parted in a library that looked like St. Pancras Station.")

B. B. C. broadcast the play on its *World Theatre* program in January 1951. In October 1952 the play was performed at the Bermuda Festival, directed by Hal Burton and starring Nora Swinburne and Esmond Knight. During the 1955-56 season, Belfast's Lyric Players Theatre staged *The Family Reunion*. It was revived again, opening on 7 June 1956, in a production by Peter Brook and Paul Scofield at London's Phoenix Theatre. That run lasted 100 performances and starred Scofield as Harry, Sybil Thorndike as Amy, and Thorndike's husband, Lewis Casson, as Warburton. Stuart Vaughan staged a revival that opened 20 October 1958 at Broadway's Phoenix Theatre—the inaugural of the theatre's season devoted to Nobel Prize writers—featuring Fritz Weaver as Harry, Florence Reed as Amy, Dorothy Sands as Ivy, silent-film star Lillian Gish as Agatha, Margaretta Warwick as Violet, Nicholas Joy as Gerald, Eric Berry as Charles, Sylvia Short as Mary, and Conrad Bain as Warburton. Settings were by Norris Houghton; costumes were by Will Steven Armstrong; and music was composed by David Amram.

In 1960 Browne directed a run of seven performances beginning on 9 December at New York's Union Theological Seminary where he had a visiting appointment. The student production was part of a curriculum in religious drama.

Michael Elliott directed the Royal Exchange Theatre Company in a revival that opened 18 April 1979 in Manchester and moved to London's New Round House. On 19 June 1979 it opened at the West End's Vaudeville Theatre; Edward Fox starred as Harry, Pauline Jameson as Amy, Constance Chapman as Ivy, Avril Elgar as Agatha, Daphne Oxenford as Violet, William Fox as Gerald, Jeffry Wickham as Charles, Joanna David as Mary, and Esmond Knight as Warburton. (Elliott had also directed a 1973 version in which Fox starred.) Technical innovations for that run included a supernatural-sounding background score of bass viol, cello, and synthesizer, arranged by Ian Gibson; and Michael Williams's lighting which, reviewer David

Mayer writes, with its "cold whites, grays, chocolates and chalky yellows, validates both the real and the long-dead but intruding past."

Critical Overview

Performance Reviews

The *Times Literary Supplement* review of the Westminster Theatre premiere finds *The Family Reunion* surprisingly similar to other current drama: Eliot clings "to naturalism of surface and the naturalistic time. For all the versification, he may be said to have hardly broken with the main tenets of Shaftesbury Avenue," that is, with the standard offerings in the theatres in London's West End. The review labels the poetry "clumsy and diffuse" in its attempts to be unpronounced; and regarding Eliot's attempts to infuse modernist intensity into a drawing-room drama, the reviewer criticizes Eliot by his own standards: claiming that the play lacks the "objective correlative," embodying an emotion which is inexpressible (R99).

In the London *Times*, reviewer Charles Morgan finds the verse quite palatable: "Mr. Eliot's dialogue is in verse which seeks in large measure the freedom of prose. And it succeeds in capturing the cadence and rhythm of our everyday conversation and in passing, without breaking its own texture, from small talk to the statement of truths which illumine the inner lives of a family of landed aristocrats. In a theatre still struggling gamely to stretch conventions that have become so oppressively rigid so bold an experiment in language . . . must command much good will" (R92). Browne confirms that, from the point of view of the play's presenters, the stylistic innovation Morgan notes is its key success. "A verse-form has been created capable of including every kind of contemporary speech, from the banal conversation of a drawing-room at teatime to the revelations of the heart's depth and the terror of eternal things" (C275, 203).

Philip Horton expresses many reviewers' misgivings when he writes in the *Kenyon Review* that the "point of adequate motivation" is the play's failure: "To be sure, we know the general subject of the play. . . . But this is not enough. In order that the action be convincing, the sin must be sufficiently defined to make clear not only the nature of the relations between the characters, but also the terms of the central conflict. Without such elementary definition, it seems to me, there can be no adequate motivation. What Eliot offers in its stead—a complex of possible sins almost Jamesian in its ambiguities—hardly constitutes, however rich its materials, a workable substitute." The play thus offers speculations about sin, rather than definitions of sin, and resembles a philosophical poem like *The Waste Land* more than a poetic drama, "with the unfortunate result that the ideas, the speculation, tend to take precedence over the characters both as the principal agents of the action and the center of interest" (R84).

Desmond MacCarthy explains his perception of the play's point, as well as its confusion: "It is a drama of the inner life. The character contrast which runs through it—the test applied to all the characters in the play—is whether he or she attempts to live on the surface and *pretends* (that is all that is possible) to ignore the spiritual destiny of man, or accepts a predicament which is essentially tragic. If I had grasped this while in the theatre instead of only when on my return home, I should not have been so perplexed by the play." MacCarthy thus addresses, though more sympathetically than Horton, the perceived absence of dramatic motivation. MacCarthy notes Eliot's affinities with Ibsen's drama in terms of blending realism and symbolism; and with O'Neill's *Strange Interlude*, which shares with *The Family Reunion* the technique "of making the characters on the stage speak their thoughts and feelings aloud, not as in traditional drama in the form of brief conversational asides or set soliloquies, but in order to convey to the audience a running contrast between what they are saying to each other, and those thoughts and feelings they are withholding or even stifling unconsciously in themselves." MacCarthy judges these devices failures, though, because they diminish the play's level of realism, and—in what he considers an ineffective Chorus—sound more like rituals than naturalistic dialogue (R88).

In the *Observer* Ivor Brown lauds an "abundance of fine, confused feeling," often expressed in exquisite passages, and performed by a fine company. The *Listener* reviewer writes that the play is probably unsuited to the stage since the main action is an unexplained mystery, a symbolic event that may not have happened, and also because the Eumenides seem too academic, not dramatic. As a literary text for reading, though, the reviewer finds the play "marvelous . . . [with] passages of great poetic beauty, and statements which are the fruits of a lifetime devoted to poetry"; Eliot's moral sensibility and layers of consciousness are called evocative of Henry James (R76).

Finally, in the *Sunday Times* James Agate reviews *The Family Reunion* in verse that parodies Eliot's: while he is untroubled by what he describes as somewhat discordant verse, he cannot accept the intricacies of the plot; he does not understand why, simply because a man's aunt should have been his mother (as he glibly summarizes Harry's dilemma), that man has to drown his wife (R71).

In partial explanation for mixed reviews of the play and complaints of incomprehension or irritatingly unusual dramatic development, Browne suggests that the period's immense political tension—Hitler had just annexed Bohemia and Moravia—made it hard for audiences and critics at the premiere to devote their minds with the intricate concentration necessary to appreciate Eliot's sometimes-elusive style. He refers to reviews of the 1946 Mercury revival that are more tolerant: in *Punch*, for example, Eric Keown writes, "Strictly speaking this is a revival, since the play had a short run in 1939 which was spoilt by the war, but to most of us it comes fresh." Lauding the play as "a new and fascinating experiment" containing "crisp, pure English, geared to modern usage and set in verse forms which combine flexibility with impelling rhythms of their own which go on ringing in one's head," Keown focuses on Agatha's passages as those in which "the play rises to its heights.

Mr. Eliot has an extraordinary power of evoking in a few words a crisis in the life of the spirit. . . . Agatha is not a character in the usual sense but a kind of summing up of how far the human intellect has succeeded in reaching its effort to meet the divine" (R86).

By the time of the 1946 production, some of the play's more surreal and macabre aspects that had put off audiences in 1939 had been validated by the war, Browne writes: "Harry's question whether the policeman was real seemed quite a natural one to those who had known the nightmares of the 1940's. . . . And why then should not the elderly relations, when they had an overwhelming common concern for the family and themselves, speak that concern in common? That the speech was labelled 'Chorus' in the text should make no difference. Why should not Agatha and Mary revolve in sad ritual round the memorial cake . . . just as we file past the coffin of a great public figure?" (C276, 63). Eliot was perhaps a few years ahead of his time with this play—though certainly, in 1939, one would not have to have been clairvoyant to sense that England was headed toward catastrophic chaos (which might be seen as the analogous macrocosm of Harry's private chaos).

The *New York Times* reviewer of the 1947 New York premiere writes, "after trying to listen to *The Family Reunion* last night, it became abundantly clear why the play has been done so rarely. . . . It isn't even a play for the theatre. It is completely lacking in any dramatic structure or conflict. . . . You have the feeling that you are being oppressed by the spirit of the late Gertrude Stein." Responding to the director's note in the program that objected to audiences' fear of the avant-garde, the reviewer argues, "It isn't sufficient . . . to object to the 'slavish commercialism' on Broadway. It should not be redoing experiments that already have failed" (R100).

American reviewers of the 1958 Phoenix production were similarly harsh. "Mr. Eliot is interested in ideas, form and ritual," writes Brooks Atkinson in the *New York Times*. "He is not much interested in human beings. It is easy to point out that the chorus passages and the speeches of warning are out of context in modern drama. It would be easy to quibble about other technical matters. But nothing technical would matter very much if the characters had flesh and blood and were involved in a situation that grew out of their own natures rather than a literary tradition." Atkinson finds the play "a wordy drama about uninteresting people engaged in a struggle that they are not eager to explain" (R73).

In the New York *World-Telegram* Frank Aston calls the play "a labored, rambling, communal introspection uttered through the author's smoky imagination" (R72). John McClain, in the New York *Journal-American*, writes, "I do not think Mr. T. S. Eliot . . . has written himself much of a play. It is oblique and diffused, and he never comes to grips with the theatre in simple, dramatic terms. The production is elegant and the cast is eminent. There is a reasonable consignment of his witty observations and some rather poetic interludes . . . but the basic story, such as it is, falls short of fulfillment" (R91).

In the New York *Post*, Richard Watts, Jr., agrees that the story is the problem: "The weakness theatrically of the play . . . is not chiefly due to its uncompromisingly enigmatic quality. It is, in truth, at its most interesting in its cryptic earlier sections, when the mood is ominous and given to dark intimations of doom and the action is vague and suggestive of sinister, unknown things to come. There the moments of comedy and the air of mystic incantation are promisingly effective. It is only when the basic problem of the narrative is presented that it proves to be disappointing" (R98).

Walter Kerr, in the New York *Herald Tribune*, finds the play successful: "The handsome, shining production . . . comes mysteriously close to bringing off the almost insuperable theatrical problem posed. If precise clarity of thought is missing, an eerie authority established itself, a sense that whatever is being said has an importance worth struggling for. . . . It seems to me that the Phoenix has performed a considerable public service in arranging an earnest, beautifully spoken, genuinely distinguished production of an extraordinarily difficult piece of work" (R87).

Robert Coleman, in the *Daily Mirror*, writes of Fritz Weaver's starring role in the 1958 production that "he played the ghost-ridden, irresolute, elder son as if he were tackling Hamlet" (R77).

Of Michael Elliott's 1979 Round House production, David Mayer in *Plays and Players* is even more uncompromisingly hostile than the 1958 reviewers: "In my view, *The Family Reunion* is one of T. S. Eliot's least deserving pieces, a failed attempt to pour trivial 20th-century guilt . . . and misplaced anguish into the mold of *The Oresteia*." By 1979, Mayer attests to the fact that the increasingly prevalent biographical criticism of Eliot has made its mark on the theatre audience; he sees Eliot ineffectively and misguidedly trying to come to terms with his mistreatment of his first wife: "Eliot, trapped in his own problems, overreached himself to find a metaphor that would explain and perhaps expiate his own troubled responsibility" (R90).

Robert Rubens, in contrast, finds Elliott's revival of the play well-suited to a contemporary audience. He writes in *Contemporary Review*: "Harry's parental problems and his hallucinations, often bordering on madness, seem to have struck a recognizable chord to our own generation of theatre-goers. For this is an era in which young people are acutely aware of the dangers of parents imposing rigid demands and specific roles on their children. We are now living in a period in which the younger generation has not hesitated to rebel against established authority and to attempt to discover the true nature of their personalities through such methods as psychoanalysis, transcendental meditation and the studying of various eastern and middle eastern religions. So Mr. Eliot's metaphysics, his mysticism and the personal horrors which his hero experiences came as no shock to the audiences of *The Family Reunion* in 1979" (R96).

Rubens quotes Elliott explaining that the play "reflects life as he himself sees it: . . . two worlds that interleave and flow through each other simultaneously and yet apart which is the product of fantasy, hallucination and something closer to mysticism.'"

Edward Fox's Harry was perhaps the most exaggerated of any interpretations of that character: Mayer describes an "extroverted and visibly mad Harry, arms flung away from his body in wide gesticulation, his body corkscrewed by a limp that almost becomes a Groucho Marx lope" (R90).

Scholarly Response

Critics have found in *The Family Reunion* numerous continuations of dramatic themes begun in *Sweeney Agonistes*: Carol H. Smith notes the pervasive Oresteian theme of purgation in both plays; the repetition of the epigraph from *Sweeney Agonistes*—the cry of Orestes in the *Choephoroi*—as Harry's terrified cry that he is being pursued by haunting spirits; the reappearance of *Sweeney*'s choral "Hoo ha's" as the Furies in *The Family Reunion*; and the girl's corpse in the bathtub full of lysol repeated in the story of Harry's drowned wife (C382, 113-14). Lyndall Gordon adds another comparison between the two plays: both are about "a man's horror, almost possession, at the discovery of his capacity for violence. The strange feeling is not guilt, but a curious contamination that bonds Sweeney and Harry with their victims—or imagined victims. Even more curious is a certain pride that they should suffer so acutely for potential wrongs" (C309, 52).

Rhythmically, too, Herbart Howarth argues, this play represents a reworking of *Sweeney Agonistes*: "He had worked, when he composed *Sweeney*, to beat the drum. Perhaps too violently. He now tells himself that a whole play to that exciting beat would have been intolerable to the ear, and that he must seek variety: sometimes the strong beat may be admitted, if more often he uses a moderated beat, often a very subtle one. In *The Family Reunion* he discovers the quieter rhythms" (C322, 324).

The play "re-casts some of the material from *Murder in the Cathedral*," writes David Ward. "Harry returns to the scene of his past after an absence of eight years, as Thomas returns after seven, to find (what he knew already) that it is not the same place because he is not the same person. . . . Like Thomas, he is faced with a challenge to make the final renunciation of the self; though here the stress is not so much upon the renunciation of the *will* as upon the renunciation of earthly ties, affection for the ghosts of family and ghosts of place" (C391, 199).

Patrick Roberts explains the relation he sees between *The Family Reunion* and Eliot's other plays: it "is a transitional play, occupying a place between the religious tragedy of *Murder in the Cathedral* and the serious comedy of *The Cocktail Party* and *The Confidential Clerk*. The spiritual crisis of its hero is expressed with an intense concentration and complexity of style that casts doubt on the feasibility of it being rendered in comprehensible dramatic terms at all, while the familiar guide-lines of history and tradition that sustained *Murder in the Cathedral* have been abandoned without the compensating advantages of a contemporary comedy of manners" (C148, 185-86).

Roberts explicates the play's psychological resonances and their relation (as one would expect from the play's title) to family: "The central action of the play, a duologue in the second scene of the second act between Harry and Agatha, sees Harry, like Orestes in *The Eumenides*, released from the overwhelming burden of past guilt and sin into a life of meaningful freedom. Release comes about through the discovery of the truth about that past, through the agency of Agatha, the spiritual intercessor and guide whose role as inhabitant of 'the neutral territory between two worlds' is to form a link between them and so reveal to the hero the way of true vocation. . . . For Harry it is a kind of spiritual birth, this time from the right mother, a woman who once loved his father and who had saved Harry, an unborn child, from his father's murderous designs on his mother. Spiritual maternity and sonship is explicitly acknowledged by both Harry and Agatha" (189). Harry at first "strikes us as mentally ill," Roberts continues, "and this impression is partially correct. The therapy Agatha provides is, rightly, powered by her love and understanding, but its essential content is the revelation of the true facts of his parents' relationship" (191), augmenting a psychoanalytic interpretation.

Cleanth Brooks, in "Sin and Expiation," finds the play quite close in tenor to Eliot's poetry: "It was to be predicted that *The Family Reunion* would contain a recapitulation of the symbols which dominate Eliot's earlier poetry. They are here: the purposeless people moving in a ring . . . of *The Waste Land*; the 'hellish sweet smell' that accompanies the apprehension of the supernatural from *Murder in the Cathedral*; the purgatorial flame of *Ash-Wednesday*. But most of all . . . the play may be said to be a restatement of 'Burnt Norton' in terms of drama" (R75, 114). John Crowe Ransom, too, in "T. S. Eliot as Dramatist," finds similarities between the play and Eliot's poetry. "He keeps a foot in each of two worlds: the new world of naturalistic or realistic psychological drama, and the old world of poetry which, for him, means metaphysics. He will soon make ordinary drama look cheap because of its lack of metaphysical interest, just as he had a part in making the ordinary shallow poetry of twenty years ago look the same way, and for the same reason"; the play's "satiric touch is devastating, and he turns it onto living English types to show their social and political silliness, among other things" (R94, 264). Ultimately, though, what the play presents "is not the Eliot we knew as a poet. It is that Eliot warmed over" (271).

Louis MacNeice calls *The Family Reunion* "a better play than *Murder in the Cathedral*, better integrated, less of a charade. This time . . . the ideas behind the play are fused into the action and the characters" (R89, 384). Referring to Eliot's well-known stern religious beliefs, MacNeice writes that the writer is in some sense "a reactionary, but he is at the same time a corrective to the facile optimism of many Leftist writers. We may regret that he seems to put all his money on the religious conscience as distinct from practical morality, but at the same time we must recognize that he asserts certain truths . . . which are now commonly neglected and whose neglect may in the long run sap the life from our utilitarian ethics." Overall, MacNeice finds,

"Technically the verse of this play is most successful. . . . this is a very moving play both as a whole and in its passing pictures, its ironic comments, its pregnant understatements, its bursts into liturgy. . . . it embodies a sincere belief and a genuine courage" (385).

Copious comparisons were made between *The Family Reunion* and the plays of W. H. Auden and Christopher Isherwood. Brooks contrasts Eliot's view of the fatuousness and complacency of the British upper classes with Auden's merciless revelations: "Harry's vision of a different world is certainly not Auden's vision, but he occupies a position with relation to society basically similar to that occupied by Auden's characters. (Auden's 'converted' characters have their problems of communication too, and their problem of expiation)" (R75, 116). MacNeice discusses the character of Amy, "who in a sense has been a vampire to her son, yet compares favorably with the Mother in Messrs. Auden and Isherwood's *Ascent of F-6*, who is almost a Freudian dummy" (R89, 385). Ransom calls Eliot's chorus "often burlesque, as in Auden's plays" (R94, 268). The *Listener* review contrasts two different directions poetic drama is taking on the contemporary stage: "one, in the plays of Auden and Isherwood, certainly towards the theatre; the other, of which this play is a striking example, towards narrative poetry" (R103, 750).

The language of the play, writes Gareth Lloyd Evans, shows a transitional fulcrum in Eliot's dramatic career. "The choric ritualism [from *Murder in the Cathedral*] is still present . . . though the line lengths are, generally, shorter, more clipped. The familiar rubs shoulders with the highly charged poetic mode. . . . But if the past is in the language in these modified ways, the future seeds are already planted too"—such as the lighter comic touch of the subsequent plays, and the fusion of a diction that combines (and jumps freely between) philosophy, wit, and Wildean epigram (C295, 161-62).

The play initiates what is generally considered Eliot's naturalistic period, which encompasses all of his subsequent drama—certainly this terminology seems appropriate considering the contrast between it and the previous plays. Yet William V. Spanos notes some methods by which Eliot "transcends the basic limitations of the naturalistic subject matter and forms—the restriction of significance to the univocal level of social commentary or psychological reality" in this and the following plays. "In each, he covertly schematizes the character groupings and the development of the action in a similar way so that despite the surface differences, all the plays are characterized by a corresponding underpattern, an archetypal image that deepens the surface realism. The characters of these plays fall into three groups. The first two groups, which on the dramatic level constitute the main characters in the action, are the more or less spiritually blind—the ordinary people who 'live and partly live' in a world devoid of spiritual significance—and the spiritually aware, those who perceive the imminent irruption of the irrational into their lives and choose to face it whatever the consequences. The third group, whose mysteriousness suggests their possession of a knowledge that transcends that of the main characters, constitutes the agents of the action, their function rendering them remote descendants of the vice figures of the medieval morality plays" (C385, 192).

Spanos categorizes the groupings in each of Eliot's last four plays: Here, Amy and the aunts and uncles form the first group; Harry, Agatha, and partly Mary the second; and the Furies the third. In *The Cocktail Party*, the Chamberlaynes and Peter form the first group; Celia the second; and the Guardians the third. In *The Confidential Clerk*, Sir Claude, Lady Elizabeth, B. Kaghan and Lucasta are in the first group; Colby in the second; and Eggerson and Mrs. Guzzard in the third. Finally, in *The Elder Statesman*, Charles, Monica, and Michael are in the first group; Lord Claverton-Ferry in the second; and Gomez and Mrs. Carghill in the third (192-93).

Vinod Sena surveys the range of critics' complaints about the play's shortcomings: "The ambiguity of the wife's murder"; "The lack of any convention to restrict the meaning of the Furies"; "The mystifying mode of guilt-transmission and the questionable spirituality of the Play's pattern of sin and atonement"; "The defective characterization of Harry"; "The inadequate and high-handed treatment of the Uncles and Aunts"; "The maladjustment of certain elements to the naturalistic setting . . . or even the basic incompatibility of such a setting for Eliot's theme" (C151, 896).

The play's naturalism is criticized by Ronald Gaskell: the supernaturalism of Eliot's previous play, with his stylized Christian form, gave it its power, he argues, and the substitution of naturalism in *The Family Reunion* "has obscured rather than clarified," because Eliot is a dramatist "uninterested in the natural world" (C132, 138), but rather, with the more abstract metaphysical and spiritual issues of time, sin, and redemption. Eliot has chosen naturalistic form as a compromise, Gaskell writes, which produces dramatic incoherence.

C. L. Barber, in the same vein, calls the play a failure because the play's spiritual concerns are unsupported by a traditional religious framework. Attempting "to begin again at the beginning, at the point where the decay of faith has left modern men," Eliot "undertakes the job of virtually creating a religious symbolism. . . . His failure is extremely interesting as an example of what can happen when, in the absence of support from society, an artist tries to do everything himself" (C122, 416-17). The play's meaning and symbolism are, consequently, "dramatically and emotionally unintelligible" (418).

The play is unsuccessful by the Aristotelian standards Denis Donoghue applies: "Nothing in *The Family Reunion* persuades us that Harry's feeling is accurately rendered by his words. . . . furthermore, Eliot makes no attempt to evade the law of probability which he breaks; there are no trances, no special dramatic conventions. It might be argued, rather desperately, that the incongruous lines are Eliot's exposition of the truth about Harry, rather than Harry's expression of his own feelings. But even if we accept this . . . the audience has no means of knowing at what point the 'speaker' is superseded by the dramatist" (C290, 98).

Ronald Bush sees Harry's nightmare visions as the culmination of a long preoccupation and fascination with "dreams, nightmares, hallucinations and visions [which] had been Eliot's interests at least since his undergraduate days, when he combined those interests with an interest in mysticism. A substantial portion of his doctoral dissertation concerns 'imaginary objects,' in which category Eliot groups' the content of dreams and hallucinations with the content of literature. Then, too, Eliot's poetry is crammed with dreams" as far back as his "Preludes" (C283, 49).

The issue of what happened between Harry and his wife, though murky, is of course vitally important. "The play teases us with the superficial mystery of murder," Gordon writes, "but that drama is undercut by the profounder mystery of guilt. Harry did not push his wife overboard, but—as Eliot pointed out in a letter to Martin Browne—he didn't call for help, nor did he jump in after her. Is passivity culpable?" (C309, 91).

The play's Chorus "differs from the traditional Greek chorus," writes Angela Belli, "because it does not comment upon the action" and "is generally indifferent to Harry's plight." Its function is to help define Eliot's conception of time: "They reveal that time has a cyclical pattern. The past gives way to the present, which gives way to the future, which becomes the past again" (C125, 54).

Albert Wertheim calls Eliot's homecoming motif an important influence for such plays as Harold Pinter's 1965 *The Homecoming*, David Storey's 1969 *In Celebration*, and Peter Nichols's 1979 *Born in the Gardens*. The theme, as Eliot shapes it, "argues the significance of house and family for the returning person's understanding and revaluation of himself. It presents the ways in which various children—Harry and his brothers—are at odds with or accept the power of family and home. It uses a particular family celebration or rite as a point of departure. And it forces the returning family member to leave with new resolve and sense of self" (C157, 154).

Four existential elements provide a valuable key to the play, argues Richard E. Palmer: "(1) The underlying mood of the play is *Angst*, that is, existential anxiety. (2) The fundamental ontological assumptions in the play are essentially the same as those asserted by the important existentialist thinkers, Kierkegaard, Heidegger, Jaspers, and even Sartre. (3) The structure of values presupposed by the play is basically existentialist. (4) Harry's situation and the pattern of his action in the play, too, are basically existentialist; indeed, Harry is the very model of the Existentialist's hero, an authentic, questing self in a world of inauthenticity. . . . Eliot's proclaimed Christian orthodoxy encourages an existentialist reading of *The Family Reunion*, for the analysis of man's predicament and potentialities by existentialist thinkers is basically similar to that submitted by orthodox Christian theology" (C144, 174). Harry shares with Nietzsche and Kierkegaard "frightful aloneness and isolation, the tragic sincerity, the restless self-torment, the vivid sense of the abyss," Palmer writes (186).

Textual Notes and Influences

Rudolf Stamm explains the aspects of the *Oresteia* of Aeschylus that led Eliot to use it as a model for this play, including, mainly, "the fact that his [Orestes'] fate and his guilt were determined by the crimes of his parents and their forbears" in the *Oresteia*, "and that the curse from which his sufferings sprang was brought to an end by the intervention of the gods." Eliot "made it the background of his play because he found analogies in it to the modern creed of determinism as well as to the Christian ideas of original sin and expiation" (C154, 250).

Angela Belli writes that "Eliot has created a hero who is separated from his God because of sin. Just as Orestes moves from exile to reunion with his people and from alienation to reconciliation with the gods, Harry progresses from spiritual exile to reconciliation with his creator" (C125, 52). Maud Bodkin compares the nature of the curse (and surmounting the curse) in Aeschylus and Eliot: "The psychological development of the story in Eliot's play guides us toward an interpretation bringing the ancient idea of the curse into line with the modern thought of a compulsion, imposed by the relation to the parents, to repeat a form of action at variance with the rational purposes of the individual. . . . in each play the Furies embody the energy of passion fixed in an evil relationship or custom—the same energy which, released from the fixation and redirected, becomes the sustaining force of a better order of individual and social life" (C127, 46).

But J. Middleton Murry questions the equivalence Eliot asserts between the *Oresteia* and *The Family Reunion*. Harry's "murder" is vague, so the resulting anagnorisis is correspondingly ambiguous. Though Eliot's Chorus states that there are "certain inflexible laws" equally relevant in Argos or in England, Murry responds, "It may be so; but I cannot help demanding to glimpse them. In *The Family Reunion* they partly elude my vision. I cannot bring the whole of it within the pattern I can discern. In that pattern what was Fate to the Greek mind is given a spiritual significance. What was savage and arbitrary in the Greek myth is made comprehensible to a Christian or post-Christian sensibility: but the transvaluation is incomplete. . . . There is an obstinate residue which seems to deny the reconciliation which is declared" (C143, 73).

Though many critics challenge the effectiveness of *The Family Reunion* as a reenactment of the *Oresteia*, largely because of the troublesome presentation of the Furies, Martha C. Carpentier finds numerous correspondences that substantiate the connection between the drama of Eliot and Aeschylus. While both works "tell of a son's defense of and identification with the father, they are dominated by female archetypes. First rapacious witch figures enforce the matriarchal blood-ties of the earth mother; they are then superseded by a purely spiritual goddess without ties to the 'dark earth,' a patroness who resolves the violence of retributive blood law" (C130, 19-20).

The Family Reunion, she continues, "is modeled on the trilogy in which the laws and customs of the old matriarchal earth-bound religion are emphatically superseded by a patriarchal religion of the spirit in which godhead is above nature. And, like Aeschylus, Eliot confronts and resolves a matricidal impulse that is as profoundly and universally human as the oedipal impulse. Not only are the two works analogous in such broad thematic ways, but . . . the scenes involving Mary, Agatha, and Dr. Warburton all have 'counterparts' in the Oresteia. Amy is clearly parallel to Clytemnestra. A great villainous character must have motives that, at least in their origin, compel our sympathy, and this is true of both these towering matriarchs. . . . Yet, while their original cause is just, both Clytemnestra and Amy become mothers who try to control too much, so that their righteous defense of fecundity becomes perverted into a dominating will that corrupts and destroys" (20-21).

Mary, who is a sister-figure to Harry, is an embodiment of Electra, Carpentier argues, and "As a servant of the mother's will, in opposition to the son, Warburton is analogous to Aegisthus, Clytemnestra's lover. While there is no explicit evidence . . . Eliot repeatedly stresses his long intimacy as 'an old friend of the family,'" (32), and Amy chides Harry for not noticing him when they enter the room, "attempting to promote an almost paternal-filial relationship between them" (32).

Eliot uses a faint echo from the play in his 1942 poem "Little Gidding." Lines 250-51—the image of half-heard voices in the stillness between the sea's waves in the poem's final verse paragraph—evoke Harry's speech to Mary (57), where her voice evokes the silence between storms. Eliot's discussion of this image in a letter to his friend John Hayward is detailed in Helen Gardner's *The Composition of Four Quartets* (C302, 223).

Eliot writes in *Poetry and Drama* (P55) that his goal for this play was to use the techniques of poetic drama he had developed in *Murder in the Cathedral* and apply them to a contemporary theme. The rhythm, he explains, was meant to approximate normal speech: stresses should come in naturally expected places; his lines, of varying lengths and numbers of syllables, were to include a caesura and three stresses anywhere in the line—the only rule being that one stress had to be on one side of the caesura, and two on the other. Later, though, Eliot admitted Auden might be right in calling his verse four-stress, not three-stress; Browne, too, called the verse four-stress. Helen Gardner calls this a return to the Old English four-stress line with an unfixed number of syllables (C341, 122).

In "The Uncommon Cocktail Party," Marjorie J. Lightfoot exhaustively examines the nature of Eliot's verse in *The Cocktail Party*, finding his form little understood and subject to striking differences of opinion in terms of interpreting his scansion; Eliot himself told Lightfoot that he wrote by ear and did not pay attention to rules of scansion (C195). Lightfoot examines the prosody of *The Family Reunion* and its possible debts to Yeats in "*Purgatory* and *The Family Reunion*: In Pursuit of Prosodic Description" (C138).

In *Poetry and Drama*, Eliot criticizes his writing in this play as being too concerned with versification at the expense of plot; the device of using actors both as individual characters and as collective members of the Chorus, he writes, was unsuccessful. In two passages a duet was set off from the rest of the dialogue, written in shorter two-stressed lines—presumably, Eliot refers to two speeches of Agatha's: the rune-like incantation at the end of Part I, and another similarly cryptic pronouncement after an appearance of the Eumenides in Part II, scene II. While they were meant to be spoken in a kind of trance, as if the character had transcended herself, Eliot feels they failed because they suspend the action and sound more like an operatic aria than a contemporary situation.

The first part, Eliot continues his self-critique, was good but too long; the second part unnecessarily explores the background further, so the audience's attention wanders; the conclusion is too abrupt after a lengthy preparation. Most seriously, the play's Greek origin and contemporary situation were not smoothly melded; Eliot feels he should have stayed closer to the *Oresteia* as a source, or else diverged more widely from it. The Furies typify this problem: in future productions, he writes, they must not be cast by actors, but instead understood as being visible only to certain characters, not to the audience. He discusses various unsuccessful attempts to present them: fully on stage, they look like uninvited guests; hidden behind gauze, they look like Walt Disney characters; lit dimly, they look like shrubs outside the window. Other innovations—having them signal from across the garden, or swarm onstage like an athletic team—have been similarly unsuccessful. A *Times Literary Supplement* review describes the Eumenides as being characters "erected like statues (made at Madame Tussaud's) here and there about the desiccated stage. They are the statues of an intellectual commentary, not bold complete figures in Greek sunshine, but tenebrous with nineteenth-century Gothic guilt" (R99).

The Eumenides present a staging problem, Browne notes, because they must appear in a window embrasure in the back wall of the set to be visible to the audience; thus, Harry is facing upstage, away from the audience, for the climactic moment. The Eumenides "cannot involve the audience in an experience which cannot be seen upon the face of the character who alone can mediate it" (C277, 117).

The problem in clearly defining the play's focus, Eliot explains in *Poetry and Drama*, leaves the audience ultimately divided: not knowing whether the play is about the mother's tragedy or the son's salvation. But Eliot does balance all his self-criticism with an important recognition of what succeeds in *The Family Reunion*, and lays the foundation for all his subsequent dramatic writing. *Murder in the Cathedral*, he writes, was a dead end because his achievements in that play were not applicable to anything else he wanted to create. *The Family Reunion* successfully brought him to the world of contemporary people in contemporary life; rather than using verse drama to bring the audience into an unreal poetic world for the duration of the play, Eliot values his technique in this play of bringing poetry into the real world of the audience.

In a 1959 *Paris Review* interview Eliot calls the play his best in terms of poetry, though he admits it is not well-constructed (P67, 60). Browne agrees with Eliot's assessment of its poetry: "Of the four modern works, *The Family Reunion* is poetically by far the finest" (C279, 43); Browne also writes that "Nowhere in his drama has Eliot plumbed so deeply the agony of the individual who feels dehumanized" as in this play (42).

Autobiographically, Lyndall Gordon connects Harry's wife with Vivienne Eliot in terms of her restlessly shivering nature and the control, through the couple's former intimacy, that the wife exerts even when no longer physically present (C309, 56, 67); and she writes, "Eliot's family, like Harry's, had looked on his marriage as an aberration" (85).   Virginia Woolf, in her diary, records that she clearly perceived Harry as Eliot.   A letter Eliot wrote to Browne about the play, Gordon asserts, "resonates with personal implications: Harry, he said, was partially de-sexed by the horror of his marriage.   He could be 'stirred up' by a lovable woman but, because of his state of mind, was unable to develop this feeling into a stable commitment.   His attraction to a particular woman warred with his general idea that all women are 'unclean creatures.'   His solution is to find refuge in an 'ambiguous relation'" (49)—the kind of relation, as Gordon details, that Eliot was having with Emily Hale during the time he worked on *The Family Reunion*.

Arthur's and John's automobile crashes, Gordon reports, have their sources in two 1937 *Evening Standard* newspaper articles Eliot had clipped: one about a Viscount arrested for speeding on a country road and another about an Oxford graduate charged with drunk driving on Coronation Night (90).

The moment at which Agatha enlightens Harry, writes M. C. Bradbrook in *English Dramatic Form*, is indebted to Jean Cocteau's 1934 play *The Infernal Machine*, a version of *Oedipus* and "the vehicle of a determinist ethic." Bradbrook cites Cocteau as "the first of his generation, even before Giraudoux, to reinterpret Greek tragedy. . . . This return to tradition, when used as a basis for 'Freudian' studies of character, gave grandeur to statements of cosmic unbelief and defiance" (C270, 168-69).

Christopher Brown suggests that a play by J. B. Priestly "is the source of several character types and relationships in *The Family Reunion*, and it also suggested to Eliot the peculiar use he makes of the Eumenides" (C279, 16). The strange temporality of the Eumenides—their location in Harry's past and present—is indebted to J. W. Dunne's theories of time shifting, as manifest in Priestly's 1937 *Time and the Conways*, Brown argues.

D. S. Bland finds Ivy Compton-Burnett's novels and sensibility an important source.   Citing her pessimistic outlook on the prevalence of selfish malice, he writes, "It is in the family that ill-doing may best avoid retribution, especially when it is done by the dominating father or mother figure.   This is what happens in *The Family Reunion*, and that is why at this point in his work Eliot is very close to Miss Compton-Burnett, whatever the ultimate difference in their beliefs may be" (C126, 26).

H. Z. Maccoby suggests Rudyard Kipling's 1909 story "The House Surgeon" as a source; that story mentions a family curse connected with a house's drains, an image which appears in *The Family Reunion* (C140).

Patrick Roberts's psychanalytic interpretation of the play makes comparisons to *Hamlet*: Harry's arguable madness is like the Prince's.   "Warburton plays Polonius to Harry's Hamlet, spying on him, as he believes, and trying to entangle him in the inessential . . . Mary, Harry's cousin, is Ophelia.   She offers Harry release from his sufferings through sexual love, but this is a mere illusion" (195); and Hamlet's Oedipal struggle, like those of Harry and his forebear Orestes, provides a potent dramatic undercurrent in all three plays. Roberts notes that just as Eliot criticized *Hamlet* for being full of material that Shakespeare could not bring to satisfying fruition or manipulate into art, many critics have faulted *The Family Reunion* on the same grounds.   William Montgomerie, for example, writes, "'Hamlet's bafflement' and 'the bafflement of his creator' are really the bafflement of Mr. Eliot.   It can be shown that in *Hamlet*, Shakespeare solves the problem he set himself, and that Hamlet solves his problem.   It can also be shown that Mr. Eliot, when he tackles a similar problem, does not solve it" (C142, 121).

Gordon catalogues the play's layers of composition—scenarios and drafts—that date back to 1934 (C309, 277-78).

Publishing History

Faber & Faber published *The Family Reunion* in 1939, as did Harcourt. It was reprinted in *The Complete Poems and Plays* (New York: Harcourt, 1952), and *Collected Plays* (London: Faber & Faber, 1962).   Faber & Faber's 1969 educational edition of the text, edited by Nevil Coghill, includes an introduction, explanatory notes, and supplementary critical material (C131).

The Cocktail Party

Characters

Edward Chamberlayne. Julia (Mrs. Shuttlethwaite). Celia Coplestone. Alexander MacColgie Gibbs. Peter Quilpe. An Unidentified Guest, later identified as Sir Henry Harcourt-Reilly. Lavinia Chamberlayne. A Nurse-Secretary. Caterer's Man.

Synopsis

The play opens with a cocktail party in progress. Against a background of fragmentary anecdotes, a sense of the characters emerges: Julia is a flighty old woman, though full of vitality and confidence in humankind; Alex is a bit of a ringleader; Peter and Celia are amenable and easygoing participants; an Unidentified Guest is excluded from the party chatter.

The hostess, Lavinia Chamberlayne, is mysteriously absent from the party. Her husband, Edward—not a very effective host—has prepared no food and is not forthcoming with his guests, especially when pressed about Lavinia's absence. Despite this Julia tries to find out what has happened to her, determined not to let Edward hush things up amid polite talk. The party dissipates, leaving Edward alone with the Unidentified Guest, to whom he unburdens himself.

That afternoon—too late to cancel the party—Edward discovered Lavinia had left him. The Guest probes for details of their relationship: five years married, no children, no suspicion of extramarital affairs. He glibly tells Edward things are all for the best; Lavinia's departure will cause only mild embarrassment and inconvenience, and the calm independence of single life will soon make him wonder how he ever endured marriage. Edward hotly insists he wants his wife back; while avoiding expressing love for her, he is perturbed by the mystery of the affair. Such a mystery, the Guest agrees, can eerily strip one of the sense of being human, reducing one to a mere object.

Edward must get Lavinia back to find out who he has been during their marriage; the Guest prophesizes she will return within a day. Julia barges in with Peter, ostensibly to find a pair of glasses she had left, and tells Edward the Guest (who is now singing a hearty drinking song about One Eyed Riley) is dreadful company. Finding her glasses in her bag, Julia departs, but Peter stays to confess to Edward that he is smitten with Celia. Interrupting Edward's lukewarm reaction to Peter's energetic passion, Alex—worried that Edward, alone, cannot take care of himself—returns to cook dinner. While he prepares a makeshift concoction out of meager provisions in Edward's kitchen, Peter pours out his heart about his devotion to Celia, which she has not reciprocated. Edward cynically congratulates Peter on having escaped what would likely have been a meaningless affair, thus passing on to Peter the same heartless advice (to let the affair drop) that the Guest initially gave Edward. But Peter, like Edward, is determined to pursue the truth and convinces Edward to intercede for him with Celia.

The next scene opens with Celia sneaking back to Edward's flat, hopeful that Lavinia's departure will facilitate what is now apparent as their own love affair. Edward staunchly insists Lavinia will return and refuses to marry Celia. Alex calls to ask about the dinner, which Edward claims was marvelous—in fact, he has forgotten about the meal, which sits burning in the oven. Once again Julia reenters, claiming to have had an inspiration to feed Edward in Lavinia's absence. Finding Celia there, Julia assumes she has had the same inspiration. As Julia fiddles in the kitchen, Edward tells Celia he has asked the Guest to bring Lavinia home; Celia accuses the Guest of having diabolical control over Edward, and accuses Edward of surrendering to fatigue and panic in his desire for Lavinia's return. Edward protests that there remains some deeper motive he gleaned from his talk with the Guest, whom he now calls Riley (because of the ballad he sang). Celia suggests that Edward is on the verge of a breakdown, and should go see a doctor she knows named Reilly.

Edward's rebuff leaves Celia feeling that she has deluded and humiliated herself. He tells Celia of Peter's affection for her, to which she had been oblivious. When Celia asks Edward what he wants, he says mystically that he is certain only that he is starting to feel old, deprived of desire and contentment; he does not seek happiness, but perhaps only the knowledge that his misery does not destroy beauty. Celia now sees Edward, whom she had thought she knew, as an entirely different person: cold, inhuman. She believes this is his real character, and that his earlier pose reflected her own fantasy. Celia proposes a toast to the Guardians—a term Edward had used to describe a facet of the self that transcends feeble will, representing a stronger deterministic order.

The next day the Unidentified Guest arrives at Edward's flat, reminding him of the consequences of the decision he made at the party: a decision that set into motion forces in his life and in the lives of others. Edward must understand that reuniting with his wife is like meeting one brought back from the dead; they must not get bogged down with questions, explanations, memories, or other residue from their tangled past. At every meeting, the Guest explains, one is meeting a stranger. The Guest leaves, announcing that Edward's visitors will be arriving soon. The first of these is Celia, who is able to laugh at the previous day's traumas and to see Edward as a stranger and a human being; she has stripped away her unpleasant memories of him and is ready to proceed with a more positive relationship toward him and others. Next comes Peter, announcing that Alex has arranged for him a job in California; he, too, seems more content than before—less confused about his place in the world. As he bids farewell, Celia mentions that she, too, plans to leave.

Finally Lavinia enters and, as the discussion of Peter's and Celia's plans continues, the scene starts to resemble the original cocktail party as it might have been had it not been disrupted by personal turmoil. Alex and Julia arrive, throwing the guests into a confused speculation about who invited whom and other minor mysteries; as soon as the party is assembled, Julia summons the crew off to her own house, intending that the Chamberlaynes should be alone. Lavinia is confused about what she calls the machine she started when she left Edward and now cannot control. Alex and Julia, though they seem to know more than Lavinia, refuse to explain, telling her she must discover things for herself.

Alone, Lavinia tells her husband she has come to see him as absurd and has taken him much too seriously. They bicker over the habits of their married life. Edward sees his life ahead as hellishly damned, and fears that the choice he made yesterday will ruin him; Lavinia, worrying that he is on the verge of a breakdown, suggests sending him to a doctor.

Act two opens in the consulting room of Sir Henry Harcourt-Reilly, who had been the Unidentified Guest. He anticipates three appointments, and arranges their arrivals with the same intricate organization Julia had applied to the comings and goings of the cocktail party guests. Alex, the first appointment, explains how he convinced Edward to come see Sir Henry—Edward believes Reilly is a psychologist who may send him to a sanitorium, where he will be safe from Lavinia's clutches. Edward enters next, shocked to see that his doctor is the strange guest from his party and suspicious that his wife has conspired to send him to someone in her confidence. Reilly convinces Edward to stay despite his misgivings. He will attempt, he explains, to save Edward from ruining his life and Lavinia's—Celia, whose life might have been ruined as well, has already been saved by her recognition in Act one. Edward, though, feels incapable of acting to avoid ruin; that, he feels, is precisely his illness. Trying to convince Reilly he is psychologically dysfunctional, Edward begins to prompt a Freudian analysis; Reilly, though, rejects dredging up the past or imbuing Edward's dreams with fascinating significance—this would only flatter his vanity. Instead, Reilly focuses on the immediate: he dismisses the psychological perspective of nurturing self-obsessions, simply imploring Edward to explain what has happened since the cocktail party.

Edward cannot live *with* his wife, because she is intolerable, nor *without* her, because she has usurped his personality. He is suffering the death of the spirit, unable to escape from it, and can do nothing but place himself in Reilly's hands. Reilly responds that he cannot treat Edward until he has received more information about his case—more information than even Edward himself can provide. So he has his third appointment brought in, explaining that this patient has similar problems, and can help explicate the complete situation: it is Lavinia. She also seeks refuge in a sanitorium, but Reilly refuses on the grounds that they are both too ill. Reilly begins to clear the air by telling Lavinia about Edward's affair with Celia, and revealing that Lavinia had also been having an affair with Peter. He diagnoses Edward's problem as the recognition that he could not love Celia, and Lavinia's as the recognition that Peter, though he could not love her, *was* capable of loving someone else, Celia. The couple, thus, has much in common: Edward cannot love, and Lavinia cannot be loved. With their condition clearly exposed, they are shown they can do nothing but make the best of a bad situation—as, Reilly counsels, everyone does.

Reilly bids the couple to go in peace and work out their salvation, then prepares for one more appointment, with Celia, whom Julia has brought. Celia's problems are, first, that she is alone and has always been. She has not chosen to be, but absolute solitude simply seems to be an immutable fact—for herself and others, though others may not realize they are alone. Her second problem is a sense of sin: not immorality or guilt about having hurt Lavinia, but rather, a failure to have helped someone outside of herself. Celia had thought there was a connection between herself and Edward, but has since discovered this to be untrue. She is not bitter, but merely wants to be cured of craving an escape from solitude. Reilly tells Celia he can guide her back to the routine human condition, to which many have returned after losing hope for transcendent human experience. Celia realizes, though, that this would be a betrayal of her knowledge that there is potentially a higher condition.

A second path exists, Reilly counsels: one that requires courage and faith to undertake a journey to an unknown destination. This path is not better than the other—both are necessary—but one must choose. Celia chooses the second, making a leap of faith. Reilly bids her farewell with the same invocation he addressed to Edward and Lavinia as they left him.

Julia and Reilly are confident of Celia's success, but Reilly still worries about the Chamberlaynes in their inauspiciously banal future routine. Though his prescription for them was a risk, Julia points out that we must always take risks, and there was no alternative. She tries to imagine Celia's future suffering—but not fear—on the path she has chosen. As she and Reilly discuss the people they have advised it becomes clear that Julia understands, spiritually, more about the large picture than Reilly. As Alex joins them, they carry out a ceremonious libation tinged with both Christian and mythically archetypal benedictions for their three charges. As an afterthought they remember Peter's path is not yet settled; Alex makes a note to check with his California connections.

Act three takes place in the Chamberlaynes' drawing room two years later as Lavinia coordinates a final cocktail party with Edward's amiable support;

they both yearn for the end of the social season when they can spend some time with just each other. Alex (uninvited) and Julia arrive first; their disjointed chatter evokes the dialogue from the play's opening, but now the discussion of monkeys, heathens, and Christian missionaries in exotic locales does have a connection to the party, Alex hints. Before he can explain, Peter enters, also uninvited: fresh from America, he recounts his Hollywood exploits. Reilly arrives, uninvited as at the first party, but this time not unidentified: Lavinia calls him the perfect guest.

Peter asks about Celia, which recalls what Alex had been about to say earlier: she is dead, he casually responds. She had gone to Kinkanja to join a Christian nursing order set up to alleviate the natives' afflictions. When a heathen insurrection broke out, Celia refused to leave her patients and was crucified near an ant-hill. Peter laments not having understood Celia's life, but Reilly tells him we can know only our own métiers. Lavinia announces that they all must learn to begin: to start finding out about themselves—deeper and more important things than they have yet discovered. Julia reminds Peter that just as Celia followed the path she had chosen, so must they all; Reilly notes that Celia's suffering is just like everyone else's. While Edward and Lavinia feel implicated in Celia's fate, Reilly counsels them to transform their guilty memories into something productively new for the future. Alex raises a final toast to the Guardians, who depart before the other guests arrive leaving the Chamberlaynes prepared to begin their party and the rest of their lives.

Production History

The play (conspicuously identified as "A Comedy") premiered at the Edinburgh International Festival on 22 August 1949, at the Royal Lyceum Theatre, which director E. Martin Browne describes as "a pleasant Victorian house with a warm atmosphere" (C277, 233). The cast featured Alec Guinness as Sir Henry Harcourt-Reilly, Cathleen Nesbitt as Julia Shuttlethwaite, Ursula Jeans as Lavinia Chamberlayne, Robert Flemyng as Edward Chamberlayne, Irene Worth as Celia Copplestone, Ernest Clark as Alexander MacColgie Gibbs, and Donald Houston as Peter Quilpe. Reviewer Peter Russell, while calling the play a great achievement, notes that "the actors neither knew their parts well nor even professed to 'understand' them" at the premiere.

Eliot had demanded a purely realistic set: he forbade anything apparently symbolic in the set design, anything that might evoke experimental theatre (C277, 232); what he tentatively called the supernatural element of the play must not be literally evident. (Similarly, Eliot wanted to avoid any religious terminology in the play for as long as possible—thus the murky allusions to the "sanitorium" [213].) Anthony Holland's design reflected this simple naturalism. Desmond Shawe-Taylor's review describes "the usual stylish flat, with a white telephone, a Marie Laurencin . . . " Pamela Sherek, wife of the play's producer Henry Sherek, designed the costumes—current trendy West End fashions—to harmonize with this setting. Mary Carson's review in the *Glasgow Herald* notes the suggestiveness of the costumes: the role of Julia "depended upon a change in type of dress to convey to the audience its first inkling that there was something unusual here. . . . Miss Cathleen Nesbitt . . . wearing a floral-patterned, fluttering dress and fussy hat, is first of all the dithering guest who provides the light relief; when she appears in a later scene quietly dressed in a plain black frock, we have our first hint that she has a dual role in the scheme of things" (R114, 233).

At the end of 1949 the play had a two-week run at Brighton's Theatre Royal, and then Gilbert Miller and Henry Sherek brought it to New York's Henry Miller's Theater, where it opened on 21 January 1950 (to an audience including Ethel Barrymore and the Duke and Duchess of Windsor), running for 409 performances. The long-run production opened first in America rather than England because of difficulties securing a commitment from a London theatre-owner; West End managers, Sherek asserted, were wary of a play celebrated as an intellectual success at an arts festival.

The cast was the same as the Edinburgh run except for Eileen Peel who took over the role of Lavinia and Grey Blake who starred as Peter. John Chapman, editor of *Burns Mantle Best Plays*, named the Broadway production one of the ten best of the 1949-1950 season (others of which included Carson McCullers's *The Member of the Wedding*, William Inge's *Come Back Little Sheba*, and Jean Giradoux's *The Enchanted*). It won the New York Drama Critics Circle award, the Newspaper Guild's Page One award for the outstanding play of the season, and three Tony awards: for play, author of a dramatic play, and producer of a dramatic play. (Broadway's blockbuster that season was *South Pacific*, which won nine Tony awards.) In the American run Browne cut nine lines Reilly quoted from *Prometheus Unbound* ("Ere Babylon was dust . . . " in Act three: from I.191-99 of Percy Bysshe Shelley's play, spoken to Prometheus by his mother, Earth), finding that Americans did not catch the source in Shelley and were confused; the lines were restored to the British production. The New York cast recorded a slightly abridged version of the play on Decca Records.

The London production opened at the New Theatre on 3 May 1950 with Rex Harrison as Harcourt-Reilly, Gladys Boot as Julia, Alison Leggatt as Lavinia, Ian Hunter as Edward, Margaret Leighton as Celia, Robin Bailey as Alex, and Houston repeating his Edinburgh role as Peter. It ran for 325 performances, and won the London *Sunday Times* literary prize.

Guinness, in a newspaper interview, calls the assumption that Reilly is a psychiatrist "an absolute misunderstanding of his role," writes Maurice Zolotow. "In preparing it, he didn't talk to any professional psychiatrists in England, or to any persons who'd been analyzed. He says neither the word 'psychiatry' nor 'psychoanalysis' is ever explicitly mentioned anywhere in the script, including the stage directions. Reilly is called a doctor, he does have a consulting room, his secretary is described as a nurse, but Guinness takes him to be a 'mental and spiritual adviser and guide, in a definitely religious sense.'" The sanitarium is not a medical institution, Guinness said. "At no time was it suggested by anybody—Eliot or Martin Browne, the director—that

Reilly is a medical psychiatrist." Guinness says the role "demands more concentration than anything I've ever attempted. . . . I've got to pay attention to what the others are saying. Of course, listening is an essential element of acting in any part. . . . But here there's an extra dimension to my listening. Reilly's listening to the inner moods of others, as well as to the words they're speaking. He's listening for hidden meanings, for overtones" (R153).

In "Eliot in the Theatre," Guinness discusses Eliot's presence on the set during rehearsals and his willingness to adapt and rewrite his scripts: "On one occasion, early in rehearsals while we were still holding our scripts, I stopped and said to [Browne] . . . 'This speech I've just said—isn't it in substance very similar to the dozen lines in my previous speech?' I didn't know Eliot was in the stalls. Martin Browne hesitated, rather nonplussed, when Eliot's voice came quietly from the darkness, 'May I see the script?' It was handed to him, and then he asked for a pencil. 'You're quite right,' he said to me, having read the passage, and penciled out sixteen lines with a smile. Shortly afterward I was in difficulty with a move that had been given me, and I suggested to Martin Browne that there would be an overemphatic silence as I crossed from one side of the stage to another. 'Would four lines cover it?' Eliot asked. 'Absolutely,' I replied. Again he asked for the script and scribbled in four lines which were witty, to the point and entirely helpful" (R126, 985-86).

In an interview discussing her role as Celia, Leighton explains something of the actors' experience of being in a play by Eliot, noting the freedom resulting from the paucity of stage directions: "I liked the part because no definite instructions are given to the actress by the author as to how Celia should look. The stage directions contain no long and involved notes about the dress and appearance of the girl, or how she walks and behaves in the presence of the other characters. A great deal is left to the producer and the actress, who, as she becomes more and more familiar with the lines, gets closer and closer to the character and is thus able to build up her own highly individual conception of the part" (R129, 27). Leighton, who would later act in *The Confidential Clerk*, explains that Eliot's dramatic verse style creates some difficulties for the actor: "Though Celia is not a long part . . . I found it comparatively difficult to learn, as the author uses a fair amount of repetition which makes cues rather difficult. There were times during rehearsal when I was not sure whether a line was my cue or merely one rather like it" (27).

Leighton is quite conscious of the intended three-foot meter of Eliot's lines: she calls the rhythm obvious, and recounts spending time at rehearsals practicing, for example, the proper stresses in a line shared by two characters "with as much care as a duet in a grand opera, because the broken or shared lines all form part of the pattern of the verse and if an artist disregards the beat, the flow of the lines is rudely arrested. The play has been so carefully constructed that even an ordinary piece of stage-business such as the opening of a door is taken into account in the writing and covered by words between beats" (27, 34). Sherek confirms Eliot's precise attention to dramatic diction:

he quotes the playwright as telling the cast, assembled for the first day of rehearsal, "I will now read the play to you to show you how I want my lines spoken" (C378, 141). In a 1938 essay, "The Future of Poetic Drama" (P49), Eliot had lamented the pervasive inability of contemporary actors to perform verse drama: because they do not appreciate the idiosyncracies and richness of each line in a poetic drama, they tend to impose a soporific drone on the script.

Numerous passages in Flemyng's acting copy of the script (in the New York Public Library's Billy Rose Theatre Collection) are marked to indicate caesurae in the middle of lines, and words are underlined—perhaps to indicate stresses—attesting to the emphasis Browne placed on the actors' attending to the script's scansion.

Leggatt adds a detail about performing in Eliot's plays: "Our producer had advised us not to ask our dramatist to explain any lines we might find obscure," she writes. "However, one member of the cast, splendidly daring, disregarded this advice and asked: 'Please, what does this mean?'—to receive the reply: 'My dear child, don't ask me, I don't know'" (C339, 79). Like Leighton, Leggatt attests to the cast's sense of challenge and richness in the play: actors "were kept on the alert all the time. The spirit of the plays allowed for no relaxation or slackness, and I can honestly say that acting in them one learnt undiscovered truths in one's parts all the time."

In 1950 *The Cocktail Party* was presented at Mexico City's Instituto Nacional, in conjunction with Teatro Aguileon, directed by Salvador Noro; in 1951, the University College, Dublin Society gave the play's first Irish production at Aula Maxima.

In America, Norman Lloyd directed a revival that opened at California's La Jolla Playhouse, starring Dennis King as Reilly, and travelled to Kansas City's Orpheum Theatre, and, in 1951, to San Fransisco's Curran Theatre, by that time starring Vincent Price as Reilly. In 1952 Lloyd's production travelled to Detroit's Cass Theatre, Cleveland's Euclid Theatre, Boston's Colonial Theatre, Rochester's Arena Theatre, and Chicago's Erlanger Theatre.

Douglas Seale produced a revival of the play that opened 2 September 1952 at the Birmingham Repertory Theatre. The Oxford Playhouse Company presented the play in September 1959, directed by Harold Lang and starring Robert Bernal as Reilly, Pat Keen as Julia, and Frank Windsor as Edward. In 1965, the year Eliot died, John Reich staged a production "in memory of T. S. Eliot" at Chicago's Goodman Theatre, starring Robert Flemyng (who had created the role of Edward) as Reilly and Brenda Forbes as Julia.

Another revival was staged for the Chichester Festival in southern England. It opened 22 May 1968, starring and directed by Alec Guinness, featuring Eileen Atkins, David Collings, Hubert Gregg, Pauline Jameson, and Nan Monro, and designed by Michael Warre; that production opened at London's Wyndham's Theatre on 6 November 1968, still starring Guinness. On 7 October 1968, the APA-Phoenix Ensemble presented a revival at Broadway's Lyceum Theatre, directed by Philip Minor, starring Sydney Walker as Reilly,

Nancy Walker as Julia, Frances Sternhagen as Lavinia, Brian Bedford as Edward, Patricia Conolly as Celia, Keene Curtis as Alex, and Ralph Williams as Peter.

The Bristol Old Vic presented the play at Theatre Royale, opening 21 April 1976. Denis Carey directed the production, starring Tenniel Evans as Reilly, Mary Griffiths as Julia, and Geoffrey Whitehead as Edward.

Eve Adamson directed a 1978 revival for the Jean Cocteau Repertory at New York's Bouwerie Lane Theatre, with Coral S. Potter (who had worked on the Cocteau's 1974 production of *Sweeney Agonistes*) as Reilly and Michelle Furr as Julia; in 1988, Adamson directed another production for the same company and theatre starring Craig Cook as Reilly and Elise Stone as Julia.

New York's Guardian Theatre Company at Westbeth Theatre, off-Broadway, staged twelve performances of the play in March 1979, under the direction of Christopher Cade, starring Tom McGreevey as Reilly, Naomi Riordan as Julia and Edward Morehouse as Edward. In June 1980 Cade's production moved to the off-Broadway Orpheum Theatre, in what was billed as "a thirtieth anniversary production," with Alexander Scourby taking over as Reilly; it closed after eight performances.

Fred Hartman directed the San Francisco Repertory Company's production that opened 27 December 1979, starring Donald Hudson as Reilly, Vicki Siegel as Julia, T. Stephens as Celia, and Jerome Marketl as Alex. The Hartford Stage Company in Hartford, Conn., also offered the play during the 1979-80 season, directed by Paul Weidner and William Stewart.

John Dexter directed a revival for the New Theatre Company that opened 28 July 1986 at London's Phoenix Theatre. Alec McCowen (who had created the role of Michael in *The Elder Statesman*) starred as Reilly; Rachel Kempson played Julia, Sheila Allen played Lavinia, Simon Ward played Edward, Sheila Gish played Celia, Robert Eddison played Alex, and Stephen Boxer played Peter. Decor was by Brian Vahey. Barbara Everett describes the musical accompaniment: "strong, sweet and persuasive accompaniment from onstage and offstage pianos." The sets are described as "Twenties design of immense claustrophobic stridency, transforming to (Thirties) white, with bowls of lilies, for the third-act finale" (R123).

Noting that the play's success turns on "whether the staging can breathe life into Eliot's theoretic and rather forced claim that a patched-up marriage is as worthy as Celia's heroic altruism," Lyndall Gordon writes that Dexter, in his production, "brought it off by having Lavinia and Edward bathe their words in the warmth of demonstrative gestures, and the curtain came down on the marital play. Lavinia's very visible swelling belly bore out the fertility of marriage," and Reilly, "played with messianic vehemence by Alec McCowen, shouted 'it is a good life' with a bang on the desk" (C309, 176).

Critical Overview

Performance Reviews

The London *Times'* A. V. Cookman, reviewing the Edinburgh debut, finds the play more refined than Eliot's previous productions: "His earlier plays have been successive moves towards simplicity; and now his thought, wholly undiluted, flows with certainty and a new sparkle of wit along present-day theatrical channels. The framework of ritual sat a little heavily in *Murder in the Cathedral*. Greek props gave an air of embarrassing artificiality to the narrative of *The Family Reunion*. These he has now dispensed with; and in lucid, unallusive verse which endows everyday speech with a delicate precision and a strictly occasional poetic intensity he presents in the shape of a fashionable West End comedy a story highly ingenious in its construction, witty in repartee, and impregnated with Christian feeling" (R120, 233-34).

Robert Speaight, who played Becket in *Murder in the Cathedral*, reviewed *The Cocktail Party* for the *Tablet* and captures the sense of the actors' performances: "Miss Irene Worth suggested, in a moving and vibrant study, the whole of Celia's capacity for sacred and profane love; Miss Ursula Jeans, with no sacrifice of natural charm, made Lavinia naturally unlovable, but yet made us realize, in the last act, how grace was doing its work; Mr. Robert Flemyng, young in years for Edward, gave us the authentic sag of middle age and a twinge of the Existentialist agony; and Miss Cathleen Nesbitt conducted Julia with both judgment and wit along the realistic and symbolic levels" (R141).

In the *Observer*, Ivor Brown pans the Edinburgh presentation. He expresses the views of the "Opposition" forces to Eliot's profundity, among whom he seems to place himself: "the Opposition were observing that it was all pretentious mystification and a blether of words. . . . Not poetry at all." Brown finds the characters unappealing: he calls Julia "Lady Sneerwell"; Alex is "a strangely unpleasant young man"; and of Reilly he writes, "I have rarely disliked anybody so much as this icy healer" (R110, 235).

Desmond Shawe-Taylor, in the *New Statesman*, also finds something forbidding about the characters and the play "which chills me: perhaps the lack of delight in the rich variety of human nature. Mr. Eliot's characters are admirably amusing puppets . . . but, like the host at his own party, he seems incapable of love: of warmth toward the particular, as opposed to a diffused benevolence" (R139, 238). Browne suggests that Eliot, aware that several critics sensed this coldness, compensated in his later plays with a mellower tone.

In *Nine*, Peter Russell describes a dichotomy in critics' reactions that would persist throughout the play's various productions: "The critics of the play have divided into two parties, each baffled. One lot felt it had had an evening of fun worthy of Oscar Wilde, or at least of Noel Coward in his better moments, but found the play clouded by gloomy Hamlet-like soliloquies, private jokes, and subversive Christian propaganda. The other lot laughed too—they could not help it, for the play is an extremely witty one—but they were really waiting for the recurring old shiver of recognition when Mr. Eliot's 'real message' came through" (R138). In a *Hudson Review* essay, William Arrowsmith finds such a dichotomy resolvable: "I believe it was the author's intention to write a play which could manage to be profound at the same time it was popular (or, in Eliot's terms, a play that was Christian at the same time that it was secular in form). By such a play, I do not mean one that is written for two separate audiences, one Christian and the other secular, but a Christian play in secular dress so constructed that it should be possible for a neutral and intelligent . . . reader to penetrate to the Christian interior from the secular surface" (C160, 411).

"Being a mystic as well as a poet," Brooks Atkinson writes in the *New York Times'* review of the Broadway run, "T. S. Eliot has written a verbose and elusive drama that has to be respected. . . . this drama about the souls of some contemporary people is closer to theatre than any of his previous plays. It comes closer to being a public expression of his private ideas"—closer, but not close enough. Atkinson finds fault in the play as stagecraft: while the script proves the worth of these ideas, "the most essential parts . . . are not resolved in terms of theatre and leave a theatregoer impressed without being enlightened" (R104).

Atkinson gives his impressions of the characters' performances: Flemyng (Edward) is at first "boorish"; he and Peel (Lavinia) both give "balanced performances of sensitive quality." Worth (Celia) "finds the lonely depths in the character of the other woman in a remarkably skillful, passionate and perceptive performance." Nesbitt (Julia) is "humorously animated as a garrulous busybody who flutters in and out of the play"; Clark (Alex) is "somewhat enigmatic." Guinness (Reilly) is "superb—casual and amusing in the early scenes but rising to considerable spiritual eminence in the last act." Of Guinness's performance, Robert Garland adds in the *Journal American* that he "is a cynical savior such as only the Atomic Age could conjure"; and William Hawkins writes that Guinness "achieves a plastic omniscient air in the manner of a peacock aping Gypsy Rose Lee, which gives the doctor a rhythmic distinction from the other characters" (R125).

In the New York *Post*, Richard Watts, Jr., writes, "Being a play of stature and thoughtfulness, *The Cocktail Party* has interests upon more than one level, and while its story is dramatically effective in itself, it serves chiefly to express Mr. Eliot's provocative and somewhat mystic ideas of God and man and modern society" (R145). Howard Barnes, in the *Herald Tribune*, lauds Eliot's prosody and symbolism, but finds, "unfortunately, there is too little emotional substance . . . and no catharsis" (R107). William Hawkins, in the *World-Telegram*, is disappointed by what he calls an "intellectual duel, devoid of physical action or overt event"; lacking charm and wit, "Eliot has written a didactic philosophical analysis, more suited to reading than hearing" (R128).

Newsweek gives a kinder interpretation, calling the play "on the surface . . . almost cold in the perfection of its writing, the completeness of its self-revelation, and the constant pressure of its impeccable wit. *The Cocktail Party* is a difficult play to listen to, but only because it creates a compulsion to let no word escape unheeded" (R159). Iain Hamilton, too, notices and justifies the play's coldness, writing in *World Review:* "To complain loosely of its coldness (for cold it is, although the thought is informed by emotion) is like grumbling because, say, a Byzantine mosaic is not a huge, rosy canvas by Rubens" (R127).

John Chapman, in the *Daily News*, speaks for many critics who found the play engrossing as both a comedy and a more moralistically potent enterprise: "It has the bounce and cynicism of a frolic by Noel Coward, which makes it very entertaining—and it has a depth of understanding which makes it extraordinarily moving and inspiring. . . . the amazing skill of this play is that it never preaches; it leaves a member of the audience, no matter what his faith, to do the preaching to himself while he is watching a sophisticated comedy being splendidly acted" (R116).

Commonweal reviewer Kappo Phelan finds Eliot's intellectual attempts pretentiously unsatisfying. "There is no doubt, I think, that the academic quiz-kids are going to be able to make something out of such a mistaken theatre evening. With script in hand, they will surely be able to match symbols, wrestle obscurities, conventionalize characters, and otherwise bask . . . in subtleties. . . . But I respect Mr. Eliot sufficiently to feel that he has currently wished for an audience rather than a number of fringe scholars. . . . The trouble is that one cannot be sure what Mr. Eliot's conception of a theatre audience is. If he thinks of such an assembly as a group of plain people (some intelligent), who wish to exchange time and money in return for information, instruction, and/or delight from him, he has failed his bargain in the present piece. If, on the other hand, he believes his aisles to be peopled by a parcel of fools, he has delivered, I suppose, a stunning success" (R134).

Harold Clurman, in the *New Republic*, finds Eliot morally dishonest: "I see in his play nothing less than a poisonously hypocritical emollient which the pseudo-serious will lap up like a God-given nostrum, a strong but sugared curative which the simple and naive will regret that they cannot take." Clurman paraphrases what he sees as Eliot's moral: "live as you are living—the ordinary miserable life—and if while doing so you confess yourself a fool and do as little harm as possible, you will be about as good as you can be. If you are one of the elect, you will choose a path of noble self-immolation." He reacts to that moral: "Well, then: Is everybody happy? Are you inspired? Eliot's message is a pessimistic and devitalized defense of the status quo, which suggests no ultimate good, except a saintliness without substance. It is basically a bloodless doctrine designed for the permanently and complacently wounded in the most expensive sanitariums" (R117). In the *American Mercury*, George Jean Nathan more glibly asserts the same general point Phelan and Clurman present: "What have we here? We have, plainly, bosh sprinkled with mystic cologne" (R132).

William Carlos Williams, who in his own poetry constantly reacts against Eliot's influence, seems more receptive to Eliot's drama in a New York *Post* review: "The cocktail party . . . you might say, is, darling, your life and mine. And there are two ways out—and it was very kind of Mr. Eliot to have provided them—the way of the Chamberlaynes and Celia's way. Without Celia and her heroism (a strange new note in Mr. Eliot's poems) the day-to-day solution by homely honesty could not have emerged quite as brilliantly as it did. But it was kind, I repeat, for Mr. Eliot to offer the poor married ones an escape also" (R150).

In the 1950 London performance, Rex Harrison's Reilly was closely compared to Guinness's tour-de-force performance. "That Mr. Harrison is miscast goes without saying," writes T. C. Worsley, drama critic for the *New Statesman*. "All the same, he very nearly wins through in the second act. It is impossible to compare him with Mr. Guinness; they are opposites. Mr. Guinness was rigid, decisive, imperial; Mr. Harrison is soft, tentative, engaging. Mr. Guinness commanded his way through; Mr. Harrison charms his way along. But in the consulting room scene in the second act he does impose a kind of ascendancy. It would surely help if he could assert some authority earlier on. We want to feel a fist behind his smart chamois leather gloves" (R151, 246). Browne himself writes of Guinness's "unfailingly accurate sensitiveness to the two levels of poetic truth, poetic and natural, in the writing, and his genius in interpreting them," compared with Harrison's "performance of brilliant polish, [but which] lacked that hieratic suggestion which Alec Guinness gave to the eccentricity of the modern Heracles" (C276, 65-66).

When the play was revived on Broadway in 1968 reviewers' reactions were mixed, but generally less kind than they had been in 1950. In the New York *Daily News*, John Chapman judges, "It is still a magnificent play, brimming with compassion, poetry, and lightning wit" (R115). Richard Watts, Jr., is only slightly less approving in the *Post*: "It no longer seems the modern masterpiece it did in the original production . . . but it still is a remarkable work that combines poetry, drawing-room comedy, psychiatry and mysticism in strange and arresting proportions" (R145).

Others, though, found the play dated. "Despite sparks of the late poet's wit and the pleasure of some of his versed cadences, this drawing room morality play is chilly and remote," writes Richard P. Cooke in the *Wall Street Journal*. "Its characters and sentiments no longer seem as mysterious as they apparently did in 1950 when the play started its run of more than 400 performances and was a prime subject for just about all other cocktail parties" (R119). And in the *New York Times*, Clive Barnes is the harshest critic: "It is difficult to say whether pomposity or pretentiousness is the more damaging to the theater. Both are the stock-in-trade of T. S. Eliot's play. . . . It seemed strange to me [at its premiere], and looking back it seems even stranger now. Of course, the English-speaking theater was at its lowest ebb at that time, and verse-plays were currently fashionable." Barnes finds the play melodramatic, "irritatingly obscurantist . . . puffed up with its own gnomic message and mystical importance. . . . Here is a man who in the dramatic fragment *Sweeney Agonistes* seemed to hold the clue of modern theater in his hands offering this tawdry and shallow nonsense" (R106).

In *Theatre Journal*, Albert Wertheim admires how the 1979 San Francisco Repertory Company's production "managed nicely to evoke the play's affinities with the famous scene in the first act of Sheridan's *The School for Scandal*, in which Mrs. Candour, Sir Benjamin Backbite, Lady Sneerwell, and Mr. Crabtree destroy the reputations of all their acquaintances" (R147).

In the *New York Times* Frank Rich calls the 1980 off-Broadway revival "an irritating and tedious play that has aged badly. . . . The play's avant-garde mannerisms, so hotly debated a generation ago, now seem like affectations that only literary historians could possibly find of interest" (R137). Michael Billington, in the *Guardian*, is slightly kinder about the 1986 London revival: it "offers a refreshing antidote to the trivial pursuits of most West End theatres. But . . . watching it revived now is like seeing the dust-sheets removed with a great flourish from some heirloom only to discover that it is chipped and mouldy with age" (R109). Lesley Chamberlain, while lauding an "admirable" production "with the most intelligent acting and attractive staging," notes that "it was hard to fill more than a few front rows in the stalls." Chamberlain suggests the play "has never been truly suited to pleasing a wide audience," and the acclaim of the 1949 and 1950 productions "was surely deceptive. All three occasions owed the excess of their popularity to Eliot's living celebrity as poet and Nobel laureate. . . . The play is, for all Eliot's ambitions on behalf of staged verse drama, probably best suited to arm-chair reading and slow digestion. On stage it fails to convey simultaneous natural and supernatural experience; and it fails to make a dynamic show of the continuity between those two worlds" (C167, 512-13).

John Dexter's 1986 production, writes Barbara Everett in the *Times Literary Supplement*, "brought the play up to date by everywhere humanizing, socially de-classing, eroticizing. The participants in what was conceived as a comedy of manners have become broader and cruder, have softened and blurred." She describes the transformations in characters from their original conceptions: "Lavinia is no longer a middle-aged middle-class battle-axe, nor Julia a well-off nuisance, nor Celia an aristocratic arrogant young idealist. Sheila Allen renders the first into a Bayswater beauty, Rachel Kempson dithers through the second as a dotty old dear, and—most surprisingly—Sheila Gish finds in Celia a friendly West End trouper. . . . Simon Ward's Edward has a nice humour and poise, but in shedding his character's cold barristerial blankness he deprives Lavinia of any reason for leaving him. . . . And Alec McCowen's psychiatrist, the great Sir Henry Harcourt-Reilly, not merely departs from the Guinness-Harrison interpretations of this enigma, but simply abandons the notion of the character as enigmatic at all. His Reilly is a totally new and studied portrayal: an extrovert, barking, manic, highly 'distinguished' doctor, sworn to save his patients even if he kills them in the process." Failing to provide moral irony, Dexter's production thus "carries within itself a sense of betrayal" (R123).

In the 1988 Cocteau Repertory production, D. J. R. Bruckner describes in the *New York Times* how director Eve Adamson "uses a fast tempo for part of the play and a much slower one for the rest, with somewhat disorienting effect. In the early scenes, characters fire lines at one another breathlessly, but, as they begin to discover the self-deceits and miseries of their lives, their delivery slows down." Bruckner notes that "there is no effort by this cast to sound British . . . and the American voice is refreshing" (R113).

Scholarly Response

Numerous connections have been made between *The Cocktail Party* and Eliot's earlier work. Robert Speaight in his *Tablet* review notes the influences of Eliot's earlier poetic characters and schemas: Edward "is our old friend J. Alfred Prufrock," and his dilemma is a reenactment of "the loneliness of Gerontion"; Celia "is already living the experience of the *Four Quartets*" (R141). The *Manchester Guardian* review, too, notes of the play, "in search of its immediate ancestry one must go, strange though it may seem, to neither *The Family Reunion* nor to *Murder in the Cathedral*—nor, for that matter, save in theatrical technique, to any comedy ancient or modern—but to the *Four Quartets*. . . . This play is largely a dialectical expression in theatrical terms of that sombre poem" (R157).

Jack Winter examines what he calls the archetypal condition of "Prufrockism" as it develops through Eliot's work and manifests itself in this play. The opening cocktail party, infused with Julia's empty chatter, evokes the world from "The Love Song of J. Alfred Prufrock" in which the women come and go with no apparent purpose. Reilly's initial appraisal of Edward's loss of personality, self, and stable reality pegs him as a Prufrock type, and Edward's own perception of himself as a middle-aged man feebly growing older (and consequent obsession with his powerless insignificance) mimics Prufrock's. The Chamberlaynes, though, eventually escape the condition of Prufrockism, Winter writes, because Reilly's "prescription" for them—couched in the more satisfyingly resolute sensibility of *Four Quartets*—allows different personae to emerge with matured and transcendent outlooks, not condemned to live in the solipsistic prison of Prufrock's world (C230).

William Barrett draws specific comparisons between this play and *Sweeney Agonistes*: "both deal, though in different ways, with the sheer overwhelming fact of human banality: in *Sweeney* the crudity of the lower orders, here the tedious chatter of the middle classes" (C162, 356); though *Sweeney Agonistes* is more successful because "in this earlier fragment Eliot fully released all his hatred of human life and really enjoyed himself in the raucous company of Doris, Sweeney, Klipstein and Krumpacker—in comparison with whose vulgar vitality the characters at the cocktail party are genteel skeletons" (358). Barrett evokes, too, Eliot's earliest poetry: "at bottom the world of

The Cocktail Party is the same empty world of *Prufrock*, except that 37 years ago Eliot did not disguise his contempt for this emptiness" (358).

C. L. Barber draws attention to the parallels between Sweeney's fantasy of cannibalism and Celia's death at the hands of cannibals. "The cannibal impulse, as it is encountered in *The Cocktail Party*, is still [as in *Sweeney Agonistes*] relevant to love and worship—as it is, of course, in the Lord's Supper, which in a Christian view is what the several sorts of primitive and primitivist aberrations point to" (C260, 232). Barber notes that Celia does indeed, in a sense, become Edward's "missionary stew" as Sweeney only threatens Doris with that fate. And John Pick, too, links this play to an earlier one, asserting that *The Cocktail Party* and *Murder in the Cathedral* "have a common theme: 'Humankind cannot bear very much reality.' Each is built around a fundamental pivot, the dramatic contrast between ordinary mediocrity on the one hand and heroic sanctity on the other. Both deal with the making of a saint"—Becket and Celia (C205, 30).

E. M. Forster, writing in the *Listener*, finds Celia's role ineffective and somewhat propagandistic: "Her sufferings are dwelt on, are indeed gloated over, and no doubt this is consonant with Mr. Eliot's religious outlook. . . . But aesthetically the sufferings disturb the reader and distract him. The Christian ethic of atonement, which has been hanging over his head since the end of the second act, comes down with too sudden a bump. He hears the doctor-priest analysing the successful martyrdom as they sip their drinks, and he wonders." Forster lauds Eliot's verse, though: "It is most beautifully and lucidly written. Mr. Eliot can do whatever he likes with the English language. This time he has selected a demure chatty verse-form which seems to be like prose, but it is full of turns and subtle echoes, and always open for the emotional intensity he occasionally needs" (R124).

While the tone in the first two acts is "urbane and sensitive," writes Mabel C. Donnelly, the casual dismissal of Celia's death in act three reflects a drastic "failure of sensibility. . . . Irony might have saved these lines," but "unfortunately for the third act of what began as an outstanding verse drama, Eliot was not able to maintain a consistent tone—to the great loss of the kind of synthesis he hoped to reach in his art in later years" (C173, 61).

In the play, Eliot recapitulates "the successive positions of his own spiritual biography," writes Vivienne Koch, "beginning with the nihilism of *Sweeney Agonistes* and going right on through the whole laborious ascent. One could, I think, almost plot each character as a projection of the various spiritual stages Eliot has objectified in each of his major phases. . . . I think we might call the play a 're-enactment' of Eliot's deepest conflicts, crises, and their final resolution" (C190, 251).

The play's resolution has been considered both as a portrayal of unmitigated triumph, involving the Guardians' beneficent control over many dysfunctional lives, and as a more tempered success because Edward and Lavinia seem to return to uneventful banality. Hildegard Hammerschmidt argues for the latter interpretation, and states that this points out the Guardians' limitations as spiritual agents: while they "apply all their magical and other power to bring about a change in Celia's consciousness, convincing her that there is another way" and making her "able to achieve higher values of enlightenment combined with charity," they are not so powerful with respect to the Chamberlaynes. "Edward and Lavinia, under the guidance of Reilly, Julia and Alex, finally agree to continue their rather shallow and even meaningless life, knowing that their relationship is totally void of love. So, in the last analysis, the role of the guardians has to be described as merely instrumental. They point out possibilities and they create certain conditions, but they cannot make decisions" (C179, 64). Implicit in Hammerschmidt's argument is the assumption that the Guardians should have created a more meaningful life for Edward and Lavinia, and would have done so had they been able.

Some critics, like John Peter, take issue with Eliot's categorization of the play as a comedy in view of its weighty moralities. "When Mr. Eliot calls his new play a comedy he seems to me to be closer to the position of a Shakespeare calling *Macbeth* a comedy on the strength of the Porter Scene. Only the incidentals in the play are, in fact, comic and, though on the stage they should be much more effective, on paper they barely deserve the adjective" (C204, 61). C. L. Barber agrees that audiences were put off by the gulf between expectations for a West End comedy and the play's actual content, objecting "to Eliot's 'smuggling in a priest in psychiatrist's clothing'" (C260, 235). But Richard Findlater suggests a response, calling Eliot's achievement "to induce in the audience an acceptance of both the idiom and the theme. He does this by a Trojan Horse technique, by concealing inside the shell of a comedy of manners about love among the middle class a serious discussion of the spiritual crisis, by using the witty analysis of marital failure as the bait for a recruiting call for the army of the saints" (C296, 143-44).

Katherine J. Worth writes that the play "has a claim to be considered the first black comedy in the postwar English theatre" (C404, 55). Eliot took the tradition of drawing-room comedy, she writes, and "darkened the material, putting it into ironical focus and drew out forcefully implications that the early master, Coward, had just touched on. The rituals of the cocktail party are pushed in a sinister direction. Reilly sipping gin and water is a Coward character poised for a leap into a Pinter scene. No wonder Eliot was appalled when he once dropped in on a performance . . . to find Rex Harrison getting an illicit laugh by sneaking an extra gin and water when he was alone on stage; how easy to wreck the effect of machine-like inevitability in the sequence of invitation, response and refusal that makes up the gin and water ritual" (63).

Eliot's intentions in calling the play a comedy were to disrupt expectations—as, in *The Family Reunion*, he subverted the audience's expectation that it was seeing a murder mystery in the mode of Agatha Christie—according to Carol H. Smith; he meant to clear away conventional modes of thought to reveal a hidden meaning, a divine plan, behind appearances (C382).

But G. W. Brandt is more willing to accept the play at face value as (at least partly) comic. "Why is the play called a comedy, when its climactic event is the death of Celia Copplestone? There is of course a certain lightness of tone, a comic note in many parts of *The Cocktail Party*: this is established at once by Julia's twitterings about whether there was, or was not, a tiger mentioned in Alex's story, and about Lady Klootz and the wedding cake. A good many lines that may look a little tame on the printed page are cunningly placed theatrical laugh-lines. The very title of the play is really a joke. . . . the cocktail party . . . is never actually shown on stage. The first party . . . is merely the fag-ends of a cancelled party, a social evening that never materialised; the second is about to start just as the final curtain comes down. In purely theatrical terms, there is a good deal of comedy business, all of it of course in an appropriately quiet key: Julia's well-timed irruptions and interruptions; Harcourt-Reilly's bursting into song; Edward's unsuccessful culinary efforts" (C164, 45). In a larger sense, the play is comic because Celia's death is "regarded not so much as a horrible event . . . but rather as a spiritual triumph. . . . the comedy is not primarily a comedy of laughter but that of a 'happy' view of the universe, in which even tragedy falls into place in a higher conciliation of opposites."

The play's comedy provides an alchemy that "transforms humiliation into humility, judgment into mercy," writes Ann P. Brady. "The world of comedy is the world of humility, where people do not fall, because they are already on the ground (*humus*) where they belong. It is a world of reality where one comes to see the self in relation to the rest of the world, where one is free to celebrate the ordinary. To enter this world, one must relinquish the primacy of self, the loss of which is often accomplished through a comedic 'fall' from eminence and experienced as humiliation, but eventually accepted as a descent to truth, to humility" (C163, 179).

M. C. Bradbrook, in *T. S. Eliot*, characterizes Reilly's tone as comic in the darkly sardonic mode of Eliot's early poetry: she notes the "mordant humour . . . a tone of mock dignity and assumed gravity which Sir Henry Harcourt-Reilly shares with Agatha [in *The Family Reunion*] and the First Priest of *Murder in the Cathedral*. It is a tone which belongs to Eliot himself" (C272, 44)—evocative, perhaps, of the ridiculously austere and self-critical Prufrock, or the comically genteel gentleman caller from "Portrait of a Lady."

Helen Gardner writes that what she sees as unabashedly comic represents a consciously new phase in Eliot's drama, one which would last until the end of his career. "In these last plays he deliberately wrote within the limits of what has been contemptuously called the 'West End play,' or what Mr. Terrence Rattigan called 'Plays for Aunt Edna.' He used the picture-frame stage, with a conventional setting: the modern flat, the library, the consulting-room, the terraces of an expensive rest-home. He made no use of chorus, soliloquy or aside, and employed for his machines the telephone and front-door bell" (C301, 43).

An essay in the *Times Literary Supplement* confirms, as many other critics did, that *The Cocktail Party* represented a culmination in Eliot's dramatic career, especially in terms of his efforts to recreate verse drama for the modern stage: he is credited with having begun to craft an "ideal of stage language in *Murder in the Cathedral*, in which he was at least not imitating Shakespeare; [in] *The Family Reunion* . . . he achieved a form of verse as close as possible to modern conversation. But here he was still employing poetic props which were not dramatic, and for the drama itself he was depending too much upon the literary association with Aeschylus. In *The Cocktail Party* he discarded alike the poetic props and the framework of classical drama. He told the kind of story which, except for its underlying spiritual implications, is the staple of fashionable entertainment in Shaftesbury Avenue. . . . And largely it fulfilled the general hope of a verse which should in the circumstances of modern social comedy say more than prose could say in the same circumstances." Eliot has succeeded, according to the *TLS*, in establishing the foundation for poetic drama. "Perhaps the most useful lesson which Mr. Eliot teaches his fellow poet-dramatists is the poet's proper place in the theatre" (R154). And Anthony S. Abbott finds the play "Eliot's masterpiece. In it he has solved successfully the problem of meeting the audience on its own ground and yet utilizing the play as a means of transfiguring the audience's daily life." His next two plays "move further in the same direction, too far I think" (C254, 101).

John Middleton Murry, comparing this play with Eliot's previous one, finds that the improvement here comes from "Reilly's insistence that there are two ways. The possibility of a return to ordinary life with 'a different vision' is not even faintly indicated in *The Family Reunion*. There the ordinary life, as presented in Harry's other aunts, his uncles, and his brothers appears to be one of stupid mechanism. . . . The absorbing interest of *The Cocktail Party* and that which to my mind makes it the more significant play is that the possibility of the transvaluation and transformation of the ordinary becomes the main theme: it is not merely suggested but dramatically demonstrated in Edward and Lavinia" (C356, 395).

While noting that Eliot's earlier work bears on this play, William Barrett, in *Partisan Review*, finds that it does so only in showing the inadequacy of the present effort. He argues that the play is well-received only because of Eliot's stature as a poet. "For my own part, I am unable to separate the play from its author; and, this being the case, I must assimilate the play by the standards that Eliot's other work invokes and often satisfies, and measuring by such standards I find *The Cocktail Party* a disappointing work: thin and unconvincing as drama and weak as poetry—perhaps the weakest poetry that Eliot has yet written" (C162, 354). For those who, like Barrett, refuse to see Eliot as anything other than a poet, his dramatic work may be judged inadequate: "the question is whether he has not succeeded by so sugar-coating his pill that very little of the poetic substance remains. . . . '*Isn't it wonderful!*' a friend said to me as we left the theater, '*It's poetry but you never know it.*' I am simple-minded enough to think that this must remain a very ambiguous compliment for the author even though he seems to have calculated some such effect" (354-55).

W. K. Wimsatt agrees that the play is watered-down poetry, but reacts more favorably to the enterprise: "Shall we say that Eliot, in his determination to put poetic drama honestly within reach of an audience, has uttered a thinner and plainer version of the themes and images of his major and more densely implicated poems? To say so need not I believe be a disparagement. A play is something which an audience is to follow from sentence to sentence and understand in the main—though certain auras of significance may be missed" (C229, 670).

The Cocktail Party is atypical of standard dramatic patterns, writes Vinod Sena, because "instead of a structure of complication, of inter-action," it "substitutes one of separation and progressive divergence" (C217, 393); from the beginning, the characters are pulled off in different directions, and the audience is made prominently aware of the gulf between them. Eliot "displays a remarkable ingenuity in overcoming" the obvious dramatic problems associated with this structure, "but his solutions are of the nature of improvisations which may at times rebound on their own inventor. At the most obvious level perhaps there is the difficulty of dramatising character in a work in which the protagonists, after the first scene or two, scarce come together in a common action." As a consequence, "we do begin to edge towards an over-verbalised kind of drama where language, instead of being an extension of action, is in danger of becoming its substitute" (393).

Michael Selmon, while noting as Sena does the prominence of language in *The Cocktail Party*, cites this as a success rather than a drawback in terms of Eliot's dramatic intention. He sees the play as a struggle with language and an attempt to forge a new language, consciously implanted in the medium of drama, that can embody Eliot's aspirations toward unity as presented in *Four Quartets*. "Speech in Act 1 remains trapped in the self. . . . In Act 2 . . . Eliot takes up the struggle again, working through Harcourt-Reilly to purify his characters' words" (C216, 500-501). Selmon continues, "It is in genre, then, that Eliot locates language's cure. Self-reference inevitably limits human speech; as Julia reminds us, we cannot know 'the process by which the human is / Transhumanized' . . . Using the theater, Eliot bypasses this limitation. He makes 'transhumanizing' drama's imperative. . . . Eliot's heroes . . . transcend human history" (504).

The repetitive conversational patter in the opening lines recalls "the rhythms and repetitions of the first fragment of *Sweeney Agonistes*," writes Nevill Coghill in the notes to his edition of the play. "Here the rhymes have been dropped and the rhythms broken a little, to approximate more closely to normal interchanges of speech, and yet retain the ghost of a feeling of comic verse-energy" (C168, 201). Of the versification generally, Coghill writes, "each line, as printed, has its own autonomous length and rhythm as a sentence, or part of a sentence, lightly indicating how it is to be spoken, where the emphasis should fall, and where the pauses (if any) are to come, if the meaning is to be fully expressed, and the quality of conversation is to be preserved. The 'poetry' (that is, the intensity) flows through the lines with varying strength, related to the situation and the character of the speaker" (290).

Textual Notes and Influences

In *Poetry and Drama*, Eliot explains that he tried to correct in this play some of his errors from *The Family Reunion*. He thus avoided choruses and ghosts; and, while using the *Alcestis* of Euripides for his theme, he did so merely as a springboard, and concealed this origin (rather than flaunting it, as he had done through the Eumenides in *The Family Reunion*)—so well, he claims, that nobody detected this influence until he disclosed it. As an example of his use of the source, he compares Reilly's eccentricity, drunken intemperance, and tendency to burst into song, with the behavior of Heracles.

Robert B. Heilman lists various other parallels: he discusses how Euripides creates a romantic comedy whose "distinction lies in its almost daring flirtation with tragedy"; the Chamberlaynes, like Admetus, are "compelled to undergo moral inspection" (106). The events that begin each play are parallel—Lavinia's departure and the death of Alcestis; Edward's incongruous hospitality to his guest is like Admetus's entertainment of Heracles, Heilman writes, and both husbands conceal the gravity of their situations. Reilly, like Heracles, promises to return the missing wife, and the game Heracles plays, trying to convince Admetus to take a new wife, is evoked by Reilly's initial attempt to point out the benefits of Edward's new freedoms (107). Reilly metaphorically speaks of bringing Lavinia back from the dead; Heracles, of course, must literally bring Alcestis back from death (108). Heracles is half-divine; and in Reilly, similarly, "there is an ambiguity which makes a limited naturalistic view of him seem continually inadequate" (115). Neither husband fully realizes his wife's worth until she is gone (C182, 111).

The main difference in Eliot's treatment of Euripides, Heilman argues, is that he "has really seen two characters in Alcestis—the ordinary woman and the saint—and has boldly split Alcestis into Lavinia and Celia" (110). Additionally, Eliot has combined two characters from Euripides into one of his own: Reilly is based not only upon Heracles, but also upon Pheres, the father of Admetus, whose attack on his son's sacrifice of Alcestis to save his own life "is in part a painfully accurate analysis of Admetus and in effect a summons to see himself as he is" (114).

John Rexine discusses "the transformation of the Alcestis myth into the ritual of Christian sacrifice. In a sense, the third act is a Christian epilogue, showing what happens to the ideas and plots of Euripides when the Christian element is added" (25). Rexine presents similarities between *Alcestis* and *The Cocktail Party*: both "were written in an era of spiritual upheaval, and each author is showing the hollowness of the contemporary life he writes about. The traditional divine machinery of each period is exhibited, and yet neither author accepts this completely on faith, but tries to form a new system of belief out of the materials at hand. . . . Both plays dwell on the inadequacy of human love" and are "tragicomedies, mixing the comic details of everyday life with a deep sense of the tragedy which lies under the surface. Both plays embody the predicament of the modern man of their time" (C211, 26).

David Paul, though, examining the relation of the two plays, argues that they offer very different experiences to their audiences, and that the modern play is deficient: *Alcestis* is a "deeply shrewd example of a free distribution of dramatic sympathy"; this sympathy "remains in even balance at the end, as it was at the beginning" (176-77). Eliot, though, is too heavy-handed: Reilly too prominently controls events, leaving the audience unable to judge events freely itself. "He is there from the beginning of things, running the whole machine" (C202, 176). Several other critics have cited Reilly's pervasive and manipulative control of the play's dynamics as a shortcoming.

The concept of Guardians, Grover Smith explains, is "of diverse provenance, from the legal use of the term to the Stoic-Christian idea of guardian angels, [and] recalls the Guardians in Plato's *Republic*, especially in view of the outline for the social role of the Community of Christians in Eliot's *The Idea of a Christian Society*" (C383, 220). In that essay, Eliot argues that social control and balance is possible only within what he calls a Christian society—one that adheres to Christian morals and values though governed by a secular structure and led, nebulously, by those of intellectual and spiritual superiority. In "On the Place and Function of the Clerisy" (P63), he expands on the role of an elite group of overseers in society—a group developed by training that helps catalyze beneficent social change. Both these essays anticipate the functions of the Guardians and serve as a kind of subtextual charter for their workings in *The Cocktail Party*. In this vein, Kenneth J. Reckford examines the Guardians' sharing of food and drink as evoking the sacrament of Communion (C209).

In an interview about the American premiere of his next play, *The Confidential Clerk*, Eliot called that play more successful than *The Cocktail Party* because none of its characters was outside the action of the drama, or lacking in character development, as, he then felt, the Guardians were (P64).

Browne's correspondence with Eliot—his critical reaction to various drafts of the play—has been preserved (C277, 176-78, e.g.), and gives a good insight into the extremely methodical dramaturgical technique Eliot was by now crafting (perhaps as a defensive measure against the critical responses his earlier plays had evoked: complaints that they were deficient in some of the essential elements of contemporary drama). Among Browne's suggestions for revision or elaboration were the smoother integration of passages of dialogue into an overall "pattern of action"; more consistent character development of Julia and Alex; more prominent instances of action wherever possible—displays of dramatic scenes, rather than descriptions thereof; and issues of realisitic and credible plot development. Eliot seemed receptive to this kind of criticism, and integrated many of Browne's suggestions. In a letter to

Browne's wife, the actress Henzie Raeburn, Eliot wrote, "When the various drafts of the play are finally collated and studied by researchers in American universities, I think that my debt to you and Martin will emerge!" (C277, 239).

In an interview with the *Glasgow Herald* after the play's premiere Eliot discussed some of his dramatic philosophy as it related to the play. He "smiled when it was suggested to him yesterday that Festival audiences had not found his meaning very plain. 'Perhaps,' he said gently, 'I did not intend that they should.' . . . 'All that one can aim at in a play of this type, which endeavours to combine the dramatic and the poetic in a somewhat new way,' he said, 'is to provide a plot and characters which are on the immediate theatrical level intelligible. That is, the immediate situation and the troubles and conflicts which agitate people should be obvious, the characters should not be on the surface unusual or different from ordinary human nature, and there should be perfectly intelligible things going on, with a reasonably intelligent conclusion.'" Like poetry, though, poetic drama must generate a range of different meanings unique to each individual spectator, Eliot continued (R162, 236).

The play's working title was "One-Eyed Riley: A Comedy," but Eliot was also mulling the eventual title while writing the play, intending (as he writes in a 1948 letter to Browne printed in Nevill Coghill's edition of the play [C168], 193-95) a parallel between a cocktail party full of guests unwelcome by the host and his previous play, which featured a family reunion lacking some of the family. Eliot drew another comparison between the two plays in the same letter, writing that he meant to give some clear indication of Celia's fate so as not to leave it uncertain, as Harry's was.

In a 1949 letter Eliot wrote to Sir Geoffrey Faber (printed in Coghill's edition, 190-92), he stated that he believed two passages near the end made it obvious that Lavinia was going to have a baby at the end of the play. One of these is probably on page 154, where Lavinia tells Edward she hopes he is not too tired to attend the final cocktail party, and he responds that she is the one who should be tired.

A tenuous but interesting link between the play and "Burnt Norton" derives from Julia's comment (37) that she can meditate in a lift. Helen Gardner (C302, 86) associates this with a letter Eliot wrote to his brother, comparing the descent into the London underground by stairs and by elevator; while both methods convey one to the same place, the elevator does so while seeming to abstain from movement. This dichotomy and its associated imagery govern Part III of "Burnt Norton"; there, the final stanza, evoking the meditative descent by lift, reflects a more spiritual journey than the one first described, which is colored by disaffection, distractions, emptily apathetic crowds, and ill souls.

Robert Langbaum associates the play's (and especially Reilly's) sensibility toward the definition and recognition of the self with F. H. Bradley's philosophy (C336).

Margaret Leighton, speaking of her role as Celia, compares it to another role she had played: that of Ellie Dunn in Shaw's *Heartbreak House*. "There is a quality of utter finality about both these young women, which makes them strangely alike" (R129). Reviewer Richard Watts, Jr., contrasts this play with Eugene O'Neill's 1946 *The Iceman Cometh*: "While O'Neill told passionately of the world's need for illusion to sustain it, Eliot insists more urbanely that our illusion must be dropped and reality faced" (R143).

Eliot's treatment of marriage builds "on a long established tradition on the modern stage," writes Katherine E. Kelly. "Beginning with Ibsen's *Doll House*, and continuing through Strindberg's *Ghost Sonata*, Chekhov's *Uncle Vanya*, Shaw's *Man and Superman*, O'Neill's *Long Day's Journey into Night*, Williams's *Streetcar Named Desire*, and Albee's *Who's Afraid of Virginia Woolf?*, to name only a few, the disappointments of marriage have taken a central place in twentieth-century drama. When writing this piece, Eliot drew particularly on Noel Coward's drawing-room comedy, best exemplified by plays such as *Blithe Spirit*, *Hay Fever*, and *Private Lives*, whose urbane characters speak a cultivated English and have the leisure necessary to permit their indulgence in witty analyses of themselves, their historical moment, and one another" (C327, 172).

Eliot diverges, though, from the mainstream of the modern marriage play tradition, Kelly argues: his "intense interest in his characters' spiritual salvation finally distinguishes his marriage play sharply from those preceding it. . . . By encouraging spectators to assess and reassess the events and language of the opening act, Eliot engages them in probing the deceptively Noel Coward-like surfaces of the play, which in turn has the effect of drawing the audience into the characters' search for salvation. Harold Pinter's comedies of menace, such as *Old Times* and *No Man's Land*, similarly use a deceptively innocent surface language to suggest another level of communication occurring among characters. But this second level in Pinter is savagely hostile and devoid of the influence of Christian grace. Tom Stoppard's more benevolent comedies, particularly his recent marriage play *The Real Thing*, while secular, come closer to Eliot's tone and use of dramatic irony in fixing the spectator's critical attention on the events unfolding on stage" (172-73).

Browne confirms that Eliot made clear, during dress rehearsals of the play, that he consciously intended a refutation of Jean-Paul Sartre in Edward's assertion (98) that Hell is oneself. "The line, and the whole story of Edward and Lavinia, are [Eliot's] reply to 'Hell is other people' in *Huis Clos*" (C277, 233). Lois G. Thrash finds parallels in Charles Williams's *The Greater Trumps* (C223), and Rossell Hope Robbins also notes the influence of Williams's *Descent into Hell* (C212). Ilse E. Hochwald sees a possible source for Celia in Goethe's Ottolie, from *Wahlverwandshaften* (C184), while Herbert Knust sees important mythical borrowings from the Norse myths in Richard Wagner's *Ring des Nibelungen*, including Wotan—one-eyed, appearing as an unknown stranger, who "obtained his wisdom from a drink, knew magical songs and figured as the god of poetry" (C189, 293)—as a source for Reilly, and his daughter Brunhild as a source for Celia.

R. Baird Shuman notes Buddhistic overtones in the characters of Reilly and Celia. Vimala Rao notes that "one of the key sentences in the play . . . 'Work out your salvation with diligence' . . . is a reference to the death-bed injunction of the Buddha to his disciples" (C218, 193); additionally, "the libation scene at the end of Act Two obviously shows the influence of Indian poetics. . . . the cryptic invocations and blessings pronounced by Alex, Reilly, and Julia are close to the invocations of Vedic hymns" (197), such as libations offered to the God of the hearth for the purification of a new house. An Indian philosophy pervades the play, which "can be read as an epitome of the situation described in the *Bhagavad-Gita*, that life is a matter of choice, of involvement in action with proper attitudes. The pattern of dialogue between Reilly and his patients resembles that between Krishna and Arjuna in the *Gita*. . . . Reilly's job, like that of Krishna . . . is to bring the questioner to a proper state of mind. This is done through detailed dialogue in both works. *The Cocktail Party* bears not a little resemblance to the *Gita* in this very didactical structure" (195-96); the play's Indian influences are perhaps subtly announced by "a cocktail conversation peppered with references to 'saffron monkeys,' 'curry powder,' and 'tigers'" (197).

Sandra Wool fits all the characters into a mythical/archetypal schema as delineated in Jessie Weston's *From Ritual to Romance*, while Thomas E. Porter matches the Guardians to comic prototypes described in Francis Cornford's *The Origins of Attic Comedy*, a study which strongly influenced Eliot's dramatic theory. Julia is the Old Woman, a Greek dramatic type portrayed as a "shrewish, drunken, amorous hag" (C232, 63); Reilly is the Doctor, whose "ancient ritual function . . . is to revive the slain hero" (63); and Alex "has an ancient ritual role which he announces himself: 'You know, I'm a rather famous cook.' What sounds like personal vanity is actually a broad hint about his character. Cornford has outlined his genealogy and the source of his fame: 'The Cook is a magician, a dealer in enchanted herbs, a medicine man.' . . . His function is related to a purgation-mode of regeneration" (64).

Lyndall Gordon writes that Eliot saw a 1946 production of Noel Coward's *Blithe Spirit*, featuring his friend Emily Hale, and that "this comedy about a husband whose dead wife's spirit returns to trouble his relationship with the new wife may have provided the germ for Eliot's first comedy, *The Cocktail Party*, where a wife disappears into a sanitorium, leaving her husband to his affair with another woman, and then returns to take possession of him" (C309, 168). Autobiographically, Gordon suggests that Hale is depicted in the character of Celia—the woman Edward perhaps truly loved (as Eliot seems to have loved Hale), but chose not to marry even when he became free to do so after Lavinia's departure (as Eliot finally rejected Hale after Vivienne's death). "In so far as Emily Hale was the source for Celia, it was Eliot's imaginative farewell: in the course of the play, Celia's fate moves off-stage. Yet, through her, Eliot expounds, with unprecedented explicitness, a very rare form of love. Never did he create so lovable a woman, at once assured and vulnerable. . . . Celia, like Emily, opens the route to reality—so long as she remains physically unattainable. . . . There lies behind this Eliot's fear that to enjoy love is to destroy it" (172-73).

The play's text includes the words and score for "One-Eyed Riley," the ballad Reilly sings in the first scene.

Eliot rejected a £30,000 offer for film rights to the play, because he considered it unfilmable.

Publishing History

Faber & Faber published *The Cocktail Party* in March 1950, as did Harcourt. The play was reprinted in *The Complete Poems and Plays* (New York: Harcourt, 1952), and *Collected Plays* (London: Faber & Faber, 1962). Robert L. Beare (C264, 36-39) discusses textual revisions and other bibliographical variants among different editions. For the first time, Eliot chose not to publish this play until after it had opened; he had published *Murder in the Cathedral* and *The Family Reunion* to coincide with their premieres, but Browne writes that Eliot "regretted not being able to learn from the experience of rehearsal and audience-reaction" in those texts (C277, 145). Faber & Faber's 1974 educational edition of the text, edited by Nevill Coghill, includes explanatory notes, supplementary critical essays, and relevant passages from Eliot's correspondence discussing the play's composition (C168).

The Confidential Clerk

Characters

Sir Claude Mulhammer. Eggerson. Colby Simpkins. B. Kaghan. Lucasta Angel. Lady Elizabeth Mulhammer. Mrs. Guzzard.

Synopsis

Eggerson, former secretary to Sir Claude Mulhammer, is preparing to fetch Sir Claude's wife, Lady Elizabeth, and bring her to their London residence as part of a mission necessitating delicacy and tact. In Sir Claude's library, anticipating the arrival of the new confidential clerk Colby Simpkins, Eggerson and Sir Claude discuss Colby's future prospects in his post: they foresee that he will need confidence, experience, and readjustment. He will also have to get over his disappointment at not being able to pursue what might have been his métier, a musical career, and instead settling down to something else. Sir Claude instructs Eggerson to make Lady Elizabeth feel as if she has had a hand in choosing Colby to replace him.

Eggerson has also helped prepare Colby to meet Lady Elizabeth. In oblique conversation the two men reveal that a secret—not yet divulged—about Colby's identity may complicate the impending meeting. They worry that Lady Elizabeth might be unhappily reminded of her own child, who was placed in the care of someone with whom she long ago lost touch, and they hope she will eventually want to adopt Colby. Finally, they reveal that Colby is, in fact, Sir Claude's own son.

Colby enters, nervously unsure about his meeting with Lady Elizabeth and alarmed by what he has learned about her from B. Kaghan. Eggerson advises him to disregard this, as Lady Elizabeth had been put off by Kaghan's rough libertine demeanour. Colby finds Kaghan affable, but Eggerson advises that he must be a different kind of character to win over Lady Elizabeth: he suggests that Colby play up his musical aptitude and present himself as a man of culture.

Kaghan enters with Lucasta Angel, who boisterously banters about being broke and losing her job through incompetence. She tells Colby, flirtingly, that taking care of her will be one of his responsibilities as clerk; Kaghan, announcing himself to be Lucasta's fiancé, promises to protect Colby from her and warns of her potential to connive. After Lucasta leaves, Eggerson tells Colby she is a ward of Sir Claude's: a friend's daughter. When Colby remarks on Lucasta's eccentricities, Eggerson tries to prepare him for even more extreme oddness and absent-mindedness on the part of Lady Elizabeth. At this moment, Lady Elizabeth herself enters, spoiling Eggerson's careful plans to prepare her for the new order of things. As explanations are hurriedly offered to explain Colby's presence, Lady Elizabeth easily accepts the notion that hiring him was her own idea and takes him under her wing, instructing that he will serve her as well as her husband.

Sir Claude, extolling the virtue of pragmatically adapting to circumstance, is eager to arrange a permanently stable household in which Colby will be recognized as their son and heir; Colby, too, hopes to put deceptions behind him. He is exhilarated, though sometimes also repelled, at the thought of becoming another character as conceived by Sir Claude. His disappointment in a musical career leads Sir Claude to speak of his own letdown: he had wanted to be a potter—to create real substantial form; his father, though, pushed him into the family's financial concern. Sir Claude promises to get Colby a good piano, encouraging him to follow his musical inclinations for his own satisfatction: to be happy as a second-rate musician, comforted by engaging even imperfectly in an real art form; Sir Claude's father had denied him this.

Colby is playing for Lucasta—the first time he has ever performed for anyone—and educating her about music and culture as Act two opens in the young man's flat. They become more intimately acquainted as they explore their insecurities, poses, and private desires. They try to discover their inner worlds, or secret gardens, of content, and ways of sharing those worlds and understanding other people. Lucasta tells Colby the common rumor about her—that she was once Sir Claude's mistress—is untrue; she is his daughter by an extramarital affair. Colby's face registers shock, because he believes Lucasta is his sister. He cannot divulge this secret, though, so Lucasta assumes he is scandalized by her illegitimacy and furiously withdraws from their newly-formed intimacy, retreating into Kaghan's care and affection.

Kaghan reveals that he was a foundling, and thus feels compelled to establish a respectable and successful reputation for himself. He and Lucasta, similarly untethered in the world, cling to each other for support. As they depart Lady Elizabeth enters to check on how Colby is getting settled and to advise him against becoming too familiar with Lucasta and Kaghan, whom she labels materialistic and vulgar—not his type. Colby wonders what is his type; Lady Elizabeth lauds his good breeding, intellect, and spirituality. They discuss the problems of one's family and agree that family is hostile to the development of individuality.

When Colby mentions the aunt, Mrs. Guzzard, who raised him in Teddington, Lady Elizabeth excitedly recalls a familiar note. After interrogating

Colby, she decides he is her lost child. The names "Guzzard" and "Teddington" had eluded her, but now she remembers that Mrs. Guzzard was the woman to whom her son (born before her marriage, and fathered by the man who was to become her husband, but was killed in Africa soon after the child's birth) had been entrusted.

Sir Claude rejects the discovery as merely coincidental or wishful thinking, and reveals to his wife that Colby is actually his own son. He had never told Lady Elizabeth about him because, he explains, it seemed fair to him that they should each have one misfortune in their past—Lucasta for him, the lost child for her; telling her about Colby, he worried, would make her wonder how many other children he had had. Lady Elizabeth, though, insists Colby is her child, and suggests that Mrs. Guzzard (who told Sir Claude Colby was her sister's child, fathered by Sir Claude) deceived him. Colby is left numb by this conversation: having lived without parents as a child, he feels indifferent about knowing his parentage—the emptiness he experienced can never be filled. Yet while Colby had been prepared to accept the fiction that was being contrived (that is, that the Mulhammers would become his parents), he is unwilling to accept the puzzling mixture of fact and fiction that has now been created; thus, he is determined to find Mrs. Guzzard and discover the truth.

Act three opens with Sir Claude preparing his library for Mrs. Guzzard's arrival and the resolution of the mysteries. Lady Elizabeth tells her husband she hopes Colby turns out to be his son, because such facts are more important to him than to her. Sir Claude disputes that: while he has tried to believe in facts, as his father had, he now realizes he had ignored the only essential fact in his life, wanting to be a potter, which he now shares with his wife for the first time. The admission charms Lady Elizabeth, who comments how strange it is that she should have lived with him for so long without knowing this; both admit the folly of taking things for granted, and Lady Elizabeth divulges her own secret desire: to have inspired an artist.

Eggerson prepares for an interrogation, suggesting the possibility that Mrs. Guzzard had raised two children: one Sir Claude's, the other Lady Elizabeth's. Lucasta interrupts the proceedings to announce that she has finally decided to marry Kaghan—not because Sir Claude has promoted this, but because she now realizes she wants to do it. She is told that Colby is her half-brother, and understands his shock when she divulged her secret earlier. She is thankful to Colby for having made her realize how much she wanted to be with Kaghan and sees Colby as comfortably isolated in his own world.

When Mrs. Guzzard arrives, Eggerson confronts her with the quandary at hand. The woman admits she had indeed once taken in another child, of unknown parentage, but had to give him up when support payments stopped because the father died without having made contingency plans for his child's continued care. That child (whom Lady Elizabeth is sure belonged to her, due to the correlations between Mrs. Guzzard's account and her own memories) was then given to childless neighbors named Kaghan.

Lady Elizabeth has thus found her son, in the person of a character she had denounced as vulgar. Kaghan is brought in to confirm this account. Though he is satisfied with Mrs. Kaghan as his mother, he accepts his biological mother as Aunt Elizabeth; she plans to invite Kaghan's adoptive parents for dinner, and takes charge of her son's impending wedding. Kaghan, too, is willing to adapt himself to the new set of facts and glad to have solved the mystery of having been a foundling.

Colby is relieved to know the truth but, as he had stated earlier, these facts have no inherent importance because the more important fact that he grew up without a mother or father remains paramount. He wishes his father could have turned out to be someone now dead and obscure—someone ordinary, whose image Colby could fashion for himself, thus legitimizing his own still-unsatisfying genesis. In a final denouement, Mrs. Guzzard grants his wish: she reveals that his father is not Sir Claude, but a dead man who had been a disappointed musician; and that she, whom he had thought of as his aunt, is in fact his mother. Her sister, whom Sir Claude believed had borne their child, died before giving birth; Mrs. Guzzard had deceived Sir Claude for 25 years, she states, because he wanted to believe that the child was his and his financial support made the difference in Colby's success or failure.

Colby believes Mrs. Guzzard and Sir Claude reconciles himself to accepting this decision, thus losing the man he had thought of as his son. Despite their mutual friendship, Colby is determined to leave Sir Claude because he is unwilling to continue living in a world of deception and confusion; he sets off to accomplish his real desire of becoming a church organist. Eggerson announces such a vacancy in his own rural parish, which excites Colby. Eggerson warns that the stipend is minimal, and the position may be a stepping stone to another vocation—perhaps a religious calling. Colby eagerly sets off for the country, under Eggerson's surrogate paternity, while the rest are left pondering their mistake: wanting Colby to be something he wasn't. Lady Elizabeth enjoins her husband to try to understand the children remaining to them, and finally a newly-formed family—the Mulhammers, Kaghan, and Lucasta—seems prepared to support and live with each other.

Production History

The play's premiere was 25 August 1953 at the Royal Lyceum Theatre, Edinburgh, as part of the Edinburgh International Festival. E. Martin Browne directed the production, which was presented by Henry Sherek. Hutchinson Scott was the designer: he created rooms that were not totally enclosed, but rather a set that would "allow scope for, so to speak, a look through or around the rooms in which the action takes place," Browne explains—"a library round which one could see a mysterious depth of shadow, and a mews-flat over the roof of which one could see the evening sky" (C277, 287). Henry Donald describes the two sets as "ingeniously contrasted. The one is dignified and formal; the other has planes and perspectives slightly but significantly out of true" (R173).

The cast featured Paul Rogers as Sir Claude Mulhammer, Denholm Elliott as Colby Simpkins, Isabel Jeans as Lady Elizabeth Mulhammer, Margaret Leighton (who had played Celia in the 1950 London run of *The Cocktail Party*) as Lucasta Angel, Peter Jones as B. Kaghan, Alan Webb as Eggerson, and Alison Leggatt (Lavinia in the 1950 London run of *The Cocktail Party*) as Mrs. Guzzard; it ran for twelve performances, and then for a week at Newcastle-on-Tyne's Theatre Royal. To stimulate interest in the play, part of an Edinburgh performance was televised in England.

On 16 September 1953 the play opened at London's Lyric Theatre with the Edinburgh cast. After 259 performances the play moved for an additional four weeks to the Duke of York's Theatre.

Robert Speaight (who created the role of Becket in *Murder in the Cathedral*) replaced Paul Rogers as Sir Claude when the play left London in 1954, touring (in English, but titled *Le Secrétaire Particulier*) to the Théâtre des Nations for the First International Festival of Dramatic Art of Paris, and later to Dublin's Olympia Theatre. Of that role he writes, "I did not greatly enjoy acting in *The Confidential Clerk*. I had read it in manuscript and seen it on the stage, but even there, in spite of a brilliant cast, it seemed to me no more than a dramatic exercise on five fingers. Distinguished but dry, it hovered uneasily between prophecy and farce. I was less disturbed by the disappearance of the poetry than I was disappointed by the stiffness of the prose. Except for a single scene with the young man he believes to be his son, Sir Claude Mulhammer is not a particularly good part" (C386, 76).

Leggatt, writing of her role as Mrs. Guzzard, remembers asking Eliot for some guidance for the part. "'She is a mixture of Pallas Athene and a suburban housewife,' Mr. Eliot told me!" (C339, 79).

The New York production was led by Sherek in association with Producers Theatre. (Sherek had announced earlier that the play would open in New York immediately after its Edinburgh debut, as *The Cocktail Party* had done, but Eliot immediately issued a statement contradicting him, insisting on a London opening first.) It opened on 11 February 1954 at the Morosco Theatre (after previews at New Haven's Shubert Theatre, Boston's Colonial Theatre, and Washington's National Theatre) where it ran for 117 shows, starring Claude Rains as Sir Claude, Douglas Watson as Colby, Ina Claire as Lady Elizabeth, Joan Greenwood as Lucasta, Richard Newton as B. Kaghan, Newton Blick as Eggerson, and Aline MacMahon as Mrs. Guzzard. Settings and costumes were by Paul Morrison.

Blick and Greenwood were British citizens, but the rest of the cast had to be American due to an Actors' Equity ruling the previous spring—an outgrowth of high unemployment among New York's actors—prohibiting more than 40 percent foreign actors in any production. The company thus assembled, Browne writes, presented the difficulty of embodying varying dramatic styles and traditions that had to be melded. Sherek had appealed to Equity for permission to stage the play with an all-British company, and threatened not to present the play on Broadway if he were refused his request. (Exceptions to the ruling were allowed for unit companies, like the English Old Vic, and "companies of special character.") When permission for an exemption was denied and the play was scheduled with a cast of mixed nationals, Sherek called the play the first victim of Equity's ruling; he felt that the mixture of English and American accents damaged the play's effect. The Broadway cast—even the British Greenwood—spoke the word "clerk" with the American pronunciation, to rhyme with "perk," rather than, as the British pronounce it, to rhyme with "park."

The producer refers to another difficulty in the Broadway production: hostility between Claire and Rains. "From the first day of rehearsals they were at each other's throats" (C378, 192).

On 23 May 1954 Lucille Lortel's White Barn Theatre in Westport, Conn., presented a reading of the *Ion* of Euripides followed by the same cast performing the last act of *The Confidential Clerk*; Bill Butler was the director.

In the 1954-55 season, German productions of the play—*Der Privatsekretär*—were given at the Dusseldorf Schauspielhaus and the Zurich Schauspielhaus. In England, the Birmingham Repertory Company presented the play in 1955. The Provincetown (Mass.) Players gave a production in 1959. College productions included performances at Montana State University in 1958; at Kenyon College in 1958; and at San Jose State College in 1959.

In November 1976 the London Academy of Music and Dramatic Art (LAMDA) presented the play starring Hal Ross as Sir Claude and Elizabeth Richardson as Lady Elizabeth.

Critical Overview

Performance Reviews

Reviewing the Edinburgh premiere in the *New York Times* W. A. Darlington writes, "From the point of view of technical achievement *The Confidential Clerk* is his best play. Not, let it be clearly stated, his most important play. It is a light comedy and though its undertones are deep they remain undertones. . . . [it] is contrived with masterly skill. Mr. Eliot brings off that miracle which only dramatists of the highest class can work—he takes a hackneyed and unreal theatrical situation such as no merely average writer could hope to get away with and makes us accept it as a basis for serious thought" (R172).

J. G. Weightman, in *Twentieth Century*, finds the play's content of dubious quality. After building a careful momentum through the first two acts, in the final act "Eliot adopts the clumsy solution of bringing in a new character to facilitate the denouement and all seven sit down to argue the matter out, without remarkable wit or any glimmer of poetry." The play "is embarrassingly full of echoes of other dramatists, including Wilde and Shaw; they, belonging to the late nineteenth century, had a grand manner, which allowed them to get away with the preposterous; Mr. Eliot . . . is not grand . . . most of the time he rises to nothing more than resigned whimsey, which irritates, because we expect something better" (R184).

Henry Donald, also writing of the Edinburgh premiere in *The Spectator*, objects to "a maddening, broken-backed play, which, with every contrivance of art and poetry, raises the highest expectations and then, perversely, fails to fulfill them"; he lambasts Eliot's failure to resolve the engaging themes "of music and craftsmanship, of loneliness, of secret gardens, of God" that are presented early in the play, and the tedious predictability of the interwoven parentage plots (R173).

T. C. Worsley, though, in the *New Statesman*, discounts the importance of these contrivances and thus finds the play more palatable: "The clue to the plot is not with the rather Gilbertian revelations of paternal and maternal mix-ups. It is not a question of who we are, but of what we choose to be." Worsley is one of the reviewers whose admiration for Eliot's innovation and expertise persists into the 1950s: "Each work is for him . . . an exploration in technique. *The Confidential Clerk* explores new territory and uses methods in some ways quite different from anything that has gone before, and yet it is able to rivet the attention of ordinary theatre audiences who could not—and should not—be expected to be interested in questions of technique" (R185).

"From the very opening of the play we feel we are on sure ground," Worsley writes, characterizing more appreciatively—as a captivating enigma—what some other critics called an absence of focus. "Yet it is a very odd sort of sure ground, this of Mr. Eliot's. It is by no means the conventional sure ground of problems posed and solutions neatly found for them. On the contrary, we are never quite sure what the problems really are; and as for the solutions, they none of them seem to us to fit at all. Why then we should be content to follow so fumbling and faltering a guide is a mystery. But so it is. His authority is such that he compels us along."

As Lady Elizabeth in the Edinburgh production, Jeans is "brilliantly funny," Worsley reports, "but she would have had to forgo some of her best laughs if she were to modulate properly into the seriousness that sometimes seems called for." Leighton plays Lucasta's second act scene with Colby "with an exquisite pathos; it brings tears to the eyes." "Sir Claude is comparatively straightforward . . . and Mr. Paul Rogers just about achieves him." As Eggerson, Webb is "a sweet, rather sugary, good old man," and Jones plays Kaghan giving "a life-like lightning sketch of the bounder with a good heart." Playing Colby, "Denholm Elliott has to be diffident and puzzled and charming; and so he is." Weightman offers a provocative appraisal of Elliott's acting (whether accurate or fanciful): he "achieves the miracle of looking, moving, and sounding exactly like a young Mr. T. S. Eliot" (R184).

Variety writes highly of the Edinburgh premiere from the commercial point of view: "This shapes up as worthwhile boxoffice for both London and New York. . . . Eliot emerges with that twist essential to the best of comedies. Here is something more lightweight than *Cocktail Party*, and more popular in its approach plus more plot." The review notes the "marquee value of the T S. Eliot name being a help" (R186). Again, the month before the Broadway debut, *Variety* predicts a strong run: "*Confidential Clerk* will probably register on Broadway because of the four-star combination of the infectious personal appeal of Ina Claire, acting skill of Claude Rains, physical attractiveness and stage presence of Joan Greenwood, and provocative writing of T. S. Eliot" (R187).

In 1954, many American reviewers found the play refreshingly accessible and similar to other contemporary Broadway fare: it is "more lucid and less pretentious" than *The Cocktail Party*, writes William Hawkins in the New York *World-Telegram and Sun* (R177). John Chapman, in the New York *Daily News*, expresses some misgivings of Eliot's American audience, which doubted "if they have the cerebral capacity to understand what the hell Eliot may be driving at," but is relieved to find the play comprehensible and "no more profound than a musical comedy libretto or a fairy tale" (R170). In the *Daily Mirror* Robert Coleman calls the play "the brightest and easiest to understand of all T. S. Eliot's plays" (R171).

John McClain, in the New York *Journal American*, complains of unfulfilling poetry and empty content. "Much of Mr. Eliot's poetry is lost, long passages are devoted to abstruse philosophy and one might easily conclude that never before had so many words been devoted to so little" (R182). Similarly, Richard Watts, Jr., in the New York *Post*, writes that the play "would be helped considerably if some of the garrulousness were sternly cut from it. This assuredly woudn't hurt the author's famous prose-like verse, because there is little sign here of the poetic touch" (R183). Claire—a "most beloved comedienne of the sophisticated audience," Browne writes (C277, 291)—was returning to Broadway after a seven-year absence, and Watts calls her performance the play's redeeming feature: "It is, I think, chiefly worth seeing because it brings Ina Claire back to the stage in a good part."

In the *New York Times* Brooks Atkinson writes, "Since T. S. Eliot is the grand panjandrum of modern letters, everyone expects another masterpiece from him. *The Confidential Clerk* . . . represents a deliberate attempt to be ordinary. Unfortunately, Mr. Eliot has succeeded." The play's blandness, mildness, and indirection represent "a repudiation of his own genius" (R164).

Walter Kerr, in the New York *Herald Tribune*, simply finds the play's farce wanting: it "is nowhere near as funny as you may have heard. It has its small, wry humors, its wan and rather rueful witticisms," but the "mockery is never emphatic enough, or whole-hearted enough, for sustained mirth"; and, because the play presents itself (albeit unsuccessfully) as a farce, Kerr continues, its more serious overtones cannot succeed (R180). The critic Bonamy Dobrée, though, wholly disagrees: for him, the play's "theatrical virtuosity" is that "Eliot has made a serious thing out of a farce. Or, from another angle, the originality of the play consists in its being a drastic pushing forward of the old critical comedy which, by making us laugh at and criticize our neighbors, aimed at making us see ourselves as others see us" (C237, 122).

In *Partisan Review*, Saul Bellow complains of the play, "It cost the play-goer six bucks to see this one. Of course it is not Mr. Eliot's fault that un-scrupulous Broadway people produce his plays, but I did expect to learn, at this price, what ways lie open to a man who has emerged from the dark night of the soul. I was sorely disappointed. *The Confidential Clerk* is Mr. Eliot's version of *The Importance of Being Earnest*, the element of farce removed, replaced with something more intellectual. . . . It remains a comedy. Yet there is very little laughter in it. The play is pervaded by a sort of emotional albinism hard to characterize" (R166, 313-14).

Hawkins captures details of the cast's performance: Claire's (whom Haw-kins, like Watts, sees as the dominant star) as Lady Elizabeth is one "of pure brilliance. Nobody in this country, and probably anywhere, has so understood the double plane on which Eliot writes. Miss Claire acts at a pitch of come-dy, but in a mood of pathos. She has such control of her role and her audi-ence, that you feel yourself being spiritually garroted when she does not choose for you to laugh." Rains, as Sir Claude, is "wistful and indulgent, but terribly anxious. . . . It is a sturdy, almost shy performance until despair illuminates the character in the end." Playing Eggerson, Blick "has a mellow haughtiness which peculiarly suits the play." MacMahon, as Mrs. Guzzard, is "something of a seeress"; Newton, as Kaghan, is "blustery." As Lucasta, Greenwood "plays in a voice that sounds like Lynn Fontanne imitating Carol Channing, and with a brittle style that is artificial but always purposeful. She is felinely captivating" (R177). Kerr adds of Greenwood's performance: she "is really an enchanted frog, just up from the lily-pond, and I love her" (R180).

Scholarly Response

Gerald Weales, contrasting this play with Eliot's previous one, finds that it "operates without the supernatural framework of *The Cocktail Par-ty*. . . . the action is not so much metaphysical as it is metaphorical" (C394, 202). Carol H. Smith further explains that Eliot intentionally did away with such "divine agents" as the Guardians from his previously play: "In *The Confidential Clerk* divine interruptions were to be eliminated and instead the work of communicating the religious meanings was to be handled entirely by the symbolic meanings of the surface events. High comedy lent itself to this method because in the artificiality and refinement of its dramatic world the ordered flatness which Eliot had long admired but had so far failed to achieve could be used to create a fable which would be read on two levels. . . . The dual meanings of Eggerson's garden and Colby's musical nature, as well as the latter's search for his true parentage, are examples. . . . Eliot took certain existing aspects of the high-comedy tradition and used them to point up his own set of spiritual meanings. He used the theme of the foundling child to express the Christian implications of the search for identity by insisting that discovering one's identity depends on discovering one's self to be a child of the heavenly Father" (C382, 187-88).

The play is Eliot's most mature confrontation of existentialism, writes Davis D. McElroy: his "treatment of the interesting problem of establishing the identity of the self"; Colby "is preoccupied throughout the work with the question Who am I? and What kind of a person am I supposed to be?" (C348, 44-45). Colby confronts this theme forthrightly "when he feels that he is being accused by the ghost of his true self, the disappointed musician," and "is forced to realize that he is not living an authentic existence—in other words that he is really, and not merely conventionally, illegitimate" (46). Eliot, like the Greek dramatists on whom he modeled his plays, realizes that all knowledge begins with self-knowledge; by the conclusion of the play, "Colby rejects his inauthentic existence as Sir Claude's natural son and secretary, and announces his legitimacy," his determination to become a musician (47).

C. L. Barber is wary of "an almost impossibly far-fetched plot"; while "the plots of many fine plays seem impossibly complicated . . . and often involve situations which are as out of the ordinary as all these illegitimate and mislaid children," the ultimate question is "whether plot pays off in dramatic meaning. Eliot's handling of his story certainly overloads the play with retrospective explanation. And there is too little relation between the quality of the Mulhammers' life in the present, where we see them, and the events recovered from their pasts. . . . But if the machinery of who's who is cumbersome, there is nevertheless a real and effective action in the play" (C260, 216).

Many critics, like Nicholas Brooke, call *The Confidential Clerk* a good play but a disappointment in terms of what one might expect of Eliot. Brooke cites the depiction of Sir Claude: "at the end of the play, Sir Claude's agony is entirely meaningless, but by its insistent presence precludes any chance there might have been that Colby's vocation could seem to matter." (Lady Elizabeth is "reduced . . . to the level of her husband, and spends the last act vaguely hoping that she and Claude will understand each other better in future.") Sir Claude's character, Brooke feels, has been made consummately theatrical: neat, symmetrical, melodramatic—he identifies "theatrical" as meaning "the kind of play at which Mr. Terrence Rattigan excels." "The effect that such trivial emotions must have on the significant ideas of the play . . . [is that] trivial emotions cannot be equated on any terms with significant feeling and so resist any valuable comment whatever." If writing is "theatrical," Brooke insists, "it does not admit of mixture with other genres," thus can be nothing but conventionally and predictably theatrical; the play "makes a good evening in the theatre, but it makes a depressing one afterwards. [Eliot's] long search for poetic drama seems to have led only to the discovering how to write a successful West-end play; a remarkable achievement indeed, but a bitterly disappointing one" (R167, 70). Eric Salmon, similarly, calls all of Eliot's last three plays curious works "that outwardly pretended to be drawing-room comedies . . . but inwardly wished themselves other and better" (C373, 83).

And Raymond Williams, in *Drama from Ibsen to Brecht*, writes that the play "represented a decadence in manner which was, in its way, startling. 'If one wanted to say something serious nowadays it was easier to say it in comedy,' Eliot remarked on its production. But though the form of this remark is an arguable critical truth, its content is a surrender to a particular social mode: that West End sense of humour which is supposed to be a saving grace. Since grace had meant something, in Eliot, this parody of a play was especially shocking. In any other circumstances, its slightness would leave it unnoticed" (C399, 194).

Richard Findlater finds the play not completely successful, but nevertheless solid dramatic fare: "the formalized plot is resolutely thick . . . the characters have theatrical substance, and the situations are sprung with deliberate precision . . . the note of portentous piety, hitherto inseparable from Mr. Eliot's plays, is virtually inaudible; and the verse is even more dextrously presented as eloquently colloquial prose" (C296, 311). Its failures, he feels, are its inability "to resolve the action on both its planes," that is, as a farce and as religious drama; and also to achieve "the direct illumination of experience with the intensity of high drama" (315).

Yet Helen Gardner calls the play not only a dramatic success but an unqualified advance in Eliot's oeuvre: it "has a unity which Mr. Eliot has not achieved before in a play. No single one of the characters has a monopoly of wisdom or virtue, and no character exists simply to be disguised or guyed. Each in his own way has glimpses of the truth and each is capable of suffering, because capable of love. . . . The element of fantasy, necessary if comedy is to rise above being a mere transcript of daily life and reach towards general truth, is not, as in *The Cocktail Party*, imposed upon a particular story by the addition of extraneous characters. It is the plot itself" (R174, 373-74). Gardner—an acclaimed scholar of *Four Quartets*—seems to see the same virtues in this play as in Eliot's last major poems: a kind of mature resolution of the moral and social issues that had been unsatisfyingly confronted in the earlier work; and a more workable, equitable, tranquil vision of the world—a vision strengthened by integrity, rather than racked by doubt or fragmentation—that surrounds the artist.

Katherine J. Worth, too, sees an advance in the play: an anticipation of themes that will become more important in drama of the next decade. *The Confidential Clerk* along with *The Cocktail Party* and *The Elder Statesman* "explore subjects that fascinate the modern theatre—role playing, the search for identity—with techniques that foreshadow those of Albee and Pinter" (C404, 55). She argues that Eliot "rediscovered farce . . . and gave it a new, Pirandellian look that propelled it well into the future. Joe Orton is one of his (unlikely) successors in this sphere. . . . the comic losing and finding of parents leads into genuinely disorienting effects and the precariousness of identity becomes an experience rather than a theme. The farcical structure sets the characters free to express their sense of being 'characters' in a spontaneous, direct way. B. Kaghan can come on saying 'Enter B. Kaghan.' Colby can be given a choice of identities: a selection from a number of possible parents and the roles that would be their legacy" (65).

Combatting judgments such as William Becker's of "very anaemic dramatism" and Saul Bellow's of "emotional albinism," Denis Donoghue staunchly defends the play as being full of vigor and strength. He cites John Crowe Ransom's critique that Eliot's early work is full of incongruous juxtapositions and discords but lacks a consistent stamina, and asserts that with this play "it is precisely by sustaining the chosen tone" that his effect is obtained (C290, 139). Donoghue finds each of Eliot's successive plays an improvement over its predecessor; his writing "has been consistently directed toward a greater range of experessiveness, greater precision, and, above all, a finer adjustment of verbal weight" (140).

The fact that the play is "neither odd nor obscure" represents a dramatic maturation on Eliot's part, writes R. T. Davies. "There is no character in this new play who is more than he seems. . . . This is the sort of straight play which was crystallizing out in *The Cocktail Party*. . . . Eliot has come to terms with us, and is no longer, I felt, putting one over on us, no longer, perhaps, pitching the note higher than we can reach" (C236, 411). The spiritual tenor, Davies continues, is less obtrusive than in the earlier plays: "No one should feel he is being got at, for at no point is the play in any respect a piece of Christian propaganda. . . . There are some few references to things religious and some fewer to things Christian," references which are "quietly illuminating" (413).

The "grab bag of parents and children on which the plot swings," writes Robert A. Colby, "is obviously Eliot's means of dramatizing the larger issue of alienation and kinship among human beings in general. . . . Eliot seems in his latest play to have moved the closest he has come so far to parable and allegory. The flesh-and-blood actuality of most of his characters conceals the fact that they are intended to be representative as well as individual. And unless one is prepared for this dual functioning of the characters, the coincidences and ingenious turns of plot are likely to seem like just so many tricky contrivances" (C235, 792-93).

One indication that Eliot is trying to encompass a large social condition, Colby continues, "lies in the unprecedented variety of the characters—in the variety, that is to say, of social strata represented. Apart from minor servant characters, *The Family Reunion* and *The Cocktail Party* are each peopled by homogenous groups, the 'upper crust' in the first play, the upper middle class in the second. *Sweeney Agonistes* is Eliot's single excursion into the opposite end of the social scale. In *The Confidential Clerk* some attempt is made at a vertical cross-section, from Sir Claude and Lady Elizabeth (with the implication that she comes from an even higher-class family than her husband), to Eggerson, the secure, unpretentious middle-class clerk, to the shabbily genteel Mrs. Guzzard, to perhaps Eliot's most engaging 'rough diamond,' the cockney B. Kaghan, and Lucasta, who with all Sir Claude's attempts to turn her into a 'lady' makes no attempt to conceal her low-life childhood" (793).

Adding to the width of the spectrum, there is "more of a sense than is usual with Eliot of the interaction of city and country. Sir Claude and Lady Elizabeth are obviously urban; Mrs. Guzzard is suburban. B. Kaghan has left the country to make his fortune in the city, whereas Eggerson habitually flees the city where he makes his living for the comfort and quiet of his cottage and patch" (794). Amid the variety of this spectrum Colby is in between, pulled in numerous different directions.

The Confidential Clerk represents the first time Eliot "depicts the birth of love," writes John Middleton Murry; but he asserts that Eliot is no more receptive to the possibility of love being enduring or meaningfully possible than when he wrote *The Waste Land*, "saturated with a scepticism of love, and a nausea of physical sex" (C357, 188). Thus in this play, having depicted an incipient love, "he has to spend a good deal of effort on destroying the possibility of love that he has created" with contrived, artificial complications and resolutions. "But he notably fails to make this withering of a nascent love inherently convincing. It almost shocks by its artificiality. It appears not to arise from anything in the characters themselves, nor from insuperable circumstance, but to be quite arbitrary" (183); in fact, Murry argues, love founders because of Eliot's occlusion rather than the play's logical development.

Joyce M. Holland sees a dichotomy between Kaghan's and Colby's sensibilities. Following St. Paul's admonition in Ephesians, "man stands as a symbol of reason and woman of emotion. Such a concept seems to be implicit in the relationship of Colby and Kaghan, for when Colby finds his true father—and his spiritual father in Eggerson—Kaghan finds his mother. Colby, as a 'son of man,' takes the path of holy isolation, while B. Kaghan remains, in a way, to take his place. It has been noted that B.'s name—Barnabas—means 'child of consolation.' He is the son of woman, and love and consolation are his province" (C320, 157). Kaghan's humanity and Colby's divinity combine to form a total dramatic unity.

Critics generally find the verse rather unpoetic: even Browne admits, "the poetry is not in the words but in the conception and the characterisation. There are very few moments at which one is aware of Eliot as the maker of immortal phrases. . . . The only time when Eliot the poet is consciously recalled is in the scene between Colby and Lucasta in Act Two" (C277, 281). Grover Smith writes, "The characters in *The Confidential Clerk*, where Eliot sacrificed poetry even more ruthlessly than in *The Cocktail Party*, speak lines which are verse in typography but prose in cadence" (C383, 228). David E. Jones writes that the play "does belong to the realm of poetic drama, if only by the fineness with which it delineates feeling, but perhaps it is only just across the border from prose" (C325, 178). And Ivor Brown's review of the Edinburgh performance attests to the fact that the effect on the audience was not strikingly poetic: "I am informed that this play like the previous Eliot plays was written in verse. But nobody need be frightened by that for the simple reason that they will not notice it. When the piece is printed for publication no doubt the text will be chopped to resemble poetry, but no poetic diction or poetic melody is discernible in the lines as spoken by the cast" (R168, 288). Donoghue, though, lauds the language as being especially well-suited to drama because it is a complete break with poetry, containing "no trace of anonymous or autonomous verse," as he characterizes Eliot's poetic diction (C290, 156).

Textual Notes and Influences

The *Ion* of Euripides—the story of a foundling hero raised in ignorance of his exalted lineage—contributed the germ of the story, Eliot revealed; Grover Smith explores how Eliot's interpretation of the Greek play is influenced by A. W. Verrall's nineteenth-century rationalistic interpretation: that Hermes and Athena are untrustworthy frauds and Ion is not really the son of Apollo or Creusa, but of Xuthus. Eliot "arranged his drama so that it might be read by Verrall's methods. That is, he let the resolution depend on imperfect evidence and even on possible trickery by certain of the characters" (C383, 240). Eliot was familiar with H. D.'s 1937 translation of the *Ion*.

Eggerson "was based on a real-life clerk, a Mr. McKnight who had been Eliot's first colleague at Lloyds Bank," Lyndall Gordon writes (C309, 225). Noting that the play's hero is "a man in search of identity, abjuring father, mother . . . so that he might fulfill a devotion to God alone," she asserts an autobiographical connection to Eliot, who told Mary Trevelyan soon after finishing the play that "a man who has not known his parents is fortunate, and that his own parents had seemed distant, like 'ancestors'" (239). John D. Mitchell, too, in his psychoanalysis of the play, calls it an "unconscious striving . . . to resolve repressed inner conflict" (C239, 263). Colby's quest to discover a place where he belongs and is accepted, Mitchell writes, dramatizes Eliot's own longing for such *gemeinschaft* as a consequence of his exile from America.

Browne calls the play "the best constructed of all the modern plays: it builds steadily (after a slow opening) to a last act which is taut and full of good surprises, and in the theatre, with a very fine team of actors, it got a warm response. Yet it has been almost forgotten [since its debut]. . . . I think this is partly because of its very success in terms of the theatre it was written for. By 1953, the wind of change was blowing through our drama . . . breeding dissatisfaction with the conventions of the upper-middle-class play which had dominated our stage for so long" (C280, 131).

Eliot agreed with Browne's assessment about the play's construction in a 1959 *Paris Review* interview, but regretted that, because the play was so well constructed, some people took it as a farce (P67, 61). He explained that because some people had complained that the third act of *The Cocktail Party* was merely an epilogue, he wanted fresh events to occur in the final act of this play (60).

Seán Lucy elaborates on the play's structure: Eliot "was determined that in its construction, the play should not share the weaknesses of its predecessors. The result of this concentration [on plot] was a play of classical proportions: Act I is exposition and statement of theme; Act II is complication and crisis; Act III is climax, revolution and solution. Within this framework the action moves purposefully and surprisingly, holding the attention of an audience with complete control" (C342, 199).

Publishing History

Faber & Faber published *The Confidential Clerk* in March 1954, as did Harcourt. The play was reprinted in *Collected Plays* (London: Faber & Faber, 1962). In America, the printed version of the play made the *New York Times* best-seller list—the first play to do so since *The Cocktail Party*, which by 1954 had sold 60,000 copies.

The Elder Statesman

Characters

Monica Claverton-Ferry. Charles Hemington. Lambert. Lord Claverton. Federico Gomez. Mrs. Piggott. Mrs. Carghill. Michael Claverton-Ferry.

Synopsis

In Lord Claverton's drawing room his daughter Monica banters with her suitor, Charles, who finally wins an admission that she reciprocates his love for her. Claverton poses an obstacle to marriage, though: Charles feels he is determined to keep Monica to himself; Monica feels committed to care for him in a convalescent home he is to enter, temporarily leaving Charles. Her father, Monica explains, is terrified of being alone, and also of being exposed to strangers; while his public persona was one of strength, his private nature is more fragile. Claverton is seriously ill, though he does not know this himself.

Claverton enters, thumbing through his empty engagement book and realizing that at 60 his energetic life is wearing down; he fears the prospect of future emptiness, lethargically waiting for death. Monica and Charles remind him of the glorious testimonials he received upon retirement and the newspaper articles predicting he would continue to serve as a sagacious elder statesman. Claverton dismisses all that as meaningless rhetoric; in actuality, those who are still active would shun him as a ghost.

A visitor described as foreign-looking sends up a note asking to be seen; the man who called himself Señor Gomez enters, but turns out to be an old Oxford classmate, Fred Culverwell (who notes that his host, too, has changed names, from Dick Ferry to Claverton-Ferry—taking his wife's name—and then Lord Claverton, as he climbed the social ladder). Gomez left England after serving a jail sentence for embezzling and forgery, and has made himself into a "respectable" citizen, through dubious means, in the Central American republic of San Marco.

Gomez says he has come to see Claverton because he is the only old friend he can trust. Feeling lonely and homesick, Gomez has returned to secure Claverton's acceptance, and thus a link to what he calls reality. At Oxford, Gomez explains, a bond arose between them as he fell under Dick Ferry's influence. Gomez accuses Claverton of having aroused in him, as a young unknowing scholarship boy, the tastes that led to his crimes. Claverton reminds Gomez that he came to his assistance after his release from jail, but Gomez claims that was only to get rid of him.

Gomez has been following Claverton's career closely and suspects some mystery behind his retirement from a successful political career at 50, and from an important financial post at 60. Though Claverton defends himself, asserting that he was never accused of making a mistake, Gomez counters that in the upper echelons of the English power structure mistakes are anonymous; people are allowed to withdraw quietly, citing health reasons, as Claverton has done.

Gomez considers himself a worldly success, he announces, though in another sense he is, like his old friend, a failure because his success is based on self-deceptions and pretense. Elucidating details about the bond between them, Gomez recalls a moonlit Oxford night when Claverton drove on after hitting an old man in the road; Gomez later gave evidence that saved Claverton from punishment. Claverton fears Gomez will sell the story to a Sunday newspaper or try to extort money; but Gomez retorts that his secret will remain safe, and that the only thing he might do if not appeased is leak the story to a few members of Claverton's social circle—which would puncture the pretense of Claverton's "success." All he demands is Claverton's friendship: to be dignified as a member of an aristocratic circle, and to spend a great deal of time in his company recreating the friendship they had had years earlier at Oxford.

Claverton is settling into a calm routine at the rest home, Badgley Court, as Act two opens, though he fears that the matron, a busybody named Mrs. Piggott, threatens his privacy. Another resident, Mrs. Carghill, approaches Claverton, disappointed that he does not remember her from their youth. Like Claverton and Gomez she had a different name then, Maisie Batterson, and also the stage name of Maisie Montjoy. She had been in love with Dick Ferry at Oxford. Like Gomez, she afflicts him with memories, forcing him to remember their liaison: she had started an action against him for breach of promise, though it had been settled out of court (expensively) to avoid damaging his future prospects. And like Gomez, she claims her youthful discretion helped ensure his own successful career. She lauds his eloquent pose as an elder statesman—she, too, has been following his career closely.

She seeks the same thing as Gomez: the legitimacy of Claverton's esteemed company. Mrs. Piggott swoops down to save Claverton from what she is sure is the lowbrow tedium of Mrs. Carghill's conversation—as a former music-hall girl Mrs. Carghill is less-than-suitable company for the famous Lord Claverton, the matron feels.

Michael Claverton-Ferry arrives to see his father, who is afraid his son needs to be rescued from the usual misadventures—he fears Michael might have hit someone driving recklessly, or might need to be disentangled from a romance or need money to pay a loan. In fact, Michael reveals that he has lost his job, which he had found dull in any case. He had borrowed money which he cannot now repay hoping to launch upon some business speculations, and was dismissed for his financial recklessness and for amorous indiscretions. He now wants to go abroad: Claverton finds the idea possibly a good one, and suggests sheep farming in New Zealand, but Michael wants something more exotic and more profitable. He longs for someplace where he can change his name and start over, out of his father's shadow. Claverton calls him a fugitive from reality and tells him one cannot escape one's past; Michael asks his father if he has lived up to his own ideal standards of conduct.

Mrs. Carghill returns, thrilled to meet Claverton's children, and she calls Michael the image of his father at that age. Gomez, too, arrives: he has persuaded his doctor to prescribe a rest cure at Badgley Court. He and Mrs. Carghill meet and look forward to trading stories of Claverton's youth; both take quickly to Michael, and plan to further their acquaintance with him. As they all leave Claverton alone with Monica, she worries about the awful people that have invaded his Badgley Court sanctuary; but in a moment of anagnorisis and self-abasement he confronts the reality that he has repressed his past. He closes the act wondering if he and Michael can, together, learn to admit their failures.

In Act three Monica fervently pledges her commitment to her lover. Charles, who has been told what has transpired at Badgley Court, worries that Claverton is a victim of blackmail and wants to help him. Claverton overhears this discussion and responds that his guilty secrets are not, as Monica argues, incomprehensible in an upright elder statesman—nearly everyone has them. Charles and Monica, though, are clearly safe from such guilt, Claverton perceives, because they love each other purely: anyone who has accomplished such a love—and would never hide from his or her companion a guilty secret—cannot become a victim of pretense in the way he has.

Claverton says he cannot escape from his ghosts—Mrs. Carghill and Señor Gomez—because they are tormentingly lodged in his own mind. He and his wife had never understood each other, so he could not share his secrets with her. Now he can admit that he was responsible for leading Fred Culverwell astray and abusing Maisie's love. He confesses the details of what his two ghosts had held over him: about the car incident at Oxford, it had later been determined that the old man in the road was already dead before he was hit by the car; but Claverton had not known that at the time, and kept driving in the belief that he had killed the man. He had been the first lover of Mrs. Carghill, and would have married her but for his father's disapproval. His father paid him off not to marry her, just as he paid her off in the breach of contract settlement.

Though Charles tells Claverton that Gomez and Mrs. Carghill are as guilty of hidden secrets as Claverton is himself, the elder statesman responds that their power lies in the fact that they each remember a time when he ran away; he will no longer run from them. His confession to his daughter, he explains, is the first step in his contrition.

Mrs. Carghill arrives, flaunting her youthful connection to Claverton though unable to shock Monica and Charles since Claverton has already explained the situation. She tells them she has conspired to save Michael from his misunderstanding father, arranging for Gomez to take him to San Marco for an exotic career. As Michael and Gomez enter, Claverton tries to dissuade his son by telling him of Gomez's shady past, but Michael already knows his new mentor's history and is all the more attracted to him because of it since Gomez, he feels, can better understand his own predicament. Mrs. Carghill agrees that Gomez is uniquely qualified to nurture Michael's abilities.

Michael departs brusquely with Gomez as the Claverton-Ferrys see their pretended bonds dissolving. Michael promises, lightly, to keep in touch with Monica and Claverton. Monica tries to imagine a happy outcome for Michael, though Claverton knows he will not live to see his son's success or failure. Monica tries to convince her father to leave Badgley Court, which turned out not to be restful, but Claverton tells her he has found peace there as a consequence of the contrition and truth he has accepted. He rejoices that his daughter is poised to enjoy an honest life of love with Charles—a life he never knew; and that he has rejected the same aspects of himself that his son rejected. Freed from a life of pretense, he can now begin to live and love. As Claverton exits, Charles sees that he has become a different person and that he seemed to bid farewell to the two lovers he has left alone. At the end of the play Monica and Charles have learned to accept vicissitude, loss, and death without fear, through the recognition of a powerful enduring love.

Production History

The Elder Statesman premiered at the Royal Lyceum Theatre, Edinburgh, as part of the Edinburgh International Festival, on 24 August 1958, where it ran for six performances (though it had had an unofficial opening the week before in Newcastle). Presented by Henry Sherek and directed by E. Martin Browne, it starred Paul Rogers as Lord Claverton, Anna Massey as Monica, Alec McCowen as Michael, Richard Gale as Charles Hemington, William Squire as Gomez, Eileen Peel (who played Lavinia in the first Broadway run of *The Cocktail Party*) as Mrs. Carghill, Dorothea Phillips as Mrs. Piggott, and Geoffrey Kerr as Lambert. Settings, by Hutchinson Scott—who had also designed the sets for *The Confidential Clerk*—"loyally hint at Attic temples and holy grottoes," writes Kenneth Tynan (R199). On 1 September 1958 the play was presented at the New Theatre, Oxford, and on 25 September it opened at London's Cambridge Theatre, where it ran for 92 performances; the cast remained as in Edinburgh, except that Dorothy Turner took over the role of Mrs. Piggott. The play was not presented on Broadway, Browne writes, because Gilbert Miller, unable to find a star to play Claverton, let his option on the play run out.

In 1959 the Birmingham Repertory Company presented the play, directed by Bernard Hepton. B. B. C. televised it in 1960 as part of the *Twentieth Century Series*; Vanessa Redgrave played Monica. In July 1961 Irene Mitchell directed the play for the Little Theatre in Melbourne, Australia.

The play's American premiere was at Milwaukee's Fred Miller Theatre—a theatre in the round with only 6 rows and 350 seats—on 27 February 1963. Paul Shyre directed the production, which starred Staats Cotsworth as Claverton, Anne Meachem as Monica, Jay Doyle as Michael, Richard Venturi as Charles, Guy Sorel as Gomez, Joanna Roos as Mrs. Carghill, Pauline Flanagan as Mrs. Piggott, and George Vogel as Lambert. Sets and costumes were by Charles Blackburn.

In June 1979 Bill Pryde directed a production for England's Malvern Festival starring Rogers in an encore performance as Claverton, Carol Drinkwater as Monica, Roger Davidson as Michael, David Collings as Charles, Robert Flemyng (who created the role of Edward in *The Cocktail Party*) as Gomez, Rosalind Boxall as Mrs. Carghill, Susan Brown as Mrs Piggott, and Lionel Taylor as Lambert.

Critical Overview

Performance Reviews

Reviewing the Edinburgh debut W. A. Darlington writes in the *New York Times*, "Because the theme is love and Mr. Eliot approaches it with a warmth of manner new to him, those critics who never cared much for *The Cocktail Party* or *The Confidential Clerk* are firmly of the opinion that the new play is better because it is less austere than either of these two" (R191). Harold Hobson, too, praises the play in the *Christian Science Monitor*, calling it "both aesthetically and financially the most successful new play offered at any Edinburgh Festival in recent years. . . . in conception and execution it reveals a spirit new to Mr. Eliot's work. It finishes upon a note of love and hope and forgiveness. . . . here for the first time he reveals a recognition of the gentler and sweeter of the Christian virtues" (R194).

The *Variety* reviewer, though, writes that this play is "not T. S. Eliot at his most brilliant. Despite a few glimmerings of Eliot wit and poetic phraseology, the play is largely mundane, and lapses into a poorish ending. Strong cast, crisp diction, excellent all-round acting, and well-lit sets are not enough to make it memorable or convincing." *Variety* describes Rogers's performance as "often tedious . . . looks worn-out and haggard" (R202).

In the *Manchester Guardian*, Philip Hope-Wallace calls Eliot's drama "profounder (if simpler) than what he propounded in *The Cocktail Party* or *The Confidential Clerk*. Is the impression given last night that the new piece, nevertheless, fails to persuade to anything like the same extent because of familiarity, which has rubbed the edge of novelty from the Eliot idiom (which is to propound metaphysical argument and preach the lay sermon of self-healing through self-knowledge in the guise of a light comedy of commercial

theatre)? Or is it more likely that, this time, we cannot at all take his characters as human? Moving around in E. Martin Browne's gentle and lenitive
production, they seem like talking waxworks, so that what should be touching
scenes of farewell in the last act amount emotionally only to tedium" (R195).

"The voice of a new Eliot" is heard in this play, Kenneth Tynan writes in
The Observer, "unexpectedly endorsing the merits of human love. It is a safe
bet that the word 'love' occurs more often in the present play than in all the
author's previous work put together. . . . Encouraging though we may find
this step in his spiritual development, it is not enough to make good theatre.
In some ways, indeed, it has the opposite effect: Mr. Eliot's Indian-summer
love-lyrics have little distinction, either literary or dramatic. A new simplicity
has certainly entered his style, but so has simplicity's half-wit brother, banality" (R199).

And from Alan Brien in *The Spectator* comes an extremely harsh review:
"*The Elder Statesman* is a zombie play designed for the living dead. Occasionally across the pallid mortuary scene flits an ironic joke or a haunting
phrase but the smell of formaldehyde hangs heavy in the air. It is a play in
which Mr. Eliot mistakes snobbery for ethics, melodrama for tragedy, vulgarity for wit, obscurity for poetry and sermonising for philosophy" (R190).

As Michael, Hobson writes, McCowen gives a "beautiful and exacting
performance," and Rogers, as Claverton, "has dignity." Derek Stanford notes
Rogers's resemblance to Prime Minister "Macmillan, with a dash of Somerset
Maugham thrown in" (R194, 683). Kenneth Tynan calls McCowen "bonily
brilliant as the rebel son," while Rogers, he writes, "lends Claverton a fine
shaggy sonority and the right look of stoic dismay, as a man staring past the
fire into his own thoughts." Brien criticizes Browne's direction, in which "all
but two of the cast . . . speak at dictation speed like an exercise in teaching
English by radio. . . . The slow-motion trivialities float down like confet-
ti. . . . Mr. Gale [as Charles] is as stiff, glazed and cold as a monument:
Miss Massey [as Monica], with her puffed cheeks and popping eyes, is torn
between ham and hamster—for the more technique she pours into this tiny role
the more it overflows into melodrama" (R199).

Reviewing the London premiere, W. Macqueen Pope epitomizes the
general popular reaction to the play in the New York *Morning Telegraph*: it
is, if not profound, at least a finely crafted piece of entertainment. "Eliot has
made a very good play out of all this, even if it is not so deep and philosophical as some of his others. It is far better theatre, and that is the job of a
dramatist, surely" (R197).

Bonamy Dobrée approves more wholeheartedly: "This has been called,
and is now advertised on the posters as being, 'Mr. Eliot's most human play.'
This may be because of the delicacy with which he treats the young lovers,
but one ventures to think it is judged to be so because of its greater clarity.
Not that the story is plainer than in, say, *The Confidential Clerk*, but that the
phrasing is absolutely sure throughout. . . . The structure of the play too is
beautifully balanced. . . . There is no dominant crisis, either in the action or

emotionally; there is a kind of inexorable movement from the beginning. . . . Has the katharsis . . . appropriate to the kind of play been achieved? Has it enlarged the bounds of one's sympathy with or understanding of other people? or in this case, has it brought about any kind of revelation of one's self to one's self? Judged by such standards, *The Elder Statesman* is Mr. Eliot's best play of the peculiar individual kind he has set himself to fashion, enduring a popular form with deeper meaning" (C243, 147-48).

The London *Times* reviews the West End opening more equivocally: "The confession [before Claverton's death] . . . is not dramatically the most satisfying passage, for it is largely a repetition of what is already known. . . . The second act, in which one major disclosure is made and both Claverton's ghosts precipitate situations that make him writhe, is the more stageworthy even though its aims are more modest. The éclat of this act is due largely to the performance of Miss Eileen Peel who plays with a wicked sprightliness. . . . Mr. Alec McCowen, as the disgruntled son, brings the act to its climax with a sustained scream of accusation against his father which brings an exhausted release of tension between the two men. Mr. Paul Rogers's Claverton, punctilious and resonant in delivery, isolates the two sides of the character with a delicate clarity thoroughly in key with the production which elsewhere (especially in the love scenes) verged on being stilted" (R203).

The 1963 American production is "a quiet play, filled with wisdom," writes Peter Jacobi in the *Christian Science Monitor*. Shyre "proves himself brilliantly; he brings movement to what basically is a talkfest. He strives to move his actors naturally, not to allow them to trespass on the poet-playwright's thoughts. . . . Particularly responsive is Staats Cotsworth [playing Claverton, who] . . . begins as a shell of a man, acting big and thinking small; he ends as a complete man, humbly filled with thoughts of a love which means bigness in a human being" (R196).

Scholarly Response

Though nearly all critics and reviewers agree that *The Elder Statesman* forthrightly confronts love—marking a significant departure from Eliot's earlier work—Barbara Everett demurs: "the statement of a new 'reality,' that of an honest and simple love between father and child, and between a young couple who become engaged, is unfortunately not presented so impressively that the shadows or figments of imagination sink away into unreality before it, leaving the reader of audience convinced emotionally as well as intellectually as to what has taken place. It is a pity that *The Elder Statesman* has become acclaimed because of this intention—to describe the discovery of real love—when this is where it most fails, in treating a subject perhaps almost impossible to reproduce on the stage. In face of it, Claverton is driven into wordiness . . . and the fiancé's explicitness is grotesque" (R192, 164).

Katherine J. Worth sees "interesting shadowings of new techniques for a new type of realism. Touches of farcical exaggeration in the characters of Gomez and Mrs. Carghill reinforce the impression made by their name changing that they are masks or ghosts rather than solid beings. The flamboyant new identities they have acquired don't ring true, but what else are they? They bring home with chilling persistence how close Lord Claverton's situation is to theirs. He has had three sets of names and identities, is almost as disconnected as they are. Names always have magic force for Eliot's characters. The way they are used in *The Elder Statesman*—as something to hide behind and to attack with—points, as so much of Eliot does, to Pinter and the swoops in and out of different names that his characters practise so alarmingly" (C404, 65).

The play "completes the cycle that *Murder in the Cathedral* had begun, both thematically and formalistically," writes Anthony S. Abbott. "Eliot continues, in this his last play, the movement away from an elitist view of life. . . . *The Elder Statesman* is a world without saints. There are no Beckets, Harrys or Celias, not even any Colbys or Eggersons. There is only everyman, Dick Ferry" (C254, 111).

Gerald Weales, too, writes that there is in the play "a new element, an attitude toward man in this world, embodied in the love of Monica and Charles, that displays a genuine warmth so far strange to Eliot's work. All of his plays have, in one way or another, been preoccupied with the separating of the sheep from the goats. Each of them has its special figure—Thomas, Harry, Celia, Colby—who operates at a level of perception not possible for the ordinary run of mankind. . . . In *The Elder Statesman* he seems finally to have got out of the wasteland. Perhaps that is because the play has no saint or martyr, no Celia or Harry, no special case to throw ordinary life into the shadow. More likely, Eliot is now willing to say that there is a possible human relationship which, in itself, gives meaning to life. . . . there is, for the first time, the suggestion that there is another genuine possibility, another kind of salvation, this side of the saints and martyrs" (C251, 477).

Joyce M. Holland notes the striking absence of the "more sympathetic divine hero" in this play, which "turns away from the elect entirely to concentrate on the problems of the human community. . . . The true divine hero accepts isolation; it is in the total isolation of the spirit that truth is revealed. So Thomas confronts his tempters, Harry the Eumenides, and Celia her crucifixion. But Claverton has protected himself against isolation and the recognition of self. His life is dominated by two fears: 'his terror of being alone' and 'his fear of being exposed to strangers.' . . . Claverton is a pitiable figure, but only at the end of the play, when he divests himself of his pretensions to being a hero with a destiny and admits his guilt, does he attain any real dignity. His dignity is his humanity, and he proves his humanity by dying" (C320, 158-59). The play "is Eliot's most nearly tragic play," she continues. "It does not have a tragic hero. . . . Rather, it presents a tragic situation which has been created by the persons in the play" (161).

"The poet's attitude of conciliation and resolution of differences," Carol H. Smith writes, is "evident in the fact that he has removed the last interference between himself and his audience by changing his dramatic tone of voice from that of farce to that of romantic comedy in order to make the mood of the surface compatible with the play's religious theme of the relationship between human and divine love" (C382, 214).

David E. Jones notes thematic correlations between this play and many of Eliot's earlier dramas: *The Elder Statesman* is faintly evocative of *Murder in the Cathedral*, "where in the days before his death a man reviews his past and finds spiritual wholeness. The danger of imposing one's will on others, demonstrated in Amy [in *The Family Reunion*], Sir Claude and Lady Elizabeth [in *The Confidential Clerk*], is seen again in Lord Claverton. Moreover, like Edward and Lavinia [in *The Cocktail Party*], like Lucasta and B. Kaghan [in *The Confidential Clerk*], he has been hiding his true self beneath a mask. The problem of change, which bulked so large in *The Cocktail Party*, is given a new dimension. But, as one would expect, the strongest links are with the play nearest in time, *The Confidential Clerk*. The problem of living in two worlds is referred to early in the play, and the central theme of the earlier play is taken up and developed in a new way; the question of inheritance is focused upon the repetition by a son of the father's mistakes" (C325, 183). For Jones, the most striking difference between this play and the earlier ones is the fact that "there is no suggestion that the hero has an exceptional spiritual destiny" (192).

Gwenn R. Boardman explains another link between this play and Eliot's earlier drama and poetry: Claverton epitomizes Eliot's recurrent theme of "the hollow man," she writes, full of fear and emptiness, and in need of regeneration. Harry, from *The Family Reunion*, is Eliot's original dramatic type of this character: "the true hollow man, an echo chamber inhabited by voices from the past" (C241, 38).

Raymond Williams describes connections between the characters in *The Elder Statesman* and manifestations of similar characterizations elsewhere in Eliot's work: "The Furies, it is true, are theatrically negotiated; the endless trouble of having them materialize in the window recess, in *The Family Reunion*, has been avoided by making them Federico Gomez and Mrs. Carghill: a cross between the grotesques of the early poems and familiar theatrical types" (C399, 197).

Grover Smith connects the play's "ghosts" from the past with characters from Eliot's earlier plays, as well as with other ghostly literary incarnations. "In Eliot's previous work, their prototypes are many. Of his seven pieces for the theatre, only *The Confidential Clerk* discloses no ghost and hints at none. . . . *Sweeney Agonistes* . . . contemplates the agony of a living ghost" in the passage about a murderer and his possible victim both fluctuating between life and death. "*The Rock* introduces a small group of conventional phantoms. *Murder in the Cathedral*, giving shape to ancient memories and desires by means of Becket's Tempters, summons up in the person of the Fourth Tempter a kind of Doppelgänger, a younger self of the Archbishop. *The Family Reunion* borrows the Eumenides of Greek tragedy to personify the family curse that haunts Harry. . . . *The Cocktail Party* established Lavinia's reunion with her husband as, metaphorically, a return from the dead" (C249, 233).

The Elder Statesman is "the most intimate of his works," writes Hugh Kenner (C246, 40), embodying extremely clear language—"coolly adequate to what it is saying" (38)—consummately written to be heard by an audience.

Textual Notes and Influences

Eliot identified the Sophocles play *Oedipus at Colonus* as a background to *The Elder Statesman*. Rudd Fleming writes that Eliot was drawn to Sophocles because he, "even more than Virgil, is the 'classic of classics'; and all his life Eliot had sought to become a classic. . . . When Eliot finally came home to Sophocles, he had already himself become as nearly 'classic' as seemed possible for a living English poet; and with his uncannily precise talent for finding and firmly occupying his own most tenable position within the literary cosmos, Eliot focused upon Sophocles' last and most self-reflective play, the *Oedipus at Colonus*, in which the aged and blind Oedipus undergoes at Athens his mysterious apotheosis within the Grove of the Eumenides. Even in antiquity this play was felt to be a mystical self-projection of the poet himself as he stood, an extremely old man, upon the very outposts of human wisdom" (C245, 60-61). Additionally, "of all Greek plays, this is the one in which Greek polytheism comes closest to the Christian mystery of love at once human and divine" (61).

"As all of Eliot's critics have noticed," Anthony S. Abbott writes, "*The Elder Statesman* is Eliot's *Oedipus at Colonus*, his *nunc dimittis*. Did the playwright have a premonition that it was to be his last play? It has the peace and serenity, the sense of completeness that is represented by Sophocles' play and Milton's *Samson Agonistes*" (C254, 112). Leo Aylen, while citing similarities to *Oedipus at Colonus*, also notes significant differences: "instead of the ferocious pessimism of Sophocles, Eliot gives an atmosphere of reconciliation and peace. The action is extremely simple. It is Claverton repenting of two past sins and relinquishing his hold on life, his hold over his scapegrace son, and his loving daughter. Although it is far from the world of [*Colonus*], we might say that it was the result of a Christian brooding on the last speech of Oedipus, and amplifying it through his hope of a final redemption" (C259, 336).

Carol H. Smith writes that the Sophoclean connection "suggests that he wished the play to express the final resolution of his theme of spiritual quest" (C382, 228); the play's atmosphere, she continues, also evokes Shakespeare's final work, *The Tempest*, with its ultimate resolution and harmony. Nona Balakian sees echoes in the final work of another poet: "the play unmistakably suggests the *Paradiso*. . . . For here, without strife or suffering, and in the presence of a loving, forgiving person, the penitent finds both freedom and bliss" (R188).

Eliot's "ghosts" are indebted to the tradition of Henry James's haunted stories, Grover Smith writes, for the "insight that the true mystery of a ghost

is revealed through a perceiver's comprehension of his own nature"; Maisie
and Fred "might be compared to the ghosts in 'The Turn of the Screw' in the
sense that they, like Peter Quint and Miss Jessel, can be wrongly interpreted
only at the price of disaster" (C249, 234).

The probable source for the name Claverton, Mark Webb writes, is "*The
Claverton Affair* (or *The Claverton Mystery*, in the English edition), a Dr.
Priestly detective novel which Cecil J. C. Street published in 1933 under the
pseudonym of John Rhode" (C252, 15). Noting Eliot's affinity for mystery
novels and the likelihood that he would have known Rhode's writing, Webb
cites several correspondences between the play and the detective novel: Both
Lord Claverton and Rhode's Sir John Claverton "are elderly men under
doctor's care who die in the course of the work. . . . Both have been successful in public life. . . . Their private lives, however, are characterized by
emptiness and isolation. . . . Both novel and play are about parent-child relationships" (16); and the novel, which includes a ghostly incarnation, essentially matches the plot of *The Elder Statesman*, Webb argues.

Vinod Sena argues that Henrik Ibsen's *The Pillars of Society* is a strong
influence on *The Elder Statesman*. In addition to numerous parallels in terms
of plot and detail, he notes the thematic congruence: "Both Eliot and Ibsen in
these plays, it is clear, are vitally concerned with man's liability to weakness
and error, and his even more lamentable incapacity to acknowledge and so
master his own shortcomings" (C248, 23). Sena admits, though, that Eliot informed him he had no recollection of *The Pillars of Society*, and stated that
any influence was unconscious.

The published text begins with a dedicatory poem, "To My Wife" (a
revised version of which is reprinted as "A Dedication to My Wife" in Eliot's
Collected Poems). The poem celebrates the delight and shared emotional bond
of a mutually supportive marriage; and it points toward a private meaning in
the play's language uniquely comprehensible to the author and his wife. Peter
Ackroyd writes that only the parts of the play written after his January 1957
marriage rescue it from being "by far the grimmest play he had ever written"
(C255, 325); and Robert Langbaum argues that the play "reflects Eliot's own
experience that an old man can be reborn and achieve a climax of happiness
even as he is dying" (C336, 578).

Lyndall Gordon asserts: "composed as Eliot fell in love with Valerie
Fletcher, it looks toward their union" (C309, 246). Monica's selfless protec-
tive devotion to the elder statesman in his declining years, Gordon suggests,
parallels Valerie's devotion to the employer who would become her husband.
Gordon also suggests that Mrs. Carghill's letters from Claverton, testifying to
the guilty secrets of his youth, may allude to the thousand letters Eliot wrote
to Emily Hale during the years of their relationship, which Hale had be-
queathed to Princeton University (under seal until 2020) to Eliot's dismay
(248).

The play's original title was "The Rest Cure."

Publishing History

Faber & Faber published *The Elder Statesman* in April 1959, as did Farrar, Straus and Cudahy in New York. It was reprinted in *Collected Plays* (London: Faber & Faber, 1962).

Bibliography

Primary Sources

Plays

The following editions of each play are most easily accessible in the United States; page numbers throughout this book refer to these editions. Abbreviations as used throughout the bibliography are indicated in parentheses. See the "Publishing history" section of the chapter on each play for additional details about publication.

P1 *Sweeney Agonistes*. In *Collected Poems: 1909-1962*. New York: Harcourt, 1970, 111-24. *(SA)*

P2 *The Rock*. New York: Harcourt, 1934.

P3 *Murder in the Cathedral*. New York: Harcourt, 1935, 1963. *(MC)*

P4 *The Family Reunion*. New York: Harcourt, 1939. *(FR)*

P5 *The Cocktail Party*. New York: Harcourt, 1950, 1978. *(CP)*

P6 *The Confidential Clerk*. New York: Harcourt, 1954. *(CC)*

P7 *The Elder Statesman*. New York: Farrar, 1959; Noonday, 1964. *(ES)*

Eliot's Essays on Drama

Eliot's critical essays show an intense study of dramatic history: often, with more of a stress on the poetic than the dramatic aspect of the works under discussion (which does not contradict Eliot's own concentrated attention to poetry in his verse drama), and more literary than dramaturgical in critical orientation. Nevertheless, Eliot consistently offers observations—about how to create character or sustain action, for example—that foreshadow his aspirations as a playwright and help illustrate what he tried to accomplish in his own plays. In *The Music of Poetry* (P51) Eliot asserts that a poet's critical writings are interesting because the poet/critic is always, at least on some level, trying to defend his own work or formulate what he wants to write; certainly Eliot realized this was true of his own criticism.

Because Eliot's essays are so prolific and so intently contemplative, they serve as an intriguing parallel—a guide or gloss, sometimes; a theoretical complement—to his poetry and plays. The essays allow us to ascertain Eliot's stances on issues he defines as central to literary art, and to follow over time the development or revision of these ideas. (Obviously, Eliot's shift from poetic to dramatic writing bears importantly on the critical attitudes that evolve.)

For example, a famous passage in one of his best-known early essays, "Tradition and the Individual Talent" (1919) is directly contradicted in *The Three Voices of Poetry* (P57, 1953). In 1919 he had written that the personal emotions are uninteresting and irrelevant to great poetry; the poet must escape from his personality, and separate his individuality from his art. In the later essay, though—written when drama rather than poetry was his literary paradigm—Eliot allows that a playwright may create the germ of a character out of some aspect of himself: some trait, strength, tendency, or eccentricity; some latent potential that becomes manifest within the character.

This shift in sensibility serves well as an emblem of Eliot's development during that period: from the self-obsessed and pessimistic solipsist of the early poetry, who rejected the possibility of productive personal interaction, ameliorative knowledge of the self or others, social support and succor; to the playwright who was much more open to the prospect that art is related to the person/personality of the artist, and that by implication dramatic literature might teach its audience—and its writer as well—something useful about daily human existence.

In fact even in a 1919 essay on drama, "Ben Jonson" (P11), Eliot hints at the position he would espouse in *The Three Voices of Poetry*, stating that a dramatic character somehow demands a "transfusion" of the author's character—but this statement is laden with caveats about how complex, devious, and strange this transfusion must be. His hesitation here to make the sort of straightforward admission he would offer in 1953 demonstrates that as a younger writer his dominant literary instinct—or, many would argue, *pose*—is to suppress the personal. Perhaps the essay on Jonson also indicates, though, that even in 1919, despite the impersonal stance expressed in "Tradition and the Individual Talent," Eliot foresaw the kind of outlook he might accept decades later.

Ronald Peacock sees three groupings in Eliot's dramatic criticism: "First the long series of Elizabethan essays presents itself solidly and importantly; here we find historical assessments, together with a cumulative enumeration of criteria for drama. Secondly, we have an assessment of the situation in the contemporary theatre, and see Eliot clarifying by adverse criticism his practical position. Thirdly, there are more direct statements about his ideal of poetic drama, and the problem of form involved" (C362, 89).

Of Eliot's hundreds of literary essays and reviews on dramatic and non-dramatic topics, those on the Elizabethans are arguably his most important: he seems to have embedded in these essays his weightiest cogitations on the past literary tradition; the Elizabethan criticism has, in turn, attracted the most serious attention from scholars looking to the essays for a key to Eliot's aesthetic. (These essays, along with a few on other dramatists such as Euripides, Seneca, and Goethe, whom Eliot included within his canonical "tradition," are from the period between 1919 and the early 1930s.)

The prominence of the Elizabethans in Eliot's dramatic canon, of course, leads ultimately to Shakespeare—Eliot spent much time coming to terms with his work, stating that anyone who tries to write poetic drama will find much of his energy exhausted in escaping Shakespeare's influence. In *Poetry and Drama* he writes of the need to avoid any echo of Shakespeare (P55, 85) and of trying to exorcise him so verse drama could be revived in the twentieth century. In "The Need for Poetic Drama" (P47) Eliot explains his own personal difficulty in getting away from Shakespeare: whenever his attention is relaxed, he finds that he writes bad imitations of Shakespearean blank verse.

"Eliot, in company with many of his contemporaries who thought about poetic drama, and wrote it, seems to have been very much afraid of allowing his working imagination to be trapped in Shakespeare's iambics," Gareth Lloyd Evans writes. "His instinct was absolutely right—and he had only to look at the dismal record of nineteenth-century poetic drama to know that it was" (C295, 143). Eliot had announced in *The Waste Land* that the modernist could not dance to the beat of the "Shakespeherian Rag": Eliot's pointed question about Shakespeare in the 1920s is evoked by the line that follows that rag in *The Waste Land*: What shall he do now?

Eliot's approach to Shakespeare, according to Ronald Bush, is heavily influenced by a 1929 essay by the Shakespearean scholar G. Wilson Knight (to whose book *The Wheel of Fire* Eliot later wrote an introduction, P38) called "Myth and Miracle." Bush summarizes what appealed to Eliot in that essay: "first, it approached the plays through their poetic fabric of theme and imagery and, as Eliot said in his introduction to *The Wheel of Fire*, searched 'for the pattern below the level of "plot" and "character." . . .' Secondly, it related the pattern of Shakespeare's late plays to the pattern of the bard's own spiritual progress from [as Knight wrote] 'pain and despairing thought through stoic acceptance to a serene and mystic joy.' And finally it put special stress on the last group of romances, particularly *Pericles*, whose experience was colored by music and whose myth reflected [again, in Knight's words] 'that mystic truth from which are born the dogmas of the Catholic Church . . . the temptation in the desert, the tragic ministry and death, and the resurrection of the Christ'" (C283, 163).

Eliot writes of Shakespeare as a figure who is generally (and not incorrectly) accepted as a genius; but he does not himself unilaterally or automatically bow down in homage. His kindest comments on Shakespeare come when he discusses *other* Elizabethan and Jacobean dramatists, who may perform a certain activity only nearly as well as Shakespeare, or, on the other hand, may pale in comparison. One may detect an anxiety of influence: perhaps Eliot felt Shakespeare was too happy an artist, too prolific, too easily and perfectly ensconsed within a literary condition and tradition, too catholic in his range. Shakespeare (reputedly) scarce blotted a line, while Eliot made a career out of brilliant blotting—as seen, for example, in *The Waste Land* manuscripts.

While one may profitably analyze Shakespeare's profound effect on Eliot, one should not neglect Eliot's corrolary effect on Shakespeare: G. K. Hunter writes in *Dramatic Identities and Cultural Tradition* that Eliot "virtually invented the twentieth-century Shakespeare in a collection of asides" (299): for example, his conclusion that *Hamlet* was an artistic failure; his attention to a unifying pattern underlying the surface; his comment in "John Ford" that all Shakespeare's work is one single poem.

Charles Warren cites Eliot's 1937 lectures on Shakespeare at Edinburgh University (unpublished, but exhaustively discussed in Warren's *T. S. Eliot on Shakespeare*) as the culmination of his meditation on the playwright. In his earlier essays on Shakespeare, Warren writes, "Eliot raises doubts about Shakespeare's attitude to life, his intellectual coherence, and even the coherence of his art. Arising from these doubts . . . Eliot's chief Shakespearean subject becomes the problem of 'meaning'—is there in Shakespeare's plays a coherence or unity in dealing with 'anarchic' material that redeems this material, so to speak, making the play a valuable *intellectual* presentation?" (C392, 2). By 1937, Warren concludes, Eliot had "moved from a view of the chaotic lifelikeness of Shakespeare's plays to a view of their coherence" (104). Kenneth Muir suggests that "Eliot came to respond more warmly to Shakespeare's plays" by 1930 because he was then "stimulated by his own ambitions as a dramatist"; in this period, Eliot writes "less about Shakespeare's failing as a purveyor of philosophical commonplaces and more about the impressiveness of his total *oeuvre*" (C353, 13).

Shakespeare, Eliot felt, never had to confront the kind of modern world in which he himself so consciously suffered—the world fraught with what Eliot perceived as extreme exacerbation of spiritual, aesthetic, and philosophical uncertainties. Perhaps Eliot fancied that he could have been Shakespeare if he had lived in the sixteenth century. In any case, Eliot's writing on Shakespeare and his contemporaries must be read with the recognition that the relation to the literary ancestors is a tangled one.

Muir explains numerous fallacies in Eliot's Elizabethan criticism: "In his early criticism Eliot had been too much influenced by the disintegrators, who now seem aberrant, and by Archer's attack on drama written before Pinero. He had complained that the dramatists were trying to be realistic, yet at the same time he criticized them for departing from colloquial speech. He complained of the lack of recognizable conventions at the very time when Muriel Bradbrook was analyzing them. He objected to Lamb's method of anthologizing scenes and speeches while ignoring their contexts; and yet one is bound to remember his own quotations of passages he admired and imitated rather than his discussion of the dramatic qualities of the plays" (13). Gian N. G. Orsini faults Eliot's essays on drama for using the catch-all term "convention"—a crucial term, because he often judges dramatists by their relation to a conventional standard—as if it were clear and absolute, when it is in fact an arbitrary abstraction (C360).

Eliot's essays on the historical dramatic tradition and dramatic theory belong to a separate and earlier stage of his career than that in which he was an active playwright: two-thirds of these essays (and nearly all the most important and critically-respected ones) were published before the first performance of his first play; fewer than one-fifth of them are from after 1939, when he established himself as a determined West End dramatist. Eliot put himself through a long period of intellectual apprenticeship at Harvard and Oxford before he began substantially publishing his poetry; in that vein, one might consider these essays indiciative of a period of dramaturgical apprenticeship and historical education in the background of drama, before he began to create his plays.

In a 1959 *Paris Review* interview Eliot said he was no longer interested in his theories about verse drama, especially those from before 1934; as he spent more time actually writing for the theatre, he said, he was less concerned with dramatic critical theory (P67, 62). His critical essays helped his poetry writing, he said, because his chosen subjects were the writers who influenced him and whom he admired; writing the essays helped make those influences more conscious and articulate (69).

The essays from the mid-1930s on, as Eliot was beginning to embrace a very public and pragmatic commitment to playwriting, thus reflect a diminished concern with drama as a largely historical artifact, and a greater interest in—and advocacy for—a contemporary reawakening of poetic drama. A number of these essays are fairly repetitive—even their titles betray a singular focus: "Audiences, Producers, Plays, Poets" (P45); "The Need for Poetic Drama" (P47); "Five Points on Dramatic Writing" (P48); "The Future of Poetic Drama" (P49); *The Aims of Poetic Drama* (P54); *Poetry and Drama* (P55). (One is reminded of Eliot's disclaimer in Part III of "East Coker": "You say I am repeating / Something I have said before. I shall say it again. / Shall I say it again?")

These practical essays of the 1930s through 1950s testify to the methodical importance and the demand for precision Eliot invested in his poetic drama. Prominently and exhaustively addressed in the later essays are ideas about the audience (what it should be shown and taught, what it is capable of understanding, what popular dramatic trends should be cultivated); production and performance; elocution and proper declamation of dramatic verse; the place of verse drama in the contemporary theatre community; the nuts and bolts of composing verse drama—what works well, what doesn't, and the relation of form and style to content.

Besides original bibliographic citations, sources are given for essays and monographs which have been reprinted (sometimes with revisions) in a more accessible collection. The essays in this section are listed in chronological order of publication.

P8 "Whether Rostand Had Something about Him." *Athenaeum* 4656 (25 July 1919): 665-66. Rpt. as "'Rhetoric' and Poetic Drama" in *The Sacred Wood* 78-85 and *Selected Essays* 25-30.

Denigration of "rhetoric" in drama is an unclear criticism; the term should not be synonymous with bad writing. A rhetoric of substance may be found that accurately expresses what it intends. In Shakespeare's and Rostand's plays, for example, fine rhetoric indicates a character seeing himself in a dramatic light—as we often do in actual life. A playwright who, in contrast, uses inarticulateness to indicate emotional intensity may betray that those emotions are unworthy of drama.

P9 "Some Notes on the Blank Verse of Christopher Marlowe." *Art & Letters* 2.4 (Autumn 1919): 194-99. Rpt. in *The Sacred Wood* 86-94, and as "Christopher Marlowe" in *Selected Essays* 100-106.

Marlowe's drama demonstrates the crafted improvements possible for versification, including economy, adaptation of earlier models (such as Spenser), melody, empowerment of the sentence within verse lineation, and vivid effective caricature.

P10 "Hamlet and His Problems." *Athenaeum* 4665 (19 September 1919): 940-41. Rpt. in *The Sacred Wood* 95-103 and *Selected Essays* 121-26.

The problem in *Hamlet* is only secondarily the title character's and mainly the play's. Critics mistakenly identify vicariously with the Prince, instead of objectively considering the play (which must be seen not as Shakespeare's individual work but as an accumulation of various revenge tragedies) as a whole. The play is an artistic failure: many scenes are unexplained, superfluous, or inconsistent; the style is variable and erratic. The "objective correlative," a crucial formula for evoking a specific emotion, is deficient; neither Shakespeare nor Hamlet can express Hamlet's emotions artistically. We do not and cannot ever know what emotions or experience led Shakespeare to write the play, since the play itself fails to divulge a coherent answer.

P11 "Ben Jonson." *Times Literary Supplement* 930 (13 November 1919): 637-38. Rpt. in *The Sacred Wood* 104-22 and *Selected Essays* 127-39.

Jonson's plays deal with the surface of life and are therefore often, mistakenly, dismissed as superficial. Jonson never sought the three-dimensionality of a Shakespearean character; his genius is that within the limitations of his scope, his characters fit perfectly with each other. His dramatic constructive skill allowed him to do away with plot and present the action of players in motion; *Bartholomew Fair*, for example, is ultimately and triumphantly the fair itself. The creation of a character demands infusing the character with the life of the author; Jonson succeeds here. More than Milton, whose *Comus* was the death of the masque, Jonson has a sense for the living art of drama; if both Jonson and Shakespeare were currently writing, the more intelligent audiences might be drawn to Jonson.

P12 "'The Duchess of Malfi' at the Lyric: and Poetic Drama." *Art & Letters* 3.1 (Winter 1919/20): 36-39.

A dull and ridiculous recent presentation of Webster's play represents a damning indictment of modern theatre, in which dramatic prose makes the actors ill at ease. Contemporary producers and actors inhibit the enjoyment of spoken poetry or the sharing of its sublime excitement. Shakespearean drama survives on the modern stage only because it is better constructed than other Elizabethan plays; his poetry is tolerated, but not venerated. Standard modern plays are made for the actors, but the successful presentation of a poetic play like Webster's or Shakespeare's demands that the actor not try to improve or interpret the script—rather, that he efface his personal vanity. Opera endures as a viable performance art because its tradition has gone on uninterrupted. Verse drama, though, has been dead for two centuries and cannot now be performed to give the audience pleasure or convey an intensity of effect. All one learns from this performance of *The Duchess of Malfi* is how dissatisfactory its conditions of production are.

P13 "The Poetic Drama." *Athenaeum* 4698 (14 May 1920): 635-36.

The noble failures of *Cinnamon and Angelica: A Play*, by John Middleton Murry, point to the difficulty of creating poetic drama at a time when the form is a lost art, and when audiences are not properly trained to appreciate it or to cooperate unconsciously with the production.

P14 "Euripides and Gilbert Murray: A Performance at the Holborn Empire." *Art & Letters* 3.2 (Spring 1920): 36-43. Rpt. as "Euripides and Professor Murray" in *The Sacred Wood* 71-77 and *Selected Essays* 46-50.

Murray's recent translation of the *Medea*, despite its successful performance by Sybil Thorndike, calls attention to the precarious state of classical literature and especially Greek drama. Murray, the most prominent Hellenist of his time, translates into an idiom that lamely approximates A. C. Swinburne's. His English is wordy, inaccurate, and blurry, presenting a barrier between Euripides and the contemporary audience. H. D. and Ezra Pound more delicately capture the essence of classical literature for the modern age.

P15 "Philip Massinger." *Times Literary Supplement* 958 (27 May 1920): 325-26; continuation, "The Old Comedy." *Athenaeum* 4702 (11 June 1920): 760-61. Rpt. in *The Sacred Wood* 123-43 and *Selected Essays* 181-95.

One must study study a dozen Elizabethan playwrights simultaneously to understand the period's drama, and examine how the writers borrow from each other as a test of their individual skill. Massinger's plays betray a dissociation of sensibility, a language divorced from its subject and dominated by received, rather than original, ideas; and they reveal an age lacking some moral fiber. While his tragic drama is dreary, his comedies, anticipating Restoration comedy, show more promising abilities.

P16 "The Possibility of a Poetic Drama." *Dial* (New York) 69.5 (November 1920): 441-47. Rpt. in *The Sacred Wood* 60-70.

The absence of poetic drama implies that the stage has lost claims to literary art. Dramatists such as Shaw and Maeterlinck are hybrids, and popularized imitations of great drama; thus they have sacrificed artistic integrity. Ibsen and Chekhov are insufficiently universal. Yet many poets want to write drama and the public seems to want verse plays. Lamb may be blamed for defining dramatic art as a dead form by emphasizing the immense gap between past and present. The Elizabethan dramatists benefited by having an extant and vigorous dramatic form, which could thus integrate realms of new thoughts and images. Contemporary culture, in a formless age, cannot successfully draw upon a received dramatic tradition.

P17 "London Letter." *Dial* (London) 73.6 (December 1922): 659-63. Rpt. as "Marie Lloyd" in *Selected Essays* 405-408.

England's most popular music-hall artist represented the exuberance of the lower class, the most vital segment of society. She controlled audiences through the sympathy she evoked; her performances created a vivid life among her spectators. Her understanding of her audience and her embodiment of their virtues gave her a moral superiority over other performers. The middle class and aristocracy, to their detriment, have no parallel figure who expresses their sensibility. With her death, the disappearance of the music-hall, and the rise of the cinema (which is impersonal because it is a mechanical aesthetic featuring senseless music and excessively rapid action), the lower class will lose a valuable medium of social participation and stimulation.

P18 "Dramatis Personae." *Criterion* 1.3 (April 1923): 303-306.

Sarah Bernhardt's death marks the end of an era of dramatic genius and might even be seen as symbolizing the "Closing of the Theatres," which are becoming obsolete as film and other popular cultural entities usurp the allure of the theatre. The modern stage is in a state of chaos due to styles of acting and styles of plays. In its presentation of long-forgotten Elizabethan plays the Phoenix Society reminds us—by the wide variations and incongruities between actors within a single play—how little we know of past dramatic traditions. Contemporary drama is not a living art because it does not satisfy our craving for ritual, but instead provides only a banal and mundane realism which is insufficient. Cinema, which luxuriates in the sensibility of photographic realism, epitomizes this banality.

P19 "The Beating of a Drum." *Nation & Athenaeum* 34.1 (6 October 1923): 11-12.

Review of *Studies in the Development of the Fool in the Elizabethan Drama*, by Olive Mary Busby. Discussion of the ritual source of the Shakespearean fool foreshadows the ritualistic structure of Eliot's later drama.

P20 "Four Elizabethan Dramatists." *Criterion* 2.6 (February 1924): 115-23. Rpt. in *Selected Essays* 91-99.

A "preface to an unwritten book" surveys critical perspectives on Elizabethan drama. Charles Lamb, while exciting interest in poetic drama, unfortunately created a distinction between drama and literature. William Archer successfully explains the dramatic faults of the Elizabethans, but fails to perceive the difference in conventions between their age and his own. Elizabethan drama, to be satisfactorily performed in the present—achieving a direct relationship between the play and the audience—demands an acting method different from contemporary method.

P21 "Shakespeare and Montaigne." *Times Literary Supplement* 1248 (24 December 1925): 895.

Review of *Shakespeare's Debt to Montaigne*, by George Coffin Taylor. While Montaigne seems to have been an important influence upon Shakespeare, it is not the influence of one philosopher upon another because Shakespeare was a craftsman and a playwright, not a philosopher.

P22 "A Popular Shakespeare." *Times Literary Supplement* 1255 (4 February 1926): 76.

Review of *The Works of Shakespeare, Chronologically Arranged*. The canon is confusingly categorized here under the heads of Comedies, Histories, and Tragedies; it is bewildering to find *Pericles* and *Cymbeline* among the Tragedies, and *Coriolanus* and *Troilus and Cressida* among the Histories. Laudably, this is a popularly accessible edition: it does not distract the reader by raising questions about the authorship of the plays or presenting esoteric theories about them.

P23   [Introduction to] *Savonarola*. Charlotte Champe Eliot.   London: R. Cobden-Sanderson, 1926, vii-xii.

A continuum of dramatic form ranges from liturgy to realism, determined by a tension between these two end-points.   Modern drama is at the extreme realistic end of this continuum, and must start to move in the other direction via verse drama.   Like a church service, drama should stimulate an audience to improve our lives.

P24   "[Review of] *All God's Chillun Got Wings, Desire Under the Elms*, and *Welded*."   *Criterion* 4.2 (April 1926): 395-96.

Review of plays by Eugene O'Neill.

P25   "Massinger."   *Times Literary Supplement* 1294 (18 November 1926): 814.

Review of *Étude sur la collaboration de Massinger avec Fletcher et son groupe*, by Maurice Chelli, and *Massinger's A New Way to Pay Old Debts*, edited by A. H. Cruikshank.   The kind of collaboration undertaken by Elizabethan playwrights does not lead to the best work; the genius of such dramatists as Middleton and Rowley makes them incompatible co-authors.   The period's best plays are by a single author; collaborative efforts, probably motivated by economic motives and need, generated many mediocre plays.

P26   "More and Tudor Drama."   *Times Literary Supplement* 1296 (2 December 1926): 880.

Review of *Early Tudor Drama: Medwall, the Rastells, Heywood, and the More Circle*, by A. W. Reed.   Sir Thomas More seems to have influenced the eleven important plays produced in his time.

P27   "A Study of Marlowe."   *Times Literary Supplement* 1309 (3 March 1927): 140.

Review of *Christopher Marlowe*, by U. M. Ellis-Fermor.   Marlowe deserves to be appreciated as more than just Shakespeare's most important predecessor; he is temperamentally very different from Shakespeare and should be recognized as having his own unique canon.   In *Tamburlaine* there is a personal facet to the presentation of Christians and Christianity—a degree of audacious revolt.

P28   *Shakespeare and the Stoicism of Seneca*. London: The De La More P, 1927. Rpt. in *Selected Essays* 107-20.

The wide range of interpretations of Shakespeare's plays is beneficial: none of them may be right, but still, it is preferable to change occasionally our ways of being wrong. Senecan principles, representing the Roman stoicism that influences Elizabethan drama, provide a model for an individual's behavior in a society that overwhelms him or treats him with indifference or hostility; such a character uses stoicism to cheer himself up. This sensibility provides an important interpretive focus for Shakespeare's plays. It is a mistake, though, to call Shakespeare a Senecan thinker, or to consider the plays as indicative of Shakespeare's philosophical thinking: it was not Shakespeare's job to think, or to invent any brilliant meaning in his plays; the best poet merely transforms into poetry the system of thought of his age.

P29 "Plays of Ben Jonson." *Times Literary Supplement* 1329 (21 July 1927): 500.

    Review of *Ben Jonson*, vol. III, edited by C. H. Herford and Percy Simpson; *Eastward Hoe*, by Chapman, Jonson, and Marston, edited by Julia Hamlet Harris; and *The Alchemist*, replica of first quarto. Jonson's texts are the most accurate Elizabethan plays extant; he cared more than any of his contemporaries for posterity, and expended a great deal of energy altering, polishing, editing, and improving his texts.

P30 "[Review of] *The Playgoers' Handbook to the English Renaissance Drama*, by Agnes Mure Mackenzie." *Times Literary Supplement* 1334 (25 August 1927): 577.

    The author injudiciously criticizes the Elizabethans excessively—for example, calling Chapman's plays only intellectually passionate; noting an emotional absence in Middleton, Rowley, Webster, and Tourneur—thus discouraging a popular cultivation of familiarity with these playwrights.

P31 [Introduction to] *Seneca His Tenne Tragedies*. Ed. Thomas Newton. London: Constable, 1927, 1.v-liv. Rpt. as "Seneca in Elizabethan Translation" in *Selected Essays* 51-88.

    Seneca, highly esteemed during the Renaissance though denigrated now, influenced Elizabethan tragedy more than anyone else. His plays were probably composed for private declamation or elocution rather than stage performance. His unacted drama does not embody, like Greek drama, a concrete tie to reality, but rather, instills dramatic power within language itself. His plays of recitation to an audience that actually sees none of the horrors described are evocative of modern radio drama. Though Seneca produced fine verse, his non-theatrical drama is not genuine drama. Roman culture, like many others, was not gifted with a vital dramatic tradition. Seneca's drama embodies a cruder, simpler sensibility than Greek drama: lacking the Greeks' moral and aesthetic complexities, it exhibits a more practical and public sensibility, and thus tends toward rhetoric. The Elizabethans—vastly more familiar with

Seneca than with Greek dramatists—transposed Senecan rhetoric and stoicism in their copious commonplaces and maxims and took from him the five-act structure. Seneca's influence on the "tragedy of blood" has been overestimated: its plot and sensibility are more indebted to an Italian tradition. His responsibility for bombast in Elizabethan diction has been misconstrued: though Senecan rhetoric certainly generated some badly overwrought dramatic verse, it was equally responsible for prompting the valuable Elizabethan exploration of the rich oratorical and declamatory resources of language, the fruits of which infuse the finest poetry of Shakespeare and Marlowe. His influence on Elizabethan thought has been undervalued. English translations of Seneca's trage-dies from 1559 to 1581 are an embryonic form of Elizabethan tragedy and demonstrate the contemporary transformation of versification, lan-guage, and sensibility—most crucially for the future course of English poetry and verse drama, the sublime aesthetic force of iambic pentameter which displaced the fourteener.

P32 "Thomas Middleton." *Times Literary Supplement* 1326 (30 June 1927): 445-46. Rpt. in *Selected Essays* 140-48.

Middleton is relatively unappreciated because it is difficult to imag-ine his personality. Though his legacy is uncertain and extremely var-ied, his greatness transcends personality and encompasses the Elizabe-than epoch. *The Changeling* is his greatest play because we see at the end that it is concerned not with only Elizabethan morality but with universal and eternal passions. Middleton understood women in tragedy better than any of his contemporaries except Shakespeare, and presented a finer woman than any Elizabethan playwright. His comedy *The Roar-ing Girle* shows his great "photographic" observation of human nature, a trait which ennobles his canon despite the fact that it embodies no message.

P33 "Stage Studies." *Times Literary Supplement* 1349 (8 December 1927): 927.

Review of *Pre-Restoration Stage Studies* and *The Physical Condi-tions of the Elizabethan Public Playhouse*, by William J. Lawrence. Elizabethan production details for *Hamlet* might be beneficially used today.

P34 "A Dialogue on Poetic Drama." Preface to Of *Dramatick Poesie: An Essay, 1688*, by John Dryden. London: Frederick Etchells & Hugh Macdonald, 1928. Rpt. as "A Dialogue on Dramatic Poetry" in *Select-ed Essays* 31-45.

Seven speakers offer a profusion of ideas about the state of drama: Aristotle's homogenous dramatic sensibility made him a better critic of the form than current critics, who have created a muddle with their knowledge of politics, history, religion, and so forth; nor was Dryden tainted by excessive knowledge or awareness of cultural differences. Aeschylus, Sophocles, Elizabethan and Restoration dramatists all had a moral attitude in common with their audiences; Pinero, Shaw, Coward, among other current playwrights, are too cleverly distanced from their audiences' sensibilities. They may have great dramatic abilities but that does not produce great drama. Though poetry is currently criticized as a formal restriction upon drama, any dramatic representation is inherently artificial. All poetry tends toward drama and vice versa. Ballet provides a valuable paradigm for drama, having committed itself to a permanent and traditional form. In the present religion and drama may be merged with the intention of satisfying and advancing both entities, but this may be a confusion of forms. The perfect and ideal drama is found in the ceremony of the Mass. Dryden, finally, may be taken as a consummate model for the modern poetic dramatist because he remained confident of the value of his enterprise despite the differences between his age and that of the greatest playwrights in the English tradition—differences he ignored.

P35 "The Oxford Jonson." *Dial* (New York) 85.1 (July 1928): 65-68.
Review of *Ben Jonson*, vols. I-III, edited by C. H. Herford and Percy Simpson. It is Jonson's personality, as much as his work, that makes him the greatest single influence on the course of English literature. His plays may leave readers repelled or indifferent because his satire is not intense and seems not to derive from sincere personal feeling; his world of unemotional satire may not have an enduring attraction, but every writer can learn from it.

P36 "Introduction to Goethe." *Nation & Athenaeum* 44.15 (12 January 1929): 527.
Review of *Goethe and Faust: An Interpretation* by F. Melian Stawell and G. Lowes Dickinson, and *Goethe's Faust*, translated by Anna Swanwick. Only beautiful poetry makes it possible to read the dreary second part of *Faust*. Goethe's work, adored by mid-Victorians, is now out of fashion but should be revived.

P37 "Cyril Tourneur." *Times Literary Supplement* 1502 (13 November 1930): 925-26. Rpt. in *Selected Essays* 159-69.
None of Tourneur's characters exhibits any notable humanistic morality, but they are all well-arranged in relation to each other. Though they are unreal, the unreality is balanced to scale so a close emotional pattern—an important dramatic attribute—is achieved. His technical innovations are remarkable: a lively style, with perfect words and rhythms, secures the status of this playwright whose biography and canon are largely cloaked in mystery.

P38 [Introduction to] *The Wheel of Fire*. George Wilson Knight. Oxford: Oxford U P, 1930, xi-xix.

Shakespearean interpretation is made difficult because Shakespeare, unlike Dante, is not a philosophical poet and is thus highly inscrutable; and because the idea of objective meaning of any poetry is perhaps ungraspable. Knight insightfully searches for patterns beneath the level of plot and character.

P39 "Thomas Heywood." *Times Literary Supplement* 1539 (30 July 1931): 589-90. Rpt. in *Selected Essays* 149-58.

Heywood's trademark is his empty exploitation of popular tastes—the resort of those unwilling to explore ethics. Because of the ordinariness of his characters, some misleadingly call him a realist; but there is no moral synthesis, vision, artistic unity, or pattern in his works.

P40 "John Ford." *Times Literary Supplement* 1579 (5 May 1932): 317-18. Rpt. in *Selected Essays* 170-80.

The characters created by a great dramatic poet must dramatize a search for harmony in the writer's soul. Shakespeare's plays, which develop continuously from beginning to end of his canon and present themselves as if they were one unified poem, are the standard. Ford's best-known play, *'Tis Pity She's a Whore*, fails in this regard. *Perkin Warbeck*, though, is one of the period's best historical plays. The cadence, tone, and rhythms of his blank verse are personal and distinct—few of his peers can match his originality. Throughout Elizabethan and Jacobean drama the playwrights are not disturbed by the sense of a changing world. They believed in their society as current writers cannot; consequently they are able to focus on the common attributes of humanity rather than the differences.

P41 "The Rock." *Spectator* 152.5528 (8 June 1934): 887.

Responding to criticism of *The Rock* in the previous week's *Spectator*, Eliot calls the pageant a revue and an advertisement for the church-building campaign, not a contribution to English dramatic literature; and defends himself against what he calls vague charges of illogic and unwillingness to substantiate his beliefs.

P42 "John Marston." *Times Literary Supplement* 1695 (26 July 1934): 517-18.

Review of *The Plays of John Marston*, vol. I, edited by H. Harvey Wood, and *The Malcontent*, edited by G. B. Harrison. While the reputations of most sixteenth- and seventeenth-century dramatists are firmly established, there is still a wide range of unsettled opinion and controversy about Marston. His work at first seems to be that of a poet with no inclination, other than economic necessity, to write plays; yet there are indications of poetic and dramatic talent that forestall this judgment. The strength of Middleton's most successful plays, such as *The Malcontent*, lies in his unique and powerful personality, marked by rebellious discontent. In his drama, as, perhaps, in all poetic drama, the action seems to take place on two levels at the same time: something is happening beyond the literal. Marston's genius lies in the way in which he brings out this sense of something underlying the surface; gradually his drama presents a pattern behind the pattern—something we rarely notice in our own lives because the modern world has destroyed our sensitivity.

P43 "Religious Drama and the Church." *Rep* [Magazine of the Croyden and Westminster Repertory Theatres] 1.6 (October 1934): 4-5.

Young poets interested in theatre must choose between the mutually exclusive alternatives of the Church and Communism. The church should prepare its members for religious drama and demand theological orthodoxy.

P44 "Shakespearian Criticism I. From Dryden to Coleridge." In *A Companion to Shakespeare Studies*. Ed. Harley Granville-Barker and G. B. Harrison. Cambridge: Cambridge U P, 1934, 287-99.

We must avail ourselves of at least some of the voluminous Shakespeare criticism because we cannot judge his greatness unaided. Every critical view is a partial one and changes with the world's changes, though we may not realize that the world 100 years hence will think differently of Shakespeare than at the present time and that previous criticism is not inherently inferior to contemporary criticism. We may discern a pattern in past criticism: Jonson gives the best contemporary reaction to Shakespeare; Dryden mixes dramatic and literary criticism, while Pope and Addison give a more poetically textual criticism; Johnson honors Shakespeare with the heights of classical rhetoric; Coleridge, influenced by the Germans, focuses on the character as an individual—transcending the play's context—and might loosely be considered a forerunner of the psychoanalytic critic.

P45 "Audiences, Producers, Plays, Poets." *New Verse* 18 (December 1935): 3-4.

A new dramatic literature cannot come about until audiences and producers can help poets write for the theatre. A poet who starts playwriting at this time will probably not be very good because the task is so unfamiliar. Dramatic poetry (like all poetry) must be interesting—exciting to audiences, and sustaining interest and form—rather than a theoretical exercise.

P46 *"Shakespeare.* By John Middleton Murry" *Criterion* 15.61 (July 1936): 708-10.

Approves of the author's assertion that Shakespeare's maturity came so rapidly as to be almost immediate, and bemoans the fact that Murry is too brief on the later plays (on which a better scholar, Eliot finds, is G. Wilson Knight).

P47 "The Need for Poetic Drama." *Listener* 16.411 (25 November 1936): 994-95.

Poetry is the natural medium for drama, providing the intense excitement that the abstractions of a prose play cannot offer. Yeats and the Abbey theatre are to be credited with the revival of the genre, along with Shakespearean scholars who have helped explain how Elizabethan plays should be properly produced. Drama should not compete with cinema, which is a medium of illusion unconnected with its audience and which does not ennoble the spoken word. Good poetic drama is not simply a play translated into verse but rather a play wholly conceived and composed in terms of poetry, embodying a pattern like that of music. It must have an immediate effect on an audience that has not previously read the poetry—otherwise it is not dramatic; and it must give pleasure to a reader of the script—otherwise it is not poetry. It must be informed by, but not a pale imitation of, drama from previous periods.

P48 "Five Points on Dramatic Writing." *Townsman* 1.3 (July 1938): 10.

A brief facetious open letter to Ezra Pound states that it is of supreme importance to keep the audience's attention; important ideas must be surreptitiously introduced; verse is a medium for something deeper, not a decoration in itself.

P49 "The Future of Poetic Drama." *Drama* [Journal of British Drama League, London] 17 (October 1938): 3-5.

While there are sufficient audiences and producers to ensure the proliferation of verse drama—at least in small productions—there is a dearth of capable authors and actors. Actors, who must truly act in verse and not simply declaim poetry, have been inadequately trained to appreciate the delicately musical nuances of prosody. Speaking lines as if the stresses were in the same position in each line, they produce a soporific drone. Perhaps poetic actors who demonstrate an ear from dramatic verse should be selected when they are very young and precluded from acting in prose plays. Poets who write for the stage cannot simply learn about the theatre and fill scripts with poetry: they must learn to write a different kind of poetry, in which the implicit speaker is not the poet himself—as is the case with ordinary poetry—but someone else. An additional reason for the short supply of verse dramatists is the tremendous dedication required to write plays; most poets have too many other claims on their time to be able to give the necessary attention to playwriting.

P50 "The Duchess of Malfy." *Listener* 26.675 (18 December 1941): 825-26.

Webster is consummately representative of Elizabethan drama in its period of decline. His characters are unreal and his best play, *The Duchess of Malfy*, embodies an inconsequential plot and inconsistent behavior though it powerfully delivers sensation and novelty, which his audience appreciated. While some of his isolated scenes express a truth, the play as a whole does not (as Shakespeare's do). He has, though, a moral and artistic seriousness, which gives his plays a unity that those of his contemporaries lack.

P51 *The Music of Poetry*. Glasgow: Jackson, 1942. Rpt. in *On Poetry and Poets* 17-33.

Poetry must cling closely to everyday common speech; it is, essentially, just a person talking to someone else. The failure of Shelley's *The Cenci* and copious other verse plays by great nineteenth-century poets is that their speech rhythms do not sound like those of any person except a poetry reader. Shakespeare did more for the English language than any other poet, adapting drama to colloquial speech and then elaborating his language without losing the connection with the colloquial.

P52 [Introduction to] *Shakespeare and the Popular Dramatic Tradition*. S. L. Bethell. Durham, NC: Duke U P, 1944, vii-x.

As Shakespearean scholarship accumulates readers must wonder what function is served by the plethora of interpretive criticism—that is, the endless relation of historical facts to the contemporary consciousness. Shakespeare looks different to every age and Shakespearean criticism can give us an insight into the consciousness of the critic's epoch. We assume that we now know more about Shakespeare than any earlier age, because we now have a greater volume of historical scholarship and we assume that such scholarship advances progressively. Shakespearean criticism affects theatrical productions of the plays, adding a historical burden unfelt by the contemporary playgoer. Writing verse drama today demands that the playwright be more conscious about his enterprise than Shakespeare was: in guessing how people would speak if they spoke in poetry, the modern verse dramatist must disclose in these characters a deeper reality and consciousness than in normal life. Poetic drama is not just a standard drama put into verse, but rather, a wholly different kind of work: it is more realistic than naturalistic drama because it removes surfaces and exposes what is inside the facade. While characters may seem to behave inconsistently, there exists a deeper consistency. Both audiences and verse playwrights today must train themselves to perceive a sensibility that came naturally to an Elizabethan audience.

P53 "A Personal Letter from T. S. Eliot." *Stage Door* [The Magazine of the Newton Abbot Repertory Company] 1 (October 1948): 4-5.
Concerns a production of *MC*.

P54 *The Aims of Poetic Drama*. London: The Poets Theatre Guild, 1949.
Early version of *Poetry and Drama*.

P55 *Poetry and Drama*. Cambridge, MA: Harvard U P, 1951. Rpt. in *On Poetry and Poets* 75-95.
There must be a dramatic purpose for poetic drama; the poetry cannot be mere decoration, and if a play can be written in prose then it should be. The play and its language should be perfectly suited to each other, not two separate things. Mixing prose and verse is undesirable in modern drama because it jolts the audience and improperly accentuates the presence of verse. Poetic drama should leave the audience unaware that it has been listening specifically to poetry. The poetic play should succeed even among an audience that may not like poetry. A poet who also writes verse drama must realize that that poetry is for other voices, not his own. While verse is more tolerated in historical or mythological dramas, modern playwrights should use poetic drama for subjects related to the real and contemporary world of the audience; the mundane present world would thus become transfigured. Ideally, poetic drama should impose a sublime order on life: action and language should combine to evoke, simultaneously, dramatic and musical order.

P56 [Preface to] *The Film of Murder in the Cathedral*. With George Hoellering. New York: Harcourt, 1952.
Discusses collaboration on the film and the difference between stage and screen: cinema is more realistic than stage; the audience contributes less to the performance; we are seized with illusion; the audience cannot follow as complex a plot, but must have a more straightforwardly episodic narrative; the camera provides a singular direction of the eye. The additions made for the film script are a tour de force.

P57 *The Three Voices of Poetry*. Cambridge: Cambridge U P, 1953. Rpt. in *On Poetry and Poets* 96-112.
Describes three kinds of communication in poetry: the poet speaking to himself; the poet communicating to an audience; and the poet creating a dramatic character who speaks in verse and represents not the poet, but some detached imaginary character in dialogue with another. This third dramatic voice, an element of which Eliot sees even in his early poetry, is very different from the other two. In *The Rock* this third voice is not attained: the actors do not embody a character of their own, but only spout Eliot's own words. Incipiently in *MC*, and more prominently by 1938, Eliot became attuned to his third voice. A play-

wright may implant in his characters some aspect of his own personality, something perhaps very latent within himself. A true dramatic character cannot emerge out of a dramatic monologue such as Browning's masterful examples; but must exist only in action, that is, arising out of communication with another character. In the plays of a great verse dramatist, such as Shakespeare, the playwright is the common element in every character: he is present everywhere, and hidden everywhere, in the plays' world.

P58 [Foreword to the English edition of] *Shakespeare*.   Henri Fluchère. New York: Longmans, Green, 1953, v-vii.

Fluchère's work, an introduction for French students to the previous 25 years of English Shakespearean criticism, fills a void that no English criticism has addressed: giving an overview of Shakespeare's drama and considering his work in relation to other Elizabethan playwrights. Fluchère's qualifications are unmatched by many other critics since he is a poet, a philosopher, and a man of the theatre—cognizant of the special conditions of drama and Elizabethan culture—who has had his own dramatic successes and knows the point of view of producer, actor, and audience.

P59 *Religious Drama: Mediaeval and Modern*.   New York: House of Books, 1954.

Modern audiences at medieval plays such as *Everyman* and the York and Beverly cycles, which flourished in the fourteenth and fifteenth centuries, may mistakenly attend them out of a sense of duty rather than for enjoyment and immediacy. Medieval actors who played in Nativity plays were unaware of the gap between Christ's time and their own, while modern audiences are made highly conscious of the difference between medieval and modern religiously emotional drama; today, we avoid the direct emotion. Medieval audiences enjoyed the combined piety, drama, and spectacular entertainment of these plays because it was all that was available; they did not look to different dramatic genres for different messages. They were fortunate in not having a diffusion of dramatic forms, as the Greek tragedians were fortunate not to have had cinemas in ancient Athens. To experience religious plays properly—medieval or modern—we must recapture the experience of the medieval audience. A religious play must not be purely religious, or it only inadequately duplicates the efforts of the liturgy. It must be a combination of religious and plainly dramatic interest; it must be related to the secular theatre. All serious drama, religious and secular, must be more fully infused with Christian faith because theatre is a forum where people can achieve, vicariously, greater dignity and meaning than is available in daily life; mere distractive amusement, such as cinema, can never satisfy this need. The decline in Greek drama from Sophocles to

Euripides reflects a less effective grasp of a communal morality. In drama, as in real life, we must integrate the religious and secular realms—as medieval people did, though in a more complex way. Cathedrals should sponsor amateur companies with cycles of modern religious plays, which would have the correlary benefit of combatting the excessively metropolitan and mechanized contemporary drama.

P60 "Gordon Craig's Socratic Dialogues." *Drama* n. s. 36 (Spring 1955): 16-21.

Craig's 1905 and 1910 dialogues in *On the Art of the Theatre*, about dramatic production, may be responsible for an overemphasis on the importance of staging and design at the expense of the script and other composite aspects of the theatre. While Craig's set designs eliminated a good deal of superfluous and distracting scenery from the English stage, the extreme simplicity he offered as replacement may attract attention too aggressively: this is a mistake because the set should attract the audience's attention for only a few seconds after the play begins and then melt into an unconscious background. Craig is to be commended, though, for his advice to the producer to ignore stage directions, which are an interference by the author into the producer's affairs and an admission of a flaw in the script.

P61 [Preface to] *Poems and Verse Plays*, vol. 2. Hugo von Hofmannsthal. Ed. Michael Hamburger. New York: Pantheon, 1961, xi-xii.

Hofmannsthal, W. B. Yeats, and Paul Claudel are the most important figures in the effort to maintain and reanimate verse drama.

Other Essays Relevant to Eliot's Plays

P62 "The Idea of a Christian Society" (1939). In *Christianity and Culture*. New York: Harcourt, 1960, 1-77.

Eliot's vision of secular social promotion of Christian values, which serves as a backdrop to most of his drama.

P63 "On the Place and Function of the Clerisy" (1944). In *T. S. Eliot's Social Criticism*. Roger Kojecky. London: Faber & Faber, 1971, 240-48.

The "clerisy," a Coleridgean concept, performs the elite vocation of serving as social overseers; relevant in terms of various characters in Eliot's plays who loosely serve in such a role (especially the Guardians in *CP*).

Interviews

P64 Blair, Raymond J. "'The Confidential Clerk': Comments by T. S. Eliot." New York *Herald Tribune* 7 February 1954: 4.1.

   Answering questions about the play, which he says may be seen as either comic or tragic, Eliot states that he feels more comfortable and satisfied with this play than with his previous one; all the characters are part of the action, unlike the Guardians in *CP* who were outside the drama. He rejects any autobiographical connections to the work.

P65 Breit, Harvey. "T. S. Eliot." In *The Writer Observed*. Cleveland: World, 1956, 35-38. (Interview conducted 21 November 1948.)

   Eliot discusses his playwriting aptitude and process, calling himself an inexpert dramatist.

P66 Hailey, Foster. "An Interview with T. S. Eliot." *New York Times* 16 April 1950: 2.1, 3.

   Eliot discusses various interpretations of *CP*.

P67 Hall, Donald. "The Art of Poetry, I: T. S. Eliot." *Paris Review* 21 (Spring/Summer 1959): 47-70.

   Eliot discusses the relationship between *MC* and "Burnt Norton"; composition habits while writing *ES*; his hiatus from playwriting during World War II; his sense of development throughout his dramatic career; and the difference between writing plays and poems.

P68 Hamilton, Iain. "Comments on *The Cocktail Party*." *World Review* (London) n. s. 9 (November 1949): 19-22.

   Obliquely answering pointed questions about the play's meaning, Eliot says that it must have more varied meanings than he perceives himself. The audience should forget that it is listening to poetry or it will become distracted. The poetic dramatist must not produce a character he has already analyzed, but rather, present a character the audience itself can analyze; his play must be about people, not ideas. Finally, Eliot asks his questioner to suppose that Shakespeare had been asked about what Hamlet meant, and suggests that it is for the best that the hypothetical answers do not exist.

Manuscripts and Archival Holdings

   Lyndall Gordon's *Eliot's New Life* (C309) and E. Martin Browne's *The Making of T. S. Eliot's Plays* (C277) detail numerous draft, scenario, composition, and manuscript developments for the plays.

• Houghton Library, Harvard University: Manuscript of *MC*, notebooks, letters. Typescript scenarios and other notes for *FR*. A typescript of Eliot's

1937 lectures at Edinburgh University, "Shakespeare as Poet and Dramatist," never published.

• John Hayward Collection, King's College, Cambridge: Drafts and manuscripts of *FR, CP, CC, ES*. Scenario for *The Superior Landlord*, an incompleted expansion of *SA*.

• Bodleian Library, Oxford: Scenarios, notes, and typescript drafts of *The Rock*.

• Performing Arts Research Center, The New York Public Library at Lincoln Center: Archival collection of programs, reviews, production details, photographs for the plays.

• The T. S. Eliot Collection of The University of Texas at Austin: Typescript with autograph revisions of *CP*; autograph manuscript of excerpts from *CC*, with queries to Eliot from Mary Trevelyan; typescript of *ES* with autograph corrections.

Secondary Sources

In compiling my bibliography I have been aided by the vital scholarship of other bibliographers. This bibliography lists only published English-language criticism. It does not wholly reproduce other bibliographies—I have not included a relatively small number of sources which I have deemed minimally relevant, especially in view of the overall profusion of material—so readers may also want to consult the sources listed below.

Bibliographies

C1   Adelman, Irving, and Rita Dworkin. *Modern Drama: A Checklist of Critical Literature on 20th Century Plays*. Metuchen, NJ: Scarecrow P, 1967, 93-103.

C2   Breed, Paul F., and Florence Sniderman, comps. *Dramatic Criticism Index: A Bibliography of Commentaries on Playwrights from Ibsen to the Avant-Garde*. Detroit: Gale, 1972, 202-14.

C3   Brooker, Jewel Spears. "Materials" and "Works Cited" in *Approaches to Teaching Eliot's Poetry and Plays*. New York: Modern Language Association, 1988.

C4   Carpenter, Charles A. "T. S. Eliot as Dramatist: Critical Studies in English, 1933-1975." *Bulletin of Bibliography and Magazine Notes* 33.1 (January 1976): 1-12.

C5   Coleman, Arthur, and Gary R. Tyler. *Drama Criticism. Vol. I: A Checklist of Interpretation Since 1940 of English and American Plays*. Denver: Alan Swallow, 1966, 56-67.

C6   Frank, Mechthild, Armin Paul Frank, and K. P. S. Jochum. *T. S. Eliot Criticism in English, 1916-1965: A Supplementary Bibliography.* Edmonton, Alberta: Yeats Eliot Review Monograph Series 1, 1978.
        Augments Ricks's bibliography.

C7   Gallup, Donald Clifford. *T. S. Eliot: A Bibliography.* New York: Harcourt, 1969.
        Primary sources.

C8   Jones, David E. "Bibliography." In *The Plays of T. S. Eliot.* Toronto: U of Toronto P, 1960, 221-38.

C9   Ludwig, Richard M. "T. S. Eliot." In *Sixteen Modern American Authors: Survey of Research and Criticism.* New York: Norton, 1973, 181-222.

C10   Martin, Mildred. *A Half-Century of Eliot Criticism; an annotated bibliography of books and articles in English, 1916-1965.* Lewisburg, PA: Bucknell U P, 1972.

C11   *Modern Language Association International Bibliography of Books and Articles on the Modern Languages and Literature.* New York: Modern Language Association.
        Print volumes 1921-present; computer index on CD-ROM 1981-present.

C12   Ricks, Beatrice. *T. S. Eliot: A Bibliography of Secondary Works.* Metuchen, NJ: Scarecrow P, 1980.

Discussions of Individual Plays

In sections I and II below are organized, by play, two categories of sources: in the first are reviews and popular discussions and in the second are scholarly essays. Section III lists more general scholarly writing: essays and sections of books that treat more than one play, or give an overview of Eliot's drama and dramatic theory.

The distinction between reviews and scholarship (which is reflected in my discussion of each play, in separate sections that summarize reviews and scholarly reactions) seems generally sensible though it is admittedly, in a few places, arbitrary. By reviews I mean to denote immediate popular reaction, focusing on audience response to performances and the effectiveness of a production. Scholarly essays provide a more intricate response to the work.

It would be disingenuous to deny that certain readers (academics, for example) might imbue the scholarship with a privileged status, while other readers (actors, drama aficianados) might similarly favor the straightforward reviews as being more important. I mean to indicate no prejudice against either of these—merely to recognize that there are different genres of response to a work, and the user of this book might benefit from having some indication of the two different types. The scholarly sources are annotated, unlike the reviews, because the former are more likely to present idiosyncratic analysis than the latter: reviews tend to break down into simply good, bad, or mixed, and consequently, sometimes repeat each other. The "Performance reviews" section for each play gives a general sense of the tenor and range of reviews.

The distinction between reviews and scholarship is not always absolute: occasionally in my discussions of each play I have included a comment from an academic source in the section on "Performance reviews" or "Production history" because it seemed to fit better there; or, conversely, a statement from a review published shortly after a play's debut may give details about production history, or may be beneficially considered in the context of a play's scholarly dialogue.

I. Reviews and Popular Discussions

About 50 of the sources in this bibliography—mainly reviews—are conveniently collected in Michael Grant's *T. S. Eliot: The Critical Heritage* (2 vols.), London: Routledge & Kegan Paul, 1982 (marked with a dagger). These essays and articles are almost exactly duplicated in Graham Clarke's *T. S. Eliot: Critical Assessments*, vol. 3, London: Christopher Helm, 1990.

Many American reviews (marked below with an asterisk) are compiled in *New York Theatre Critics' Reviews*, published annually by Critics' Theatre Reviews, Inc., New York. A number of other reviews below are excerpted throughout E. Martin Browne's *The Making of T. S. Eliot's Plays*, and are cited as they appear there.

In parentheses following each citation of a review is the specific production (or text) discussed therein.

Sweeney Agonistes

R1   Arnott, Paul. *Independent* 24 August 1988. Rpt. in *London Theatre Record* 8.16 (29 July - 11 August 1988): 1042-43. (Old Red Lion)

R2   †Barker, George. Review. *Adelphi* 5 (January 1933): 310-11. (Text)

R3   Bishop, George W. "Plays by Modern Poets." London *Daily Telegraph* 2 October 1935. (Group Theatre)

R4   †Bridson, D. G. "Views and Reviews: Sweeney Agonistes." *New English Weekly* 2 (12 January 1933): 304. (Text)

R5   Edwards, Christopher. Review. *Spectator* 13 August 1988. Rpt. in *London Theatre Record* 8.16 (29 July - 11 August 1988): 1042. (Old Red Lion)

R6   Lipton, Victor. "Good Light Entertainment." *Show Business* 2 May 1974: 12. (Cocteau Repertory)

R7   MacCarthy, Desmond. "Sweeney Agonistes." *Listener* 13.313 (9 January 1935): 80-81. (Group Theatre)

R8   †Moore, Marianne. "Review." *Poetry* 42 (May 1933): 106-109. (Text)

R9   Panter-Downes, Mollie. "Letter from London." *New Yorker* 41 (26 June 1965): 82-89. (Globe)

R10 Sayers, Michael. "A Year in the Theatre." *Criterion* 15.61 (July 1936): 648-62. (Westminster)

R11 Watt, Douglass. "Musical Events: Tell it to Eliot." *New Yorker* 29.15 (30 May 1953): 93-94. (Columbia)

R12 †Zabel, Morton D. "A Modern Purgatorio." *Commonweal* 17 (19 April 1933): 696-97. (Text)

R13 unsigned. "At the Play." *Punch* 189 (9 October 1935): 412. (Westminster)

R14 unsigned. "Vassar Players Mix Classics with Moderns." New York *Herald Tribune* 7 May 1933: 1.22. (Vassar)

The Rock

R15 Birrell, Francis. Review. *New Statesman* 2 June 1934. In Browne 33. (Sadler's Wells)

R16 Moore, Harry Thornton. Review. *Adelphi* 9.3 (December 1934): 188-89. (Text)

R17 †Sayers, Michael. "Mr. T. S. Eliot's 'The Rock.'" *New English Weekly* 5 (21 June 1934): 230-31. (Sadler's Wells)

R18 Sewell, J. E. "Satire in Church Pageant-Play." London *Daily Telegraph* 29 May 1933: 4. (Sadler's Wells)

R19 Verschoyle, Derek. "The Theatre." *Spectator* 152.5527 (1 June 1934): 851. (Sadler's Wells)

R20 unsigned. "Church Pageant at Sadler's Wells." *Times* (London) 29 May 1934: 12. (Sadler's Wells)

R21   †unsigned. "Mr. Eliot's Pageant Play." *Times Literary Supplement* 1688 (7 June 1934): 404. (Sadler's Wells)

R22   unsigned. "The Rock at Sadler's Wells: a Provocative Passion Play." London *Church Times* 1 June 1934: 677. (Sadler's Wells)

R23   †unsigned. Editorial. *Theology* 29 (July 1934): 4-5. (Sadler's Wells and text)

R24   unsigned. Review. *Blackfriars* 15.172 (July 1934): 499-500. (Sadler's Wells)

R25   †unsigned. Review. *Blackfriars* 15.174 (September 1934): 642-43. (Text)

R26   unsigned. Review. *Catholic World* 140.835 (October 1934): 119-20. (Text)

R27   †unsigned. Review. *Everyman* 47 (17 August 1934): 189. (Sadler's Wells and text)

R28   †unsigned. Review. *Listener* 11 (6 June 1934): 945. (Sadler's Wells)

R29   †unsigned. Review. *Sunday Times* (London) 30 September 1934: 12. (Text)

R30   †unsigned. Review. *Tablet* 164 (4 August 1934): 138. (Text)

Murder in the Cathedral

R31   Arvin, Newton. "About T. S. Eliot." *New Republic* 85.1102 (15 January 1936): 290. (Text)

R32   Atkinson, Brooks. "Meditation of a Martyr in T. S. Eliot's 'Murder in the Cathedral.'" *New York Times* 21 March 1936: 13. (FTP)

R33   _____. "The Play." *New York Times* 17 February 1938: 16. (Ritz)

R34   _____. "Strange Images of Death." *New York Times* 29 March 1936: 9.1. (FTP)

R35   _____. "Triumph at Old Vic." *New York Times* 26 April 1953. (Old Vic)

R36   Barnes, Howard. "'Murder in the Cathedral.' T. S. Eliot's Poetic Melodrama Opens at the Manhattan." New York *Herald Tribune* 21 March 1936: 12. (FTP)

R37   Barnes, T. R. "Poets and the Drama." *Scrutiny* 4.2 (September 1935): 189-93.

R38   Brown, Ivor. "Murder in the Cathedral." *Observer* 15 November 1936. (Duchess)

R39   Colum, Mary M. "Life and Literature: Revival in the Theater." *Forum and Century* 95.6 (June 1936): 344-47. (FTP)

R40   Crowther, Bosley. "The Screen in Review." *New York Times* 26 March 1952: 35. (Film)

R41   Esslin, Martin. "Murder in the Cathedral." *Plays and Players* 20.1 (October 1972): 44-45. (Aldwych)

R42   Gabriel, Gilbert W. "Murder in the Cathedral." New York *American* 21 March 1936: 11. (FTP)

R43   Gerlando Jay. "Mr. Eliot's Encyclical." *The Daily Worker* 26 March 1936. (FTP)

R44   Gregory, Horace. "Poets in the Theatre." *Poetry* 48.4 (July 1936): 221-28.

R45   Guernsey, Otis L., Jr. "Murder in the Cathedral." New York *Herald Tribune* 26 March 1952. (Film)

R46   Isaacs, Edith J. R. "Fresh Fields: Broadway in Review." *Theatre Arts Monthly* 22.4 (April 1938): 247-55. (Ritz)

R47   Jack, Peter Monro. "T. S. Eliot's Drama of Beauty and Momentous Decision." *New York Times Book Review* 27 October 1935: 11. (Text)

R48   Jacobs, Arthur. "'Murder in the Cathedral' as an Opera." *Listener* 59 (20 March 1958): 504-505. (La Scala)

R49   Jeake, Samuel, Jr. [pseudonym for Conrad Aiken]. "London Letter." *New Yorker* 11 (13 July 1935): 61-63. (Canterbury)

R50   †Laughlin, James. "Mr. Eliot on Holy Ground." *New English Weekly* 7 (11 July 1935): 250-51. (Text)

R51 †Matthiessen, F. O. "T. S. Eliot's Drama of Becket." *Saturday Review* 12 (12 October 1935): 10-11. (Text)

R52 †Muir, Edwin. "New Literature." *London Mercury* 32 (July 1935): 281-83. (Text)

R53 Panter-Downes, Mollie. "Letter from London." *New Yorker* 29 (2 May 1953): 87. (Old Vic)

R54 †Parsons, I. M. "Poetry, Drama and Satire." *Spectator* 154.5583 (28 June 1935): 1112. (Text)

R55 Pollock, Arthur. "The Theatre." Brooklyn *Eagle* 17 February 1938. (Ritz)

R56 Pope, W. Macqueen. "Robert Donat Welcomed Back in 'Murder in the Cathedral.'" *Morning Telegraph* (London) 14 April 1953. (Old Vic)

R57 †Pottle, Frederick A. "Drama of Action." *Yale Review* 25 (December 1935): 426-29. (Text)

R58 Putt, S. Gorley. "This Modern Poetry." *Voices* 85 (Spring 1936): 57-61. (Text)

R59 Rahv, Philip. "A Season in Heaven." *Partisan Review* 3.5 (June 1936): 11-14. (Text)

R60 Sayers, Michael. "A Year in the Theatre." *Criterion* 15.61 (July 1936): 648-62.

R61 †Shillito, Edward. "Review." *Christian Century* 52 (2 October 1935): 1249-50. (Text)

R62 Stone, Gregory. "Plays by Eliot and Auden." *American Review* 6.1 (November 1935): 121-28. (Text)

R63 †Van Doren, Mark. "The Holy Blissful Martir." *Nation* 141 (9 October 1935): 417. (Text)

R64 Watts, Richard Jr. "Bringing the Middle Ages to Broadway." New York *Herald Tribune* 29 March 1936: 5.1, 5. (FTP)

R65 _____. "Martyr of Canterbury." New York *Herald Tribune* 17 February 1938. (Ritz)

R66 Young, Stark. "Government and Guild." *New Republic* 86.1114 (8 April 1936): 253. (FTP)

R67 _____. "Mr. Miller's Importations." *New Republic* 94.1213 (2 March 1938): 101. (Text)

R68 †unsigned. "Mr. Eliot's New Play." *Times Literary Supplement* 1741 (13 June 1935): 376. (Text)

R69 unsigned. "Murder in the Cathedral." *Times* (London) 16 September 1936. (Mercury)

R70 unsigned. "New Plays & Old in Manhattan." *Time* 31.9 (28 February 1938): 34. (Ritz)

The Family Reunion

R71 Agate, James. "The Eumenides at Home, Audience at Sea." *Sunday Times* (London) 26 March 1939: 4. (Westminster)

R72 *Aston, Frank. "T. S. Eliot Play a Ghostly Tale." New York *World-Telegram* 21 October 1958. (Phoenix)

R73 *Atkinson, Brooks. "Theatre: Eliot's 'The Family Reunion.'" *New York Times* 21 October 1958: 39. (Phoenix)

R74 †Bodkin, Maud. "The Eumenides and Present-Day Consciousness." *Adelphi* 15 (May 1939): 411-13. (Westminster and text)

R75 †Brooks, Cleanth. "Sin and Expiation." *Partisan Review* 6 (Summer 1939): 114-16. (Text)

R76 †Brown, Ivor. Review. *Observer* 26 March 1939: 15. (Westminster)

R77 *Coleman, Robert. "'Reunion' a Mental Exercise." New York *Daily Mirror* 21 October 1958. (Phoenix)

R78 Darlington, W. A. "T. S. Eliot's New Verse Play." London *Morning Post* 22 March 1939. (Westminster)

R79 Driver, Tom F. "Eliot in Transit." *Christian Century* 75.48 (26 November 1958): 1380-82. (Phoenix)

R80   Fergusson, Francis. "Notes on the Theatre." *Southern Review* 5.3 (1939-40): 562-64.

R81   Gassner, John. "Broadway in Review." *Educational Theatre Journal* 11 (March 1959): 33. (Phoenix)

R82   †Gregory, Horace. "The Unities and Eliot." *Life and Letters* 23 (October 1939): 53-60. (Text)

R83   Hewes, Henry. "Reunions That Don't Reune." *Saturday Review of Literature* 41.45 (8 November 1958): 25. (Phoenix)

R84   †Horton, Philip. "Speculations on Sin." *Kenyon Review* 1 (Summer 1939): 330-33. (Text)

R85   Kelly, Bernard. "The Family Reunion." *Blackfriars* 20.231 (June 1939): 469-71. (Text)

R86   Keown, Eric. "At the Play." *Punch* 211:5525 (13 Nov 1946): 434-35. (Mercury)

R87   *Kerr, Walter. "T. S. Eliot's 2-Act Drama 'The Family Reunion' Opens." New York *Herald Tribune* 21 October 1958: 20. (Phoenix)

R88   †MacCarthy, Desmond. "Some Notes on Mr. Eliot's New Play." *New Statesman* 17 (25 March 1939): 455-56. (Westminster)

R89   †MacNeice, Louis. "Original Sin." *New Republic* 98 (3 May 1939): 384-85. (Text)

R90   Mayer, David. "The Family Reunion." *Plays and Players* 26.8 (May 1979): 29. (Round House)

R91   *McClain, John. "Eliot Play Misses." New York *Journal American* 21 October 1958. (Phoenix)

R92   Morgan, Charles. "The Family Reunion." *Times* (London) 22 March 1939: 12. (Westminster)

R93   †Pottle, Frederick A. "A Modern Verse Play." *Yale Review* 28 (June 1939): 836-39. (Text)

R94   †Ransom, John Crowe. "T. S. Eliot as Dramatist." *Poetry* 54.5 (August 1939): 264-71. (Text)

R95   †Roberts, Michael. "Mr. Eliot's New Play." *London Mercury* 39.234 (April 1939): 641-42. (Text)

R96   Rubens, Robert. "T. S. Eliot's *The Family Reunion*—Forty Years Later." *Contemporary Review* 236.1373 (June 1980): 321-22. (Vaudeville)

R97   Schwartz, Delmore. "Orestes in England." *Nation* 148 (10 June 1939): 676-77. (Text)

R98   *Watts, Richard, Jr. "T. S. Eliot's 'The Family Reunion.'" New York *Post* 21 Oct 1958. (Phoenix)

R99   †unsigned. "Mr. Eliot in Search of the Present." *Times Literary Supplement* 1938 (25 March 1939): 176. (Westminster)

R100 unsigned. "T. S. Eliot's 'Family Reunion' in Cherry Lane." *New York Times* 29 November 1947: 9. (Cherry Lane)

R101 unsigned. "T. S. Eliot's Modern Variation on the Eumenides Myth." *New York Times Book Review* 9 April 1939: 2, 20. (Text)

R102 unsigned. "T. S. Eliot's New Play." *Manchester Guardian* 22 March 1939: 13. (Westminster)

R103 †unsigned. Review. *Listener* 21 (6 April 1939): 750. (Text)

The Cocktail Party

R104 *Atkinson, Brooks. "At the Theatre." *New York Times* 23 January 1950: 17. (Miller's)

R105 Barber, John. "T. S. Eliot's 'Party' Witty, Brutal . . . Valuable." London *Daily Express* 4 May 1950. (New)

R106 *Barnes, Clive. "Theater: The A. P. A.'s 'Cocktail Party.'" *New York Times* 8 October 1968. (Lyceum)

R107 *Barnes, Howard. "Modern Morality Play." New York *Herald Tribune* 23 January 1950: 12. (Miller's)

R108 Baxter, Beverly. "I'm Not Drinking." London *Evening Standard* 5 May 1950. (New)

R109 Billington, Michael. Review. *Guardian* 30 July 1986. (Phoenix)

R110 Brown, Ivor. Review. *Observer* 28 August 1949. In Browne 235. (Edinburgh)

R111 Brown, John Mason. "Honorable Intentions." *Saturday Review* 33 (4 February 1950): 28-30. (Miller's)

R112 Brown, Ray C. B. "Alcoholic Allegory." *Voices* Summer 1950-51: 33-40. (Text)

R113 Bruckner, D. J. R. "Stage: 'Cocktail Party' By the Cocteau Troupe." *New York Times* 2 March 1988: C17. (Cocteau)

R114 Carson, Mary. *Glasgow Herald* 31 August 1949. In Browne 233. (Edinburgh)

R115 *Chapman, John. "'Cocktail Party' Back." New York *Daily News* 8 October 1968. (Lyceum)

R116 *____. "'Cocktail Party' a Masterpiece; Cast Gives Superb Performance." New York *Daily News* 23 January 1950: 39. (Miller's)

R117 Clurman, Harold. "Theatre: Cocktail Party." *New Republic* 122 (13 February 1950): 30-31. (Miller's)

R118 Coleman, Robert. "Eliot's Fine 'Cocktail Party' Goes Right to the Head." New York *Daily Mirror* 23 January 1950: 20. (Miller's)

R119 *Cooke, Richard P. "A Conversation Piece." *Wall Street Journal* 9 October 1968. (Lyceum)

R120 Cookman, A. V. Review. *Times* (London) 24 August 1949. In Browne 233-34. (Edinburgh)

R121 Dobrée, Bonamy. "Books and Writers." *Spectator* 184.6356 (21 April 1950): 541. (Text)

R122 Edman, Irwin. "Incantations by Eliot." *Saturday Review* 33.25 (24 June 1950): 56-57. (Decca recording)

R123 Everett, Barbara. "A Congregation of Solitaries." *Times Literary Supplement* 4350 (15 August 1986): 891. (Phoenix)

R124 †Forster, E. M. "Mr. Eliot's Comedy." *Listener* 43 (23 March 1950): 533. (Text)

R125 *Garland, Robert. "Here's a Masterpiece; A Comedie Humaine." New York *Journal American* 23 January 1950. (Miller's)

R126 Guinness, Alec. "Eliot in the Theatre." *Southern Review* 21.4 (October 1985): 985-86. (Reminiscences about play's first production)

R127 Hamilton, Iain. "A Critic's View." *World Review* n. s. 9 (November 1949): 23. (Edinburgh)

R128 *Hawkins, William. "T. S. Eliot Analyzes 'The Cocktail Party.'" New York *World-Telegraph* 23 January 1950: 16. (Miller's)

R129 Johns, Eric. "Creating a T. S. Eliot Role." *Theatre World* 46.306 (July 1950): 27, 34. (Interview with Margaret Leighton)

R130 Marshall, Margaret. "Drama." *The Nation* 170 (28 January 1950): 94-95.

R131 Nathan, George Jean. "The Cocktail Party." *The Theatre Book of the Year: 1949-50*. New York: Knopf, 1950, 197-203. (Miller's)

R132 _____. "The Theatre: Clinical Notes." *American Mercury* 70.317 (May 1950): 557-58.

R133 Peter, John. "Sin and Soda." *Scrutiny* 17 (Spring 1950): 61-66. (Text)

R134 Phelan, Kappo. "The Stage." *Commonweal* 51 (3 February 1950): 463. (Miller's)

R135 Pollock, Arthur. "Eliot's 'The Cocktail Party' Engrossing and Skillful." New York *Daily Compass* 23 January 1950: 2.15. (Miller's)

R136 Popkin, Henry. "Theatre Letter." *Kenyon Review* 12.2 (Spring 1950): 331-9. (Miller's)

R137 Rich, Frank. "Stage: T. S. Eliot's 'Cocktail Party' Revisited." *New York Times* 13 June 1980: C5. (Orpheum)

R138 †Russell, Peter. "A Note on T. S. Eliot's New Play." *Nine* 1 (October 1949): 28-29. (Edinburgh)

R139 †Shawe-Taylor, Desmond. Review. *New Statesman* 38 (3 September 1949): 243. (Edinburgh)

R140 Sherek, Henry. "On Giving a Cocktail Party." *Theatre Arts* 34 (April 1950): 24-26. (Play's producer recounts his involvement with the production and the author)

R141 †Speaight, Robert. Review. *Tablet* 194 (3 September 1949): 154-55. (Edinburgh)

R142 Spender, Stephen. "After the Cocktail Party." *New York Times Book Review* 19 March 1950: 7, 20.

R143 Thurber, James. "What Cocktail Party?" *New Yorker* 26 (1 April 1950): 26-29. (Satirizes reactions of people at a cocktail party to Eliot's play)

R144 Trewin, J. C. "'The Cocktail Party' Opens in London." *New York Times* 7 May 1950: 2.2. (New)

R145 *Watts, Richard, Jr. "The Theatre Event of the Season." New York *Post* 23 January 1950. (Miller's)

R146 *_____. "T. S. Eliot's Modern Mysticism." New York *Post* 8 October 1968. (Phoenix)

R147 Wertheim, Albert. "The Cocktail Party." *Theatre Journal* 32.3 (October 1980): 393-94.

R148 White, John Minchip. "What a Party!" *Poetry London* 5.19 (August 1950): 24-27. (Text)

R149 Williams, Stephen. "Why Call It Poetic?" London *Evening News* 5 May 1950. (New)

R150 †Williams, William Carlos. "It's About 'Your Life and Mine, Darling.'" New York *Post* 12 March 1950: M18. (Text)

R151 Worsley, T. C. "The Second Cocktail Party." *New Statesman* 39 (13 May 1950): 543. In Browne 245-46. (New)

R152 Wyatt, Euphemia van Rensselaer. "Theater." *Catholic World* 170 (March 1950): 466-67.

R153 Zolotow, Maurice. "Psychoanalyzing the Doctor." *New York Times* 26 February 1950: 2.3. (Alec Guinness discusses his role as Reilly)

R154 unsigned. "Entertainment and Reality." *Times Literary Supplement* 2513 (31 March 1950): 198. (Text)

R155 unsigned. "The Edinburgh Festival, 'The Cocktail Party.'" *Times* (London) 24 August 1949, 8. (Edinburgh)

R156 unsigned. "First Irish Production of 'The Cocktail Party.'" *Irish Times* 18 April 1951: 3. (Aula Maxima)

R157 †unsigned. "Mr. T. S. Eliot's New Play." *Manchester Guardian* 23 August 1949: 3. (Edinburgh)

R158 unsigned. "New Play in Edinburgh." *Time* 54 (5 September 1949): 58. (Edinburgh)

R159 unsigned. "New Plays." *Newsweek* 35.5 (30 January 1950): 66. (Miller's)

R160 unsigned. "New Plays in Manhattan." *Time* 55 (30 January 1950): 37. (Miller's)

R161 unsigned. "New Theatre. The Cocktail Party." *Times* (London) 4 May 1950: 2. (New)

R162 unsigned. "T. S. Eliot Discusses His New Play." *Glasgow Herald.* 27 August 1949: 4. In Browne 236-37. (Interview with Eliot)

R163 unsigned. Review. *Aberdeen Press.* 23 August 1949. In Browne 234-35. (Edinburgh)

The Confidential Clerk

R164 *Atkinson, Brooks. "Comedy by T. S. Eliot With Ina Claire, Claude Rains and Joan Greenwood." *New York Times* 12 February 1954: 22. (Morosco)

R165 Beaufort, John. "'The Confidential Clerk' on Broadway." *Christian Science Monitor* 20 February 1954: 16. (Morosco)

R166 Bellow, Saul. "Pleasures and Pains of Playgoing." *Partisan Review* 21.3 (May-June 1954): 312-15.

R167 †Brooke, Nicholas. "*The Confidential Clerk*: A Theatrical Review." *Durham University Journal* 96 (March 1954): 66-70. (Lyric)

R168 Brown Ivor. Review. New York *Herald Tribune* 30 August 1953. In Browne 288. (Edinburgh)

R169 Brown, Spencer. "T. S. Eliot's Latest Poetic Drama." *Commentary* 17 (April 1954): 367-72.

R170 *Chapman, John. "T. S. Eliot's 'The Confidential Clerk' A Stimulating, Enjoyable Comedy." New York *Daily News* 12 February 1954. (Morosco)

R171 *Coleman, Robert. "Eliot's 'Confidential Clerk' Is Superlative Theatre." New York *Daily Mirror* 12 February 1954. (Morosco)

R172 Darlington, W. A. Review. *New York Times* 30 August 1953. In Browne 288. (Edinburgh)

R173 †Donald, Henry. "Edinburgh Festival." *Spectator* 191 (4 September 1953): 238. (Edinburgh)

R174 †Gardner, Helen. Review. *New Statesman* 47 (20 March 1954): 373-74. (Text)

R175 Gibbs, Wolcott. "The Importance of Being Eliot." *New Yorker* 30 (20 February 1954): 62-66. (Morosco)

R176 Hartley, Anthony. "The Drama and Mr. Eliot." *Spectator* 192.6561 (26 March 1954): 364-65. (Text)

R177 *Hawkins, William. "Comedy, Pathos Mix in 'Confidential Clerk.'" New York *World-Telegram and Sun* 12 February 1954. (Morosco)

R178 Hivnor, Mary. "Theatre Letter." *Kenyon Review* 16.3 (Summer 1954): 463-67. (Morosco)

R179 Hobson, Harold. "Mr. Eliot in the Saddles." *Sunday Times* (London) 30 August 1953: 4. (Edinburgh)

R180 *Kerr, Walter. "The Confidential Clerk." New York *Herald Tribune* 12 February 1954. (Morosco)

R181 Kirk, Russell. "Two Plays of Resignation." *Month* 10 (October 1953): 223-29. (Edinburgh)

R182 *McClain, John. "Rewarding Drama." New York *Journal American* 12 February 1954. (Morosco)

R183 *Watts, Richard, Jr. "T. S. Eliot's 'Confidential Clerk.'" New York *Post* 12 February 1954. (Morosco)

R184 †Weightman, J. G. "Edinburgh, Elsinore and Chelsea." *Twentieth Century* October 1953: 302-10. (Edinburgh)

R185 †Worsley, T. C. Review. *New Statesman* 46 (5 September 1953): 256. (Edinburgh)

R186 unsigned. "The Confidential Clerk." *Variety* 2 September 1953. (Edinburgh)

R187 unsigned. "The Confidential Clerk." *Variety* 13 January 1954.

The Elder Statesman

R188 †Balakian, Nona. "Affirmation and Love in Eliot." *New Leader* 42 (24 May 1959): 20-21. (Text)

R189 Brahms, Caryl. "The Elder Statesman." *Plays and Players* 6.2 (November 1958): 11. (Cambridge)

R190 Brien, Alan. Review. *Spectator* 201.6793 (5 September 1958): 305-306. Rpt. in *Plays in Review 1956-1980: British Drama and the Critics*. Ed. Gareth and Barbara Lloyd Evans. London: Batsford Academic and Educational, 1985, 75-76. (Edinburgh)

R191 Darlington, W. A. "By T. S. Eliot." *New York Times* 31 August 1958: 2.3. (Edinburgh).

R192 Everett, Barbara. Review. *Critical Quarterly* 1.2 (Summer 1959): 163-64, 166. (Text)

R193 †Hewes, Henry. "T. S. Eliot at Seventy, and an Interview with Eliot." *Saturday Review* 41 (13 September 1958): 30-32. (Interview)

R194 Hobson, Harold. "T. S. Eliot's 'The Elder Statesman.'" *Christian Science Monitor* 6 September 1958: 4. (Edinburgh)

R195 Hope-Wallace, Philip. "T. S. Eliot's New Play: 'The Elder Statesman.'" *Manchester Guardian*: 27 August 1958. (Edinburgh)

R196 Jacobi, Peter. "Eliot Play Given U. S. Premiere." *Christian Science Monitor* 6 March 1963: 6. (Miller)

R197 Pope, W. Macqueen. "O'Neill, Eliot Represented On West End." New York *Morning Telegraph* 9 October 1958. (Cambridge)

R198 Salmon, Christopher, and Leslie Paul. "Two Views of Mr. Eliot's New Play." *Listener* 60.1536 (4 September 1958): 340-41. (Edinburgh)

R199 Tynan, Kenneth. Review. *Observer* 31 August 1958. Rpt. in *Plays in Review 1956-1980: British Drama and the Critics*. Ed. Gareth and Barbara Lloyd Evans. London: Batsford Academic and Educational, 1985, 73-75. (Edinburgh)

R200 Unger, Leonard. "Deceptively Simple—and Too Simple." *Virginia Quarterly Review* 35.3 (Summer 1959): 501-504. (Text)

R201 †Weightman, J. G. "After Edinburgh." *Twentieth Century* 164 (October 1958): 342-44. (Edinburgh)

R202 unsigned. "Elder Statesman." *Variety* 19 September 1958. (Edinburgh)

R203 unsigned. "London Opening of an Eliot Play." *Times* (London) 26 September 1958. (Cambridge)

R204 unsigned. "Mr. Eliot's Most Human Play." *Times* (London) 26 August 1958: 11. (Edinburgh)

Cats

R205 *Barnes, Clive. "Cats." New York *Post* 8 October 1982. (Winter Garden)

R206 *Kissel, Howard. "Cats." *Women's Wear Daily* 8 October 1982. (Winter Garden)

R207 *Rich, Frank. "Theater: Lloyd Webber's Cats." *New York Times* 8 October 1982. (Winter Garden)

R208 Wardle, Irving. "Flash Cats and Little Sense." *Times* (London) 12 May 1981: 8. (New London)

R209 *unsigned. "The 'Cats' Meow on Broadway." *Newsweek* 11 October 1982. (Winter Garden)

II. Scholarly Criticism of a Single Play

The bulk of critical writing on individual plays is about *Murder in the Cathedral* and *The Cocktail Party*; *Sweeney Agonistes* and *The Family Reunion* are individually covered in a sizable number of essays, while *The Rock*, *The Confidential Clerk*, and *The Elder Statesman* have relatively few essays devoted solely to them. Researchers looking for criticism of plays other than those most exhaustively covered individually, however, will find ample treatment of the entire dramatic canon in the general discussions and surveys of Eliot's plays listed in section III.

Sweeney Agonistes

C13   Barker, Jonathan. "'Wanna Go Home, Baby?': 'Sweeney Agonistes.'" *Agenda* 23.1-2 (Spring-Summer 1985): 103-10.

        Analyzes *SA* in terms of its position within Eliot's canon and its relation to other poetry and plays; closely examines the characters of Sweeney and Doris.

C14   Bentley, Eric, ed. *From the Modern Repertoire, Series One*. Bloomington: U of Indiana P, 1949.

        Anthology of plays includes notes on Bentley's production of *SA*.

C15   Bentley, Joanne. *Hallie Flanagan: A Life in the American Theatre*. New York: Knopf, 1988.

        Includes details about the first performance of *SA*.

C16   Coghill, Nevill. "*Sweeney Agonistes* (An Anecdote or Two)." In *T. S. Eliot: A Symposium*. Eds. Richard March and Tambimuttu. Freeport, NY: Books for Libraries P, 1968: 82-87. Rpt. in *Critical Essays on T. S. Eliot: The Sweeney Motif*. Ed. Kinley E. Roby. Boston: G. K. Hall, 1985, 115-19.

        Reminiscences of an early encounter with *SA* and a discussion about it with Eliot.

C17   Dorris, George E. "Two Allusions in the Poetry of T. S. Eliot." *English Language Notes* 2.1 (September 1964): 54-57.

        Suggests a passage of dialogue in Henry James's *The Ambassadors* as a source for the exchange about cannibalism and conversion.

C18   Everett, Barbara. "The New Style of *Sweeney Agonistes*." *Yearbook of English Studies* 14 (1984): 243-63.

        A vast range of stylistic borrowings—mainly American—infuse the play's language and tenor; these influences create "a new and essentially modern satiric style" in *SA*.

C19   Freedman, Morris. "Jazz Rhythms and T. S. Eliot." *South Atlantic Quarterly* 51.3 (July 1952): 419-35.
       SA is the most prominent example of Eliot's use of jazz rhythms, with their patterns of repetition, to evoke conversational idiom.

C20   _____. "The Meaning of T. S. Eliot's Jew." *South Atlantic Quarterly* 55.2 (April 1956): 198-206.
       Examination of Eliot's anti-Semitic characterizations includes discussion of "At least two of the clients of Dusty and Doris's bordello . . . [who] have Jewish names."

C21   Galef, David. "Fragments of a Journey: The Drama in T. S. Eliot's *Sweeney Agonistes*." *English Studies* 69.6 (December 1988): 481-96.
       Suggests an underlying Christian structure and a more coherent unity than the fragmentary appearance suggests.

C22   Hargrove, Nancy D. "The Symbolism of Sweeney in the Works of T. S. Eliot." In *Critical Essays on T. S. Eliot: The Sweeney Motif.* Ed. Kinley E. Roby. Boston: G. K. Hall, 1985, 147-69.
       Intricate examination of Eliot's use of the Sweeney character.

C23   Hauge, Hans. "Arnold Bennett and T. S. Eliot: What Happened to *Sweeney Agonistes*?" In *T. S. Eliot Annual No. 1.* Ed. Shyamal Bagchee. London: Macmillan, 1990, 145-52.
       Details possible genesis (as early as 1920) and early drafts of *SA*, and suggests contributions by Bennett and Vivienne Eliot.

C24   Holt, Charles Lloyd. "On Structure and *Sweeney Agonistes*." *Modern Drama* 10 (1967): 43-47. Rpt. in *Critical Essays on T. S. Eliot: The Sweeney Motif.* Ed. Kinley E. Roby. Boston: G. K. Hall, 1985, 130-34.
       Classical backgrounds and structure.

C25   Jayne, Sears. "Mr. Eliot's Agon. *Philological Quarterly* 34 (October 1955): 395-414. Rpt. in *Critical Essays on T. S. Eliot: The Sweeney Motif.* Ed. Kinley E. Roby. Boston: G. K. Hall, 1985, 100-15.
       Exegesis and allusive backgrounds of *SA*.

C26   Morse, Jonathan. "Sweeney, the Sties of the Irish, and *The Waste Land*." In *Critical Essays on T. S. Eliot: The Sweeney Motif.* Ed. Kinley E. Roby. Boston: G. K. Hall, 1985, 135-46.
       Overview of Eliot's and general English stereotypes of the Irish, with reference to *SA*.

C27   Roby, Kinley E. "Introduction." *Critical Essays on T. S. Eliot: The Sweeney Motif.* Boston: G. K. Hall, 1985, 1-29.
      Overview of Eliot's development of the Sweeney character from the early poems up to *SA*.

C28   Schneider, Elisabeth. *T. S. Eliot: The Pattern in the Carpet.* Berkeley: U of California P, 1975.
      Section on *SA* in a survey of Eliot's poetry discusses its genesis and relation to *The Waste Land* and "The Hollow Men."

C29   Sidnell, Michael J. *Dances of Death: The Group Theatre of London in the Thirties.* London: Faber & Faber, 1984.
      Performance details for *SA*, and influences of Rupert Doone's avant-garde Group Theatre company upon Eliot's early drama.

C30   Smith, Carol H. "Sweeney and the Jazz Age." In *Critical Essays on T. S. Eliot: The Sweeney Motif.* Ed. Kinley E. Roby. Boston: G. K. Hall, 1985, 87-99.
      Interplay in *SA* between drama, jazz rhythms and sensibility, and the idea of ritual.

C31   Spanos, William V. "God and the Detective: The Christian Tradition and the Drama of the Absurd." *Newsletter of the Conference on Christianity and Literature* 20.2 (1971): 16-22.
      "One of the most consequential mistakes in modern literary history was Eliot's decision to abandon the formal experiments" in *SA* "in favor of an increasingly subtle naturalistic surface that unfolds a mythic underpattern . . . if the Christian tradition is to recover a place in the modern theater, its dramatists must return to *Sweeney Agonistes* as their model."

C32   _____. "'Wanna Go Home, Baby?': *Sweeney Agonistes* as Drama of the Absurd." *PMLA* 85.1 (October 1970): 8-20.
      Existential aspects of *SA* compared to other examples of this movement. Eliot's "choice of what we might call the anti-Aristotelian form and the Pop Art style of the music hall is itself rooted in his larger desire to project—in all its detail—his version of the metaphysics and ontology of absurdity in a form that becomes a metaphor of it. And this form . . . turns out, not accidentally, to be something remarkably like the comic-tragic anti-art form of the absurdists."

C33   Thompson, T. H. "The Bloody Wood." *London Mercury* 29 (January 1934): 233-39. Rpt. in *T. S. Eliot: A Selected Critique*. Ed. Leonard Unger. New York: Rinehart, 1948, 161-69.

Sweeney's evolution from the early poems to *SA* is extremely unified: the poems contain clues that prove him to be a murderer.

The Rock

C34   Aiken, Conrad. "After 'Ash-Wednesday.'" *Poetry* 45 (December 1934): 161-65.

The Rock makes Eliot's audience uncomfortable about his present direction: it is too glibly rhetorical.

C35   Fox, Arthur W. "Collected Poems of T. S. Eliot." *Papers of the Manchester Literary Club* 63 (1937): 23-40.

"Choruses from 'The Rock,'" included in the 1936 volume of Eliot's collected poetry, embodies a meaningful social satire and morality; its clear simplicity alone redeems an otherwise enigmatic volume.

C36   Harding, D. W. "The Rock." *Scrutiny* 3 (September 1934): 180-83.

The pageant's absolute conviction in the power of the church is unconvincing. It "forms a transition to a stage of Mr. Eliot's work which has not yet fully defined itself."

C37   Olshin, Toby. "A Consideration of *The Rock*." *University of Toronto Quarterly* 39.4 (July 1970): 310-23.

The Rock is a more significant element of Eliot's canon than most critics recognize, and better unified—by a kind of invisible structure appropriate to its spiritual sensibility—than it might seem by conventional dramatic standards.

Murder in the Cathedral

C38   Adair, Patricia M. "Mr. Eliot's 'Murder in the Cathedral.'" *Cambridge Journal* 4.2 (November 1950): 83-95. Excerpted in *Twentieth Century Interpretations of Murder in the Cathedral*. Ed. David R. Clark. Englewood Cliffs, NJ: Prentice-Hall, 1971, 73-74.

MC, intentionally cold and rarefied, can be properly appreciated only in the Canterbury Cathedral setting. Sainthood and the exclusion of humanity in Becket's character universalize him.

C39   Adams, John F. "The Fourth Temptation in *Murder in the Cathedral*." *Modern Drama* 5.4 (February 1963): 381-88.

The Fourth Tempter presents a paradox surrounding Becket's understanding of the problems that may contaminate the martyrdom—preventing Becket from participating in his martyrdom sincerely.

C40   Auden, W. H. *Secondary Worlds: The T. S. Eliot Memorial Lectures*. London: Faber & Faber, 1968.

Chapter entitled "The Martyr as Dramatic Hero" compares *MC* and Charles Williams's *Thomas Cranmer*; the latter play's martyrdom is free of the suspicion of pride, while Becket's is "one of those cases of martyrdom over which the question of motive" and accident must arise.

C41   Ayers, Robert W. "*Murder in the Cathedral*: A 'Liturgy Less Divine.'" *Texas Studies in Literature and Language* 20.4 (Winter 197-8): 579-98. Rpt. in *T. S. Eliot's Murder in the Cathedral*. Ed. Harold Bloom. New York: Chelsea House, 1988, 105-22.

Analyzes *MC* as liturgy, comparing its structure to the structure of the Mass and Becket's experience to the life of Christ. The play's structure is based on the church's annual cycle, culminating with a vision of the second coming.

C42   Badenhausen, Richard. "'When the Poet Speaks Only for Himself': The Poet as 'First Voice' in *Murder in the Cathedral*." In *T. S. Eliot: Man and Poet*, vol. 1. Ed. Laura Cowan. Orono, ME: National Poetry Foundation, U of Maine, 1990, 239-52.

Eliot was troubled in his early drama by the elusiveness of a single expressive authorial voice; the Chorus serves that function.

C43   Batson, E. Beatrice. "A Christian View of Tragedy." In *The Christian Imagination: Essays on Literature and the Arts*. Ed. Leland Ryken. Grand Rapids, MI: Baker Book House, 1981, 211-26.

Overview of Christian tragedy briefly discusses how *MC* fits into this genre.

C44   Beehler, Michael T. "*Murder in the Cathedral*: The Countersacramental Play of Signs." *Genre* 10.3 (Fall 1977): 329-38. Rpt. in *T. S. Eliot's Murder in the Cathedral*. Ed. Harold Bloom. New York: Chelsea House, 1988, 95-103.

The historical "sign" at the center of *MC* challenges the creation of an "authorizing presence"; Eliot creates this presence by shifting away from Becket's death, a historical moment, to the moment when he allows himself to become a martyr for the right reason.

C45   Billman, Carol.   "History Versus Mystery: The Test of Time in *Murder in the Cathedral.*" *Clio* 10.1 (Fall 1980): 47-56.
       MC is "riddled with unresolved oppositions—time and timelessness, saint and sinner, action and suffering, joy and mourning," to indicate "the divine mystery overriding human history."

C46   Bloom, Harold. *T. S. Eliot's Murder in the Cathedral.* New York: Chelsea House, 1988.
       Reprints several important critical discussions.

C47   Boulton, J. T. "The Use of Original Sources for the Development of a Theme: Eliot in *Murder in the Cathedral.*" *English* 11.61 (Spring 1956): 2-8. Rpt. in *Twentieth Century Interpretations of Murder in the Cathedral.* Ed. David R. Clark. Englewood Cliffs, NJ: Prentice-Hall, 1971, 74-79.
       The narrative of Edward Grim, a contemporary of Becket, is a source for *MC*—especially for its theme of conflict between Christianity and secularism.

C48   Brannon, Lil. "The Possibilities of Sainthood: A Study of the Moral Dilemma in Graham Greene's *The Power and the Glory* and T. S. Eliot's *Murder in the Cathedral.*" *Publications of the Arkansas Philological Association* 4.3 (1978): 66-70.
       Compares the criteria for sainthood in the two works, and the temptations of Becket and Greene's priest.

C49   Browne, E. Martin. "The Two Beckets." *Drama* 60 (Spring 1961): 27-30.
       Director of *MC* compares Eliot's drama of Becket with Jean Anouilh's.

C50   _____. "The Variations in the Text." In *Twentieth Century Interpretations of Murder in the Cathedral.* Ed. David R. Clark. Englewood Cliffs, NJ: Prentice-Hall, 1971, 99-106.
       Reprint of passage from *The Making of T. S. Eliot's Plays* discusses revisions (and reasons for some of the alterations) in different editions of the text.

C51   Butler, John F. "Tragedy, Salvation, and the Ordinary Man." *London Quarterly and Holborn Review* 162 (October 1937): 489-97.
       Uses *MC* as a point of departure for comparing the salvation of a tragic hero and that of a saint.

C52   Campbell, Douglas G. "Drama as Monument: Eliot's *Murder in the Cathedral*." *Liberal and Fine Arts Review* 1.1 (January 1981): 9-17.

      In terms of structure, symbolism, and verse, *MC* is characterized as a "monument," as determined by "1) memorial intention, 2) permanence, 3) a timeless message or subject matter, 4) clarity of message presentation, 5) clarity of structural organization, 6) eminence of location, 7) richness of materials or means used in presentation."

C53   Clark, David R., ed. *Twentieth Century Interpretations of Murder in the Cathedral*. Englewood Cliffs, NJ: Prentice-Hall, 1971.

      Reprints several important critical discussions.

C54   Clausen, Christopher. "A Source for Thomas Becket's Temptation in 'Murder in the Cathedral.'" *Notes and Queries* n. s. 21.10 (October 1974): 373-74.

      Cites Sir Edwin Arnold's 1879 poem *The Light of Asia* as a source for the First Tempter.

C55   Clougherty, R. J., Jr. "T. S. Eliot's *Murder in the Cathedral*: A Chorus Divided." *Yeats Eliot Review* 10.1 (Winter-Spring 1989): 13-16.

      Study of the Mercury Theatre's production copy of the script shows the nature and significance of the play's choral divisions, which are not indicated in most texts.

C56   Coghill, Nevill, ed. *Murder in the Cathedral*. London: Faber & Faber, 1965.

      Text of the play, along with introduction (approved by Eliot), extensive notes, and brief critical essays about its background.

C57   Cutts, John P. "Evidence for Ambivalence of Motives in *Murder in the Cathedral*." *Comparative Drama* 8.2 (Summer 1974): 199-210.

      Eliot's use of historical and liturgical sources suggests ambivalent motives for Becket's martyrdom.

C58   Davidson, Clifford. "T. S. Eliot's *Murder in the Cathedral* and the Saint's Play Tradition." *Papers on Language and Literature* 21.2 (Spring 1985): 152-69. Rpt. in *T. S. Eliot's Murder in the Cathedral*. Ed. Harold Bloom. New York: Chelsea House, 1988, 123-36.

      MC is a modern version of a saint's play, indicating Eliot's "choice of 'medievalism' over 'modernism' . . . the result of his conversion to Anglo-Catholicism." The medieval fusion of drama and ritual is especially germane to Eliot's intentions.

C59   Fergusson, Francis. "Action as Passion: *Tristan* and *Murder in the Cathedral*." *Kenyon Review* 9.2 (Spring 1947): 201-21.
    Compares Eliot's use of pathos with Richard Wagner's and concludes that *MC* goes beyond *Tristan und Isolde* in sophistication.

C60   _____. *The Idea of a Theater: A Study of Ten Plays*. Princeton: Princeton U P, 1949. Excerpted as "*Murder in the Cathedral*: The Theological Scene" in *Twentieth Century Interpretations of Murder in the Cathedral*. Ed. David R. Clark. Englewood Cliffs, NJ: Prentice-Hall, 1971, 27-37. Also in *T. S. Eliot's Murder in the Cathedral*. Ed. Harold Bloom. New York: Chelsea House, 1988, 5-15.
    Section on *MC* considers it poetically theological more than poetically dramatic, and thus different from such plays as André Obey's *Noah* and Jean Cocteau's *The Infernal Machine*, which are dramatic reenactments of myths.

C61   Flanagan, Hallie. *Arena: The History of the Federal Theatre*. New York: Benjamin Blom, 1965.
    Background on the company that presented the American premiere of *MC*.

C62   Geraldine, M. "The Rhetoric of Repetition in *Murder in the Cathedral*." *Renascence* 19.3 (Spring 1967): 132-41.
    Examines "recurrences of figures, phrases, and ideas" in *MC*, and the intended effects of such repetitions.

C63   Gerstenberger, Donna. "The Saint and the Circle: The Dramatic Potential of an Image." *Criticism* 2 (Fall 1960): 336-41.
    W. B. Yeats, Stephen Spender, and Eliot all use the traditional image of the turning wheel and the still point, but Eliot does so most fully as *MC* formally mirrors the image. Spender's *Trial of a Judge*, written three years after *MC*, borrows the image from Eliot.

C64   Gielgud, Val. "Radio Play: In the Age of Television." *Theatre Arts Monthly* 21.2 (February 1937): 108-12.
    B. B. C.'s radio adaptation of *MC* is discussed in a survey of contemporary radio plays.

C65   Grimes, Ronald L. "Victor Turner's Social Drama and T. S. Eliot's Ritual Drama." *Anthropologica* 27.1-2 (1985): 79-99.
    Turner applied his theory of social drama—which considers it as social interaction separated into phases of breach, crisis, redress, and reintegration—to the historical story of Becket in *Dramas, Fields and Metaphors*. Comparing that study and *MC* "leads to a discussion of the mutual critiques they imply, and reveals the dominant metaphors

that organize" Turner's and Eliot's treatment of the same event—Turner's are "linear and processual," while Eliot's are "static and circular."

C66 Harben, Niloufer. *Twentieth-Century English History Plays.* London: Macmillan, 1988.

Chapter on *MC* suggests a Brechtian influence in terms of Eliot's "distancing the audience from the surface of the action in order to involve it on a rational plane," and examines the play's relation to history and its "fine and subtle balance between inner and outer reality."

C67 Hayter, Althea. "Thomas à Becket and the Dramatists." *Essays by Divers Hands* n. s. 34 (1966): 90-105.

Becket's martyrdom is such a popular dramatic theme because "Such a story as Thomas Becket's—such events and such personalities—could not fail in the theatre. The struggle between temporal and spiritual power, and the martyr's victory—it is one of the archetypal dramatic situations, from Antigone onwards. . . . Then, too, there is something essentially theatrical about the personality of the historical Becket." The martyr as witness correlates to the poet as witness.

C68 Holloway, Patricia Mosco. "T. S. Eliot's *Murder in the Cathedral.*" *Explicator* 43.2 (Winter 1985): 35-36.

The Chorus of women presents a birth metaphor, implying that the making of a martyr is like the act of birth.

C69 Jennings, Humphrey. "Eliot and Auden and Shakespeare." *New Verse* 18 (December 1935): 4-7.

MC and W. H. Auden's *The Dance of Death* are inferior to Shakespeare's drama because they "oversystematise," presenting a manufactured theatrical artifact rather than the complexity of real life.

C70 Kantra, Robert A. "Satiric Theme and Structure in *Murder in the Cathedral.*" *Modern Drama* 10.4 (February 1968): 387-93.

MC, neither tragedy nor morality, is organized satirically around the theme of conflict between church and state; the Knights are comic archetypes.

C71 Kinneavy, Gerald B. "Becket, the Chorus and the Redemption of Waiting." *Language Quarterly* 22.3-4 (Spring-Summer 1984): 25-29.

Examines the motif of waiting: its role in Becket's martyrdom and in the development of the Chorus.

C72   Koppenhaver, Allen J. "The Musical Design of T. S. Eliot's *Murder in the Cathedral.*" *Husson Review* 5.1 (1971): 4-10. (Continued in May 1972)

   MC takes the form of a sonata, having two opposing major themes. The play's structure is specifically compared to Beethoven's *Appassionata Sonata*, Op. 57.

C73   Kornbluth, Martin L. "A Twentieth-Century *Everyman.*" *College English* 21.1 (October 1959): 26-29.

   MC is similar to the medieval morality play in structure and style: Becket is a type of *Everyman*, and the Tempters are like the allegorical characters with which the sinner must vie.

C74   Krieger, Murray. *The Classic Vision: The Retreat from Extremity in Modern Literature.* Baltimore: Johns Hopkins P, 1971.

   Chapter on *MC*, "The Limits of Drama and the Freedom of Vision," examines the problem of sainthood given the inevitable presence of the Fourth Tempter, representing will and pride, and compares the perspectives of Becket and the Chorus on guilt and salvation.

C75   LeCroy, Anne. "*Murder in the Cathedral*: A Question of Structure." In *Essays in Memory of Christine Burleson.* Ed. Thomas G. Burton. Johnson City, TN: Research Advisory Council, East Tennessee State U, 1969, 57-70.

   Examines liturgical structure—reenactment of the Communion service—in *MC*, viewing audience as congregation and the martyrdom as a sign of God's life and the church's strength.

C76   Maccoby, H. Z. "Two Notes on '*Murder in the Cathedral.*'" *Notes and Queries* n. s. 14.7 (July 1967): 253-56. Rpt. in *Twentieth Century Interpretations of Murder in the Cathedral.* Ed. David R. Clark. Englewood Cliffs, NJ: Prentice-Hall, 1971, 93-96.

   The Fourth Tempter is not a mere seducer from virtue but rather, following Jewish tradition, "a devil who is the servant of God, using temptation to awaken men to the knowledge of their own souls."

C77   Martz, Louis L. "The Saint as Tragic Hero: *Saint Joan* and *Murder in the Cathedral.*" In *Tragic Themes in Western Literature.* Ed. Cleanth Brooks. New Haven: Yale U P, 1955, 150-78. Rpt. in *T. S. Eliot's Murder in the Cathedral.* Ed. Harold Bloom. New York: Chelsea House, 1988, 23-39.

   Though saints and martyrs seem inappropriate subjects for tragedy because they are apt to be immobile and uncombative, "the saint may become a figure well adapted to arouse something very close to a tragic experience. . . . the uncertainty of the audience's attitude—and to some extent the dramatist's own—may enable him to deal also with the painful and pitiful aspects of experience that form the other side of the tragic tension."

C78   _____. "The Wheel and the Point: Aspects of Imagery and Theme in Eliot's Later Poetry." *Sewanee Review* 55 (Winter 1947): 126-47. Rpt. in *Twentieth Century Interpretations of Murder in the Cathedral.* Ed. David R. Clark. Englewood Cliffs, NJ: Prentice-Hall, 1971, 15-26; and in *T. S. Eliot: A Selected Critique.* Ed. Leonard Unger. New York: Rinehart, 1948, 444-62.
        The central quest for "peace" in *MC*—analogous to "the still point" in *Four Quartets*—presents an experience that infuses all Eliot's works.

C79   Mason, W. H. *Murder in the Cathedral.* Oxford: Basil Blackwell, 1962.
        Students' guide to *MC* includes coverage of dramatic and verse technique; historical background; and focused emphasis on the Knights, Tempters, and Chorus.

C80   McCarthy, Patrick A. "Eliot's *Murder in the Cathedral.*" *Explicator* 33.1 (September 1974): Item 7.
        The Four Tempters' actions are compared to the temptations of Christ. The Fourth Tempter expresses Becket's real desire because he presents a temptation not expected in terms of Christ's experience.

C81   McCormick, Peter. After Foundationalism: Interpreting Intentional Actions." In *Anti-Foundationalism and Practical Reasoning.* Ed. Evan Simpson. Edmonton, Alberta: Academic Printing & Publishing, 1987, 59-75.
        Becket's assertion to the Chorus that waiting is an intentional action (rather than passive inaction), examined through a foundationalist philosophy, shows the inadequacy of that construct.

C82   McGill, William J. "Voices in the Cathedral: The Chorus in Eliot's *Murder in the Cathedral.*" *Modern Drama* 23.3 (September 1980): 292-96.
        The choral odes embody three distinct voices, each representing a motif developed in *MC*: "The first with its recurrent appeal to destiny emphasizes that the women are but passive witnesses; the second with its recitation of the mundane preoccupations of the poor emphasizes that they are drawn unwillingly to fulfill the role of witness; and the third with its darksome, surreal vision emphasizes the pessimism, the fatalism of their witness."

C83   Moore, Marianne. "'If I Am Worthy, There Is No Danger.'" *Poetry* 47.5 (February 1936): 279-81.
        Lauds the verse's effectiveness and the reverent austerity of Eliot's tone.

C84   Mueller, William R. "*Murder in the Cathedral*: An Imitation of Christ." *Religion in Life* 27.3 (Summer 1958): 414-26.
        Becket is a Christ figure: "He undergoes a series of temptations which serve to make perfect his will. He forces the hands of those hostile to him to bring him to a martyr's death. His death is followed by a kind of resurrection which strengthens the Body of Christ. . . . His triumphant death and resurrection serve as a source of truth and light for those who have unwillingly borne witness to his last days."

C85   Nicholas, Constance. "The Murders of Doyle and Eliot." *Modern Language Notes* 70.4 (April 1955): 269-71.
        Arthur Conan Doyle's "The Musgrave Ritual" is a source for part of a speech by the Second Tempter.

C86   O'Brien, Bernard. "Notes on *Murder in the Cathedral*." *Meanjin Papers* 4.3 (Spring 1945): 212-15.
        MC is "not so much a play of action as a philosophical drama"; Becket's sermon "has some resemblance to the discourse at the Last Supper."

C87   Pankow, Edith. "The 'Eternal Design' of *Murder in the Cathedral*." *Papers on Language and Literature* 9.1 (Winter 1973): 35-47.
        Eliot's use of conventions, such as allegory and liturgy, expresses the play's "divine realities," while his verse and musical structure express its "human realities."

C88   Peter, John. "*Murder in the Cathedral*." *Sewanee Review* 61.3 (1953): 362-83. Rpt. in *T. S. Eliot: A Collection of Critical Essays*. Ed. Hugh Kenner. Englewood Cliffs, NJ: Prentice-Hall, 1962, 155-72.
        MC, better than Eliot's subsequent plays in terms of its verse and inner coherence, also compares favorably to Tennyson's *Becket* because it abandons Elizabethan tragedy as a model.

C89   Pickering, Jerry V. "Form as Agent: Eliot's *Murder in the Cathedral*." *Educational Theatre Journal* 20 (May 1968): 198-207.
        Eliot's dramatic form relates to his perception of Dante's work as an emotional framework within an external structure. This form involves the audience in the play, with the Chorus as mediator.

C90   Pickering, Kenneth W. *Drama in the Cathedral: The Canterbury Festival Plays 1928-1948*. Worthing, West Sussex: Churchman Publishing, 1985.

   Chapter on *MC* presents a basic overview of the play and details on its original performance. Other chapters examine the history and context of the play's sponsor, the Canterbury Festival, describing other lesser-known plays featured there and extensively exploring the background of modern British Christian drama.

C91   Pike, Lionel J. "Liturgy and Time in Counterpoint: A View of T. S. Eliot's *Murder in the Cathedral*." *Modern Drama* 23.3 (September 1980): 277-91.

   MC is stylistically and structurally closer to medieval liturgical drama than to modern theatre because "events of great dramatic possibility (whose impact is upon men of all times) are performed in a ritualistic language which, by its very nature, lacks immediacy." The play's opposition of church and state is mirrored in the oppositions of modern and liturgucal language, and of eternity versus people's limited time.

C92   Ransom, John Crowe. "Autumn of Poetry." *Southern Review* 1 (1935-36): 619-23.

   Criticizes the play's "snappiness" but calls this a fault related to the age rather than the author, and finds *MC* inferior to another religious historical drama, Milton's *Samson Agonistes*.

C93   Rehak, Louise Rouse. "On the Use of Martyrs: Tennyson and Eliot on Thomas Becket." *University of Toronto Quarterly* 33.1 (October 1963): 43-60.

   Compares the two plays' use of historical facts, characterization, versification, language, and use of symbol and imagery, concluding that *MC* is more theatrically successful.

C94   Renner, Stanley. "Affirmations of Faith in *Victory* and *Murder in the Cathedral*." *Christian Scholar's Review* 4 (1974): 110-19.

   In both Conrad's novel and *MC* the protagonist is faced with the modern problem of how to act in this world while avoiding the immorality inherent in any human action. Both writers finally affirm their faith in the value of action: Conrad in secular terms and Eliot within a Christian schema.

C95   Rickey, Mary Ellen. "'Christabel' and 'Murder in the Cathedral.'"
        Notes and Queries n. s. 10.4 (April 1963): 151.
            Coleridge's poem may provide a source for the passage in Part I
        of *MC* in which the Chorus, Priests, and Tempters warn Becket of
        danger.

C96   Robinson, James E. *"Murder in the Cathedral* as Theatre of the
        Spirit." *Religion and Literature* 18.2 (Summer 1986): 31-45.
            MC transcends the religious drama to become "Theatre of the
        Spirit," which involves "the paradoxical quest of the time-and-place
        bound artist to give voice to the timeless and placeless, the arena of
        theatre itself serving as metaphor of the confinement in which the
        human spirit seeks expression and from which it may struggle for
        release."

C97   von Rosador, Kurt Tetzeli. "Christian Historical Drama: The Exem-
        plariness of *Murder in the Cathedral.*" *Modern Drama* 29.4 (Decem-
        ber 1986): 516-31.
            Analyzes the play's Christian historicity and traces Becket's de-
        velopment, viewing the sermon as an explanation of Christian history
        and Becket as a Christ figure.

C98   Roy, Émil. "The Becket Plays: Eliot, Fry, and Anouilh." *Modern
        Drama* 8.3 (December 1965): 268-76.
            Compares *MC* with Christopher Fry's *Curtmantle* and Jean An-
        ouilh's *Becket, or the Honor of God.* Fry's Becket play is Christian
        and Shavian; Anouilh's Pirandellian and existentialist. While Eliot's
        construction is "focused and ritualistic, Fry's is panoramic and histor-
        ical, and Anouilh's is musical and choreographic. . . . [which] would
        place *Murder* in a 'theater of ideas,' *Curtmantle* in a 'theater of char-
        acters,' and *Becket* in a 'theater of situations.'"

C99   Samuelson, Scott. "The Word as Sword: Power and Paradox in
        Murder in the Cathedral." *Literature and Belief* 7 (1987): 73-81.
            MC is a "conflict of interpretation" which contrasts the Knights'
        strategy of creating a controllable stereotype with Becket's strategy of
        inviting the individual to participate in the archetype through the
        Christian paradox of sacrifice. Becket's strategy expresses Eliot's
        ideas about faith and art.

C100   Seed, David. "Eliot's Use of Tennyson in *Murder in the Cathedral.*"
        Yeats Eliot Review 7.1-2 (1982): 42-49.
            Eliot diverges widely from the nearest contemporary treatment of
        the Becket story, Tennyson's, in terms of his repudiation of blank
        verse and what he considered inflexible dramatic language, and a

narrowing of the range of issues presented; he did, though, borrow certain lines and phrases from Tennyson. "On the level of simple dramatic effectiveness Eliot shows a greater awareness of suspense, of how to manage a climax, and of how to maintain stature."

C101   Sharoni, Edna G. "'Peace' and 'Unbar the Door': T. S. Eliot's *Murder in the Cathedral* and Some Stoic Forebears." *Comparative Drama* 6.2 (Summer 1972): 135-53.

Compares *MC* with the poetic dramas of Stoicism of Chapman, Shakespeare, and Milton, examining the ideas of patience, peace, temptation, and fate versus free will.

C102   Shorter, Robert N. "Becket as Job: T. S. Eliot's *Murder in the Cathedral.*" *South Atlantic Quarterly* 67.4 (Autumn 1968): 627-35. Rpt. in *Twentieth Century Interpretations of Murder in the Cathedral.* Ed. David R. Clark. Englewood Cliffs, NJ: Prentice-Hall, 1971, 86-93.

In Part I Becket is a type not of Christ, as is often argued, but of Job, in terms of suffering as a result of devotion to God.

C103   Smith, Grover. "Mr. Eliot's New Murder." *New Mexico Quarterly Review* 22 (Autumn 1952): 331-39.

Examines differences between film and theatrical versions of *MC*, concluding that the film does more justice to the play than any theatre production and specifically praising Eliot's modification of the Knights' speeches.

C104   _____. "T. S. Eliot and Sherlock Holmes." *Notes and Queries* 193 (2 October 1948): 431-32.

Parallels between Arthur Conan Doyle's "The Musgrave Ritual" and *MC*.

C105   Smith, Stevie. "History or Poetic Drama?" In *T. S. Eliot: A Symposium for his Seventieth Birthday*. Ed. Neville Braybrooke. Freeport, NY: Books for Libraries P, 1968, 170-75.

Criticizes the use of history in *MC* to instill fear in the audience.

C106   Sochatoff, A. Fred. "Four Variations on the Becket Theme in Modern Drama." *Modern Drama* 12.1 (May 1969): 83-91.

Compared to dramatizations of the same historical event by Fry, Anouilh, and Tennyson, *MC* is the most austere and unified; Eliot concentrates on Becket's state of mind and his martyrdom by such devices as exclusion of the character of King Henry II.

C107   Spanos, William V. *"Murder in the Cathedral*: The *Figura* as Mimetic Principle." *Drama Survey* 3.2 (October 1963): 206-23. Rpt. in *Twentieth Century Interpretations of Murder in the Cathedral*. Ed. David R. Clark. Englewood Cliffs, NJ: Prentice-Hall, 1971, 54-72.

    Erich Auerbach's typological analysis of the *figura* shows how Eliot has presented in *MC* "a sacramental action . . . that confirms or fulfills in a moment of time the redemptive figure of the real and archetypal sacrifice of Christ and that prefigures at the same time the final fulfillment of the eternal pattern"; the figural aesthetic unites the play's spiritual sensibility with its concrete naturalism.

C108   Speaight, Robert. *The Property Basket: Recollections of a Divided Life*. London: Collins, 1970.

    Memoirs of the actor who created (and spent his career playing) the role of Becket.

C109   _____. "With Becket in *Murder in the Cathedral*." *Sewanee Review* 74.1 (Winter 1966): 176-87. Rpt. in *T. S. Eliot: The Man and His Work*. Ed. Allen Tate. New York: Delacorte P, 1966, 182-93.

    Discusses experiences playing the role of Becket over 25 years and "the problem of giving concrete shape to a character which had been conceived, designedly, in the abstract."

C110   Spencer, Theodore. "On 'Murder in the Cathedral.'" *Harvard Advocate* 125.3 (December 1938): 21-22.

    MC is "spiritual exaltation against the background of the world," in which four levels of reality are represented by Becket, the Priests, the Chorus of women, and the murderers. The Christian tradition emphasizes the contrast of values.

C111   Spender, Stephen. "Martyrdom and Motive." In *T. S. Eliot: Plays*. Ed. Arnold Hinchliffe. London: Macmillan, 1985, 96-101.

    Explores Becket's temptations and motive for action in *MC*.

C112   Tremaine, Louis. "Witness to the Event in *Ma'sat al-Hallaj* and *Murder in the Cathedral*." *Muslim World* 67.1 (January 1977): 33-46.

    Compares the plays and examines Eliot's possible influence on Salāh 'Abd al-Sabūr.

C113   Turner, A. J. "A Note on 'Murder in the Cathedral.'" *Notes and Queries* n. s. 17.2 (February 1970): 51-53.

    Eliot's revisions in the fourth edition of *MC* are intended to diminish the sense that Becket provoked his own death; this prideful sense, though, is inherent within the contemporary narratives Eliot followed.

C114   Virsis, Rasma. "The Christian Concept in *Murder in the Cathedral.*" *Modern Drama* 14.4 (February 1972): 405-407.

MC presents two struggles: "Becket's to do the right deed for the wrong reason, and the Chorus's to witness, to accept, and to consent to the suffering and insecurity the martyrdom of Thomas will bring. The second ends in acceptance at the end of the play: the first ends in success at the end of the first section."

C115   Weiher, Carol. "'Sometimes Hesitating at the Angles of Stairs': Becket's Treasonous Thoughts in *Murder in the Cathedral.*" *Notes on Modern American Literature* 2.1 (Winter 1977): note 1.

The moment of Becket's reflection when he faces the Fourth Tempter evokes the theme and tenor of *Ash-Wednesday.*

C116   Whitaker, Thomas R. *Fields of Play in Modern Drama.* Princeton: Princeton U P, 1977.

Postmodern theoretical meditation on participative dramatic interaction includes section on *MC*.

C117   Williams, Pieter D. "The Function of the Chorus in T. S. Eliot's *Murder in the Cathedral.*" *American Benedictine Review* 23.4 (1972): 499-511.

Exhaustively explores the role of the Chorus in terms of its dramatic, structural, visual, and vocal contributions to *MC*, and the formal and thematic contrast of its stasis compared to Becket's change and action.

C118   Wingate, Gifford W. "*Murder in the Cathedral*: A Step Toward Articulate Theatre." *Greyfriar* 3 (1960): 22-35.

Discusses two types of human action portrayed in *MC*: free will in the world of time and subordination of will to God. The play's success is in the way it uses modern imagery to define these two levels.

C119   Worthen, W. B. "*Murder in the Cathedral* and the Work of Acting." In *T. S. Eliot: Man and Poet*, vol. 1. Ed. Laura Cowan. Orono, ME: National Poetry Foundation, U of Maine, 1990, 253-73.

In an early version of the essay on Marie Lloyd, Eliot includes a phrase about the audience's "work of acting"; the nature of his drama is explored with reference to this idea. "As poetic theater, *Murder in the Cathedral* participates in the dialectic between 'the act' and 'the work of acting,' organizing the fictive 'personalities' of the theater—actor, character, spectator—as the expression of the 'poetic' formalities of the text. For *Murder in the Cathedral* is a play *about* its audience."

C120 Wyman, Linda. "On Teaching *Murder in the Cathedral*." In *Approaches to Teaching Eliot's Poetry and Plays*. Ed. Jewel Spears Brooker. New York: Modern Language Association, 1988, 174-78. Adapted from "*Murder in the Cathedral*: The Plot of Diction." *Modern Drama* 19.2 (June 1976): 135-45.

   MC needs to be taught as having a "plot of diction," meaning that "while we are shown a change in the situation of the protagonist . . . and a change in his thought and feeling . . . we are shown, in the total design of the language, a meaning more comprehensive than that encompassed by the protagonist alone."

The Family Reunion

C121 Avery, Helen P. "*The Family Reunion* Reconsidered." *Educational Theatre Journal* 17 (March 1965): 10-18.

   Director of a community theatre production of *FR* argues for its relevance to audiences in 1965, comparing it to the works of more contemporary dramatists. Refutes Eliot's own critiques of the play and discusses defects in earlier productions.

C122 Barber, C. L. "T. S. Eliot After Strange Gods." *Southern Review* 6.2 (Autumn 1940): 387-416. Rpt. in *T. S. Eliot: A Selected Critique*. Ed. Leonard Unger. New York, Rinehart, 1948, 415-43.

   Eliot's decision to eschew a traditional Christian framework for *FR*—because he felt religious meaning had decayed for modern society—results in an unintelligible drama in which he cannot recreate a system of religious symbolism.

C123 Battenhouse, Roy W. "Eliot's *The Family Reunion* as Christian Prophecy." *Christendom* 10.3 (Summer 1945): 307-21.

   Use of Greek myth and the supernatural are attempts to revitalize faith by refreshing the meanings of language and Christian terminology.

C124 Beehler, Michael T. "Troping the Topic: Dis-closing the Circle of *The Family Reunion*." *Boundary 2* 8.3 (1980): 19-42.

   Deconstructive analysis "seeks to partially extract the play from the circumscription of its title and to de-mystify that title's previously privileged metaphors. What is disclosed by such a reading is not the closure of the hermeneutical circle, but rather a certain prodigality, a wandering or excess that ultimately dis-closes the circle traced by the title."

C125   Belli, Angela. *Ancient Greek Myths and Modern Drama: A Study in Continuity.* New York: New York U P, 1969.

Study of modern renditions of Greek myths includes a section on *FR*; in that play, Eliot's interest in myth is centered on the issue of how the past exerts an influence upon the present. Devices and themes are compared with the Aeschylean model.

C126   Bland, D. S. "T. S. Eliot's Case-Book." *Modern Language Notes* 75.1 (January 1960): 23-26.

Compares names, language, plot, and technique of *FR* to the novels of Ivy Compton-Burnett, specifically *Men and Wives*.

C127   Bodkin, Maud. *The Quest for Salvation in an Ancient and a Modern Play.* London: Oxford U P, 1941.

Extensively developed comparison between *FR* and its Aeschylean source finds that Eliot's use of myth "keeps us aware of the necessity that the new order, which Eliot shows realized in an individual spiritual experience, should find expression also on the plane of history."

C128   Brooks, Harold F. "*The Family Reunion* and *Columbe's Birthday.*" *Times Literary Supplement* 2654 (12 December 1952): 819.

Suggests Robert Browning's play as an influence.

C129   Brown, Christopher. "J. B. Priestly and *The Family Reunion.*" *Yeats Eliot Review* 6.1 (1979): 16-20.

Suggests Priestly's 1937 play *Time and the Conways* as a source for *FR*.

C130   Carpentier, M. C. "Orestes in the Drawing Room: Aeschylean Parallels in T. S. Eliot's *The Family Reunion.*" *Twentieth Century Literature* 35.1 (1989): 17-42.

Though *FR* is often criticized as being a failed transformation of its Greek source, critics have not sufficiently noted the extent of Eliot's parallelism of Aeschylus.

C131   Coghill, Nevill, ed. *The Family Reunion.* London: Faber & Faber, 1969.

Text with introduction, explanatory notes, and supplementary critical material including an inferential chronological table of events at Wishwood.

C132   Gaskell, Ronald. "*The Family Reunion.*" *Essays in Criticism* 12 (July 1962): 292-301. Rpt. in *Drama and Reality: The European Theatre Since Ibsen.* London: Routledge & Kegan Paul, 1972.

       Examination of perspectives on reality argues that Eliot's acceptance of naturalism in *FR* initiates the the trend toward limited conventionalities that hampered all his later dramatic work.

C133   Hamalian, Leo. "The Figures in the Window: Design in T. S. Eliot's *The Family Reunion.*" *College Literature* 4.2 (Spring 1977): 107-21.

       Discusses the function of the Eumenides, the use of time, ties to the *Oresteia*, and the musical design of *FR*.

C134   _____. "Wishwood Revisited." *Renascence* 12.4 (Summer 1960): 167-73.

       Harry's story of expiation "is brought about in the presence of certain mysterious forces represented by the Eumenides" who "are pivots in the pattern of the play, the turning point of Eliot's mosaic, the touchstones to character, and not merely adjuncts to the action."

C135   Häusermann, H. W. "'East Coker' and 'The Family Reunion.'" *Life and Letters Today* 47 (October 1945): 32-38.

       In the poem and FR "Eliot was chiefly concerned with the following two aspects. First, that we tend to overrate reality and the world of will and action. . . . Secondly, that we have, as individuals, as little power over the evil as over the good." "East Coker" expresses these themes more intensely.

C136   Isaacs, Jennifer I. "Eliot the Poet-Playwright: As Seen in *The Family Reunion.*" *English* 16.93 (Autumn 1966): 100-105.

       Discusses the contrast between inner significance and outer action, finding *FR* a quest for spiritual enlightenment in which Harry serves as a "meeting point" for different states of awareness.

C137   Jamil, Maya. "*Hamlet* and *The Family Reunion.*" *Venture* 5.1 (June 1968): 21-29.

       While Eliot "completely misunderstood" *Hamlet* in his famous essay, that play and *FR* are "essentially the same in concept, theme and structure." The mother's sin, which is clear in *Hamlet*, is ambiguous in *FR*; this makes her death seem inappropriate.

C138   Lightfoot, Marjorie J. *"Purgatory* and *The Family Reunion*: In Pursuit of Prosodic Description." *Modern Drama* 7.3 (December 1964): 256-66.

Examines the meter of W. B. Yeats's and Eliot's plays, concluding that the four-stress measured accentual verse predominates although Yeats maintains it more consistently than Eliot.

C139   Maccoby, H. Z. "Difficulties in the Plot of 'The Family Reunion.'" *Notes and Queries* n. s. 15.8 (August 1968): 296-302.

Numerous factual, logical, and chronological inconsistencies in *FR* may reflect Eliot's intricate process of composition, or may be intentional errors to indicate that "underneath the facade of regularity symbolized by the ticking of the clock, the reality of life is chaos."

C140   _____. "'The Family Reunion' and Kipling's 'The House Surgeon.'" *Notes and Queries* n. s. 15.2 (February 1968): 48-50.

Suggests Rudyard Kipling's story as a source for *FR*.

C141   MacVean, Jean. "In Argos or in England." *Agenda* 23.1-2 (Spring-Summer 1985): 111-30.

General summary and analysis of *FR*.

C142   Montgomerie, William. "Harry, Meet Mr. Prufrock (T. S. Eliot's Dilemma)." *Life and Letters Today* 31.51 (November 1941): 115-28.

Loosely psychoanalytic examination of *FR* considers Eliot's references to *Hamlet* in his poetry and concludes that his "failure to force the solution of *Hamlet* into complete consciousness" continues in *FR*, which fails because Eliot creates an abnormal family and cannot return it to normalcy.

C143   Murry, J. Middleton. "A Note on the 'Family Reunion.'" *Essays in Criticism* 1.1 (January 1951): 67-73.

Harry's intent to murder, or actual murder of, his wife is a "problem": the vagueness of his motivations reflects an incomplete transition from Greek myth to modern Christianity; "the curse is not wholly transformed into sin." (Stephen Floersheimer's response, in 1.3 [July 1951]: 298-301, disputes the degree of vagueness.)

C144   Palmer, Richard E. "Existentialism in T. S. Eliot's *The Family Reunion*." *Modern Drama* 5.2 (September 1962): 174-86.

Existentialism helps explain aspects of *FR* that have been judged inadequate.

C145 Peter, John. "'The Family Reunion.'" *Scrutiny* 16.3 (September 1949): 219-30.

Overview considers the play's references to Greek mythology and psychological theory.

C146 Porter, David H. "Ancient Myth and Modern Play: A Significant Counterpoint." *Classical Bulletin* 48.1 (November 1971): 1-9.

Eliot's change in the Orestes myth—having Harry chased by the Furies for killing his wife rather than his mother—emphasizes the connection between wife and mother.

C147 Ransom, John Crowe. "T. S. Eliot as Dramatist." *Poetry* 54.5 (August 1939): 264-71.

Early critical appraisal of *FR* and its relation to Eliot's poetry.

C148 Roberts, Patrick. *The Psychology of Tragic Drama*. London: Routledge & Kegan Paul, 1975.

Chapter offers intricate explication of *FR* and its place in Eliot's dramatic development, with focus on the modern adaptation and interpretation of the *Oresteia*. Psychoanalytic critical interpretation includes comparison of Harry and Hamlet: "Harry, like Hamlet, is mad, even if only north-north-west; and in his distress he shows, like Hamlet, suspicious resentment of the wrong kind of interference."

C149 Scott, Nathan A., Jr. *Rehearsals of Discomposure: Alienation and Reconciliation in Modern Literature*. New York: King's Crown P, 1952.

Chapter on Eliot includes discussion of a technique in *FR* new to his writing: "the dramatization of the religious problem without visibly relying on a structure of dogma, a strategy obviously intended to disarm the modern theatre audience of its usual secular defenses."

C150 Scrimgeour, C. A. "The Family Reunion." *Essays in Criticism* 13.1 (January 1963): 104-106.

Disagrees with Ronald Gaskell's assertion that the natural world is not real in *FR*, proposing that Eliot integrates the natural and supernatural in the conflict between Amy and Agatha as they "struggle to be Harry's mentor."

C151 Sena, Vinod. "Eliot's *The Family Reunion*: A Study in Disintegration." *Southern Review* 3 (Autumn 1967): 895-921.

Meticulously details and examines the faults of *FR*, "an exercise in disintegration" and artistically incoherent.

C152   Smith, R. Gregor. "Mr. Eliot's *The Family Reunion* in the Light of Martin Buber's *I and Thou*." *Theology* 50.319 (January 1947): 59-64.
        Eliot, like Buber, "ignores the traditional limits of philosophical and poetic activity—and attempts to answer anew the old question, *What is Man?*" Both works deal "with the crucial situation of our age, with the critical sickness of civilization."

C153   Spanos, William V. "T. S. Eliot's *The Family Reunion*: The Strategy of Sacramental Transfiguration." *Drama Survey* 4.1 (Spring 1965):·3-27.
        In *FR* Eliot presents "the implications of a sacramental poetic, which reconciles poetry and everyday reality."

C154   Stamm, Rudolf. "The Orestes Theme in Three Plays by Eugene O'Neill, T. S. Eliot and Jean-Paul Sartre." *English Studies* 30.5 (1949): 244-55.
        Explores Harry's thematic and characteristic roots in the play of Aeschylus.

C155   Unger, Leonard. "T. S. Eliot's Rose Garden." *Southern Review* 7 (Spring 1942): 667-89. Rpt. in *T. S. Eliot: A Selected Critique*. New York: Rinehart, 1948, 374-94.
        Thematic examination of perceptions of past and future experience in Eliot's writing, and the metaphorical construct of the garden, considers *FR* as the exposition of Harry's "spiritual problem. . . . He is beset by a peculiar need" manifested in "the advance toward spiritual rebirth and the peace of religious love."

C156   Ward, Anne. "Speculations on Eliot's Time-World: An Analysis of *The Family Reunion* in Relation to Hulme and Bergson." *American Literature* 21.1 (March 1949): 18-34.
        Discusses "Hulme's summary of Bergson's threefold division" of time, showing how Eliot uses and rearranges these kinds of time in *FR*. Addresses the concreteness of poetic language, comparing Eliot's views to Hulme's.

C157   Wertheim, Albert. "The Modern British Homecoming Play." *Comparative Drama* 19.2 (Summer 1985): 151-65.
        FR is a forerunner in creating a modern resuscitation of a dramatic form, based upon the ramifications of "one or more family members returning home after a period of absence."

C158   Wood, Grace A. "Crime and Contrition in Literature." *Contempo-rary Review* 198 (June 1960): 391-97.
Examines the Orestes myth in Jean-Paul Sartre's *The Flies*, Eugene O'Neill's *Mourning Becomes Electra*, and *FR*, focusing on the peace-making impulse at the end of *FR*.

The Cocktail Party

C159   Adler, Jacob H. "A Source for Eliot in Shaw." *Notes and Queries* n. s. 14.7 (July 1967): 256-57.
The effect of describing Celia's death amid banal chatter is similar to the revelation of a death in George Bernard Shaw's *Arms and the Man*.

C160   Arrowsmith, William. "Notes on English Verse Drama." *Hudson Review* 3 (Autumn 1950): 411-30.
Considers the dramatic creation of a possible Christian society.

C161   Bain, Donald. "The Cocktail Party." *Nine* 2.1 (January 1950): 16-22.
CP exists on two levels: as an artificial social comedy and as a sublime attempt to justify the ways of God to people.

C162   Barrett, William. "Dry Land, Dry Martini." *Partisan Review* 17 (April 1950): 354-59.
Judging *CP* by the standard of Eliot's poetry, it must be found thin and disappointing.

C163   Brady, Ann P. "The Alchemy of Humor in *The Cocktail Party*." In *Approaches to Teaching Eliot's Poetry and Plays*. Ed. Jewel Spears Brooker. New York: Modern Language Association, 1988, 179-82.
Examines the use of comedy and its transformations.

C164   Brandt, G. W. "Realism and Parables: From Brecht to Arden." In *Contemporary Theatre*. Eds. John Russell Brown and Bernard Harris. London: Edward Arnold, 1962, 33-56.
Analyzes *CP* by the standards of parable: wit, allegory, poetic obliqueness.

C165   Browne, E. Martin. *The Making of a Play: T. S. Eliot's 'The Cocktail Party.'* Cambridge: Cambridge U P, 1966.
An earlier version of the chapter on *CP* in *The Making of T. S. Eliot's Plays*, and the germ of that book.

C166 Carter, Paul J., Jr. "Who Understands 'The Cocktail Party'?" *Colorado Quarterly* 2.2 (Autumn 1953): 193-205.

Survey of various critical responses shows the diversity of perhaps unresolvably conflicting or ambiguous interpretations.

C167 Chamberlain, Lesley. "Through a Cocktail Glass Darkly." *Modern Drama* 31.4 (December 1988): 512-19.

CP, though full of successful symbolic resonances such as the role of the Guardians, fails on stage because audiences cannot properly appreciate the nuances of the verse and because of insufficiently humanized characters.

C168 Coghill, Nevill, ed. *The Cocktail Party*. London: Faber & Faber, 1974.

Text of the play, along with comments on it from Eliot's correspondence; exhaustive explanatory notes; and "An Essay on the Structure and Meaning of the Play" which treats the themes of comedy and love, the Guardians, the libation, and Eliot's verse style.

C169 Colby, Robert A. "The Three Worlds of *The Cocktail Party*: The Wit of T. S. Eliot." *University of Toronto Quarterly* 24.1 (October 1954): 56-69.

Concerned with the interplay of home, society, and church, *CP* presents a fusion of the three elements of an ideal Christian society: the Community of Christians, the Christian State, and the Christian Community.

C170 Davenport, Gary T. "Eliot's *The Cocktail Party*: Comic Perspective as Salvation. *Modern Drama* 17.3 (September 1974): 301-306.

The Chamberlaynes' salvation depends on their ability to achieve a comic perspective of themselves and life. Henri Bergson's 1900 essay "Laughter" seems to influence Eliot's creation of this detached comic perspective and the "one-eyed" motif.

C171 Dick, Bernard F. "Sartre and *The Cocktail Party*." *Yeats Eliot Review* 5.1 (1978): 25-26.

Suggests sources in Jean-Paul Sartre's *Nausea* and *No Exit* for Edward's image of hell.

C172 Dickinson, Donald Hugh. "Mr. Eliot's Hotel Universe." *Drama Critique* 1 (February 1958): 33-44.

CP resembles Philip Barry's religious drama *Hotel Universe* in terms of realism and its failure.

C173   Donnelly, Mabel C. "The Failure of Act III of Eliot's *The Cocktail Party*." *College Language Association Journal* 21.1 (September 1977): 58-61.
Criticizes the inconsistency of tone in which characters react to Celia's death.

C173a   Dunkel, Wilbur Dwight. "T. S. Eliot's Quest for Certitude." *Theology Today* 7.2 (July 1950): 228-36.
Views the characters as either materialistic or spiritual—mostly materialistic, as is most of the Broadway audience. Reilly is an ordinary man, rather than a mystic; even Celia does not have enough guilt to validate her spirituality. Eliot offers no answers that cannot be found in Christian theology. R. Gregor Smith refutes Dunkel's interpretation in a subsequent issue ("An Exchange of Notes on T. S. Eliot: A Critique." 7.4 [January 1951]: 503-506), finding that *CP* provides Christian understanding, and criticizing Dunkel's character analyses. Dunkel responds in the same issue ("An Exchange of Notes on T. S. Eliot: A Rejoinder," 507-508) that he finds the play lacking in Christ's idea of love.

C174   Enright, D. J. *The Apothecary Shop*. London: Secker & Warburg, 1957.
An essay, "On Not Teaching *The Cocktail Party*: A Professorial Dialogue," charges that *CP* is uninspiring, unpoetic, unrealistic, and bullying.

C175   Fallon, Gabriel. "After the Party." *Irish Monthly* 79.939 (September 1951): 389-93.
CP fails because it is not based in the real world of experience. The audience cannot accept Reilly on two levels; Eliot lacks tolerance and impartiality toward his characters and concludes the play with his own judgment, denying the audience the chance to judge for itself.

C176   Gardner, Helen. "The Cocktail Party." *Time and Tide* 31.12 (25 March 1950): 284-85.
CP is meant to be understood on two levels: as a comedy of manners and as a divine comedy, though these levels fail to merge because Eliot aspires to "a romantic conception of sanctity" as opposed to "the classic idea of holiness."

C177   Gillett, Eric. "Mr. Eliot Throws a Party." *National Review* 134.804 (February 1950): 140-47.
CP, while reaching at eternal Christian verities, is not an artistic success and will be forgotten.

C178   Hamalian, Leo. "Mr. Eliot's Saturday Evening Service." *Accent* 10.4 (Autumn 1950): 195-206.

        Connections are presented between *CP* and Eliot's earlier plays and poetry. Jessie Weston's *From Ritual to Romance* is a source, or model, for some of the play's symbolism.

C179   Hammerschmidt, Hildegard. "The Role of the 'Guardians' in T. S. Eliot's *Cocktail Party*." *Modern Drama* 24.1 (March 1981): 54-66.

        Focus on magical elements presents Reilly as the magus, and suggests that he is modeled on Dr. John Dee, a possible Shakespearean source for Prospero in *The Tempest*. The magic, naturally beneficent or malevolent, is ambivalent except with regard to Alex who may be a mysteriously diabolical accomplice to Celia's death. Her martyrdom is challenged because of the Guardians' manipulative influence.

C180   Hanzo, Thomas. "Eliot and Kierkegaard: 'The Meaning of Happening' in *The Cocktail Party*." *Modern Drama* 3.1 (May 1960): 52-59.

        CP shows a closer relationship between event and idea than *FR*. This expression of meaning can be understood in terms of Sören Kierkegaard's formula for despair from *The Sickness Unto Death*, which is applied to Edward as a means of understanding his salvation.

C181   Hardy, John Edward. "An Antic Disposition." *Sewanee Review* 65 (Winter 1957): 50-60.

        Reilly's heroic character makes him a kind of Christ-figure, though at the same time that role is in some ways undercut.

C182   Heilman, Robert B. "*Alcestis* and *The Cocktail Party*." *Comparative Literature* 5.2 (Spring 1953): 105-16.

        Parallels between the two works include the motif of desertion and death and the nature of a successful marriage. Lavinia and Celia are two halves of the character of Alcestis, while Reilly evokes both Heracles and Pheres. The doubleness of Heracles may have suggested Eliot's theme of the dualism of world and spirit.

C183   Heywood, Robert. "Everybody's Cocktail Party." *Renascence* 3.1 (Autumn 1950): 28-30.

        There is no unilaterally authoritative interpretation of *CP*; its power lies in the multiplicity of possible interpretations.

C184   Hochwald, Ilse E.   "Eliot's *Cocktail Party* and Goethe's *Wahlver-wandtschaften.*" *Germanic Review* 29.4 (December 1954): 254-59.
    Compares Celia with Goethe's Ottolie and suggests that the different endings of the two works reflect Eliot's critique of the novel.

C185   Holland, Norman N.   "Realism and the Psychological Critic; Or, How Many Complexes Had Lady Macbeth?" *Literature and Psychology* 10 (Winter 1960): 5-10.
    Dialogue questions whether psychological criticism offers a too strongly realistic interpretation of Reilly, whose function is primarily dramatic as opposed to human.

C186   Hollis, Christopher.   "Saints of the Cocktail Bar?" *Listener* 46:1174 (30 August 1951): 337-38.
    Cautions against trying to ask larger moral questions of *CP* than Eliot chooses to confront.

C187   Hovey, Richard B.   "Psychiatrist and Saint in *The Cocktail Party.*" *Literature and Psychology* 9.3-4 (Sumer-Fall 1959): 51-55.
    Reilly's psychoanalysis reflects Eliot's inadequate understanding of psychiatry, which points to a limitation of his insight into Christianity and spiritual love.

C188   Kee, Howard C.   "The Bible and the Work of Eliot and Sitwell." *Friends Intelligencer* 109.45 (8 November 1952): 641-43.
    Examines the nature of the play's biblical allusions, such as those to Paul's Letter to the Philippians, and criticizes Eliot for scuttling "the New Testament conception of individual moral autonomy" by a Thomistic rigidity that may derive from an unconsciously Calvinistic determinism.

C189   Knust, Herbert.   "What's the Matter With One-Eyed Reilly?" *Comparative Literature* 17.4 (Fall 1965): 289-98.
    Raises questions about *Alcestis* as a source and proposes the Norse myths from Richard Wagner's *Ring des Nibelungen* as an additional source.

C190   Koch, Vivienne.   "Program Notes on *The Cocktail Party.*" *Poetry Quarterly* 11.4 (Winter 1949): 248-51.
    CP—each act of which is described in terms of tone, character development, and theme—is a study of redemption, in secular rather than institutional terms. Each character represents a stage in Eliot's spiritual ascent, and the play reenacts his conflicts, crises, and resolutions.

C191   Kramer, Hilton. "T. S. Eliot in New York (Notes on the End of Something)." *Western Review* 14.4 (Summer 1950): 303-305.

      CP is thematically integrated with Eliot's earlier work; its success indicates that an increasingly widespread audience is capable of appreciating New Criticism and serious literature.

C192   Lawlor, John. "The Formal Achievement of 'The Cocktail Party.'" *Virginia Quarterly Review* 30.3 (Summer 1954): 431-51.

      Eliot's satire lies within the Shakespearean tradition of high comedy; those who are disappointed by *CP* have not considered it within the parameters of comedy.

C193   Levine, George. "*The Cocktail Party* and *Clara Hopgood.*" *Graduate Student of English* 1.2 (Winter 1958): 4-11.

      Comparing the theme of personal salvation in both works, concludes that Mark Rutherford's novel more successfully portrays sainthood and self-sacrifice; Eliot, assuming that the cocktail party embodies the play's only reality, deprives his characters of real choices.

C194   Lewis, Allan. *The Contemporary Theatre: The Significant Playwrights of Our Time.* New York: Crown, 1962.

      Chapter on *CP* explores its role as "the basis for extended discussions on the importance of the theatre as temple" and examines the themes of atonement, salvation, and communion.

C195   Lightfoot, Marjorie J. "The Uncommon Cocktail Party." *Modern Drama* 11.4 (February 1969): 382-95.

      Examines the play's prosody based upon the Decca recording and presents widely-varied hypotheses about the meter. The predominant measure is four-stress measured accentual verse, which is well-suited to capturing the rhythms of common contemporary speech.

C196   Lund, Mary Graham. "The Androgynous Moment: Woolf and Eliot." *Renascence* 12.2 (Winter 1960): 74-78.

      Like Virginia Woolf's *The Waves*, *CP* is concerned with "the painful process of individuation, which means not only differentiation from others but relationship with them." Both present the possibility of the individual's return to society at a higher level, which reflects an androgynous synthesis.

C197   Manning, Hugo. "Mr. Eliot's Strange Party." *Norseman* 9.2 (March-April 1951): 128-30.

      Eliot is a spent force, as this play demonstrates with its smug, insidious, and cynical sensibility that forestalls faith and ideology.

C198   McLaughlin, John J. "A Daring Metaphysic: *The Cocktail Party.*"
       Renascence 3.1 (Autumn 1950): 15-28.
       The different levels of perfection in *CP* illustrate the Thomist
       principles of Potency and Act: change occurs beause a subject is
       capable of receiving or losing various perfections.

C199   Morgan, Frederick. "Chronicles: Notes on the Theater." *Hudson
       Review* 3.2 (Summer 1950): 289-97.
       The play's concern is mystical experience in the modern world.

C200   Munz, Peter. "The Devil's Dialectic or *The Cocktail Party.*" *Hib-
       bert Journal* 49 (April 1951): 256-63.
       Theologically-based critique laments the fact that Eliot, lacking
       an understanding of Christian love, sees Christianity as focusing on
       people's depravity. The idea that absolute Christian love can be
       modified for human weaknesses comes from the devil, so Eliot's
       premise that there are two paths shows that he has succumbed to the
       devil's trickery and prevents him from understanding or describing
       saintliness.

C201   Oberg, Arthur K. "*The Cocktail Party* and the Illusion of Autono-
       my." *Modern Drama* 11.2 (September 1968): 187-94.
       The movement of speech is the action of *CP*. Eliot attempts to
       create, through speech in the play, "self-sufficiency of lan-
       guage"—words portraying consummate meaning and emotion, sepa-
       rate from action; but this cannot be finally achieved, for some things
       cannot be reduced to words.

C202   Paul, David. "Euripides and Mr. Eliot." *Twentieth Century*
       152.906 (August 1952): 174-80.
       The play is less successful than its Greek source because Reilly
       forces the audience to consider only the author's moral position, and
       does not permit viewers to exercise their own judgments or sympa-
       thies.

C203   Peschmann, Hermann. "*The Cocktail Party*: Some Links Between the
       Poems and Plays of T. S. Eliot." *The Wind and the Rain* 7.1 (Au-
       tumn 1950): 53-58.
       CP dramatizes the doctrines of *Four Quartets* as earlier plays
       dramatize issues from the earlier poetry; it is the culmination of El-
       iot's concern with the ideas of reconciliation to the human condition
       and salvation.

C204   Peter, John. "Sin and Soda." *Scrutiny* 17.1 (Spring 1950): 61-66.
       Examines spiritual and secular connections.

C205   Pick, John. "A Note on *The Cocktail Party*." *Renascence* 3.1 (Autumn 1950): 30-32.

        CP, like *MC*, has the theme that "Humankind cannot bear very much reality"; both plays deal with the making of a saint: Becket and Celia.

C206   Porter, Thomas E. "The Old Woman, the Doctor and the Cook: *The Cocktail Party*." In *Myth and Modern American Drama*. Detroit: Wayne State U P, 1969, 53-76.

        Discusses the play's numerous mythic intentions: concealing a classcial foundation; merging Greek ritual with Christian detail; combining conventional comic form with Euripidean satyr-drama. Explains the mythological and ritualistic resonances of the Guardians' types as described in Francis Cornford's *The Origins of Attic Comedy*.

C207   Quin, I. T. "'The Cocktail Party': A Criticism." *Irish Monthly* 79.936 (June 1951): 259-63.

        CP fails as drama because its truths are implanted by the author rather than realized by the audience; still, it may be considered great moral literature.

C208   Rao, Vimala. "T. S. Eliot's *The Cocktail Party* and the *Bhagavad-Gita*." *Comparative Literature Studies* 18.2 (June 1981): 191-98.

        CP is indebted to the sensibility of the *Bhagavad-Gita* and to the tenor of some of its passages and rhythms; the Guardians especially evoke the *Bhagavad-Gita* in their attitude toward choice and action.

C209   Reckford, Kenneth J. "Heracles and Mr. Eliot." *Comparative Literature* 16.1 (Winter 1964): 1-18.

        Eliot's themes of folly and humility have roots in Euripides. Examines sharing of food and drink and its relation to Christian sacrament; analyzes Reilly's song; and discusses the element of the author's own laughter in the play.

C210   Reed, Henry. "Towards 'The Cocktail Party.'" *Listener* 45 (10 May 1951, 17 May 1951): 763-64, 803-804.

        CP has elevated dramatic poetry to a level as important as that of the novel. Through the triumphant creation of a form "equidistant between prose and poetry," Eliot has solved the problem of writing verse for the modern stage.

C211 Rexine, John E. "Classical and Christian Foundations of T. S. Eliot's *The Cocktail Party*." *Books Abroad* 39.1 (Winter 1965): 21-26.

Discusses plot parallels from the *Alcestis* and possible derivations of Eliot's characters' names in the Greek source. Eliot ultimately departs from the Greek model by transforming myth into Christian terms of sacrifice.

C212 Robbins, Rossell Hope. "A Possible Analogue for 'The Cocktail Party.'" *English Studies* 34 (August 1953): 165-67.

Charles Williams's 1937 novel *Descent into Hell* may be a more direct source for the play than *Alcestis*, based upon similarities in language and characters and use of a passage from Percy Bysshe Shelley's *Prometheus Unbound*.

C213 Rothbard, Lorraine. "Eliot." *Diameter* 1 (March 1951): 31-38.

CP, though intellectually dense, shows a diminution of Eliot's poetic power; the characters are ideas rather than human beings and Eliot tries to approach truth by reason alone.

C214 Schwartz, Edward. "Eliot's *Cocktail Party* and the New Humanism." *Philological Quarterly* 32.1 (January 1953): 58-68.

Though Eliot objected to Irving Babbitt's focus on human reason and will to the exclusion of the supernatural, he nevertheless draws upon both Christian and humanistic ideas of people's moral responsibility in *CP*; the humanism takes the form of a dualism between a person's natural and moral facets, and between the fact that people are natural objects but also have qualities that set them apart from nature.

C215 Scott, Nathan A. "T. S. Eliot's 'The Cocktail Party': Of Redemption and Vocation." *Religion in Life* 20.2 (Spring 1951): 274-85.

CP shows the growth of Eliot's dramatic style: the atmosphere and its effect on the characters are "fully realized." The play's comment on the human situation is linked to the Christian idea of vocation.

C216 Selmon, Michael. "Logician, Heal Thy Self: Poetry and Drama in Eliot's *The Cocktail Party*." *Modern Drama* 31.4 (December 1988): 498-511.

CP is an investigation of "our struggle with language," infused with linguistic self-reference. Ultimately Eliot discovers a language that transcends the self, finding fruition in the genre of drama.

C217   Sena, Vinod. "The Ambivalence of *The Cocktail Party*." *Modern Drama* 14.4 (February 1972): 392-404.

The Guardians subvert the idea of free will that Eliot envisaged for *CP* by manipulating the other characters; Reilly, Alex, and Julia represent a comic and theatrical success but a dramatic failure.

C218   Shuman, R. Baird. "Buddhistic Overtones in Eliot's *The Cocktail Party*." *Modern Language Notes* 72.6 (June 1957): 426-27.

Reilly's advice to his patients evokes the language of the Buddha; Celia's actions parallel the four noble truths of Buddhism.

C219   _____. "Eliot's *The Cocktail Party*." *Explicator* 17.7 (April 1959): Item 46.

Reilly is cast in the role of celebrant or high priest.

C220   Speaight, Robert. "Sartre and Eliot." *Drama* n. s. 17 (Summer 1950): 15-17.

Comparing Jean-Paul Sartre's plays *Crime Passionel, Men Without Shadows*, and *The Respectable Prostitute* with *CP* shows that Sartre "makes a mockery of the human will while Eliot restores it to honour."

C221   Stein, Walter. "After the Cocktails." *Essays in Criticism* 3.1 (January 1953): 85-104.

CP fails because of its unintentional and desperate Manicheism and its inability to achieve a poetically immediate embodied vision.

C222   Styan, J. L. *The Elements of Drama*. Cambridge: Cambridge U P, 1960.

Study of dramaturgical technique analyzes *CP*, in a chapter called "Passing Judgment," as an example of how to examine a play critically; finds it "a play about happiness, happiness to be conceived at the highest spiritual level that each of Mr. Eliot's samples from contemporary sophisticated humanity is capable of," but technically haphazard, imbalanced, and unintegrated.

C223   Thrash, Lois G. "A Source for the Redemption Theme in *The Cocktail Party*." *Texas Studies in Language and Literature* 9.4 (Winter 1968): 547-53.

Charles Williams's 1932 novel *The Greater Trumps* may be a source for *CP* in terms of character parallels and the idea of two distinct paths to salvation.

C224   Toms, Newby. "Eliot's *The Cocktail Party*: Salvation and the Common Routine." *Christian Scholar* 47.2 (Summer 1964): 125-38.

   Examines Eliot's theology in terms of the Chamberlaynes' salvation, and explores the technique of combining poetic drama with comedy to yield the same themes present in Eliot's poetry.

C225   Vassilieff, Elizabeth. "Piers to Cocktails." *Meanjin* 9.3 (Spring 1950): 193-203.

   Links *CP* to *Piers Plowman* metrically and discusses both works as religious allegories.

C226   Vincent, C. J. "A Modern Pilgrim's Progress." *Queen's Quarterly* 57.3 (Autumn 1950): 346-52.

   CP, Sophoclean rather than Euripidean, is, like *Four Quartets*, religious art. Celia's journey parallels Dante's in the *Divine Comedy*.

C227   Wade, Stephen. "The Orchestration of Monologues: 'The Cocktail Party' and a Developing Genre." *Agenda* 23.3-4 (Autumn-Winter 1985-86): 202-209.

   Praises Eliot's use of the monologue as a medium for presenting the theme of self-knowledge; the language is fluent enough to sustain the play's momentum and simultaneously versatile enough to embody profound religious discovery.

C228   Weisstein, Ulrich. "*The Cocktail Party*: An Attempt at Interpretation on Mythological Grounds." *Western Review* 16.3 (Spring 1952): 232-41.

   Details correspondences with Euripides, Sartre, Dante, Vico, Shakespeare, and the Bible.

C229   Wimsatt, W. K., Jr. "Eliot's Comedy." *Sewanee Review* 58 (Autumn 1950): 666-78. Rpt. in *Hateful Contraries: Studies in Literature and Criticism*. Lexington, KY: U of Kentucky P, 1965, 184-200.

   Eliot has made verse drama attainable for his audience by presenting a "thinner" version of his poetry; *CP* is a "comical-morality" with semi-allegorical elements.

C230   Winter, Jack. "'Prufrockism' in *The Cocktail Party*." *Modern London Quarterly* 22.2 (June 1961): 135-48.

   The Prufrock archetype, which develops through Eliot's work, manifests itself in the characters' misery, particularly Edward's. By the end of *CP*, though, the characters mature beyond this condition to a resolution evocative of the serenity of *Four Quartets*.

C231   Wiseman, James. "Of Loneliness . . . and Communion." *Drama Critique* 5.1 (February 1962): 14-21.

        The play's repetition, especially about the devil and hell, is meant to evoke deceit and miscommunication; these are remedied by a communion that must be fostered by a stranger.

C232   Wool, Sandra. "Weston Revisited." *Accent* 10.4 (Autumn 1950): 207-12.

        Interprets the play's symbolism through Jessie Weston's *From Ritual to Romance* (which Eliot identified as a key to *The Waste Land*). Edward is the Fisher King; Reilly is the Quester and Medicine Man; Alex is the Templar; Julia, Alex, and Reilly are the Guardians of the Grail; Celia is the Saint and Hanged God; and Peter is the Apostle.

C233   Wren-Lewis, John. "The Passing of Puritanism." *Critical Quarterly* 5.4 (Winter 1963): 295-305.

        Dichotomy between romantic love, which denies a worldly connection, and a tradition of love according to natural law, based upon procreation, is explored with relation to *CP*.

C234   Yoklavich, John M. "Eliot's 'Cocktail Party' and Plato's 'Symposium.'" *Notes and Queries* 196.25 (8 December 1951): 541-42.

        Both works are a series of dramatic dialogues about love; Reilly's speeches evoke Socrates, and his quotation from Percy Bysshe Shelley has Platonic resonances.

The Confidential Clerk

C235   Colby, Robert A. "Orpheus in the Counting House: *The Confidential Clerk*." *PMLA* 72.4 (September 1957): 791-802.

        CC is an allegory of social interaction and compassion. Stylistically and formally it owes much to a musical theory of composition.

C236   Davies, R. T. "Mr. T. S. Eliot's 'The Confidential Clerk.'" *Theology* 56.400 (October 1953): 411-14.

        Unlike Eliot's earlier plays, *CC* is marked by easy naturalism and satisfying conventionality.

C237   Dobrée, Bonamy. "*The Confidential Clerk*." *Sewanee Review* 62 (Winter 1954): 117-31. Rpt. in *The Lamp and the Lute*. London: Frank Cass, 1964, 122-41.

        "Eliot has made a serious thing out of a farce. . . . the originality of the play consists in its being a drastic pushing forward of the old critical comedy which, by making us laugh at and criticize our neighbors, is aimed at making us see ourselves as others see us."

C238   Findlater, Richard. "The Camouflaged Drama." *Twentieth Century* 154 (October 1953): 311-16.

        CC lacks emotional unity, which Eliot himself described in a critical essay as a strong, dominant tone.

C239   Mitchell, John D. "Applied Psychoanalysis in the Drama." *American Imago* 14.3 (Fall 1957): 263-80.

        Considers *CC* as Eliot's hidden wish-fulfillment fantasy. His rejection of his homeland led to his need to find a place where he belonged and was accepted; *CC* dramatizes that sensibility via Colby's quest to discover a home and family.

C240   Weedon, William S. "Mr. Eliot's Voices." *Virginia Quarterly Review* 30.4 (Autumn 1954): 610-13.

        CC is a dramatic articulation of the ideas expressed in "The Three Voices of Poetry."

The Elder Statesman

C241   Boardman, Gwenn R. "Restoring the Hollow Man." *Review* 4 (November 1962): 34-45.

        The peace at the play's end "expresses Eliot's recurrent theme of the restoration of the hollow man." As a hollow man, Claverton "fears strangers, loneliness, and his memories," but as he begins to face his fears, "Meditating in the quiet garden, he eventually makes an act of contrition and finds happiness through his final confession."

C242   van Boheemen, Christel. "Old Possum at Colonus: T. S. Eliot's *The Elder Statesman*." *Dutch Quarterly Review* 11.2 (1981): 119-32.

        ES, while "not interesting for aesthetic reasons . . . offers us an easy insight into Eliot's method of dramatic composition," especially regarding "the thematic and structural adaptation of the two Oedipus plays to a Christian view of the world."

C243   Dobrée, Bonamy. "The London Stage." *Sewanee Review* 67.1 (Winter 1959): 109-15. Rpt. in *The Lamp and the Lute*. London: Frank Cass, 1964, 141-49.

        Eliot's most human play, *ES* is more contemplative than dramatic with "a kind of inexorable movement from the beginning" rather than standard plot and action.

C244   Donoghue, Denis. "Eliot in Fair Colonus: *The Elder Statesman*." *Studies* 48 (Spring 1959): 49-58.

        ES is an extension of *FR*: an "attempt to accost that guilt-ridden experience which has been in the shadows of Eliot's world" for decades; this play more successfully "commits itself firmly to the possibility of an individual moral act" and represents what Northrop Frye would call "an ideal play": "gently drawing forth, from an ambiguous situation, an image of communal order."

C245   Fleming, Rudd. "*The Elder Statesman* and Eliot's 'Programme for the Métier of Poetry.'" *Wisconsin Studies in Contemporary Literature* 2.1 (Winter 1961): 54–64.

         ES presents the "consummate expression of the poet's awareness of himself and of his place within the European tradition," because of its ascension to the realm of love.

C246   Kenner, Hugh. "For Other Voices." *Poetry* 95.1 (October 1959): 36–40.

         Discusses the play's language, intimacy, and clarity.

C247   Padmanabhan, P. S. "The Irritant and the Pearl: 'Jones's Karma' and the Poetry and Drama of T. S. Eliot." *Canadian Review of Comparative Literature* 9.2 (June 1982): 188–99.

         Explores Eliot's interest in a short story by May Sinclair about an Indian philsophical examination of fate versus free will and briefly suggests its influence on *ES*.

C248   Sena, Vinod. "Henrik Ibsen and the Latest Eliot." *Literary Criterion* 6 (1965): 19–25.

         Ibsen's *The Pillars of Society* is a closer source for *ES* than *Oedipus at Colonus*.

C249   Smith, Grover. "The Ghosts in T. S. Eliot's 'The Elder Statesman.'" *Notes and Queries* n. s. 7.6 (June 1960): 233–35.

         Analyzes the nature and characterization of the play's "ghosts" with comparisons to ghostly evocations of characters from the past in Eliot's other plays and in Henry James's haunted tales.

C250   Stanford, Derek. "T. S. Eliot's New Play." *Queen's Quarterly* 65.4 (Winter 1958-59): 682–89.

         Examines the play's meaning, its "artistic fitness," and its "contribution to contemporary English drama."

C251   Weales, Gerald. "The Latest Eliot." *Kenyon Review* 21.3 (Summer 1959): 473–78.

         The appeal of Eliot's plays is intellectual rather than dramatic; *ES* fails because it is too strongly concerned with character and plot at the expense of intellectual dimensions.

C252   Webb, Mark. "John Rhode and the Naming of Eliot's *Elder States-man*." *Yeats Eliot Review* 6.2 (1979): 15-18.

Numerous correspondences between *ES* and Rhode's Dr. Priestly detective novel *The Claverton Mystery* make it probable that the novel is the source for Claverton's name.

Cats

C253   Kirk, Russell. "Cats, Eliot, and the Dance of Life." *Renascence* 40.3 (Spring 1988): 197-203.

Surprisingly, the dramatic adaptation of Eliot's poems is quite consonant with Eliot's aesthetic especially in terms of its emphasis on the dance, which was central for him.

III. General Scholarly Criticism

C254   Abbott, Anthony S. *The Vital Lie: Reality and Illusion in Modern Drama*. Tuscaloosa: U of Alabama P, 1989.

Reality and illusion within a Christian schema are the plays' focus; exploration of the difference between a saint and a common person is the foundation for this paradigm.

C255   Ackroyd, Peter. *T. S. Eliot: A Life*. New York: Simon and Schuster, 1984.

Biography includes background on the plays' composition and performance, and connections to autobiographical aspects of the plays.

C256   Andreach, Robert J. *Studies in Structure: The Stages of the Spiritual Life in Four Modern Authors*. New York: Fordham U P, 1964.

Chapter on Eliot examines the plays' spiritual sensibility and their relation to the post-conversion poetry.

C257   ApIvor, Denis. "Setting *The Hollow Men* to Music." In *T. S. Eliot: A Symposium for His Seventieth Birthday*. Ed. Neville Braybrooke. Freeport, NY: Books for Libraries P, 1958, 89-91.

Composer discusses the musical nature of Eliot's poetry and the process of scoring it.

C258   Arrowsmith, William. "Eliot and Euripides." *Arion* 4.1 (1965): 21-35. Rpt. from *English Stage Comedy*. Ed. W. K. Wimsatt. New York: Columbia U P, 1955.

Both playwrights' work are sometimes interpreted as taking place on two levels: one secular or superficial and the other spiritual or more profound; Eliot's levels, though, are not as substantially developed or satisfying as those of Euripides.

C259   Aylen, Leo. *Greek Tragedy and the Modern World*. London: Methuen, 1964.

        Chapter on Eliot in a study of modern tragedy and its affinities with Greek models credits him with having "made it possible to think of a modern English tragic drama."

C260   Barber, C. L. "The Power of Development . . . In a Different World." In *The Achievement of T. S. Eliot*. F. O. Matthiessen. New York: Oxford U P, 1959, 198-243.

        Discusses *CP* and *CC* in relation to Eliot's dramatic criticism, his religious sensibility, and classical dramatic analogues. Basic general explication and discussion.

C261   Barry, Michael. "Televising *The Cocktail Party*." In *T. S. Eliot: A Symposium for His Seventieth Birthday*. Ed. Neville Braybrooke. Freeport, NY: Books for Libraries P, 1958, 85-88.

        Details about presenting the plays for television.

C262   Barth, J. Robert. "T. S. Eliot's Image of Man: A Thematic Study of his Drama." *Renascence* 14.3 (Spring 1962): 126-38, 165.

        Examines "the problem of isolation from reality, leading to the thematic action of striving for union with reality—oneself, the world, other men, God."

C263   Bayley, John. "The Collected Plays." *Review* 4 (November 1962): 3-11.

        An overview of Eliot's dramatic aspirations, successes, and failures on the occasion of the publication of his collected plays, which brings his career to a close.

C264   Beare, Robert L. "Notes on the Text of T. S. Eliot: Variants from Russell Square." *Studies in Bibliography* 9 (1957): 21-49.

        Exhaustively catalogues textual variants (revisions, unauthoritative editorial changes, and possible errors) in different editions of the plays, chiefly *MC* and *CP*.

C265   Beehler, Michael. "Metaphysics and Dramatic *Praxis*: Eliot on the Rhetoric of Drama." *CEA Critic* 51.1 (Fall 1988): 103-13.

        In arguments resembling Martin Heidegger's about "the objectifying realism that defines modernity by shaping its metaphysics . . . Eliot highlights the realism of the Western theater as a central indicator of the pernicious mental habits characteristic of modernism's metaphysics of the world picture. From his earliest *Egoist* essays on drama to his late theoretical and practical reappraisals of his own dramatic work, Eliot's critical attention was repeatedly drawn to questions concerning the drama: its performability, its conventions, and particularly its rhetoric."

C266   Bergonzi, Bernard. *T. S. Eliot*. New York: Macmillan, 1972.
        Critical overview of Eliot's career includes discussion of the plays.

C267   Blackmur, R. P. *The Double Agent*. New York: Arrow Editions, 1935. Excerpt, "From *Ash Wednesday* to *Murder in the Cathedral*," in *T. S. Eliot: A Selected Critique*. Ed. Leonard Unger. New York: Rinehart, 1948, 236-62.
        Examination of the religious element in Eliot's development includes discussion of *The Rock* and *MC*.

C268   Bland, D. S. "The Tragic Hero in Modern Literature." *Cambridge Journal* 3.4 (January 1950): 214-23.
        Eliot's plays (especially *FR*) are considered as examples, though isolated ones, showing that the tragic hero still exists in modern literature; more generally, individual heroism has vanished.

C269   Bloomfield, B. C. "An Unrecorded Article by T. S. Eliot." *Book Collector* 11 (Autumn 1962): 350.
        Briefly paraphrases a newly-discovered 1934 essay, "Religious Drama and the Church," in which Eliot argues for a strong religious influence on dramatists.

C270   Bradbrook, M. C. *English Dramatic Form: A History of Its Development*. London: Chatto & Windus, 1965.
        Chapter on Eliot's plays examines structural unities, and their relation to such traditions as W. B. Yeats's, French Existential drama, and classical myth.

C271   _____. "The Lyric and Dramatic in the Latest Verse of T. S. Eliot." *Theology* 46.259 (January 1942): 81-90.
        Considers *MC* and *FR* in relation to Eliot's late explicit Christian poetry.

C272   _____. *T. S. Eliot*. London: Longmans, Green, 1950.
        Section surveys Eliot's dramatic development and literary criticism.

C273   Brooks, Cleanth. *The Hidden God: Studies in Hemingway, Faulkner, Yeats, Eliot, and Warren*. New Haven: Yale U P, 1963.
        Chapter entitled "T. S. Eliot: Discourse to the Gentiles" examines the indirection of the Christian sensibility in the plays and po-

ems, which are "conceived in terms of the following problem: how is revealed truth to be mediated to the gentiles? How is that which is by definition ineffable to be translated into words, no direct transmission of the vision being possible?"

C274   Broussard, Louis. *American Drama: Contemporary Allegory from Eugene O'Neill to Tennessee Williams.* Norman: U of Oklahoma P, 1962.
        Chapter on Eliot surveys his work in the context of allegorical drama.

C275   Browne, E. Martin. "The Dramatic Verse of T. S. Eliot." In *T. S. Eliot: A Symposium.* Eds. Richard March and Tambimuttu. Freeport, NY: Books for Libraries P, 1968, 196-207.
        Formal observations on the development of Eliot's dramatic verse up to *FR*.

C276   _____. "From *The Rock* to *The Confidential Clerk*." In *T. S. Eliot: A Symposium for His Seventieth Birthday.* Ed. Neville Braybrooke. Freeport, NY: Books for Libraries P, 1958, 57-69.
        A brief overview of Eliot's dramatic career by his director.

C277   _____. *The Making of T. S. Eliot's Plays.* Cambridge: Cambridge U P, 1969.
        The plays' director extensively describes business, production, and performance details; conception and composition; textual revisions; biographical background and personal reminiscences; and numerous other germane aspects in this definitive work.

C278   _____. "The Permanent Contribution of T. S. Eliot to the Drama." *Gordon Review* 6.4 (Winter 1962-63): 150-66.
        Details about the plays that are repeated, more fully developed, in *The Making of T. S. Eliot's Plays.*

C279   _____. "T. S. Eliot as Dramatist." *Drama* 76 (Spring 1965): 41-43.
        Appreciation of Eliot's drama and the tenor of the theatre for which he wrote, on the occasion of his death.

C280   _____. "T. S. Eliot in the Theatre: The Director's Memories." *In T. S. Eliot: The Man and his Work.* Ed. Allen Tate. New York: Delacorte P, 1966, 116-32.
        Reminiscences of personal and professional contacts with Eliot throughout his dramatic career.

C281   _____ with Henzie Browne. *Two in One*. Cambridge: Cambridge U P, 1981.

Reminiscences of the Brownes' career, including extensive work with Eliot. Covers the same ground as *The Making of T. S. Eliot's Plays* with minimal new information about Eliot, though more background on their other endeavors.

C282   Bullough, Geoffrey. "Christopher Fry and the 'Revolt' against Eliot." In *Experimental Drama*. Ed. William A. Armstrong. London: G. Bell, 1963, 56-78.

Eliot's drama was experimentally an important precursor to Fry's success, but Fry's plays are "much more technically accomplished"; he, unlike Eliot, is "first and foremost a man of the theatre" and more full of "the miraculous wonder of living" than the puritanical Eliot.

C283   Bush, Ronald. *T. S. Eliot: A Study in Character and Style*. New York: Oxford U P, 1983.

Biographical and psychoanalytically-based exegesis covers Eliot's entire oeuvre emphasizing how his character, impulses, and repressions shape his writing.

C284   Carnell, Corbin S. "Creation's Lonely Flesh: T. S. Eliot and Christopher Fry on the Life of the Senses." *Modern Drama* 6.2 (September 1963): 141-49.

Eliot, though more praised than Fry, is "less orthodox and less successful in his handling of Christian belief. He has failed conspicuously in one important area—in his handling of the the relation between the natural world and God, that is, in his doctrine of Creation," which is understated, fearful, devoid of joy.

C285   Chiari, Joseph. *Landmarks of Contemporary Drama*. New York: Gordian P, 1965.

Chapter on poetic drama in a survey of modern drama highlights Eliot's formative contributions.

C286   _____. *T. S. Eliot: Poet and Dramatist*. London: Vision P, 1972.

Conventional exegetical study includes a chapter on the plays.

C287   Cornwell, Ethel F. *The "Still Point."* New Brunswick, NJ: Rutgers U P, 1962.

Chapter on Eliot in a study of literary manifestations of the dialectic between the writer's "desire to preserve and develop his individual identity, and the desire to merge himself with something greater than and outside himself" examines attempts to present this dialectic in *Four Quartets* and in the plays.

C288   Daniells, Roy. "The Christian Drama of T. S. Eliot." *Canadian Forum* 16 (August 1936): 20-21.
    The dogma in Eliot's essays is inquisitorial and heavy-handed, as compared with the "cadenced beauty" of the dogma in *The Rock* and *MC*.

C289   Dickinson, Hugh. "Eliot's Dramatic Use of Myth." *Drama Critique* 5.2 (May 1962): 50-58. Rpt. in *Myth on the Modern Stage*. Urbana, IL: U of Illinois P, 1969.
    In Eliot's plays, "myth seems to serve him as private guide or referent as he tries to impose order and form on his own creation," even though "the myth itself is not apparent in the plays as dramatic experience." Eliot's use of myth is very different from his famous discussion of Joyce's mythic method in "Ulysses, Order, and Myth."

C290   Donoghue, Denis. *The Third Voice: Modern British and American Verse Drama*. Princeton: Princeton U P, 1959.
    Finds the earlier plays awash in Empsonian chaos or elusively ephemeral structure, and sees increasing precision, control, and dramatic success in the later plays.

C291   Downey, Harris. "T. S. Eliot—Poet as Playwright." *Virginia Quarterly Review* 12.1 (January 1936): 142-45.
    An early application of Eliot's poetic and dramatic theories to his own plays (*The Rock* and *MC*).

C292   Dukes, Ashley. "Re-enter the Chorus." *Theatre Arts* 22 (May 1938): 335-40.
    Discusses Eliot's use of the chorus in the context of a revival of choral drama.

C293   _____. "T. S. Eliot in the Theatre." In *T. S. Eliot: A Symposium*. Eds. Richard March and Tambimuttu. Freeport, NY: Books for Libraries P, 1968: 111-18.
    Theatre-owner and early champion of Eliot's drama appraises his works up to *FR*.

C294   Emery, Sarah Watson. "Saints and Mr. Eliot." *Emory University Quarterly* 7.3 (October 1951): 129-42.
    Describes the theme of sainthood as portrayed in *MC*, *FR*, and *CP*, from "the first awareness of the call to sainthood," which is "a

haunting consciousness of sin which must be atoned," to the trans-humanizing election of a saint's destiny.

C295   Evans, Gareth Lloyd. *The Language of Modern Drama*. London: J. M. Dent, 1977.
        Eliot's cultivation of diction and style.

C296   Findlater, Richard. *The Unholy Trade*. London: Victor Gollancz, 1952.
        Surveys the first five plays in light of an argument that stagnation and decline afflict the modern British stage.

C297   Flannery, James. "In Search of a Poetic Drama for the Post-Modernist Age." In *The Modernists: Studies in a Literary Phenomenon*. Ed. Lawrence B. Gamache and Ian S. MacNiven. Rutherford, NJ: Fairleigh Dickinson U P, 1987, 75-91.
        Survey of modern poetic drama finds that Eliot "fell short as a dramatist precisely because he ignored the language of theatre as it might have served his vision." The genre has benefited from the experiments and energy of Gordon Craig's formalism; mime and a language of actions; and Yeats's vision that "poetry could not return to the stage until there was an entire reform of all the arts of the theatre." Poetry, as Jean Cocteau writes, "lacks sufficient power to engage the spectator's full attention"; the conventional plays of Christopher Fry, Maxwell Anderson, and Eliot "are, from a theatrical standpoint, dull and ineffective."

C298   Frankenberg, Lloyd. *Pleasure Dome: On Reading Modern Poetry*. Boston: Houghton Mifflin, 1949.
        A section surveys Eliot's first four plays with a loose focus on time.

C299   Freedman, Morris. *American Drama in Social Context*. Carbondale, IL: Southern Illinois U P, 1971.
        Chapter on Eliot's drama examines its relationship to the sensibility of his poems especially with regard to the image of the Jew and the anti-emotional barrenness.

C300   Gardner, Helen. *The Art of T. S. Eliot*. New York: Dutton, 1959 (originally published 1950). Excerpt (on *MC*), "The Language of Drama," in *T. S. Eliot's Murder in the Cathedral*. Ed. Harold Bloom. New York: Chelsea House, 1988, 17-22.
        Chapter entitled "The Language of Drama" asserts that the plays "are full of dramatic moments and of dramatic poetry," but these "do not necessarily add up to a drama"; nevertheless, in spite of such

generic deficiencies, important connections between the plays and poetry are explored.

C301   ____. "The Comedies of T. S. Eliot." *Sewanee Review* 74.1 (1966): 153-75. Rpt. in *T. S. Eliot: Plays*. Ed. Arnold P. Hinchliffe. London: Macmillan, 1985, 42-60.
Discussion of classical theory of dramatic comedy demonstrates how the final three plays adhere to this and have integrity within this genre.

C302   ____. *The Composition of Four Quartets*. New York: Oxford U P, 1978.
Describes occasional connections between the poetry and plays Eliot was writing in the 1930s and 1940s.

C303   Gascoigne, Bamber. *Twentieth-Century Drama*. London: Hutchinson, 1962.
Chapter on Eliot argues that his increasing conformity to the conventions of drawing-room drama "in some fiendish way overwhelmed him" with its prosaic naturalism.

C304   Gassner, John. *The Theatre in our Times*. New York: Crown, 1954.
Chapter on Eliot, "The Poet as Anti-Modernist," in a survey of modern drama, calls critical attention to his plays disproportionate and undeserved; they are important, though, as representative of "the most definite break with modern playwriting" in his insistence on a non-psychological drama—that is, an anti-rationalism which holds that "there are things in life that cannot be explained."

C305   Glicksberg, Charles I. "The Journey That Must Be Taken: Spiritual Quest in T. S. Eliot's Plays." *Southwest Review* 40 (Summer 1955): 203-10.
Each play's focus is the "higher reality" of spiritual liberation.

C306   ____. "The Spirit of Irony in Eliot's Plays." *Prairie Schooner* 29 (Fall 1955): 222-37.
Generic examination of Eliot's ironic insights and their relation to his comedy.

C307   Goldman, Michael. "Fear in the Way: The Design of Eliot's Drama." In *Eliot in His Time*. Ed. A. Walton Litz. Princeton: Princeton U P, 1973, 155-80. Excerpt (on *MC*) in *T. S. Eliot's Murder in the Cathedral*. Ed. Harold Bloom. New York: Chelsea House, 1988, 63-68.

    Eliot's drama is all patterned on "the calamitous loss of self and imprisonment in self that haunts our era, a dis-ease that may drive the fortunate man to glimpse transcendence, but which even those glimpses cannot cure." The plays engage and haunt the audience by casually defeating our expectations about what we think we fear and what we think we know.

C308   Gordon, Lyndall. *Eliot's Early Years*. Oxford: Oxford U P, 1977.

    Biographical study, generally considered the most reliable to date, of Eliot up to his 1927 conversion.

C309   _____. *Eliot's New Life*. Oxford: Oxford U P, 1988.

    Continues biographical study from the late 1920s to the end of Eliot's life, covering the period in which he did most of his dramatic work; explores numerous provocative autobiographical aspects of the plays, showing how Eliot may have expressed in his scripts echoes of his spiritual and emotional trials and resolutions.

C310   Graves, Robert, with Laura Riding. "Poetic Drama." In *The Common Asphodel: Collected Essays on Poetry*. New York: Haskell House, 1970, 284-94 (originally published 1949).

    Critical overview of the genre laments the "widening of the unbridgeable gap between dramatic and poetic realities"; calls Eliot's attempts to reconcile these two realities in *The Rock* and *MC* profane, infused with "a cynical candour with which Eliot uses drama as a means of journalizing a poetic theme."

C311   Gray, Ronald. "The Success and Failure of Poetic Drama in Austria and Britain: Hugo von Hofmannsthal and T. S. Eliot." In *Patterns of Change: German Drama and the European Tradition*. Ed. Dorothy James and Silvia Ranawake. New York: Peter Lang, 1990, 241.53.

    Eliot's attraction to Hofmannsthal is based upon a mutual interest in making verse drama popularly accessible, a desire to unite Europe, and religious concerns. "The indebtedness of *The Cocktail Party* to *Der Schwierige* is well established"; *CC*, too, is related to that play.

C312   Gross, John. "Eliot: From Ritual to Realism." *Encounter* 24.3
        (March 1965): 48-50.
        "Eliot's true importance to the theatre lies . . . in his essays, in
        Murder in the Cathedral, and in his non-dramatic poetry." His pro-
        gression from ritualistic to realistic drama in the later plays was a
        mistake.

C313   Hall, John. "Eliot as Dramatist." *Christian Drama* 2.11 (Autumn
        1954): 7-11.
        Lauds the Christian sensibility of the plays, which tell us "that
        the Christian way is the true way, and of the Christian ways, the
        Anglo-Catholic the truest; that we must take life as seriously as possi-
        ble, and also laugh at it unmercifully. He tells us these great truths
        in such a manner that we can both say, I never thought of that, and
        also, that is just what I thought."

C314   Harding, D. W. "Progression of Theme in Eliot's Modern Plays."
        Kenyon Review 18.3 (Summer 1956): 337-60.
        FR, *CP*, and *CC* deal with the theme of separation, in terms of
        "the Christian idea of longing to be at one with God by overcoming
        separation from him" and the loneliness of people separated from
        sexual or familial love—an isolation that must be endured by those
        who accept a spiritual vocation.

C315   Harding, Joan N. "T. S. Eliot, O. M." *Contemporary Review*
        187.1072 (April 1955): 239-43.
        Examines the humanist and Christian influences on Eliot.

C316   Henn, T. R. *The Harvest of Tragedy*. London: Methuen, 1956.
        Genre study examines *MC*, *FR*, and *CP* as tragedies.

C317   Hinchliffe, Arnold P. *Modern Verse Drama*. London: Methuen,
        1977.
        Surveys the development and practice of modern verse drama,
        including a general overview of Eliot's plays.

C318   _____. *T. S. Eliot: Plays*. London: Macmillan, 1985.
        A comprehensive collection of critical essays about the plays.
        Several essays on each play and overviews of Eliot's drama provide a
        survey of three decades of scholarship.

C319   Hirsch, Foster. "The Hearth and the Journey: The Mingling of Orders in the Drama of Yeats and Eliot." *Arizona Quarterly* 27.4 (Winter 1971): 293-307.

Compares Eliot's and W. B. Yeats's drama in terms of their opposition to confining Ibsenian realism and affirmation of a more profuse poetic expression; "both look beyond the limits of the purely natural world in their search for the mysterious and eternal." Explores how both use the symbols of building a hearth (finding redemption in human terms) versus going on a journey—(seeking salvation on a higher order) to this end.

C320   Holland, Joyce M. "Human Relations in Eliot's Drama." *Renascence* 22 (1970): 151-61.

Eliot's emphasis on personal relationships defines and creates a Christian community. By the end of Eliot's career, "the choice for Eliot's people is no longer between community and isolation, but between creative community and a 'community' of mutual destruction. . . . Human beings will inevitably act on one another—if not for good, then for evil."

C321   Howarth, Herbert. "Eliot and Hofmannsthal." *South Atlantic Quarterly* 59 (Autumn 1960): 500-509. Rpt. in *Notes on Some Figures Behind T. S. Eliot*.

Discusses Hugo von Hofmannsthal's influence on Eliot's drama.

C322   _____. *Notes on Some Figures Behind T. S. Eliot*. Boston: Houghton Mifflin, 1964.

Biographical, scholarly, cultural, and other exegetical sources give backgrounds or more tentatively suggest influences for Eliot's poetry and drama.

C323   Inserillo, Charles R. "Wish and Desire: Two Poles of the Imagination in the Drama of Arthur Miller and T. S. Eliot." *Xavier University Studies* 1 (Summer-Fall 1962): 247-58.

In *FR*, *CP*, and *CC*, "the audience is invited to participate in a transformation from wish into desire . . . and to see the necessity of an insight into the objective order through which the imagination can give birth to possibilities that are permissible, real, and fertile"; "wish" arises "out of the mind's natural appetite for infinite possibility," while "desire" is "born of the realizable potentialities of the self." Eliot's classicism contrasts with Miller's romanticism in this regard.

C324   Isaacs, J. *An Assessment of Twentieth-Century Literature*. London: Secker and Warburg, 1951.

        Chapter on "T. S. Eliot and Poetic Drama" posits that "Poetic drama is the literary form of the future."

C325   Jones, David E. *The Plays of T. S. Eliot*. Toronto: U of Toronto P, 1960.

        A comprehensive study of the plays focuses on detailed exegesis with attention to dramatic structure and interrelations between the plays.

C326   Kaul, R. K. "Rhyme and Blank Verse in Drama: A Note on Eliot." *English* 15.87 (Autumn 1964): 96-99.

        Examines Eliot's views on the suitability of rhymed verse as a dramatic medium, applied to the period from Dryden to Johnson.

C327   Kelly, Katherine E. "An Unnatural Eloquence: Eliot's Plays in the Course on Modern Drama." In *Approaches to Teaching Eliot's Poetry and Plays*. Ed. Jewel Spears Brooker. New York: Modern Language Association, 1988, 169-73.

        The plays offer "a valuable record of the competing claims of naturalism and poetic stylization on the modern stage. The radical style shifts in the work of Ibsen, Strindberg, and Shaw, as well as the tension between poetic depth and banal surface language in Chekhov, Beckett, and Pinter, can be anatomized for the student with the help of Eliot's dramatic theory and practice."

C328   Kennedy, Andrew K. *Six Dramatists in Search of a Language*. Cambridge: Cambridge U P, 1975.

        Chapter on Eliot discusses how his dictum on tradition and his "borrowed language" affect his mission of creating "new possibilities of expression in drama."

C329   Kennedy, Richard S. "Working Out Salvation With Diligence: The Plays of T. S. Eliot." *University of Wichita Bulletin* 40.2 (May 1964): 3-11.

        MC represents a "peak of magnificent passion" that Eliot has never again reached.

C330   Kenner, Hugh. *The Invisible Poet*. New York: McDowell, Obolensky, 1959.

        MC articulates the sensibility of *Ash-Wednesday*. A chapter, "Supplementary Dialogue on Dramatic Poetry," examines Eliot's movement toward dramatic verse through his own dicta from essays on drama; another chapter, "Prepared Faces," explains how Eliot's drama serves as a coda to his poetic career.

C331   Kermode, Frank.   "What Became of Sweeney?"   *Spectator* 202 (10 April 1959): 513.
Survey of Eliot's dramatic evolution on the occasion of his final play finds that his increasingly close attention to the audience has "sabotaged" his plays.

C332   Kline, Peter.   "The Spiritual Center in Eliot's Plays."   *Kenyon Review* 21.3 (Summer 1959): 457-72.
Though Eliot's drama is, as he admits, "inexpert," its profound spiritual strength "brings to the stage a depth profounder in its implications than anything previously realized in successful drama."

C333   Kneiger, Bernard.   "The Dramatic Achievement of T. S. Eliot."   *Modern Drama* 3.4 (February 1961): 387-92.
The major plays are all about "the gaining of knowledge by the protagonist about the nature of his moral struggle, but in no case is this knowledge attained dramatically, that is, through struggle and conflict"; the plays, thus, are all static—offering only "automatic" rather than dramatic enlightenment—to their detriment.

C334   Kojecky, Roger.   *T. S. Eliot's Social Criticism.*   London: Faber & Faber, 1971.
Chapter on drama discusses the plays' social dimensions such as attitudes toward the unemployed and Social Credit in *The Rock*, the clash of church and state in *MC*, and the Community of Christians in *CP*.

C335   Lambert, J. C.   "The Verse Drama."   In *Theatre Programme*.   Ed. J. C. Trewin.   London: Frederick Muller, 1954, 51-72.
Examines Eliot's influence at the heart of the revival of verse drama.

C336   Langbaum, Robert.   "The Mysteries of Identity as a Theme in T. S. Eliot's Plays."   *Virginia Quarterly Review* 49 (Autumn 1973): 560-80.
The plays confront and solve the problem of loss of self as Eliot "Christianizes Freud's doctrine of the therapeutic value of conscious self-recognition." By the end of his career, "Eliot makes his life-size characters emerge from the phantoms of their much larger potential selves."

C337   Leavell, Linda. "Nietzsche's Theory of Tragedy in the Plays of T.
        S. Eliot." *Twentieth Century Literature* 31.1 (Spring 1985): 111-26.
             Correlations between Eliot's and Friedrich Nietzsche's dramatic
        theories include "the presupposition that contemporary society lacks
        cultural unity" which is "directly dependent upon a fundamental
        myth"; the idea of theatrical experience as ritual; and extensive use of
        Apollonian and Dionysian themes. Eliot seems to have found *The
        Birth of Tragedy* provocative in light of the attention it drew from
        such scholars as Frazer, Harrison, and Cornford—whom he drew
        upon for his own dramatic theory.

C338   Leeming, Glenda. *Poetic Drama*. New York: St. Martin's, 1989.
             Close analysis of Eliot's plays in a survey of twentieth-century
        poetic drama that also highlights Christopher Fry and W. B. Yeats.

C339   Leggatt, Alison. "A Postscript from Mrs. Chamberlayne and Mrs.
        Guzzard." In *T. S. Eliot: A Symposium for His Seventieth Birthday*.
        Ed. Neville Braybrooke. Freeport, NY: Books for Libraries P, 1958,
        79-80.
             Reminiscences about acting in *CP* and *CC*.

C340   Levi, Peter. "Eliot's Late Plays." *Agenda* 23.1-2 (Spring-Summer
        1985): 131-36.
             The late plays are "liberating . . . a transformation of the every-
        day world into a world of spiritual meanings" with "a peculiarly
        Anglican humility."

C341   Lightfoot, Marjorie J. "Charting Eliot's Course in Drama." *Educa-
        tional Theatre Journal* 22 (1968): 186-97.   Excerpt in *Critical Es-
        says on T. S. Eliot: The Sweeney Motif*. Ed. Kinley E. Roby. Bos-
        ton: G. K. Hall, 1985, 119-23.
             Conventions, rhythms, and prosody of Eliot's verse drama.

C342   Lucy, Seán. *T. S. Eliot and the Idea of Tradition*. New York:
        Barnes and Noble, 1960.
             Study of Eliot's critical theory applies it to his drama, focusing
        on ritual and realism, and giving a comprehesive overview of his
        program for verse drama.

C343   Lumley, Frederick. *New Trends in 20th Century Drama: A Survey
        Since Ibsen and Shaw*. New York: Oxford U P, 1972.
             Brief and conventional overview of Eliot's dramatic career in a
        survey of modern drama.

C344   MacLeish, Archibald. "The Poet as Playwright." *Atlantic Monthly* 195.2 (February 1955): 49-52.
    Challenges Eliot's defensive attitude toward the appropriateness of verse drama and his idea that most plays should be written in prose.

C345   Marcus, Philip. "T. S. Eliot and Shakespeare." *Criticism* 9 (Winter 1967): 63-79.
    As a young man Eliot was repelled by Shakespeare's Senecan philosophy but later began a reappraisal sparked by G. Wilson Knight's *The Wheel of Fire* (1930) and came to appreciate particularly Shakespeare's late romances.

C346   Matlaw, Myron. "Eliot the Dramatist." *College Language Association Journal* 12.2 (December 1968): 116-22.
    Conventional overview and critique.

C347   Matthiessen, F. O. "For an Unwritten Chapter." *Harvard Advocate* 125.3 (December 1938): 22-24.
    Discusses Eliot's increasing sense of the dramatic in the 1930s and his role in the revival of verse drama.

C348   McElroy, Davis D. *Existentialism and Modern Literature.* New York: Philosophical Library, 1963.
    Section discusses *CP* and *CC* as platforms for the existentialist quests of Celia, the Chamberlaynes, and Colby—searches for an authentically meaningful life in the face of barriers to truth.

C349   Melchiori, Giorgio. *The Tightrope Walkers: Studies of Mannerism in Modern English Literature.* New York: Macmillan, 1956.
    Chapter on Eliot's drama finds the plays increasingly open in terms of their statement of his aims; "obviousness is achieved at the expense of intensity."

C350   Miller, Arthur. "Morality and Modern Drama." *Educational Theatre Journal* 10.3 (October 1958): 190-202.
    Discussing his own plays in an interview with Phillip Gelb, Miller briefly mentions Eliot's drama, characterizing it as lacking character: "I don't think T. S. Eliot would even claim that he is creating characters, in the realistic sense of the word. It is a different aim. It doesn't mean that he can't do it; I don't think he can, but I don't think he is trying to do it. I think he is trying to dramatize quite simply a moral, a religious dilemma."

C351 Moody, A. D. "Artful Voices: Eliot's Dramatic Verse." *Agenda* 18.4 (Winter-Spring 1981): 112-19.
Traces the development of Eliot's verse drama technique.

C352 Mudford, P. G. "T. S. Eliot's Plays and the Tradition of 'High Comedy.'" *Critical Quarterly* 16.2 (Summer 1974): 127-42.
Examines the importance of the comic genre in the final four plays and its relevance to a more sombre sensibility which is also present.

C353 Muir, Kenneth. "Poetic Drama in Transition: The Later Plays of T. S. Eliot." In *Patterns of Change: German Drama and the European Tradition*. Ed. Dorothy James and Silvia Ranawake. New York: Peter Lang, 1990, 257-67.
Discusses weaknesses in the later plays: Eliot's possible disappointment because he came to the theatre too late in life; superficial links to classical drama; uneven characterization; and prosaic language.

C354 _____. "T. S. Eliot's Criticism of Elizabethan Drama." In *Mirror up to Shakespeare: Essays in Honour of G. R. Hibbard*. Ed. J. C. Gray. Toronto: U of Toronto P, 1984, 3-14.
Traces Eliot's critical writings about the Elizabethans, detailing numerous fallacies of scholarship and sensibility and finding that some of Eliot's own drama is flawed by the faults for which he criticized his predecessors.

C355 Muller, Herbert J. *The Spirit of Tragedy*. New York: Knopf, 1956.
Genre study includes section discussing the spirit of *MC*, *FR*, and *CP* as a "modern equivalent of the mythical, ritual patterns underlying Greek tragedy."

C356 Murry, John Middleton. "Mr. Eliot's Cocktail Party." *Fortnightly* 168.1008 (December 1950): 391-98.
The difficulties of understanding Harry's consciousness in *FR* do not arise in *CP*, where "the drama seems to arise directly out of the scheme of salvation."

C357 _____. "The Plays of T. S. Eliot." In *Unprofessional Essays*. London: Jonathan Cape, 1956, 149-91.
The plays, like Eliot's poetry, show his "inhuman detachment" from the condition of common human love.

C358   Newton, Stella Mary.   "The First Three Plays by T. S. Eliot: Designs for Settings and Costumes." *Costume* 24 (1990): 97-110.
Designer for *The Rock*, *MC*, and *FR* recounts details about the
design for those plays and *CP*, with six illustrations of costumes.

C359   Nicholson, Norman.   "Modern Verse-Drama and the Folk Tradition." *Critical Quarterly* 2.2 (Summer 1960): 166-70.
Eliot's and W. H. Auden's verse drama fulfill the psychological
and social needs which gave rise to medieval Mystery and Miracle
plays.

C360   Orsini, Gian N. G.   "T. S. Eliot and the Doctrine of Dramatic Conventions." *Transactions of the Wisconsin Academy of Sciences, Arts
and Letters* 43 (1954): 189-200.
Criticizes indiscriminate and arbitrary use of the term "convention" in Eliot's essays on dramatic theory.

C361   Patrides, C. A.   "T. S. Eliot: Alliances of Levity and Seriousness."
Sewanee Review 96.1 (Winter 1988): 77-94.
Eliot's plays and poetry defy simple categorization as comedy or
tragedy, grave or amusing; "the two modes can coexist in one and
the same work as a matter of course." The effect—as, for example,
in the way the living come to terms with Celia's death in *CP*—is that
"the gaiety transfigures the dread."

C362   Peacock, Ronald   "Eliot's Contribution to Criticism of Drama."   In
The Literary Criticism of T. S. Eliot.   Ed. David Newton-De Molina.
London: Athlone P, 1977, 89-110.
A comprehensive examination of Eliot's dramatic criticism shows
how the essays set out the details of his dramatic theory, how they
relate to his own enterprises in the theatre, and how they show the
importance Eliot accorded generally to drama. This criticism is "directed also by his powerful, insistent interest in the nature of all
poetry, and a critical understanding of its variant forms."

C363   _____.   *The Poet in the Theatre*.   London: Routledge & Kegan Paul,
1946.
Survey on poetic influences in the modern theatre includes a
chapter that gives a general overview of Eliot's drama through *FR*
and its connection to his earlier poetry and criticism.

C364 _____. "Public and Private Problems in Modern Drama." *Tulane Drama Review* 3.3 (March 1959): 58-72.

Social criticism in Eliot's drama is compared to that of Jean Giraudoux, Henrik Ibsen, and Georg Kaiser, with attention to his conception of cultural integration and Christian structures of belief.

C365 Pietersma, H. "The Overwhelming Question." *Folio* 21 (Summer 1956): 19-32.

"Eliot, as well as Pascal and Kierkegaard, believes that if people know their own real situations they will come to an acknowledgement of God. . . . Thus in all his plays Mr. Eliot is attempting to show not so much what it is *to be* a Christian as what it is to *become one*."

C366 Pinion, F. B. *A T. S. Eliot Companion*. London: Macmillan, 1986.

Includes exegesis of Eliot's plays and dramatic criticism.

C367 Rahv, Philip. "T. S. Eliot: The Poet as Playwright." In *Literature and the Sixth Sense*. Boston: Houghton Mifflin, 1969, 345-50.

Recounts Eliot's dicta on poetic plays and appraises his dramatic career, faulting him with reference to his own standards.

C368 Reynolds, Ernest. *Modern English Drama: A Survey of the Theatre from 1900*. Norman: U of Oklahoma P, 1949.

Eliot's drama through *FR* is examined in the context of an extensive study of British dramatic styles and trends in the first half of the twentieth century.

C369 Richman, Robert. "The Quiet Conflict: The Plays of T. S. Eliot." *New Republic* 127 (8 December 1952): 17-18.

The private intimacy of Eliot's plays reflects his experimental attempt to "create the metaphysical play, in which the dramatic conflicts among characters, or the momentous spiritual torment within the central character, yield their mystery."

C370 Robbins, Rossell Hope. *The Myth of T. S. Eliot*. New York: Henry Schuman, 1951.

Discusses inadequacies in the plays as part of a harsh critique of Eliot's entire work, calling him "a poet of minor achievement, emotionally sterile and with a mind coarsened by snobbery and constricted by bigotry," and exploring the historical and aesthetic factors that have deluded modern audiences as to his importance.

C371   Roberson, Susan L. "T. S. Eliot's Symbolical Woman: From Tempt-
ress to Priestess." *Midwest Quarterly* 27.4 (Summer 1986): 476-86.
        Analysis of the women in Eliot's poetry and plays shows that "In
effect, it took Eliot his entire literary career to reach a more or less
normal attitude toward woman" as he does in *ES*.

C372   Roy, Emil. *British Drama Since Shaw*. Carbondale, IL: Southern
Illinois U P, 1972.
        Includes a routine discussion of the plays.

C373   Salmon, Eric. *Is the Theatre Still Dying?* Westport, CT: Greenwood
P, 1985.
        Surveys trends in the contemporary theatre with reference to
Eliot's plays in the contexts of drawing-room comedies and verse
drama.

C374   Sampley, Arthur M. "The Woman Who Wasn't There: Lacuna in T.
S. Eliot." *South Atlantic Quarterly* 67 (Autumn 1968): 603-12.
        The women in Eliot's plays generally reflect the same misogynis-
tic characterization as in the poetry, marked by the absence of com-
passion, humanity, fertility; but the more benevolent portrayals of
Julia in *CP* and Agatha in *FR* evince some sympathy, and finally in
ES, Monica presents an emotionally satistfying female character.

C375   Semaan, Khalil I. H. "T. S. Eliot's Influence on Arabic Poetry and
Theater." *Comparative Literature Studies* 6.4 (1969): 472-89.
        The Egyptian poet and dramatist Salāh 'Abd al-Sabūr is structur-
ally and thematically indebted to Eliot; "he deals with basic material
that is radically different from that of Eliot, and yet he uses Eliot's
techniques to interpret and present Arabic and Islamic events and
concepts."

C376   Sewell, Elizabeth. "Lewis Carroll and T. S. Eliot as Nonsense Poets." In *T. S. Eliot: A Symposium for His Seventieth Birthday*. Ed.
Neville Braybrooke. Freeport, NY: Books for Libraries P, 1958,
49-56.
        Examines the element of nonsense in Eliot's poetry and plays,
within the tradition of Stéphane Mallarmé, Edward Lear, and Lewis
Carroll.

C377   Shapiro, Leo. "The Medievalism of T. S. Eliot." *Poetry* 56.4 (July
1940): 202-13.
        Discusses Eliot's medieval sensibility about "the problem of
God's foreknowledge and man's free will" in the poetry and early
plays.

C378   Sherek, Henry. *Not in Front of the Children*. London: Heinemann, 1959.
       The producer of Eliot's final three plays recounts (mostly gossipy) details about various productions, and his acquaintance with the author; gives a sense of the period's atmosphere and manners on the business side of theatre.

C379   Skaff, William. *The Philosophy of T. S. Eliot*. Philadelphia: U of Pennsylvania P, 1986.
       Brief discussion of Eliot's drama considers it as a tool to bring his writing closer to the primitive and ritualistic origins of poetry and art.

C380   Smith, Carol H. "Eliot as Playwright." *Nation* 203.10 (3 October 1966): 325-28.
       General overview of Eliot's dramatic intentions and unity.

C381   _____. "Reluctant Saints and Modern Shamans: Teaching Eliot's Christian Comedies." In *Approaches to Teaching Eliot's Poetry and Plays*. Ed. Jewel Spears Brooker. New York: Modern Language Association, 1988, 162-68.
       Pedagogical advice for teaching Eliot's dramatic oeuvre; teachers "must be persuaded of the importance of drama to Eliot and of its relation to his religious and poetic growth."

C382   _____. *T. S. Eliot's Dramatic Theory and Practice*. Princeton: Princeton U P, 1963.   Excerpt (on *MC*), "The New Rhythm," in *T. S. Eliot's Murder in the Cathedral*. Ed. Harold Bloom. New York: Chelsea House, 1988, 41-53.
       The definitive critical work on the plays explores how Eliot's dramatic theory creates "personal order out of the chaos which he found around him as a young man"; this theory grows out of Francis Cornford's work on ritual roots of drama and what Eliot called the mythical method, and develops with stylistic and formalistic precision into a drama of multilayered levels, each embodying a different realm of meaning—the highest of which is wholeheartedly religious.

C383   Smith, Grover. *T. S. Eliot's Poetry and Plays: A Study in Sources and Meaning*. Chicago: U of Chicago P, 1960.
       The definitive exegetical guide to Eliot's canon, most useful for its exhaustive elucidation of Eliot's ubiquitous obscurities, allusions, references, and sources.

C384   Sochatoff, A. Fred. "The Use of Verse in the Drama of T. S. Eliot." *Carnegie Series in English* 2 (1955): 59-75.

Applies Eliot's dramatic theories to his own plays and examines details of his technique for poetic drama.

C385   Spanos, William V. *The Christian Tradition in Modern British Verse Drama: The Poetics of Sacramental Time.* New Brunswick, NJ: Rutgers U P, 1967.

Eliot, like writers such as Christopher Fry, Charles Williams, and the Mercury Poets, is at the center of a new strand of Christian humanism which is not (as some critics would assert) hostile to art or the celebration of human life. Contrary to the alleged "medievalism" of this verse, it speaks to the modern condition. Elaborate theological analysis is applied to all Eliot's plays.

C386   Speaight, Robert. "Interpreting Becket and Other Parts." In *T. S. Eliot: A Symposium for His Seventieth Birthday.* Ed. Neville Braybrooke. Freeport, NY: Books for Libraries P, 1958, 70-78.

Recounts experiences acting in Eliot's plays.

C387   _____. "The Plays of T. S. Eliot." *Month* 30 (October 1963): 209-13.

Eliot's plays generate "a mental rather than a theatrical excitement. . . . You have only to compare *The Cocktail Party* with Pirandello . . . to see the difference between a dramatist who is a native of the theatre and one who, there too, is a naturalised citizen. It remains true, however, that no plays written for the English theatre in our time are so worth discussion as these."

C388   Stelzmann, Rainulf A. "The Theology of T. S. Eliot's Dramas." *Xavier University Studies* 1.1 (February 1961): 7-17.

Eliot's "theology is incomplete in so far as it does not show an attempt to solve the difficult problem of grace and free will. It is slightly 'antisocial' in so far as it overemphasizes the preponderance of a spiritual elite.. But still, we should take this modern writer seriously. Much of our situation is focused in his dramas."

C389   Torrens, James. "T. S. Eliot and Shakespeare: 'This Music Crept By.'" *Bucknell Review* 19.1 (Spring 1971): 77-96.

Surveys Eliot's writings and thoughts about Shakespeare throughout his career.

C390   Tydeman, William. *Murder in the Cathedral and The Cocktail Party: Text and Performance*. London: Macmillan, 1988.
       Close and intensive exegesis of textual and performance aspects of the two best-known plays.

C391   Ward, David. *T. S. Eliot Between Two Worlds*. London: Routledge & Kegan Paul, 1973. Excerpt (on *MC*) in *T. S. Eliot's Murder in the Cathedral*. Ed. Harold Bloom. New York: Chelsea House, 1988, 69-85.
       Meticulous analysis of the plays in a chapter of a book covering Eliot's career.

C392   Warren, Charles. *T. S. Eliot on Shakespeare*. Ann Arbor: UMI Research P, 1987.
       Examination of Eliot's writings about and attitudes toward Shakespeare—especially "the problem of meaning"—up to 1937 illustrates how he learned from and reacted against his most important dramatic precursor.

C393   Wasson, Richard. "The Rhetoric of Theatre: The Contemporaneity of T. S. Eliot." *Drama Survey* 6.3 (Spring 1968): 231-43.
       Examines Eliot's consciousness of rhetoric and dramaturgy.

C394   Weales, Gerald. *Religion in Modern English Drama*. Philadelphia: U of Pennsylvania P, 1961.
       Treats Eliot as part of a tradition dating back to Henry Arthur Jones's 1884 *Saints and Sinners*, which presented religious drama on the commercial stage, and William Poel's 1901 production of *Everyman*, which began the semiprofessional church drama movement that nurtured Eliot's first plays. An extensive bibliography documents nearly a century of religious plays.

C395   Webster, Clifford J. "The Chorus: T. S. Eliot" *McMaster University Quarterly* 48.1 (November 1948): 40-49.
       "The chorus, in the hands of T. S. Eliot, has become a vital element of modern drama. Perhaps its meaning is best defined in its function, which is generally considered three-fold: interpretation, anticipation and excitation." In Eliot's hands, the chorus "is recreated, it is refashioned and it is consecrated to a new task."

C396   Weisstein, Ulrich. "Form as Content in the Drama of T. S. Eliot." *Western Review* 23.3 (Spring 1959): 239-46.
       "Rhythm, meter and rhyme serve to heighten the emotional and, hence, tragic impact of the action; they are co-ordinated with, not subordinated to, sheer content."

C397   West, Paul. *The Wine of Absurdity: Essays on Literature and Conso-lation.* University Park: Pennsylvania State U P, 1966.

Chapter about Eliot's late poetry and plays examines how "in-creasing security of faith (plus some worldly success) enabled Eliot to discard severity for benignity and . . . brought to the fore Eliot the romantic who was always there in disguise."

C398   Wilder, Amos. *The Spiritual Aspects of the New Poetry.* New York: Harper, 1940.

Chapter examining religious influences in Eliot's poetry and plays through *FR* argues that "The total impression . . . suggests that while his chosen theological affiliation may be Catholic, his deeper personal debts and insights are not so easily assigned. The evident eclectic quality of his literary culture points to a deeper eclecticism in his thinking. . . . Eliot has the same large freedom in his church that Mauriac, Claudel and Maritain have in theirs, indeed more."

C399   Williams, Raymond. *Drama from Ibsen to Brecht.* New York: Ox-ford U P, 1969. (Revised edition of *Drama from Ibsen to Eliot*, 1952.)

Chapter examines Eliot's plays in the context of a meticulous survey of modern European drama.

C400   _____. "Tragic Resignation and Sacrifice." *Critical Quarterly* 5.1 (Spring 1963): 5-19.

In *MC* and *CP* Eliot presents a pattern of sacrifice which, unlike the Christian paradigm, "does not redeem the world, or bring new life to the waste land. Rather, in an obscure way, it ratifies the world as it is," presenting resignation rather than redemption.

C401   Williamson, Audrey. *Theatre of Two Decades.* London: Rockliff, 1951.

Survey of the London stage in the 1930s and 1940s includes an overview of Eliot's plays and discussion of the resurgence of poetic drama.

C402   Wilson, Frank. *Six Essays in the Development of T. S. Eliot.* Lon-don: Fortune P, 1948.

Chapter on Eliot's drama presents observations about the early plays.

C403   Worth, Katherine J. "Eliot and the Living Theatre." In *Eliot in Perspective: A Symposium.* Ed. Graham Martin. New York: Hu-manities P, 1970, 148-66. Excerpt (on *MC*) in *T. S. Eliot's Murder in the Cathedral.* Ed. Harold Bloom. New York: Chelsea House,

1988, 55-61. Excerpt (on *SA*) in *Critical Essays on T. S. Eliot: The Sweeney Motif.* Ed. Kinley E. Roby. Boston: G. K. Hall, 1985, 123-30.

Eliot's plays are not arcane, or exclusively religious or poetic, but rather experimental, powerful, vividly immediate.

C404   _____. *Revolutions in Modern English Drama.* London: G. Bell, 1973.

Chapter on Eliot explores beyond conventional interpretations of the plays and finds provocative and "revolutionary" dramatic practices that link him to Harold Pinter, Edward Albee, John Arden, and Luigi Pirandello.

C405   Wyatt, Euphemia van Rensselaer. "What Religious Drama Owes to E. Martin Browne." *Drama Critique* 4.1 (February 1961): 31-37.

Surveys the career of the director most prominently known for presenting six of Eliot's plays.

C406   Wyman, Linda. "'Common Liberation': The Idea of Salvation in the Plays of T. S. Eliot." *Christianity and Literature* 29.4 (Summer 1980): 46-52.

The plays "have as their subject the necessary and saving interrelatedness of human beings."

C407   Zabel, Morton D. "Poetry for the Theatre." *Poetry* 45.3 (December 1934): 152-58.

Eliot's first two experiments in poetic drama (along with other works by such writers as Sean O'Casey and W. B. Yeats) herald a reawakening of interest in the genre, but also evoke a warning: poetic dramatists must be careful not to produce trivial or ridiculous fare, and not to apply poetry to barren or non-poetic material; their drama "must be grounded in the deepest nature and intelligence of the poet."

Appendices

Additional Adaptations

Cats

Musical adaptations of the poems from *Old Possum's Book of Practical Cats* (1939) include Dorothy Howell's *The Song of the Jellicles, Two-Part Song* (London: Edward Arnold, 1953); Alan Rawsthorne's 1954 *Practical Cats* (recorded by Angel Records with Robert Donat as the speaker and The Philharmonia Orchestra conducted by Rawsthorne; Angel Record 30002); Humphrey Searle's *Two Practical Cats for Speaker, Flute (doubling Piccolo), Guitar and 'Cello: Macavity: The Mystery Cat and Growltiger's Last Stand* (London: Oxford U P, 1956); and Donald Keats's *The Naming of Cats* (New York: Boosey & Hawkes, 1962).

The most famous production, *Cats*, opened at the West End's New London Theatre on 11 May 1981 and on Broadway at the Winter Garden on 7 October 1982; both runs, which garnered enormous popular acclaim, were still underway in 1992 and spawned numerous international road companies. Valerie Eliot gave composer Andrew Lloyd Webber some unpublished material including eight lines about Grizabella that Eliot had considered too sad; the musical's book also uses Eliot's early poem "Rhapsody on a Windy Night" for a song not in the *Old Possum* collection, "Memory."

In the London production, directed by Trevor Nunn and choreographed by Gillian Lynne, Elaine Page played Grizabella, Brian Blessed played Old Deuteronomy, and Wayne Sleep played the principal dancing role of Mistoffolees.

The Broadway musical won seven Tony awards in 1983: Eliot was posthumously awarded the Tony for musical book, and shared with Lloyd Webber the award for score; in addition Betty Buckley, who played Grizabella, won the Tony for best actress; producers Cameron Mackintosh, The Really Useful Company Ltd., David Geffen, and the Shubert Organization won for best musical; Trevor Nunn won for best director; John Napier of the Royal Shakespeare Company won the award for costume design (and also did scenic design); and David Hersey won for lighting design.

Choreography for the Broadway show was again by Gillian Lynne. Featured actors included Stephen Hanan as Bustopher Jones, Asparagus, and Growltiger; Rene Clements as Coricopat and Mungojerrie; Christine Langer as Etcetera and Rumpleteazer; Bonnie Simmons as Jellylorum and Griddlebone; Anne McNeeley as Jennyanydots; Timothy Scott as Mistoffolees; Ken Page as Old Deuteronomy; Kenneth Ard as Plato, Macavity, and Rumpus Cat; Terrence V. Mann as Rum Tum Tugger; and Reed Jones as Skimbleshanks. Like several of Eliot's earlier plays, this one features a prominent Chorus.

The set was a landmark in contemporary theatre: Frank Rich describes "a huge nocturnal junkyard for Eliot's flighty jellicle cats," in which Napier made the entire theatre seem like an extension of the stage: he "obliterated the proscenium arch, lowered the ceiling and stage floor and filled every cranny of the place with a Red Grooms-esque collage of outsized rubbish (from old Red Seal records to squeezed out toothpaste tubes) as seen from a cat's eye perspective. Well before the lights go down, one feels as if one has entered a mysterious spaceship on a journey through the stars to a cloud-streaked moon" (R207). The transformation of the theatre's interior cost $2.5 million.

"What Eliot himself would have thought of the idea," writes Clive Barnes in his New York *Post* review, "which has Eliot's widow's enthusiastic sanction, is anyone's guess. When Alan Rawsthorne once wrote a background score to the same poems, Eliot commented: 'I like the idea that they are read *against* the musical background and not themselves set to music'" (R205). In *Women's Wear Daily* Howard Kissel writes: "It is impossible to view without irony the fact that one of the most austere poets of the 20th century, admittedly in one of his lighter moments, should have provided the pretext for such a gigantic extravaganza" (R206). But *Newsweek* concludes that "the original genius behind *Cats* remains, of course, T. S. Eliot. . . . Old Possum would have enjoyed the spectacle of his Grizabella escaping hell, rising to heaven amid a stageful of happy cats and a theater-ful of happy people" (R209).

Russell Kirk asserts that Eliot never could have expected "that his cat poems, dramatized, somehow would reach audiences larger far than the combined total of persons who ever attended performances of *Murder in the Cathedral*, *The Family Reunion*, *The Cocktail Party*, *The Confidential Clerk*, and *The Elder Statesman*—indeed, that more people would pay for costly tickets to Cats than ever bought his books during his lifetime. He had hoped to renew the public's taste for the poetic drama—but scarcely through poetry resembling Edward Lear's verses about pussycats, owls, and runcible spoons" (C253, 198).

An important fact about the poems, Kirk writes, is that they "were written as civilization was about to explode; when the state of public affairs induced in Eliot a 'depression of spirits so different from any other experience of fifty years'; when he found it necessary to extinguish his noble quarterly *The Criterion*. . . . Britain declared war against Germany on September 3, 1939; *Old Possum's Book of Practical Cats* was published precisely a month later" (198). Given this, Kirk suggests that there is an appropriate sensibility in Lloyd Webber's arrangement of the spectacle of *Cats*, and especially in its alliance of poetry and dance. *Cats* allows a metaphorical examination of personal and social conditions—which is parallel to those of the cats—yet one which is distanced and disguised, as Eliot might have felt such an expression must have been in late 1939. "Andrew Lloyd Webber's remarkable imagination has seized upon this parallel and, through the power of the dance, has enabled us to perceive ourselves as so many cats: felines laughable and tragic, lustful, heroic, pitiable, furious, evanescent, meant for eternity" (199).

Dance, so prominent in *Cats*, "is implicit in Eliot's poetry," Kirk writes, "and rises to the surface with the ghostly peasant dance in 'East Coker'" (199). Eliot's critical writing frequently attests to the centrality of dance in artistic expression, and his poetry, too, often invokes images of dance. "Of these dances, the grand ball is at the still point of the turning world, where time and the timeless intersect; 'Except for the point, the still point, there would be no dance, and there is only the dance.' . . . the dance of the turning world lies at the heart of Eliot's beliefs" (201).

Other Musical Settings

Martin Shaw's score of *The Builders: Song from 'The Rock,'* an arrangement for chorus, was published in 1934 (London: J. B. Cramer); a setting for Shaw's music for part of Chorus X from *The Rock*, called *The Greater Light Anthem*, was published in 1966 (London: J. Curwen; New York: G. Schirmer); that setting is for tenor solo, double choir, and organ.

Vincent Persichetti wrote a composition for *The Hollow Men* for a trumpet and string orchestra (Philadelphia: Elkan-Vogel, 1948), as did Kees van Baaren, for soprano, baritone solo, choir, and small orchestra (Amsterdam: Donemus, 1948).

Denis ApIvor set *The Hollow Men* to music in 1950 (published by Oxford U P, 1951). "The poem employs, deliberately or unconsciously, musical devices," he writes, citing as examples the recurrent theme of eyes, and the "subtle variation—augmentation, diminution, inversion, echoes, mirror-images, and reappearances for dramatic effect" in the language used to describe death's kingdom. "It becomes clear very quickly, therefore, that this kind of verse imposes its own musical form very precisely," ApIvor writes, calling the verse "already half-way to music." ApIvor used a baritone solo for what he calls the poet's personal voice in the poem, and a male-voice chorus for the impersonal voice. Eleven years later, ApIvor set Eliot's poems from *Landscapes* to music for one singer and a small group of instruments. "To me no poet writing in English this century can offer the equal of his musicality, his sonorous lyricism and his dramatic impact," ApIvor writes of Eliot's appeal (C257, 89-91).

The *Landscapes* group of poems has also been set to music by Alan Thomas (Bryn Mawr: Theodore Presser, 1957) and Gregg Smith (New York: G. Schirmer, 1962, Octavo No. 10818).

Igor Stravinsky's *Anthem: The Dove Descending Breaks the Air*, is based upon "Little Gidding" (London: Boosey & Hawkes, 1962).

Benjamin Britten's *Canticle IV: Journey of the Magi*, op. 86, is for countertenor, tenor, baritone, and piano (London: Faber Music, 1972; New York: G. Schirmer, 1972). His *Canticle V: The Death of Saint Narcissus*, op. 89, is for tenor and harp (London: Faber Music, 1976; New York: G. Schirmer, 1976).

Don Freund wrote an instrumental ensemble of suites called *The Waste Land: Four Movements after T. S. Eliot for Winds and Percussion* (New York: Seesaw Music, 1977), an interpretation of *The Waste Land* Parts I to IV.

Ballet/Opera

In May 1951 the Sadler's Wells Theatre Ballet presented John Cranko's *Harlequin in April*, based on the first two lines of *The Waste Land*. David Blair danced as Harlequin.

Sweeney Agonistes was performed as a chamber opera under the direction of Richard Winslow at Columbia University in 1953.

Murder in the Cathedral was staged as an opera (*Assassinio nella Catedrale*) by Ildebrando Pizzetti, produced by Margherita Wallman (with some consultation from Eliot), conducted by Gianandrea Gavazzeni, and designed by Piero Zuffi, at La Scala in Milan in 1958. The piano-vocal score was published by G. Ricordi, Milan, 1958. The bass-baritone Nicola Rossi-Lemeni sang as Becket. Arthur Jacobs, reviewing the production in *The Listener*, writes that Pizzetti mistakenly lost some of Eliot's dramatic power (by omitting, for example, a musical analogue to the anti-climactic effect of the Knights' speeches after the murder of Becket). Italian poet Eugenio Montale, reviewing the opera (as recounted in *The Listener* review), writes that Pizzetti perhaps miscalculated the applicability of an operatic treatment to a play that is not primarily one of emotion, narrative, or characterization, but rather of argumentation (R48).

The opera opened at London's Sadler's Wells, with Don Garrard as Becket, on 3 July 1962. Colin Davis conducted the Sadler's Wells Opera Company.

Film

Murder in the Cathedral was filmed by George Hoellering and released in 1952 (after its debut at the Venice International Film Festival in June 1951, where it won prizes for Best Film in Costume and Best Art Direction). Eliot had begun working with Hoellering on the project as early as 1942. Eliot made a film recording of his reading of the entire play to give the actors guidance about the rhythms and emphases of the verse; this gave Hoellering the idea of using Eliot's own voice for the role of the Fourth Tempter. Eliot wrote the screenplay, which involved considerable changes from the stage version.

"I did not approach Mr. Eliot's text as that of a stage play," Hoellering writes. "I saw in it a great dramatic poem which had a definite literary form but was 'open' as far as its adaptation to any other medium was concerned. As a film director, I am grateful that in writing *Murder in the Cathedral* Mr. Eliot was obliged to keep in mind conditions of production different from those of the normal stage" (P56, xi).

King Henry II is introduced as a character—as Eliot explains, there is not room in the play for another character as dominating as Becket, but in the film his presence is essential. The Knights' closing speeches, addressed to the audience in the stage play, were shortened and addressed to a crowd, except for a final speech to the cinema audience. At Hoellering's suggestion, Eliot added several scenes that explain the action before the beginning of the play's text—Becket's appearance before Henry's court, his judgment by the bishops, his departure for France. Among other changes, the Chorus of women is transformed from a self-consciously dramatic presence into a group of real Canterbury women, going about their daily business and integrated with the screenplay's action. Hoellering added such cinematographic devices as a close-up of a chess game between Becket and the First Tempter during that temptation, in which the Archbishop checkmates the Tempter to signal his rejection of the temptation.

The film's music, by Laszlo Lajtha, was recorded by the London Philharmonic Orchestra and the Renaissance Singers. The film featured Father John Groser—an Anglican priest in his first acting role—as Becket, Alexander Gauge as King Henry II, David Ward, George Woodbridge, and Basil Burton as the three visible Tempters, and Mark Dignam, Michael Aldridge, Leo McKern, and Paul Rogers (who would create the role of Lord Claverton in *The Elder Statesman*) as the Knights.

The film "is an illustrated poem which has converted the 60th St. Trans-Lux into a shrine where the poet's admirers may come to exchange homage for renewed experience," writes reviewer Otis L. Guernsey Jr. in the New York *Herald Tribune*. Groser "maintains the immobile but calm and dignified expression of a saint in a niche, letting the language express all the color of his personality," Guernsey adds. Describing the film's atmosphere, he writes that it is all "filmed in twilight on the edge of deep shadow," achieving effects by having "characters step out of obscurity into half-lit attention." He finds the production more of a poem than a film, subordinating "the values of the screen to the values of verbal imagery wherever they conflict" (R45).

New York Times reviewer Bosley Crowther, though, finds the film "not felicitous material for the screen. . . . [it] completely eludes projection in cohesive and exciting visual terms." While there are "flashes of stark pictorial beauty," Crowther finds the film generally cold, static, and tedious (R40).

Television

Murder in the Cathedral, The Family Reunion, The Cocktail Party, The

Confidential Clerk, and *The Elder Statesman* have been broadcast on B. B. C. television.   Producer and Head of Television Drama Michael Barry writes about broadcasting *The Cocktail Party* in January 1952 for an estimated audience of three and a half million, and repeating the show in April 1957 to eight million viewers. The text of that play was shortened to a 90-minute performance "to bring the spectator closely into the play. He would be present in the same room, sitting at the same desk as the players. He would look across a shoulder and perceive immediately the tremor of an eyelid on occasions when a speech might be required to carry the same meaning to the back of a theatre dress-circle" (C261, 86). Vanessa Redgrave starred in the televised production of *The Elder Statesman*.

Dramatic Adaptation

In 1966, Edinburgh's Traverse Theatre presented *The Waste Land*. Another production of that poem as a play was given in 1976 by New York's Shared Forms Theatre—an expressionist interpretation starring Duncan Kegerreis, Rob McBrien, and Wendy Wasdahl. A videotape of the 1976 play is preserved in the archives of the New York Public Library's Performing Arts Research Center at Lincoln Center, as part of the Theatre on Film and Tape collection.

The Fire and the Rose, a program of Eliot's poetry with text by Ralynn Stadler and music composed by Teijo Ito, was given on 24 May 1966 by the Equity Library Theater Company and performed at New York's Master Theater.

A play about Vivienne and T. S. Eliot, Michael Hastings's *Tom and Viv*, opened at London's Royal Court Theatre on 3 February 1984, starring Julie Covington as Viv and Tom Wilkinson as Tom; it opened off-Broadway at the Public Theater on 6 February 1985, with Edward Herrmann taking over the role of Tom. Though the play has absolutely no textual connection with any of Eliot's writing, many Eliot scholars found the drama, a biographical recreation, full of some speculatively provocative depictions of the Eliots' lives and marriage. Especially with regard to the life and fledgling artistic career of Vivienne Eliot, about whom little substantial critical information has been published, the play stimulated interest. The play reestablished T. S. Eliot's presence in the West End, though certainly in a very different way than in the 1940s and 1950s. In an introduction to the play's published text (London: Penguin, 1985), Hastings discusses his biographical/dramatic research and methodology.

Recordings

A recording was made of the 1950 New York production of *The Cocktail Party*, slightly abridged (Decca Record DX-100). "On the technical side, the recording is excellent" writes Irwin Edman. "Not only do the sounds of the voices come rich and accurate; every clipped cadence of educated British speech is finely and firmly caught. As well as may be, the editors have made the play intelligible without the visual frame of action to give identification to the speakers of the words." The actors, Edman continues, "speak their lines with a sense of the music that is in them and even when T. S. Eliot is dubious as a thinker (as in my judgment he frequently is), even when the play falters (as I think it sometimes does), Eliot's own special incantatory quality of writing is present. And that incantation is heard on the records even more patently, for one is more concentrated on listening than one is when hearing actors on a watched stage. These records show how wonderful an instrument recording may be to remind listeners what they forget on the printed page, that a beautiful half of poetry is the art of the spoken word, that a beautiful half of acting is in articulation, in cadence, in rhythm" (R122).

The 1953 Old Vic production of *Murder in the Cathedral* was also recorded (Angel Record 3505). In 1965 Howard Sackler directed a recording of *The Family Reunion* (Caedmon TRS 308M) featuring Flora Robson, Paul Scofield and Sybil Thorndike, and in 1968 Sackler directed a recording of *Murder in the Cathedral* (Caedmon TRS 330) again starring Scofield.

The Memorial Record of Homage to T. S. Eliot at the Globe Theatre, London, on 13 June 1965, is on HMV [His Master's Voice—the British imprint of RCA/Victor] Record CLP 1924; that recording includes a production of *Sweeney Agonistes*.

Eliot's own readings of his texts can be found on the following records:

T. S. Eliot Reading His Own Poem. As recorded for The Poetry Room, Harvard College Library 1947. Cambridge: The Harvard Film Service, 1948. 78 r.p.m., 12-inch record. Recording of *Sweeney Agonistes*, "Fragment of an Agon"; made available in 1951 on a long-playing record.

T. S. Eliot Reading Poems and Choruses. New York: Caedmon, 1955. Long-playing record (Caedmon TC 1045) includes "O Light Invisible" from *The Rock*, the opening chorus from *Murder in the Cathedral*, and a selection from *The Family Reunion*.

T. S. Eliot Reads Old Possum's Book of Practical Cats. An Argo Production. Recorded under the Auspices of the British Council. New York: Spoken Arts, 1959. Long-playing record (Spoken Arts 758) includes all 15 poems from *Old Possum's Book of Practical Cats*.

Photographs

Photographs of productions of Eliot's plays can be found in the following sources, for which full citations (unless listed) are given in the bibliography:

Sweeney Agonistes

• 1933 Vassar production: Bentley, *Hallie Flanagan*, following 170.
• 1934 Group Theatre production: Gordon, *Eliot's New Life*, following 52. Sidnell, *Dances of Death*, following 160. MacCarthy, "Sweeney Agonistes," 80.

The Rock
• 1934 Sadler's Wells production: Browne, *Two in One*, 81, 85.

Murder in the Cathedral
• 1935 Canterbury production: Gordon, *Eliot's New Life*, following 52. Speaight, *The Property Basket*, following 176. Reynolds, *Modern English Drama*, following 196. Ackroyd, *T. S. Eliot*, following 256. Browne, *Two in One*, 94; costume designs, 97, 99. Leeming, *Poetic Drama*, following 102. Site of production (Canterbury Cathedral Chapter House): Tydeman, *Text and Performance*, following 66. Pickering, *Drama in the Cathedral*, 109.
• 1935 London production: J. C. Trewin, *The Turbulent Thirties: A Further Decade in the Theatre* (London: Macdonald, 1960), following 80. Tydeman, *Text and Performance*, following 66.
• 1952 film: Eliot and Hoellering, *The Film of Murder in the Cathedral.*
• 1953 London production: Tydeman, *Text and Performance*, following 66.
• 1958 Milan opera: Jacobs, "'Murder in the Cathedral' as an Opera."
• 1970 Canterbury production: Browne, *Two in One*, 237.
• 1972 London production: Leeming, *Poetic Drama*, following 102. Esslin, *Plays and Players*, 44-45.

The Family Reunion
• 1939 London production: Gordon, *Eliot's New Life*, following 84. Ackroyd, *T. S. Eliot*, following 256.
• 1947 London production: Browne, *Two in One*, 164.
• 1956 London production: Elizabeth Sprigge, *Sybil Thorndike Casson* (London: Victor Gollancz, 1971), following 320. Eric Johns, ed., *Theatre Review '73* (London: W. H. Allen, 1973), 41. *Theatre World* 52.379 (August 1956): 19-22.
• 1958 New York production: Louis Broussard, *American Drama*, facing 73.
• 1979 London production: *Plays and Players* 26.8 (May 1979): 32-33.

The Cocktail Party
• 1949 Edinburgh production: *World Review* n.s. 9 (November 1949): 18.
• 1950 London production: *Theatre World* 46.305 (June 1950): 11-18. Ackroyd, *T. S. Eliot*, following 256. Tydeman, *Text and Performance*, following 66.
• 1950 New York production: *Time* 16 March 1950: 25. *Theatre Arts* 34.4 (April 1950): 10, 24-25. John Chapman, ed., *The Burns Mantle Best Plays of 1949-50* (New York: Dodd, Mead, 1950), following 86. *Saturday Review* 48 (23 January 1965): 54.
• 1968 Chichester production: Tydeman, *Text and Performance*, following 66.

The Confidential Clerk

• 1953 London production: *Theatre World* 49.345 (October 1953): 9-14. Ackroyd, *T. S. Eliot*, following 256. Browne, *Two in One*, 205.
• 1954 New York production: *Life* 11 February 1954: 57, 61, 62, 64. *Saturday Review* 48 (23 January 1965): 54.

The Elder Statesman

• 1958 Edinburgh production: *Listener* 60.1536 (4 September 1958): 340.
• 1958 London production: *Theatre World* 54.406 (November 1958): 31-35. *Plays and Players* 6.2 (November 1958): 11.   Gordon, *Eliot's New Life*, following 180. Ackroyd, *T. S. Eliot*, following 256. *Life* 24 November 1958: 108.   Peter Roberts, ed., *The Best of Plays and Players: 1953-1968* (London: Methuen, 1988), 87.

Chronological Bibliography

The sources annotated in the bibliography of secondary sources are listed below by year of publication, for readers who wish to trace the chronological trends and development of scholarship.

1933   R2, R4, R8, R14, R18.
1934   R15, R16, R17, R19, R20, R30, C33, C34, C36, C407.
1935   R3, R7, R13, R37, R47, R49, R50, R51, R52, R54, R57, R61, R62, R63, R68, C69, C92.
1936   R10, R31, R32, R34, R36, R38, R39, R42, R43, R44, R58, R59, R60, R64, R66, R69, C83, C288, C291.
1937   C35, C51, C64.
1938   R33, R46, R55, R65, R67, R70, R99, C110, C292, C347.
1939   R71, R74, R75, R76, R78, R80, R82, R84, R85, R88, R89, R92, R93, R94, R95, R97, R101, R102, R103, C147.
1940   C122, C377, C398.
1941   C127, C142.
1942   C155, C271.
1945   C86, C123, C135..
1946   R86, C363.
1947   R100, C59, C78, C152.
1948   C104, C267, C395, C402.
1949   R110 R114, R120, R127, R138, R139, R141, R155, R157, R158, R162, R163, C14, C60, C145, C154, C156, C190, C298, C310, C368.
1950   R104, R107, R108, R111, R112, R116, R117, R118, R121, R122, R124, R125, R128, R129, R130, R131, R132, R133, R134, R135, R136, R140, R142, R143, R144, R145, R148, R149, R150, R151, R152, R153, R154, R159, R160, R161, C38, C160, C161, C162, C173a, C176, C177, C178, C183, C191, C198, C199, C203, C204,

C205, C220, C225, C226, C229, C232, C268, C272, C300, C356.
1951   R156, C143, C175, C186, C197, C200, C207, C210, C213, C215, C234, C294, C324, C370, C401.
1952   R40, R45, C19, C128, C149, C188, C202, C228, C296, C369.
1953   R11, R35, R53, R56, R168, R172, R173, R179, R181, R184, R185, R186, C88, C166, C182, C212, C214, C221, C236, C238.
1954   R164, R165, R166, R167, R169, R170, R171, R174, R175, R176, R177, R178, R180, R182, R183, R187, C169, C184, C192, C237, C240, C304, C313, C335, C360.
1955   C25, C77, C85, C258, C305, C306, C315, C344, C384.
1956   C20, C47, C314, C317, C349, C355, C357, C365.
1957   C174, C181, C218, C235, C239, C264.
1958   R48, R72, R73, R77, R79, R83, R87, R91, R98, R189, R190, R191, R193, R194, R195, R197, R198, R199, R201, R202, R203, R204, C84, C172, C193, C250, C257, C261, C276, C339, C350, C376, C386.
1959   R81, R188, R192, R200, C73, C187, C219, C243, C244, C246, C251, C260, C290, C330, C331, C332, C364, C378, C396.
1960   C8, C63, C118, C126, C134, C158, C180, C185, C196, C222, C249, C321, C325, C342, C359, C383.
1961   C49, C230, C245, C333, C388, C394, C405.
1962   C79, C132, C144, C164, C194, C231, C241, C262, C263, C269, C274, C278, C287, C289, C303, C323.
1963   R196, C39, C93, C95, C107, C150, C233, C273, C282, C284, C348, C382, C387, C400.
1964   C17, C138, C209, C224, C256, C259, C322, C326, C329.
1965   R9, C56, C61, C98, C121, C153, C189, C211, C248, C270, C279, C285, C312.
1966   C5, C67, C109, C136, C165, C280, C301, C380, C397.
1967   C1, C24, C62, C76, C151, C159, C345, C385.
1968   R106, R115, R119, R146, C16, C40, C70, C89, C102, C105, C137, C139, C140, C201, C223, C275, C293, C341, C346, C374, C393.
1969   C7, C75, C106, C131, C195, C206, C277, C367, C375, C399.
1970   C32, C37, C108, C113, C320, C403.
1971   C31, C50, C53, C72, C74, C146, C299, C319, C334, C389.
1972   R41, C2, C10, C101, C114, C117, C217, C266, C286, C343, C372.
1973   C9, C87, C307, C336, C404.
1974   R6, C54, C57, C80, C94, C168, C170, C352.
1975   C28, C148, C328.
1976   C4.
1977   C44, C112, C115, C116, C133, C173, C295, C308, C317, C362.
1978   C6, C41, C48, C171, C302.
1979   R90, C129, C252.
1980   R96, R137, R147, C12, C45, C82, C91, C124, C406.
1981   R208, C43, C52, C179, C208, C242, C281, C351.

1982   R205, R206, R207, R209, C100, C247.
1983   C283.
1984   C18, C29, C71, C255, C354.
1985   R126, C13, C22, C26, C27, C30, C58, C65, C68, C90, C111, C141, C157, C227, C318, C337, C340, C373.
1986   R109, R123, C96, C97, C366, C371, C379.
1987   C81, C99, C297, C392.
1988   R1, R5, R113, C3, C15, C21, C46, C66, C120, C163, C167, C216, C253, C265, C309, C327, C361, C381, C390, C391.
1989   C55, C130, C254, C338.
1990   C23, C42, C119, C311, C353, C358.

Productions and Credits

The following is a list of major productions of Eliot's plays. Production and cast lists are provided to the extent available.

P1 *Sweeney Agonistes*

P1.1 Vassar Experimental Theatre (Poughkeepsie, NY). 6 May 1933. Directed by Hallie Flanagan.

P1.2 Group Theatre Rooms (London). 11 November 1934. (Opened at Westminster Theatre on 1 October 1935.) Directed by Rupert Doone; music by William Alwyn; masks and decor by Robert Medley.

   Dusty—Ruth Wynn Owen
   Doris—Isobel Scaife
   Sam Wauchope—Mervyn Blake
   Klipstein—Desmond Walter-Ellis
   Krumpacker—John Ormerod Greenwood
   Horsfall—Patrick Ross
   Snow—Rupert Doone
   Sweeney—John Moody

P1.3 Cherry Lane Theater (NY). 2 March 1952. Directed by Judith Malina; costumes by Julian Beck.

   Dusty—Christina French
   Doris—Shirley Gleaner
   Sam Wauchope—Mihran Chobania
   Klipstein—J. E. Duane
   Krumpacker—Angelo Laiacona
   Swarts—Henri Sulaiman
   Snow—Cecil Cunningham

Sweeney—Walter Mullen

P1.4   Globe Theatre (London). 13 June 1965. Produced by Peter Wood; directed by Vera Lindsay; score written and conducted by John Dankworth; settings by Bridget Riley.
Dusty—Cleo Laine
Doris—Anna Quayle
Sweeney—Nicol Williamson

P1.5   Old Red Lion Theatre (London). 4 August 1988. Birkenhead Exchange company, directed by Richard Williams; music by Stephen McNeff; decor by Simon Ash; costumes by Hilary Peyton.
Dusty—Maggie Saunders
Doris—Liz Brailsford
Sam Wauchope—Iain Armstrong
Klipstein—Michael Rigg
Krumpacker—Christopher Snell
Horsfall—Mark Lindridge
Sweeney—Jack Ellis

P2 *The Rock: A Pageant Play*

P2.1   Sadler's Wells Theatre (London). 28 May 1934. Directed by E. Martin Browne; costumes by Stella Mary Pearce; sets by Eric Newton; chorus trained and directed by Elsie Fogerty and Gwynneth Thurburn. Cast of over 300 amateur actors from church parishes.

P3 *Murder in the Cathedral*

P3.1   Chapter House (Canterbury). 15 June 1935. Directed by E. Martin Browne; costumes by Stella Mary Pearce; settings by Laurence Irving; chorus trained by Elsie Fogerty and Gwynnyth Thurburn. Cast of largely amateur actors.
Becket—Robert Speaight
Second Tempter/Knight—Frank Napier
Fourth Tempter/Knight—E. Martin Browne

P3.2   Mercury Theatre (London). 1 November 1935. (Opened at Duchess Theatre on 30 October 1936; reopened in March 1937.) Directed by E. Martin Browne.
Becket—Robert Speaight
First Priest—Alfred Clark
Second Priest—Charles Petry

Third Priest—Frank Napier
First Tempter/Knight—Guy Spaull
Second Tempter/Knight—G. R. Schjelderup
Third Tempter/Knight—Norman Chidgey
Fourth Tempter/Knight—E. Martin Browne

P3.3   Manhattan Theater (NY).   20 March 1936.   Popular Price Theater company of the WPA's Federal Theatre Project, produced by Hallie Flanagan; directed by Halsted Welles; music by A. Lehman Engel; scenery and costumes by Tom Adrian Cracraft.
  Becket—Harry Irvine
  First Tempter—Tom Greenway
  Second Tempter—Joseph Draper
  Third Tempter—George LeSoir
  Fourth Tempter—Robert Bruce
  First Knight—Roger DeKoven
  Second Knight—Stephen Courtleigh
  Third Knight—Jon Loriner
  Fourth Knight—Frederick Tozere

P3.4 Ritz Theatre (NY). 16 February 1938. Produced by Gilbert Miller and Ashley Dukes; directed by E. Martin Browne.

P3.5   Gateway Theatre (Edinburgh). 1947 Edinburgh International Festival. Directed by E. Martin Browne.
  Becket—Robert Speaight

P3.6   Old Vic Theatre (London).   1953 season.   Produced by Robert Helpmann; music by Christopher Whelen; sets and costumes by Alan Barlow.
  Becket—Robert Donat

P3.7   American Shakespeare Festival Theatre (Stratford, Conn.). 18 June 1966. Directed by John Houseman with Pearl Lang.
  Becket—Joseph Wiseman

P3.8   Aldwych Theatre (London).   31 August 1972.   Royal Shakespeare Company directed by Terry Hands; music by Ian Kellam, conducted by Gordon Kember; sets by Abdul Farrah.
  Becket—Richard Pasco

P3.9   Avon Theatre (Stratford, Ont.). 1988 Stratford Festival. Directed by David William.
  Becket—Nicholas Pennell

P4 *The Family Reunion*

P4.1 Westminster Theatre (London). 21 March 1939. Directed by E. Martin Browne; decor by Peter Goffin; costumes by Stella Mary Pearce.
　　Harry—Michael Redgrave
　　Amy—Helen Haye
　　Ivy—Henzie Raeburn
　　Agatha—Catherine Lacey
　　Violet—Marjorie Gabain
　　Gerald—Colin Keith-Johnston
　　Charles—Stephen Murray
　　Mary—Ruth Lodge
　　Warburton—E. Martin Browne

P4.2 Mercury Theatre (London). 31 October 1946. Directed by E. Martin Browne; costumes by Stella Mary Pearce.
　　Harry—Alan Wheatley
　　Amy—Eileen Thorndike
　　Ivy—Henzie Raeburn
　　Agatha—Catherine Lacey
　　Gerald—John Burch
　　Charles—Frank Napier

P4.3 Gateway Theatre (Edinburgh). 1947 Edinburgh International Festival. Directed by E. Martin Browne.
　　Harry—Patrick Troughton
　　Mary—Yvonne Coulette
　　Agatha—Henzie Raeburn
　　Amy—Eileen Thorndike

P4.4 Cherry Lane Theatre (NY). 1947 season. Directed by Frank Corsaro; settings by Michael Mear.
　　Harry—John Christie
　　Amy—Olivia
　　Ivy—Laviah Lucking
　　Agatha—Roberta Dixon
　　Violet—Roberta Unger
　　Gerald—Jeffrie Weaver
　　Charles—James Linn
　　Mary—Julia Meade
　　Warburton—David Perkins

P4.5 Phoenix Theatre (London). 7 June 1956. Produced by Peter Brook and Paul Scofield; settings by Norris Houghton; costumes by Will Steven Armstrong; music composed by David Amram.

Harry—Fritz Weaver
Amy—Florence Reed
Ivy—Dorothy Sands
Agatha—Lillian Gish
Violet—Margaretta Warwick
Gerald—Nicholas Joy
Charles—Eric Berry
Mary—Sylvia Short
Warburton—Conrad Bain

P4.6 Vaudeville Theatre (London). 19 June 1979. Royal Exchange Theatre Company directed by Michael Elliott; score by Ian Gibson.

Harry—Edward Fox
Amy—Pauline Jameson
Ivy—Constance Chapman
Agatha—Avril Elgar
Violet—Daphne Oxenford
Gerald—William Fox
Charles—Jeffry Wickham
Mary—Joanna David
Warburton—Esmond Knight

P5 *The Cocktail Party*

P5.1 Royal Lyceum Theatre (Edinburgh). Edinburgh International Festival, 22 August 1949. Produced by Gilbert Miller and Henry Sherek; directed by E. Martin Browne; directed by E. Martin Browne; design by Anthony Holland; costumes by Pamela Sherek.

Sir Henry Harcourt-Reilly—Alec Guinness
Julia Shuttlethwaite—Cathleen Nesbitt
Lavinia Chamberlayne—Ursula Jeans
Edward Chamberlayne—Robert Flemyng
Celia Copplestone—Irene Worth
Alexander MacColgie Gibbs—Ernest Clark
Peter Quilpe—Donald Houston

P5.2 Henry Miller's Theater (NY). 21 January 1950. Same cast as Edinburgh production except for Eileen Peel who took over the role of Lavinia and Grey Blake who took over the role of Peter.

P5.3 New Theatre (London). 3 May 1950. Directed by E. Martin Browne.
   Sir Henry Harcourt-Reilly—Rex Harrison
   Julia Shuttlethwaite—Gladys Boot
   Lavinia Chamberlayne—Alison Leggatt
   Edward Chamberlayne—Ian Hunter
   Celia Copplestone—Margaret Leighton
   Alexander MacColgie Gibbs—Robin Bailey
   Peter Quilpe—Donald Houston

P5.4 Wyndham's Theatre (London). 6 November 1968. Directed by Alec Guinness; design by Michael Warre.
   Edward Chamberlayne—Alec Guinness

P5.5 Lyceum Theatre (NY). 7 October 1968. APA-Phoenix Ensemble directed by Philip Minor.
   Sir Henry Harcourt-Reilly—Sydney Walker
   Julia Shuttlethwaite—Nancy Walker
   Lavinia Chamberlayne—Frances Sternhagen
   Edward Chamberlayne—Brian Bedford
   Celia Copplestone—Patricia Conolly
   Alexander MacColgie Gibbs—Keene Curtis
   Peter Quilpe—Ralph Williams

P5.6 Phoenix Theatre (London). 28 July 1986. New Theatre Company directed by John Dexter; decor by Brian Vahey.
   Sir Henry Harcourt-Reilly—Alec McCowen
   Julia Shuttlethwaite—Rachel Kempson
   Lavinia Chamberlayne—Sheila Allen
   Edward Chamberlayne—Simon Ward
   Celia Copplestone—Sheila Gish
   Alexander MacColgie Gibbs—Robert Eddison
   Peter Quilpe—Stephen Boxer

P6 *The Confidential Clerk*

P6.1 Royal Lyceum Theatre (Edinburgh). Edinburgh International Festival, 25 August 1953. Presented by Henry Sherek; directed by E. Martin Browne; design by Hutchinson Scott.
   Sir Claude Mulhammer—Paul Rogers
   Colby Simpkins—Denholm Elliott
   Lady Elizabeth Mulhammer—Isabel Jeans
   Lucasta Angel—Margaret Leighton
   B. Kaghan—Peter Jones
   Eggerson—Alan Webb

Mrs. Guzzard—Alison Leggatt

P6.2 Lyric Theatre (London). 16 September 1953. Same cast as Edinburgh production.

P6.3 Morosco Theatre (NY). 11 February 1954. Presented by Henry Sherek; directed by E. Martin Browne; settings and costumes by Paul Morrison.
Sir Claude Mulhammer—Claude Rains
Colby Simpkins—Douglas Watson
Lady Elizabeth Mulhammer—Ina Claire
Lucasta Angel—Joan Greenwood
B. Kaghan—Richard Newton
Eggerson—Newton Blick
Mrs. Guzzard—Aline MacMahon

P7 *The Elder Statesman*

P7.1 Royal Lyceum Theatre (Edinburgh). Edinburgh International Festival, 24 August 1958. Presented by Henry Sherek; directed by E. Martin Browne; settings by Hutchinson Scott.
Lord Claverton—Paul Rogers
Monica—Anna Massey
Michael—Alec McCowen
Charles Hemington—Richard Gale
Gomez—William Squire
Mrs. Carghill—Eileen Peel
Mrs. Piggott—Dorothea Phillips

P7.2 Cambridge Theatre (London). 25 September 1958. Same cast as Edinburgh production, except for Dorothy Turner who took over the role of Mrs. Piggott.

P7.3 Fred Miller Theatre (Milwaukee). 27 February 1963. Directed by Paul Shyre.
Lord Claverton—Staats Cotsworth
Monica—Anne Meachem
Michael—Jay Doyle
Charles Hemington—Richard Venturi
Gomez—Robert Flemyng
Mrs. Carghill—Rosalind Boxall
Mrs. Piggott—Susan Brown

Author Index

The following index lists all critics and scholars included in the bibliography of secondary sources. The references are keyed to the numbers assigned to each entry; page numbers are given first, with coded entry numbers following.

General Index

The entries listing Eliot's plays and non-fiction prose are followed, parenthetically, by code numbers keyed to the bibliography entries.

About the Author

RANDY MALAMUD is Assistant Professor of English at Georgia State University, specializing in modern literature and modernism. He is author of *The Language of Modernism* (1989) and numerous reference and journal articles on Eliot, James Joyce, Virginia Woolf, and others. He is at present completing a critical study of Eliot's drama and working on a study of modernism in literature and other arts.

Also Available in
Modern Dramatist Research and Production Sourcebooks

Clifford Odets: A Research and Production Sourcebook
William W. Demastes